The Politics of Urban and Regional Development and the American Exception

The Politics of Urban and Regional Development and the American Exception

Kevin R. Cox

SU

Syracuse University Press

Copyright © 2016 by Syracuse University Press
Syracuse, New York 13244-5290

All Rights Reserved

First Edition 2016

16 17 18 19 20 21   6 5 4 3 2 1

∞ The paper used in this publication meets the minimum requirements
of the American National Standard for Information Sciences—Permanence
of Paper for Printed Library Materials, ANSI Z39.48-1992.

For a listing of books published and distributed by Syracuse University Press,
visit www.SyracuseUniversityPress.syr.edu.

ISBN: 978-0-8156-3456-0 (hardcover)
978-0-8156-3439-3 (paperback)
978-0-8156-5361-5 (e-book)

Library of Congress Cataloging-in-Publication Data

Available upon request from publisher.

Manufactured in the United States of America

Contents

Illustrations

Tables

Preface

This is a book about the American politics of urban and regional development. Much has been written about this topic. There are numerous case studies as well as some more theoretical statements that have been highly influential; those of Molotch, Elkin, and Stone come readily to mind. There has been critical review. Among others, a common claim is that the literature has had difficulty bringing together the local forces that are at the heart of the American politics and forces of a more global nature. In this book, this claim will be of only incidental concern. My focus lies elsewhere. For one thing that is rarely remarked on is the sheer distinctiveness of the American politics: its utter peculiarity when compared with what transpires in the countries of Western Europe and even compared with Canada. It is, for a start, a very bottom-up politics in which interests in rent dominate. The object is to channel value through real estate investments, something that necessarily takes on a competitive character, not just within metropolitan areas but between them and between regions. The American politics is bottom-up because it works by mobilizing different agencies of the state to very local purposes: local government is called on to provide the infrastructure for a particular office park project; or local governments, aided and abetted by developers, bring pressure to bear on state government for some sort of favor. In Western Europe the balance between bottom-up and top-down, between private and public interests, has tended to be quite different. Central branches of the state have played a preponderant role relative to local government. Private interests have seemingly been subordinated to planners, and local planners to some sort of central oversight. There have certainly been changes in a more American direction over the last thirty or so years, but how things are done in France, Germany, Italy, and so forth, remains quite different. In short, the West European case provides a useful counterpoint to the American one, and our understanding of the latter stands to be deepened by an examination of these differences. That is what I have had in mind in writing this book.

This study has opened up other questions. Understanding why the United States is different cannot be reduced to the synchronic. Structures of social relations have a history. The very idea of "urban and regional development" has to be examined from that standpoint. Intriguingly, it begins to emerge on both sides of the North Atlantic at a very similar time, to blossom forth in clear ensembles of institutions and practices after the Second World War. There are certainly similarities in the conditions, not least the unevenness of geographical development and its politicization, along with, at more concrete levels, the emergence of city planning, of property capital and, of new real estate products like the garden suburb and the industrial estate. But how the latter get combined in a response to the former is very different.

There are also questions around what is meant when reference is made to "urban and regional development." A related term often used is "local development." In addition there is the problem of usages that vary from one country to another. "Urban," "regional," and "local" development each have distinctive meanings, associations, and contexts within which they are drawn on, but they also overlap. "Urban development" is both "local" and "regional," for example; but one can also talk about the development of particular localities—hence "local development" within an urban area and contributing to "urban" development.

The terms "development" and "local development" are used particularly loosely by those directly responsible: by the "developers" and by those who define themselves as "local economic development professionals"— the people who work in the economic development departments of the utilities in the United States, the site selection consultants like Fantus and Real Estate Research Corporation, or those attached to city planning departments whose brief is to facilitate inward investment. They are unlikely to use the term "urban development" either to describe to each other what they do or to justify themselves to wider constituencies. Again "development" here can refer either to housing, to inward investment in employment-creating activities, or to both; it depends on the context.

"Urban development," on the other hand, is a favored category of state officials. This can be very direct, as in the federal "Department of Housing and Urban Development" or "urban renewal," or more indirect, as in "the development of our city." Since the 1960s and the efflorescence of social science interest in the urban, it has also been a favored category of the academics. The attention given to "urban regimes" and "urban growth coalitions" are instances of this, as are the titles of the journals: "urban this," "urban that," or "urban and regional." Curiously, "local" is the poor relation.

"Urban" and "regional" are used in the title of this book because they are more effective in capturing the imperatives and consequences of development in a capitalist society. Both express the socialization of production, which is at the heart of capitalist development: the agglomeration of related activities is fundamental to the contemporary meaning of the city as a form that facilitates accumulation, just as "region" connotes distinctive roles in the geographic division of labor. In addition, regional development is reflected in and is stimulated by urban development. The protagonists of urban development cannot ignore what is happening in the wider region.

To talk of "Western Europe" also requires comment. In the first place, I am referring to the more developed countries of Europe; so not those of the former Soviet bloc or of southeastern Europe, including Greece. Second, I am aware that France is not Great Britain[1] and that development in Germany is characterized by different practices and institutional forms than, say, Belgium. As a federal state, Germany is in some contrast to France and Great Britain, as indeed is Spain. Particular practices emerge at different times in different countries. To address localized unemployment, the British government was intervening in industrial location as early as the 1930s, a practice to be taken up elsewhere in Western Europe

---

1. I use the term "Great Britain" throughout the book and in preference to the "United Kingdom." Neither is without unfortunate baggage, but of the two the first is slightly less so.

only after the Second World War. Each country has unique qualities, but my point will be that they have been and remain more alike in their approaches to urban and regional development than they are like the American case. To justify this claim is not straightforward. This is because one's knowledge of the different countries and of the development practices and institutions found there is inevitably uneven. I know more about Great Britain than I do of France; more about France and the Netherlands than Germany; and least about Italy, Spain, and Switzerland. The degree to which I have overgeneralized— and clearly I think it is very limited— will be for the reader to judge.

In drawing on Western Europe to shed light on the American case, the *tabula* is not entirely *rasa*. There have been a number of book-length comparative studies though with an Anglo-American emphasis. The work of Hall and Clawson (1973) on comparative urban development in the United States and Great Britain comes to mind, as does Susan Fainstein's (2001) comparison of property development, its planning, and its politics in London and New York. The 1989 book by Barnekov, Boyle, and Rich on privatism and urban policy in the United States and in Britain is also to be noted. In some other important instances the comparative standpoint is more implicit: Stephen Elkin's (1974) book on planning in London is a good example.

Finally, there is the question of method. I see the book as a contribution to what David Harvey has called "historical geographical materialism." This means that in understanding the politics of urban and regional development I prioritize the accumulation process to the extent that it both creates a distinctive geography and mobilizes it to its purposes. In the mainstream literature on the politics of development there is a concept of capitalism. Competition is to the fore and so, therefore, are markets. Popular resistance also figures into the discussion as indeed does the state. But the failure to situate them with respect to the accumulation process allows incoherence to take over. Local government, competition, notions of social justice, even uneven development, become so many independent forces unshackled from any overriding structuring rooted in the imperatives of production; and emphatically that is *not* to be deterministic.

The emphasis on accumulation means, in turn, that class relations and struggles are paramount. In the Western democracies, these have typically assumed a strongly distributional character. The logic of accumulation has not been at stake; rather it is how the product gets allocated. These struggles can certainly map on to the basic production relations between a class that, in effect, puts the means of production in motion and those who subsequently do the labor. But just as clearly, distributional struggle occurs within the latter; how else would those whose revenues come primarily from returns on investments ever come to have a predominant say in the way the state functions if it was not for a coalition with those of the working class who see advantages to themselves over the remainder?

But beyond this basic division—typically between those who have significant property, even if it is largely of a consumptive sort, and those who do not—distributional struggle becomes much more complex and much, much more contingent upon differences in, for example, matters of religion, ethnicity, gender, native born versus immigrants, and even generation, judging from recent writing in the British press. Every country has such divisions. Some are more enduring than others and some more central to contemporary politics, including, it might seem, that of development. In the American case, one might argue this for racial division, and I pay some attention to it. I do not regard it, though, as fundamental. If you take race out of the picture, the American politics remains much as it is: there would still be a politics of suburban exclusion, a politics of downtown redevelopment, and a politics in which those with limited resources to draw on in the struggle are disadvantaged, and this persistence would be for very good structural reasons having to do with the nature of the accumulation process.

This is not to say that the accumulation process has not experienced important mutations that are absolutely crucial to understanding any politics of urban and regional development. Property capital, and the conflicts it enters into with people in both their work- and living-places, occupies a major place in my argument. It is, though, a historical creation. The practice and recognition of a separate branch of capital servicing the needs for premises of capital as a whole is relatively new; likewise the provision of shelter for workers. Equally central to my argument will be the mobility of those buying or renting real estate: the retail chains, the light assembly industries, the back offices, the home buyers liberated from the old kinship and mutual aid relations of the working-class community. A fundamental condition for the politics of urban and regional development has been what I call the new mobility, and this as a result of the way it has entered into contradiction with the fixity of real property. This condition is, to repeat, fundamental. Not least it means that *any* such politics necessarily involves a dialectic between class tensions on the one hand and those of territory on the other. In popular consciousness in the United States, this dialectic has tended to be resolved more in the territorial direction. It is with an exploration of some instances of this that this investigation to the very peculiar practice that is the American politics of local and regional development will commence.

Acknowledgments

Numerous people helped in different ways in the preparation of this book and going back a very long time. Not least, I want to record the continuing inspiration I have drawn from numerous students whom I have worked with on their graduate research. These include: Delphine Ancien, Golden Jackson-Mergler, Andy Jonas, Felicity Kitchin, Andy Mair, Jeff McCarthy, Emily Nosse-Leirer, Bae-Gyoon Park, Michael Sutcliffe, and Andrew Wood. They have taught me a great deal perhaps more than they can ever know. Thinking through the problems posed in the book has benefited hugely, and in different ways, from the work of Jamie Gough, David Harvey, Ray Hudson, Ron Martin, and Richard Walker. Jim DeGrand of the Geography Department at Ohio State University prepared the figures in both timely and original fashion. Syracuse University Press has been brilliant. Deanna McCay commissioned extremely useful reviews, and I owe the reviewers a debt of thanks. Suzanne Guiod then brought the project to fruition with careful and sympathetic guidance. Elizabeth Myers helped to make everything much clearer through her superb copyediting. Finally, and certainly not least, I want to acknowledge the support given to me in the form of a fellowship by the Guggenheim Foundation. Since this was well over ten years ago, they can be excused if they have long given up ever seeing any concrete results from their support. They have been extraordinarily patient and I am grateful for that, too. I was clearly far too optimistic in my original plans. Working out the ideas took much longer than I ever would have imagined. I hope that it was worth the wait.

The Politics of Urban and Regional
Development and the American Exception

1

A Very Peculiar Practice

Context

In the United States, the public interest in issues of what has come to be known as local economic development is nothing short of extraordinary. Americans may take political drama in this arena for granted, but the fixation seems unusual to those whose experience is rooted in other countries. This major focus of local and state government attracts remarkable degrees of US media attention: the steady dribble of news items on controversies around rezonings, highway widenings, annexations, and the provision of tax incentives to new investors is, for Americans, a familiar one. Equally indicative are the various referenda on development issues—to approve the sale of bonds for new convention centers, to rescind rezoning decisions, and the like—on which Americans are asked to vote and whose contestation is equally highly publicized.

This is a politics that has also attracted more than its fair share of social science interest. It is a central theme in urban studies, where it has found a series of distinct expressions, such as the politics of downtown revitalization, of suburbanization, or of inward investment and plant closures. It is, I will want to claim, utterly distinctive, and the attention it attracts contributes to that distinctiveness. It is part of the warp and weft of local life in a way that is duplicated nowhere else in the developed world. This is the American politics of urban and regional development, a politics whose basic lineaments first appeared as a complex whole subsequent to the Second World War and which endures. It has forms, material and discursive, that make it distinctive nationally as well as historically. There is nothing quite like it in the advanced capitalist countries. In this book, I

1

set out just what that politics amounts to, demonstrate its distinctiveness, and then provide an explanation. The experience of the Western European countries will provide the necessary foil.

To briefly set the scene: It is a politics generated by intense local interests of a business sort. These focus on a struggle for that component of revenue which is rent: rent derived from both land and from the improvements to it. The utilities, the property developers, and local governments are typically at the forefront, but so too—to varying and lesser degrees, depending on the issue—are the banks, small retailers, builders, and local newspapers and media empires. The balance between rent and other sources of revenue varies, but for all of them it is a central consideration: more so for the property companies and the developers, certainly, but a very considerable proportion of the revenue streams of utilities, retailers, local media, and banks depends on exactly where they are, and changing that where-ness has been an enduring preoccupation.

For these businesses, space relations must occur in a particular place by virtue of the fact that they are so locally embedded as to find it difficult, even impossible, to take advantage of growth elsewhere. Accordingly, coalitions may form around particular development initiatives and programs to attract final users, whether industrial, commercial, or residential, or simply to attract investors with no particular idea as to where they will be accommodated. To facilitate this investment, various financial and regulatory incentives are typically offered, and these commonly ignite so-called bidding wars with similar coalitions of forces elsewhere. But the coalitional form of this politics is not essential. Coalitions cannibalize each other, relegating particular places to yesteryear; but so too do individual developers as they struggle with each other for the various infrastructural investments that the state can provide and which will make all the difference to the rents that they can extract. And there again, this is a *class* politics. A common scenario is one in which the growth protagonists try to socialize the costs of their projects while at the same time privatizing any and all of the subsequent benefits—something that can generate opposition from the more popular forces footing the bill. The federal government or the individual states may then be called on for some sort of fiscal or regulatory relief. But this always risks the opposition of growth interests elsewhere that stand to lose.

Most significant of all, bathing the US phenomenon in its distinctive light, this is a politics of *capitalist* development, and it is this which allows contrast and comparison with its trans-Atlantic cousins. Capitalism and its inherent logics are crucial to the story told in this book. Capitalism has turned out to be *the* engine of development: piling up the wealth, revolutionizing labor processes, generating one new product after another, and transforming culture, politics, and institutions, as well as geography. Capitalism revolutionizes social relations as they are experienced across space. It urbanizes; it develops in ways that are geographically uneven; it extends itself across new frontiers pushing back precapitalist forms before it; it *displaces* and *replaces* with new forms of itself—technical, social, and institutional; it despoils environments and then makes more money from cleaning up the mess. To understand why means coming to terms with capitalism's contradictions: its constant tendency to erect barriers to its own continuing development, technical, social, geographic or whatever, and then to suspend them.

Some might argue that the barriers different capitals erect to each other's expansion is the ultimate contradiction, and certainly competition looms large in many accounts of capitalist history. But underlying this competition, providing its necessary condition, is the more fundamental contradiction between the classes, a contradiction that often gets obscured. Capital piles up wealth and then recycles it by virtue of its exploitation of the masses, which is all made possible by their utter need, and hence their vulnerability. This vulnerability owes in turn to their historical separation from the means of production and the concentration of the latter, or at least the possibility of buying them, in the hands of the few. But once workers are so separated and have to sell their labor power for a wage, then everything entering into production has to be bought for money—money that then must be retrieved through the sale of finished products and which may not be. So while separation from the means of production makes workers vulnerable to exploitation, competition makes that exploitation a reality as capitalists as a class seek to lower their costs of production.

Historically, of course, and with varying degrees of vigor and in highly variable ways, both through the labor movement and by simply seeking out another employer, the working class has resisted: capital has entered into contradiction with the necessary condition of its own profitability. To continue to accumulate, capital must overcome the barrier. Concessions are made, and these then become the condition for new ways of extracting more product from the workers, ways that inevitably have some sort of spatial expression; such as new divisions of labor and new *spatial* divisions of labor.

In an important sense, the contradictions of capitalist development get expressed spatially: fixity versus mobility, competition over space versus spatial monopoly, inclusion versus exclusion, concentration versus dispersion, local versus global. Urbanization concentrates the working class and lays down the conditions for an enhanced consciousness of their condition, producing forms of resistance that in turn generate attempts to disperse production. The goal of competition is always to seek a monopoly, and the particularity of locations in space creates opportunities for achieving that goal, which is then to be challenged by the arrival of newcomers attracted by the super-profits or super-rents being appropriated.

These spatial contradictions are then grasped more succinctly as urban and regional questions regarding, that is, the opportunity and the challenge of concentration in cities and of uneven development over space. This suggests that in the barriers that they raise, and in the diverse ways those barriers are suspended, they are at a fundamental level territorial in character. They certainly have a territorial form and are typically represented as such; for example, as in how the "international challenge" can only be met through unity around some conception of the national interest. But in turn that territorialization needs to be situated with respect to the more fundamental struggles identified above: class, to be sure, and the competitive forces for which it is the necessary condition.

In resolving capital's contradictions, the state has always assumed a crucial role. This is as true of the urban and regional questions as it is elsewhere. Early forms of city planning, like the use of the right of eminent domain to bring the railways into the heart of the city, gave new impetus to the advantages of agglomeration by facilitating some commuting and an easing of pressure on urban housing markets (Kellett 1969). Urbanization always brought with it the threat of worker organization. In the famous Flanders example, this was anticipated through measures aimed at keeping the workers at home in the countryside: subsidies to purchase housing and also to commute to work in the city (De Decker 2008). One thinks also of the role that the US federal government played in opening up the West and so securing cheaper food for the cities of the East, if at the cost of agriculture in New England and the mid-Atlantic states: the land grants to railways, the land grant universities, the Homestead Act.

But these federal initiatives are in a sense misleading. Rather, what takes institutional shape in the United States as *the* vehicle for delivering urban and regional development is much, much more decentralized and stands in stark contrast with what would unfold in Western Europe. For in the United States it would be property capitals and others with strong interests in rent who—sometimes alone, sometimes in what have come to be called local growth coalitions, but always in alliance with, even subsuming, local government—would spearhead initiatives aimed at suspending the spatial contradictions of capital. These contradictions were therefore seen as threatening to, even giving rise to the very notion of, specifically *local* or *urban* economies. the viability of which the continued extraction of rents has tended to depend upon. In Western Europe, on the other hand, the vision would be much more national; a question, as we shall see, of fashioning the "good geography." But before broaching these questions we need some more concrete sense of what the American politics of local and regional development has amounted to. This is the purpose of the case studies that follow.

The Contradictions of Geographically Uneven Development

In his critique of economic growth originally published in 1967, Edward Mishan provides a nice spatial metaphor that with a little reworking does much to sum up the process of geographically uneven development. In Mishan words, "as the carpet of 'increased choice' is being unrolled before us by the foot, it is simultaneously being rolled up behind us by the yard" (1969, 119). In the United States that is certainly how the changing map of employment looked from the early 1970s onward. And it also applied to processes of suburbanization and urban decline, processes that had been apprehended long before people were talking about rust belts. Both instances provide vivid entrées into much that constitutes the American politics of urban and regional development.

The Rise of the Rust Belt

The emergence of the Rust Belt has to start with what has been called, in discussions of the global economy, "the long downturn" (R. Brenner 1998) starting in the early 1970s. Before then, the label Rust Belt had no currency. During the so-called golden years of the 1950s and 1960s the economies of the advanced capitalist countries, including the United States, experienced growth that was unprecedented. But from about 1973 onward there was a sharp turn for the worse. Investment slowed down, as indeed did the growth of employment; wages started to stagnate; and, most crucially, rates of profitability declined. The change, while general, was geographically uneven: the United States and Great Britain were much more affected than France, Japan, or West Germany. And, of course, the changes were felt in regionally differentiated ways.

In the United States it was the emergence of a regional problem in what had been the old Manufacturing Belt in the Midwest and Northeast that attracted attention. This was dramatized by a number of highly mediatized events, including the near bankruptcy of New York City in 1975 and the actual bankruptcy of Cleveland three years later. Prior to the Cleveland debacle, what became known as Black Monday in 1977 heralded the implosion of the steel industry in Youngstown, Ohio, followed by more moderated declines in other classic steel towns like Gary and those in Western Pennsylvania around Pittsburgh. A decade later, the 1989 movie *Roger and Me* would draw attention to the plight of Flint, Michigan, a town that had relied almost entirely on the automobile industry; employment in that sector plummeted from 80,000 in 1978 to an amazing tenth of that just over twenty years later.

Meanwhile the West and South were relatively less affected, due in significant part to the disproportional presence of the new growth sectors of the time, particularly in the West. During the 1970s the term "Silicon Valley" first became part of the popular argot. There would then be talk of Silicon Prairies, the most notable of which by far was focused on the Dallas–Fort Worth area. Most aircraft production was on the West Coast, in Seattle and Southern California. Rapidly growing retirement and tourist industries brought the South into this new penumbra of growth, as indeed did federal spending on weapons, something already apparent during the 1950s and 1960s.[1] And the South was being discovered as a low-wage location for branch plant operations.

To a degree these regional differences had been apparent for some time. In fact the growth of employment in the West and South had been outstripping that in the old Manufacturing Belt since at least the immediate postwar period. It was just that until the early 1970s it had been a matter of differences in growth rates, all of which remained positive. With the onset of the long downturn, modest growth in many local economies in the Midwest and the Northeast would turn into absolute decline, characterized by business failures, growing unemployment, and falling local tax revenues.

The issue then was how to restore profitability, something that would of course be close to the hearts of local growth coalitions and interests in rents—housing developers, banks with mortgages extended, utilities fearing underused facilities in place—scattered across what would quickly become known as the Rust Belt or, and in contrast to the Sun Belt, where growth was continuing, the Cold Belt. Several tendencies quickly became clear. The one that would grab most attention and particularly affect the union movement, whose membership was heavily concentrated there and was obviously being impacted by plant closures and bankruptcies, was the low-wage route: corporate headquarters, research and development, even possibly some higher skill employment would stay where they had always been, but the lower-skill work would be decanted to small towns scattered across the South, the Plains states, and the Mountain West. Here

---

1. Ann Markusen (1991a; 1991b) is particularly good on this; though as she points out, parts of the Northeast, like Connecticut, Massachusetts, and Long Island, also tended to be beneficiaries of this federal largesse.

corporations could take advantage of lower wages: a result of the monopsony advantages bestowed by being the big employer in town, lower costs of living (particularly housing), and a union movement whose growth had been stymied by right-to-work laws courtesy of the Taft-Hartley Act of 1947. This tendency was not entirely new. The rubber tire companies of Akron, Ohio, had pioneered this particular strategy in the second half of the 1960s when they decentralized the manufacturing bit to small towns in Alabama, Mississippi, Oklahoma, and Tennessee. But it became a tidal wave in the mid to late 1970s, a central ingredient in the making of what would be referred to as "the rural turnaround."

There were countertendencies. The rural turnaround was not confined to the South, the Plains, and the Mountain West. It happened in the Midwest, too, and for some of the same reasons: lower wages and a weak union presence. The trend was exemplified by the choices of Japanese auto transplants, which located in places that few had heard of before, like Anna and Marysville in Ohio, Georgetown in Kentucky, and Normal, Illinois, along with more recognizable ones like Lafayette, Indiana; but definitely not in the auto industry's unionized heartlands of Southern Michigan, Northern Ohio, and Indiana. Later the center of gravity would shift more unambiguously in a southern direction. Changes in the steel industry were also emblematic if on a smaller scale. Who, after all, had heard of Crawfordsville, Indiana, or Auburn, New York? But these would be new steel producing centers based on the reduction of scrap metal and helping to undermine the former dominance of Gary, Pittsburgh, Buffalo, and Sparrow's Point next to Baltimore in Maryland.

The second tendency for corporate America was, and remains, to go with the flow: the flow, that is, in the form of the logic of what was becoming known at the time as the New International Division of Labor. It was no coincidence that as Western economies slumped in the 1970s, attention turned to the way in which a geographic skills division in manufacturing seemed to be emerging; these economies were on one side of the emergent divide and the so-called Newly Industrializing Countries (NICs)—at that time notably Brazil, Mexico, South Korea, and Taiwan, to be joined later by China, Malaysia, and Thailand—were on the other. The shift was both technical and sectoral: the decanting of the less skills-intensive parts of the labor process to sites in the global South, as well as the relative expansion of sectors like shoes, garments, steel, and then shipbuilding, which had long been monopolies of the advanced capitalist countries. As the NICs grew, though, so too did their need for the more technically sophisticated products of the global North: machine tools, airplanes, medical equipment, locomotives, engines, and pumps and switching gear of all sorts. So while the steel-producing areas of Eastern Ohio and Western Pennsylvania went into a long decline, the passenger aircraft industry in the state of Washington and in Southern California enjoyed boom times. As new markets in the NICs developed, so too would arguments in favor of lowering the barriers to those of their products that were undermining local economies elsewhere in the United States. In fairness, this did not work entirely to the disadvantage of the old Manufacturing Belt. The aircraft producers needed jet engines, and these were produced in Hartford, Connecticut, and Cincinnati, Ohio. The American machine tool belt stayed exactly where it had always been, in an area stretching from Rockford in Northern Illinois through Southern Wisconsin to Milwaukee. But the fact that the Rust Belt experience was spotty did not make its implications for labor much more palatable in the old heartlands of iron and steel, coal, automobiles, and later, as the container revolution hit, dock workers.

Class would be central to the way in which the regional crisis was imagined. For the organized labor movement, the evidence was clear. The South had become the new attraction for corporate America because of its low labor costs and the weakness of the union movement there. Coal mining was in disarray in its old center of gravity in the Appalachians because in the Mountain West the labor costs of a ton of coal were so much lower.[2] And so on. The solutions were clear: first, organize workers outside the union heartland of the Midwest and Northeast. This, it was argued, would slow down the hemorrhage of jobs by reducing the incentive for firms to relocate. A second approach was to promote plant closure laws, both at federal and state level, to make it more difficult for firms to

---

2. This was only part of the comparative advantage of western coal, as we will see below.

close plants in the older industrial areas of the Midwest and Northeast and open new ones in the rest of the country.[3] Yet a third approach was to give the unions control of their pension funds so they could invest the money in more regionally strategic ways (Rifkin and Barber 1978.) None of these would be especially effective in countering the loss of well-paid, unionized jobs.

Meanwhile there were businesses in the old Manufacturing Belt that found themselves marooned as the tide went out. A lot of business was dependent on the health of local economies and was in no position to move: not just the utilities and the banks, limited at that time from branching out into more lucrative pastures by antitrust legislation, but also the retailers, car dealers, beverage franchises, and construction industries that tended to cluster around local chambers of commerce and whose bread and butter was wholly or in large part land rent in some form or other. Faced with plant closures and sluggish investment in economic bases, their problem was how to return the local market to the vigor experienced during the golden years. Like the labor movement, these businesses too recognized the lure of Sun Belt wages and weak unions for corporations and their initial response was to counterattack: not by joining the labor movement in its distinctive attempt to offset regional disadvantage but by outdoing the Sun Belt—in other words, by forcing wages in the struggling local economies of the Midwest and Northeast down to the same levels.

3. The goal here was to exact penalties of a sufficiently dissuasive character. These could take the form of generous severance payments to existing employees and, less dissuasive, advance notice of plant closures to give workers the opportunity to find alternative work. Corporations objected to the first, as expected, but they also saw notice of imminent closure as problematic because any workforce attrition subsequent to the announcement would compromise plant efficiency. The federal Worker Adjustment and Retraining and Notification Act of 1988 (WARN) mandated a sixty-day notification period for firms employing five hundred workers or more with a penalty of up to sixty days' pay for failure to provide proper notice. Enforcement, though, has proven difficult: not only did the legislation fail to assign enforcement of the law to any government agency (thus forcing workers to bring legal suit), but firms have found numerous ways around it, exploiting various loopholes or slowly running employment down until the workforce totals less than five hundred.

The new watchword became "business climate," a term that, if not quite so new to the 1970s and 1980s as Silicon Valley or "high-tech," would certainly experience a remarkable rise in its fortunes. Creating a favorable business climate meant reducing state taxation of corporations, revising labor law by pressing for the same right-to-work provisions that seemed to have burnished the star of Southern, Plains, and Mountain West states, weakening workers' compensation laws, and opposing plant closure laws that, in their view, would deter investment; in short, it meant attacking organized labor through the power of the states.

Both of these class projects continue down to the present day. The new frontier for labor organizing is the auto industry in the South. The right-to-work advocates have succeeded in Indiana and Michigan but have been turned back in Ohio and Pennsylvania. In addition to these class responses to the crisis in the Manufacturing Belt—a crisis renewed since the great recession that started in 2007—there have been approaches of a very different sort: ones of a *cross*-class nature that have brought territorial conflict into greater prominence in the ongoing struggle around the country's regional problem. One of these approaches took the form of something called the Northeast-Midwest Congressional Coalition, and the target was the fiscal redistribution of the federal government. The focus was, and remains, something called "fiscal balance."

This refers to the difference between what a particular state or region sends to the federal government in the form of taxes and what it gets back in the form of federal government spending. It is not that difficult to calculate the amount of taxes paid by the residents and firms located in a given state. Using some not-too-heroic assumptions, it is also possible to calculate how much is returned to the region in the form of, for example, subsidies to local governments, pension payments, research grants awarded to universities, government orders for goods and services, federal government employees (civil servants, military personnel) living there. Interest then focuses on the difference or balance; and in particular how it varies from one region to another, supposedly shedding light on the degree to which some regions are benefitting at the expense of others. Obviously this bears on local economic development since spending by the federal government affords a boost to local economies.

Statistics and maps were (and still are) prepared by a research organization set up for the purpose—the Northeast Midwest Institute— purportedly showing serious inequalities between the regions. Particularly during the 1980s it was argued that the Midwest and the Northeast sent more money to Washington than they got in return; the converse applied to the South and the West. This was the background to a push for legislative acts that would favor a redistribution of federal largesse toward the Cold Belt rather than the Sun Belt. These statistical exercises, it should be noted, are thoroughly questionable on diverse grounds, not least the challenge of tracing the geography of the federal money flow as, for instance, it works its way from a federal contractor in one state to their subcontractors scattered, quite typically, across the rest of the country (Markusen and Fastrup 1978).

Nevertheless, the claims were and are treated in grim earnest and stimulated, in turn, the formation of a counter-coalition acting on behalf of the Sun Belt: the Sunbelt Council. This coalition has not challenged, as well it might, the data on fiscal balance. By and large these seem to be accepted. Rather the response, particularly from the Southern states, is to resort to geographical equality arguments: that for many, many years, and still today, much of the Sun Belt was, and remains, relatively deprived compared with the states of the US industrial heartland in the Midwest and the Northeast. The immediate significance of this particular framing is that regional lobbies select the particular concept of territorial justice they will draw on according to circumstances. But the more general significance is the way in which class responses to regional crisis were displaced by ones of a territorial sort: an enduring theme in the American politics of urban and regional development and one that calls for explanation.

Tales of the City

A different sort of uneven development has emerged within metropolitan areas, the origins of which were creating tension and conflict long before the discovery of the Rust Belt. This phenomenon was highlighted more recently by a case that came before the Supreme Court in 2005. *Kelo v. City of New London* revolved around what might seem the rather arcane issue of whether a municipality, in this case the City of New London, could make use of the right of eminent domain in assembling land for purposes of economic development. Kelo's argument was that this was not a permissible use. Permissible uses were "public uses." Accordingly the question for the court was whether economic development could be defined as a public use. The view of the City of New London was that it could be, and this was sustained by the Supreme Court. The decision led to widespread public dismay, particularly among property rights advocates, of whom there are many in the United States, and to pressure on different states to change their eminent domain laws. Opposed to these changes, though, were the local governments of what have become known as "first suburbs," older suburbs that adjoin central cities and have struggled to rebuild their tax bases. To them, the use of eminent domain for purposes of economic development has been of particular interest. Some historical perspective is useful.

The opposition of central city to suburb has a long history in the United States. Legislation around the turn of the twentieth century made it easier to establish new municipalities on the edge of the big American cities to facilitate escape from what was seen as the obnoxious influence of the urban machine (Teaford 1979). During the 1930s, though, the dispersion of the residential population and employment into the independent suburbs and beyond would generate a central city problem of a quite different nature. The problem was one of rents; dispersion was making it harder to find buyers and tenants, so rents and land values were threatened. As Marc Weiss (1980) showed, this would be the necessary condition for what would come to be known as urban renewal. Legislation would provide federal subsidies for what was essentially a restructuring of the central city to make room, it was hoped, for major developments—office, institutional, residential, hospitality, or whatever might materialize—that would then provide anchors for the revival of the fortunes of land owners. Weiss has explained how this legislative action was pushed by central city land owners, galvanized by their national lobbying body, the wonderfully neutral-sounding Urban Land Institute, until it bore fruit in the federal Housing Act of 1949. This essentially gave a hefty two-thirds subsidy to the cost of acquiring supposedly "deteriorated" properties through eminent domain—typically the houses of the poor—and of clearing these properties and subsequently redeveloping the physical infrastructure of roads and utility lines.

This approach to countering the central city problem—a problem that arguably existed because of other federal policies that had promoted suburbanization—was then supplemented by additional federal action: the Highway Act of 1956. This was a huge public works program aimed at creating a system of multilane, limited-access highways that would come to be known as freeways, joining up the major urban centers of the country. The original goal had been to facilitate evacuation of cities in case of the threat of nuclear attack. But land-owning interests in central cities spotted an opportunity and put pressure on the federal government to take the freeways through downtown areas. This, it was hoped, would revive central city retailing and the rents from the land on which it stood. It would also put the downtown more effectively at the center of metropolitan labor markets, which was important for the office building boom that was already beginning to take shape.

What is also clear, though, is that these restructurings of the downtown would be on the back of the masses. Housing was declared "deteriorated," and people had to leave, which created a need for housing elsewhere even as the removal of units had altered the balance of advantage between landlord and tenant. Communities, often with a markedly ethnic character, were disrupted.[4] People were dispersed, separated from their churches and from other aspects of the community infrastructure. The insertion of freeways through the hearts of downtowns had similar effects, except that now communities might find themselves divided. Academics wrote of "grieving for a lost home" (Fried 1966).

Eventually, particularly with the development of the civil rights movement, urban renewal would become a very contentious program: a target for what were becoming known as "urban social movements" and an issue in city elections. Some concessions were made, not least provision for resettlement of the displaced and for some participation of those to be

---

4. At the time, the critics of urban renewal summarized it as "Negro removal."

affected in decisions on new projects. But by the early 1970s, and from the federal standpoint, the game was no longer worth the candle and the program came to an end. It had, though, lasted for over a quarter of a century.

Meanwhile urban renewal had been absorbed into a new definition of the central city problem: the problem of metropolitan fiscal disparities that attracted the attention of central city mayors, the federal government, and academics during the 1960s The focus now had shifted. Although there was a sense in which the concern was still property values, there was now also an anxiety about the effect on city tax takes. The geographic scale of the problem had changed, too: no longer the downtown but the political central city as a whole. The disparity in question was between central cities on the one hand and the independent suburbs on the other. The fiscal part referred to the relation between tax bases and revenue needs: suburbs, it was argued, had the tax base but without huge demands for expenditures on public safety, municipal hospitals (where they existed), mass transit, and welfare services, while the reverse applied to the central city. This outcome was widely interpreted as a byproduct of the suburbanization, essentially of taxable land uses, but in the context of the jurisdictionally fragmented American metropolitan area. The geography of the property tax base in metropolitan areas was changing as property values increased in the suburbs along with larger houses and to a lesser extent larger lots. Property values were going down in the central city as a consequence of the declining demand for housing there from people with money. New industrial and office parks in the suburbs added to their tax bases while firms abandoned sites in the central city. The growth of large suburban shopping centers at the expense of downtown retailing contributed something extra to this mix: a shift in the geography of sales tax revenues. On the other hand, the massive in-movement of poor and poorly educated African-Americans from the Deep South during the 1940s and 1950s added to the expenditure burdens on central cities (Piven and Cloward 1971). The metropolitan fiscal disparities problem was *the* urban question of the time (Cox 1973, chapter 3)

Various approaches were used in an attempt to "fix" the problem. The rebuilding of downtown tax bases through urban renewal drawing on the federal legislation of 1949 was one response. The federal government provided its own palliatives, particularly in the wake of the civil rights movement, easing the financial burden on central city governments through initiatives like the War on Poverty. Remedying what would become known as "spatial mismatch" was seen as an additional key to a solution. The argument here was that the combination of residential exclusivity and growing employment in the suburbs meant that the unemployed of the central city had difficulty accessing jobs. "Opening up the suburbs" then became the battle cry. All of these policies were vigorously espoused by central city and particularly downtown growth interests.[5]

Nowadays no one refers to the metropolitan fiscal disparities problem; the term is almost archaic.[6] The foreground is now occupied by the way in which the fiscal problems of the central city have become those of the inner ring of older suburbs that adjoin the central city, the first suburbs referred to above. In other words, the seemingly inexorable outward movement of population and employment has caught up with these older, inner or inner-ring suburbs: those independent suburbs that, while bordering the central city, found themselves surrounded by other suburbs, limiting their ability to expand via annexation. This has exposed them to the worst of all possible worlds. They have been in direct line of the export of the

---

5. Later the analytic lens would shift again, though without breaching the boundaries of the central city. This time the issue was redlining, sometimes connected to neighborhood change further out. The redlining question drew attention to the critical role that lenders play in maintaining the buoyancy of real estate markets. What started to attract public attention in the 1970s was their increasing aversion to lending for home purchase in areas close to the downtown. Compared to the suburbs, where residential values were increasing year after year, home mortgages there were not seen as good investments, and so they were redlined. Just as urban renewal and highway projects had generated opposition, so too did redlining, but mainly among existing home owners for whom it meant that there was no market for their houses if they should want to leave. Much ink was spilt at the time about its implications for home *buyers*, but they were already casting their eye on housing further out where mortgages *were* available. This then generated a cottage industry in urban sociology looking at the implications for neighborhood change.

6. Oddly, most analyses of Detroit's decline and fall seem to avoid mention of it, preferring to focus, often through thinly veiled racist argument, on the inadequacies of a succession of local governments.

central city's "social problems"—what had attracted attention in the 1970s so euphemistically as "neighborhood change,"—but without the ability to annex developable land available to the newer suburbs further out. This dilemma has been hugely significant from the standpoint of their fiscal capacities. This in turn owes to the space-extensive forms of all manner of new real estate developments, not to mention the demands for more space of industrial and office uses that had once found a home in the inner suburbs. Putting together those sorts of spaces in first suburbs is extremely difficult as a result of the patchwork of ownership, the paucity of large undeveloped spaces and the time and expense of land assembly: hence the interest in *Kelo v. City of New London*.

Ongoing change in the character of real estate products—housing, shopping centers, office parks—continually places older vintages at a disadvantage. Older, typically smaller, housing, perhaps without off-street parking, lacking modern insulation, and contemporary design features means, for existing residents at least, the danger that it will filter down to, horror of horrors, "them" and that the residential tax base will undergo some attrition. Inner suburbs often have their shopping centers, but they are usually on far too small a scale to compete with the newer mega malls appearing further out. And their expansion possibilities are distinctly limited due to the fact that they are often already surrounded by other development. A fairly well-defined "entertainment" district may emerge around some restaurants, perhaps alongside art galleries and a boutique hotel, all promising additional tax revenues. But parking, particularly when compared with the new entertainment complexes appearing further out, is almost invariably an issue.

Additionally, inner suburbs often have a different balance of land uses, one that is biased more toward residential than is the case in many outer suburbs. Inner suburbs came into existence at a time when demands on local governments, and hence their revenue needs, were very strictly limited, and when employment was still found predominantly in the central city. With pressures for money for social services, libraries, parks and recreation, and schools, some inner suburbs now find themselves quite desperately in need of nonresidential uses and all the fiscal benefits that they can bring. For other inner suburbs that had an industrial component, deindustrialization has left its mark, decimating the local tax base. In still other cases, firms faced space needs that could not be met locally and were forced to move further out. Other, somewhat exclusive, inner suburbs have been less seriously affected; for while housing might be smaller and inappropriate to modern tastes the answer has been a rash of demolition and reconstruction on a larger scale: the advent of the so-called McMansions.

The responses on the part of local governments have been diverse. Shopping centers have been redeveloped. Support has been given to private initiatives that have coalesced in seeming organic fashion around new niches in the wider spatial division of consumption: clusters of trendy restaurants along with an art cinema and cramped book stores with a nice musty smell. Older industrial or warehouse sites may be redeveloped with offices and expensive apartments. But what is possible clearly depends on the wider legacy of the suburb: a particular built environment and social composition conducive to these transformations. Blue collar suburbs will struggle.[7]

In a number of states, first suburbs have come together in coalition and formulated legislative programs for state consideration (Puentes 2006). In Ohio this has taken the form of the First Suburbs Consortium, a statewide group seeking to mitigate through state policy what they see as a competitive disadvantage compared with the outer suburbs. One of their major demands has been reallocation of highway money away from the periphery and in their direction (i.e., money for the construction of new freeway interchanges that can spark redevelopment). Another key strategy has been to join forces with an emergent agricultural land preservation lobby spearheaded by farmers (who are not yet ready to sell but want the tax advantages that a preservation policy would bring, bless their hearts) and environmentalists to push for change in annexation law. The intent here has been to try to limit the advantage that outer suburbs enjoy from their relatively large acreages of undeveloped land and of annexing still more of it.

---

7. On the other hand, the position of some inner suburbs is quite exceptional: the City of Vernon in California, to be discussed below, immediately comes to mind—no problem of development there.

This policy program clearly contains within it the seeds of conflict between inner and outer suburbs. Indeed, the potential here is already evident in isolated skirmishes over the allocation of state money for new freeway interchanges and quite apart from any concerted effort on the part of the First Suburbs Consortium. The argument is that new interchanges further out simply reproduce urban sprawl and that there are very real economic gains to be made from taking advantage of a physical infrastructure of streets, houses, and utility lines that already exists further in.[8]

The Contradictions of Urbanization

That capitalist development is accompanied by the growth of cities is a commonplace. For manufacturing and for service industries, the clustering of firms has huge advantages. As cities grow, the division of labor can deepen, allowing the cost advantages of specialization both within and between firms. In some respects cities are like shared means of production: the bigger the city the cheaper the provision, at least as far as things like water and sewerage are concerned, and sometimes airline service.[9] As more firms move in, there is a pooling of workers to be drawn on as one firm expands and another contracts.

In short, cities are those places where firms can most effectively take advantage of the way in which, under capital, production gets socialized. But alongside that socialization of production is a privatization of what comes out of it; not to put too fine a point on it, a struggle over the division of the product in which might is right and which is the focus of so much of what is understood as urban politics. Most obviously this has

8. There is also a national organization called the First Tier Suburbs Council, which seems to operate under the umbrella of the National League of Cities. According to its website it represents "cities and towns outside of central cities and inside the ring of developing suburbs and rural areas. We share unique challenges and strengths that should be included in national, state and regional policy discussions" (National League of Cities 2015).

9. And while airline hubs can bring higher fares in their wake, for corporations the attractions of direct flights to international destinations can more than compensate.

been a struggle between capital and labor, a conflict intensified by the fact that urbanization brings together workers in a situation where they can share their grievances and more effectively organize and then contest the division of the pie: a major reason why, from the standpoint of industrial firms, the dispersal of production has often seemed attractive, particularly for those parts of the labor process that are relatively separable from big city divisions of labor; as in the decanting of low-skill work to small towns discussed earlier.

But the lesson should be clear: through its characteristic socialization of production and subsequent expansion, capital throws up barriers to continuing along the same path; and the removal of those barriers is, among other things, the historical origin of the impulse to city planning (Preteceille 1976). Just how this contradiction expresses itself, though, can vary a great deal depending on exactly what sorts of opportunities and limits there are, and these can be institutional in character. From this standpoint, one of the most distinctive features of metropolitan areas in the United States has been their fragmentation into numerous independent local governments, each with quite formidable powers of land use planning as well as reasons to use those powers. Production is metropolitan in character: firms connect with clients and suppliers across jurisdictional boundaries; workers live within the boundaries of one local government and work in another; some services are provided on a metropolitan basis— a single airport, perhaps a metropolitan water and sewer authority. But how that product is divided up depends to some degree on the competitive actions of local governments; and from the standpoint of furthering the metropolitan development process on which they all ultimately depend, this competition can be far from productive, as we will now see.

Hard Times in Silicon Valley

> Farther south in Menlo Park, Facebook raised billions of dollars in an IPO, instantly putting millions of dollars in the hands of early employees and investors. But as Trulia's economist Jed Kolko notes, the surge of cash will create losers, by bidding up the cost of local housing. "If Facebook were in Texas or North Carolina," he observes, "developers

would have been building new homes in anticipation of this day," but in Silicon Valley—as in San Francisco and Marin County farther north—it's essentially impossible for new construction to meet rising demand for living space. So some of the people living in the area who *didn't* just reap a financial windfall are poised to be priced out of their homes as high rents get even higher. (Yglesias 2012)

Why is this happening? In a nutshell, it's because high-density development is illegal. The city of San Jose has 350 pages of regulations that place an effective ceiling on building density. The regulations include minimum lot sizes, minimum building setbacks, maximum building heights, minimum parking requirements, and so on. Of course, developers can apply for exceptions to these rules, but when they do so, city officials are besieged by what Avent calls NIMBYs ("Not In My Back Yard"), local activists who strenuously oppose having more people live or work in their neighborhoods. (Lee 2011)

A major focus of local development policy in the United States is promoting investment, typically from the outside, in a large lump, and in a locality's economic base: new office developments, new industrial employment, a branch of the state university—in other words, whatever will result in circulating more value through the local economy in the form of retail sales, housing sales, electricity and gas, and taxes to local government. This reflects the typical lobby for local economic development in the United States: the usual cast of characters in local growth coalitions.

In some cases, though, employers in the economic base itself take the initiative, coming together not to secure or defend demand for their products, as in the case of the local retailers and the utilities, but to ensure the future of what might be called their supply side: inputs on terms that will facilitate their profitability. Silicon Valley is a case in point, owing to its massive housing cost problem. On the one hand, there is explosive job growth as a result of the expansion of the computer design and software industries; on the other, there is a huge shortage of affordable housing. This has long been an issue, and clearly a very contradictory one, but one that, if anything, has become more rather than less aggravated over time.

Housing shortage affects the IT businesses not only directly, through the wages that they have to pay to attract the "right" workers (wages that must be set to compensate for extraordinarily high housing costs), but also *in*directly. The computer geeks earning sums of money large enough to allow them to bid housing away from others are a small minority. Most of those working in Silicon Valley are in much humbler positions; more replaceable, perhaps, but as a category absolutely indispensable. These are the people working for the subcontractors who do the assembling, as well as the municipal workers: the fire fighters, the teachers, the garbage collectors. Without them, Silicon Valley is a less desirable place in which to live, which means that it becomes still harder to attract the "right" people.

This is a crisis of shelter that has had impacts beyond the locality. Demand has been pushed out further afield, bringing along with it issues of highway capacity as extensive commutes become commonplace. Competition for available housing in places fifty miles away is creating housing problems for those who happen to already work there. Although the computer industry is concentrated in San Mateo and Santa Clara counties, it is now impacting the adjacent counties of Monterrey and Salinas. In Monterrey this means very stiff competition for housing for workers in the tourist industry, who are already poorly paid. Environmental anxieties there also make expanding the housing supply a fraught matter. In Salinas County it is a question of competition with another classically poorly paid group: agricultural workers. This then displaces housing demand still further out.

The quotes at the beginning of this section give some indication as to exactly *why* there is a housing problem. In fact, it has long been recognized that the effects of the land use policies of the myriad local governments in the area have been thoroughly perverse. Limits on housing density, the exclusion of rental, and limits on building upward all conspire to make it hard to cope with high levels of demand for housing. There is a beggar-thy-neighbor attitude, too. Some local governments have inherited, in their view, more than their fair share of residents and less than their fair share of employment. Nonresidential uses in the United States are always regarded as more fiscally desirable: they bring in property taxes and, in the case of retailing, sales taxes while, unlike residential households, making limited demands on public services. These are important considerations in a country where local governments are obliged to do things, and dependence on locally raised revenues reaches exaggerated proportions. So there is a view among some local governments that they are being dumped on by others—others who have been successful in the struggle for industrial and commercial uses and who are not about to share the loot with those local governments that are, apparently, supposed to house the workers.

On top of that has been the effect of Proposition 13, a quite radical overhaul of state and local taxation that occurred in California in 1978. The most dramatic of the changes from the standpoint of local government was a severe limit on assessed values for property tax purposes. Annual changes could not exceed the rate of inflation, with an absolute cap of 2 percent. This has led to a further reassessment of the tax revenue implications of different land uses. Residential uses, which pay only property taxes, have been further devalued. Instead, and on account of the sales taxes that they generate, it is the commercial uses that have been most desperately sought.

What this has meant is a challenge to the future viability of the computer industry in the area. In part, firms have responded by relocating those parts of their labor processes that call for less than the most highly skilled, highly qualified workers. The more standardized operations have been moved out to smaller towns in the western United States, from Oregon and Idaho in the north through Utah to Arizona and New Mexico. Meanwhile, the research and development operations have remained in Silicon Valley with its advantages of access to collaborators, to upstream firms important to designing new products, and to the lenders who know the industry.[10] This is a development that has been going on at least since the 1970s when housing first emerged as a problem (Saxenian 1984).

There have also been more collective responses. It was the housing question that originally led to businesses coming together: first the Santa Clara Valley Manufacturing Group, which then morphed into the Silicon Valley Manufacturing Group (SVMG), and then later into the Silicon

---

10. For a theoretical elaboration of this point see Gough (2012, 102–103).

Valley Leadership Group. This is a growth coalition with a difference. Instead of focusing on attracting new investment, it has different anxieties: trying to mitigate the housing constraints that threaten the viability of its members.

Part of the coalition's focus has been directly on housing supply. Some of this is a matter of lobbying local government on particular residential developments and raising awareness more generally of an issue that threatens the area's economic base. In addition, the coalition has sponsored research into the problem as a basis for focusing the attention of not just local but also state government. Much has also been made of a $20 million housing trust fund to assist first-time homebuyers and for the provision of affordable rental housing, though in light of the magnitude of the problem this is a drop in the bucket. Earlier the SVMG worked through a number of other organizations. These included a Housing Action Coalition, whose advocacy has, according to SVMG press releases, "either helped or directly resulted in the approval of 72 housing projects, representing 24,000 new homes in 17 different Silicon Valley cities; the projects provide a mix of affordable, market rate and single-room occupancy units" (Association of Bay Area Governments 2016). There has been collaboration with school districts over the provision of housing for teachers, who find themselves increasingly priced out of the local housing market. The SVMG also found itself working with what might seem at first glance to be surprising bedroom partners. One such group is the Greenbelt Alliance. But its goals of limiting peripheral expansion through densification and infill development clearly jibe with the SVMG's agenda of limiting wage increases by reining in not just housing costs but also those of commuting. At the same time, the coalition's goal is to maintain what is left of a highly attractive physical environment and therefore an additional reason for wanting to work in Silicon Valley, as well as something to be traded off against wage demands.

The other relevant area of policy emphasis has been transportation. This tackles the housing question by facilitating access to housing at greater distances though not without effects on people already living there, as noted above. A good deal of energy was put into a referendum in Santa Clara County in 2000 to extend a half-cent sales tax for thirty years that would connect the it to the Bay Area Rapid Transit system or BART. But bottom line: the urbanization process is a contradictory one, and in the United States the jurisdictional fragmentation so characteristic of metropolitan areas has given it distinctive expression. This in turn can mean that the local economic development agenda is not necessarily monopolized by the usual cast of characters anxious to boost demand by bringing more investment into the area regardless of, say, consequences for local housing markets. Rather, the contradictions of urbanization can be directly felt by the major export businesses of the area, which can give local development policy a very different slant.

The Significance of Vernon, California

> Each day tens of thousands of workers pour into Vernon, then return home at night to their bedroom communities. While local government is funded in California by property taxes, the great wealth in Vernon can't be touched by other cities. Commuting workers must tax their homes to pay for the municipal services they need. (Ralph Shaffer, "It's Now Time to Dismantle City of Vernon," *Los Angeles Daily News*, Oct. 15, 2010)

Vernon is part of the Los Angeles metropolitan area, situated just a little to the south of the Los Angeles Central Business District. From one angle it is just one more of the numerous local governments into which American metropolitan areas are divided. But from another it seems very different. This is because Vernon, like one other municipality in the same metro area, the City of Industry, has virtually no residents. Rather, it functions almost entirely as a business site, and this is how those with businesses there like it. Vernon has, in fact, ninety residents and almost two thousand businesses. Quite extraordinary.

Vernon attracted public attention in 2006 when the district attorney announced plans to try to get the city disincorporated: in other words, dissolved. This would require action on the part of the state of California. Municipalities were not always municipalities. Rather they had to be proposed and their boundaries carved out of what had been unincorporated land. In this case what the district attorney had in mind, though, was not to return it to the unincorporated state. The question up for debate was what should be done with it, of which other city it should henceforth become a part, although this is not the aspect of the case that will concern us here.

The ostensible reason for disincorporating Vernon, underline *ostensible*, was the charge of corruption. Its city officials were rewarding themselves with massive salaries and perks. This was held to be due to a lack of accountability. The few residents who voted either worked for the city or lived in city-owned housing. County prosecutors did, however, also argue that what was happening in the case of Vernon was a sequestering of tax base so that the revenues that might otherwise have flowed to schools, hospitals, and other services in the county were retained by the businesses there as profits—which sounds a bit more like it.

From the standpoint of business, the low taxes resulting from this sequestering were a major raison d'être for a city like Vernon. Why locate there rather than somewhere else in the greater Los Angeles area if not for tax attractions? So, not surprisingly, businesses were opposed to the disincorporation move. One "interesting" suggestion came from the president of the Vernon Property Association, according to whom many of the owners thought that if accountability was the problem then the (nonresident) property owners of the city—i.e., them—should be allowed to vote in local elections, even though this is typically not allowed in US municipalities. Another point made was that those who worked in Vernon were taxed elsewhere, so the wealth produced there did in fact add to municipal revenues beyond the city's boundaries. As always in the United States, when future streams of land rent are at stake, as they were here, the imaginations of those who stand to make a juicy buck run riot.

This particular case raises at least two interesting questions for the American politics of local development. The first is whether only residents should be allowed to vote in elections. The second involves the creation of what one might call "fiscal enclaves": areas that can sequester taxable wealth from those elsewhere who could usefully do with it. Obviously these topics are closely connected.

First point to be made: Despite all the invidious attention it attracted, on closer inspection the Vernon case of fiscal sequestering seems little different from what is commonplace across American metropolitan areas—something so commonplace that it tends to be taken for granted. Of course Vernon was deliberately created in order to keep the property taxes of businesses down and thereby preempt appropriation of their land rents by others. There would be no school taxes to pay—no taxes to support, for example, a city park system. But the practice of exclusionary zoning, whereby the more affluent residents use zoning ordinances to prevent the movement of the less affluent into a municipality (typically a suburban one) and thus keep *their* taxes down, is typical. Though not for general consumption, the argument is that by keeping out the poor you keep out people who would make the same demands on city services as those who are better off—people who would live in smaller houses and pay less in property taxes, and thus would essentially be subsidized by the affluent. Through zoning ordinances it is possible to exclude apartments since the tax that an apartment pays through property taxation is typically less than that paid by a single family house. Likewise, through low density zoning for single family housing, only those who can afford more land and who are likely, therefore, to reside in an appropriately more elaborate and therefore higher-value house can live there. Those who cannot afford such homes are excluded. If the Vernon case is different, therefore, it is only as a matter of degree: fiscal exclusion rules.

Some have argued that a general goal of local governments in the urban areas of the United States is encapsulated in the optimization of a simple ratio: maximize the tax base (typically the value of real property but also in many cases sales tax revenues) per person while minimizing municipal expenditures. A bizarre consequence is school districts that do not want children. There is also a whole consulting industry dedicated to producing so-called cost-revenue analyses for local governments. These evaluate the revenues that particular land uses are likely to bring in relative to the costs of providing city services to them. Housing for the aged is a nice genuflection to those who tiresomely talk social justice since it keeps out maladroit youth and so holds down police costs. One-bedroom apartments are more desirable than two-bedroom ones since the latter are likely to include children who have to be educated at public expense. Shopping centers, on the other hand, bring in sales taxes but require little in terms of city expenditures: just the occasional visit from the police or the fire service, perhaps, but certainly no school children.

This tactic of purposeful exclusion of people, preventing them grazing on the rich tax bases of some suburbs, and raised to a high art, poses the issue of whether only residents should have the vote in municipal elections; or should they have to share it with the excluded? To return to what I said at the beginning of this section on the socialization of production in urban areas, one way to look at this question is indeed in terms of the geography of wealth production. If each municipality was an island in that regard, a self-sufficient economy producing all its needs, there would be no problem. But clearly this is not the case. In a metropolitan area, wealth is a cooperative product involving a division of labor that brings together people who live scattered across the various municipalities into which the area is typically divided. This cooperative character of the product raises the question of the principles according to which that product should be divided among those party to its production. This is a legitimate question for debate among all those whose labor entered into the product. Should a county judge be paid more than a shop assistant? Or a real estate sales person more than the person who laid the concrete for the houses she sells? How legitimate is the wealth commanded by the residents of some exclusive suburb? Again this seems a reasonable question for debate, and to some degree that debate occurs. But to some degree it is also pre-empted by the sorts of practices of municipal incorporation and exclusion that occur without any debate regarding their distributional effects. And exclusion *does* have redistributional effects: the very fact of exclusion, keeping out "them," means that real estate values will be higher regardless of the size or character of the house occupied—something that the owner can cash out in future if she so wishes.

This distributional question should not distract from the implications of this sort of fiscal segregation for urban development. The possibilities of residential exclusion certainly open up new avenues of accumulation for the development industry itself, as it draws on the virtues of particular school districts to sell houses; and as obsolescence, social and physical, sets in, developers move further out in search of the same marketing advantages. But, as in the case of Silicon Valley, there are implications for social reproduction: not least housing and schools. Exclusionary zoning limits housing supply, forcing up prices and so creating labor shortages: in some cases this produces the odd juxtaposition of central city unemployment and a shortage of workers in the suburbs because of the difficulty that the car-less have in accessing jobs there—what urban geographers refer to as spatial mismatch. Likewise employers depend on the public sector for a supply of reasonably formed workers: something not helped by the tax avoidance of businesses that seek refuge in the likes of Vernon, California.

In other countries, this is not such a big problem. In France some of the services typically provided by local government in the United States are responsibilities of the central state, and the central state pays for them. Such is the case of education and schools. There are no local school boards in France. Teachers are appointed by the central government and they get paid by it. There is no question of finding the money to pay them locally. The same applies to the police, hence no operating levies of the sort that litter the political landscape of the American metropolitan area. In Great Britain local governments provide many of the same services provided by local government in the United States, but they do not have to rely on local taxation to nearly the same degree. Rather, there is a central government grant to each local government designed to make up for a locally weak tax base and the particular character of the population to be provided for (so, for example, more money for services to the aged to local governments with a higher proportion of old people).

In the cases of both France and Great Britain, it is still, as in Vernon or any other local government in the United States, only local residents who get to vote. The difference is the sheer geographic scope of the jurisdiction within which they vote and how it approximates more closely to the space in which the wealth to be divided actually gets produced: that is, the country as a whole and the elections are, accordingly, national ones.

There is, of course, a common retort to this logic, and it will be typically offered by the wealthy beneficiaries of fiscal home rule and the ability to exclude. Rather, they will claim, local provision and local taxation, contra the French and British cases, have an overriding virtue: that the people who are going to consume public services are the ones who know best what they want and how much they are willing to be taxed for it.

This was, in fact, the basis for a very influential argument put forward in 1956 by the American economist Charles Tiebout. With local discretion regarding what was provided and at what price, people could move around until they found the local government most approximating in its policies of provision and taxation to their preferences. They would in effect be "voting with their feet." This is obviously and thoroughly disingenuous. It is not just that Tiebout omitted the locational choices of businesses from his calculation—clearly important if we are to make sense of the Vernon instance. Rather he ignored the way—perfectly evident at the time he was writing—in which the municipal fragmentation of American metropolitan areas for which he was trying to provide a rationale is mobilized by those with wealth not just to protect themselves from taxation but also to grow the tax base even more. As I noted above, property values are enhanced simply by virtue of exclusion. The assets so accumulated can then be used to advantage elsewhere: selling up a house in a wealthy Californian suburb in order to retire somewhere in the non-urban West, where home values are lower (and, if it is Nevada, no taxes to pay either). And just as exclusion has negative effects on the poor back in Los Angeles, so does the enhanced purchasing power of retirees on those among whom they come to live, driving up values there and making it harder for *them* to find housing at a price they can afford.

Most significant of all is the way in which the exclusionary suburb is used by the households wealthy enough to live there to enhance the life chances of their offspring. They are going to compete for employment not just in a metropolitan labor market but, for some at least, in one that is national. The large sums of money that the (exclusionary) suburban school district can afford to invest in the education of each of their pupils, along with the less quantifiable cultural capital acquired from mixing with those who share your own ambition and the assurance that you can achieve it (because of Mom and Dad's money, among other things), places them at a tremendous advantage. So the Vernon case has a very wide resonance indeed. It *should* be a Pandora's box. Important questions are: Can it be? Will it be? But this is to move the debate on from the contradictions of urbanization to what might be called the "good geography": something that has been very much in the sights of those responsible for urban and regional development in Western Europe but which, in its absence, underlines once more the distinctiveness of the American case.

The Pursuit of Monopoly Rents

The idea of competition over space has loomed large in the cases discussed so far. It is, though, far from an end in itself. The end is accumulation: amassing wealth through profits, interest, and rent, and recycling the money so as to make more. Curtailing competition— driving out the competitors and keeping them out—must in consequence be a major goal, and not least for those businesses and local governments that, as a result of their interest in rent, have stakes in particular places and form the growth coalitions so characteristic of the American politics of urban and regional development. This goal becomes all the more significant to the extent that they have investments of long life to protect: investments to be amortized by that stream of revenue that can be threatened by the arrival of others who would take business away from them. So when one talks about rent and its pursuit, the defense of some monopolistic privilege is never far away, as will now become evident.

A Tale of Two Cities and Two Airports

Airline service is a crucial condition for the economic growth of larger cities. The common view in local economic development circles is that it makes cities attractive to firms seeking sites for corporate headquarters or indeed for any operation that requires rapid and timely access to other firms and major markets elsewhere. Airline service can place them on the map as a significant site for conventions, enhancing the flow of revenue to the local government, which typically owns the convention center, as well as generating demand for local hotel rooms. The airport itself can be a major source of city revenue via various fees from airlines, concessions, and parking areas, among others; in other words, a variety of rents. On the other hand, airports represent considerable physical investments and ones of long life. Very large sums of money are borrowed to build them, and the investment is then only slowly amortized. In addition, airport expansion, and certainly the creation of entirely new airports, can be very risky. What if the traffic projected does not materialize? The case of Dallas-Fort Worth International Airport provides some powerful lessons.

The background was a decision taken in the 1960s to create a new regional airport that would serve both Fort Worth and Dallas and that would become known as Dallas–Fort Worth International, or DFWI. The two cities were to be the joint owners of the airport and so ultimately responsible for paying the bonds sold to raise the money. As is usual in these cases, the bonds would be serviced by various fees paid by the airlines, including fees for landing and the rental of space, and by the rents returned from concessions and parking. In an attempt to ensure the necessary flow of revenue, both cities agreed to restrict passenger service from their own existing airports, and all the airlines serving them at that time signed an agreement to relocate to DFWI. In other words, the threat of competition had already loomed its ugly head, but it seemed to be under control.

The new airport opened in 1974. But prior to that an airline whose creation postdated the agreement—Southwest Airlines—started using Dallas's old airport, Love Field, one of the airports that had been abandoned by other airlines corralled into using DFWI. This development was of limited interest to those planning the new airport, since at that time Southwest operated purely within Texas, which enabled it to avoid the federal regulation applying to interstate airlines. Once deregulation occurred in 1978, though, and Southwest started flying to destinations in other states, the picture changed entirely. This had not been planned for. It became a cause of considerable angst on the part of the major tenant at DFWI, American Airlines, and consequently for the major bond issuers and therefore debtors, the cities of Dallas and Fort Worth. But not far down the road it would also be a condition for an eventual parting of the ways between Fort Worth and Dallas once it became clear that Dallas had something to gain from airline traffic at Love Field, notably because the older airport happened to be much closer than DFWI to the Dallas central business district. This realization would take some time, though.

The immediate response to the challenge was the Wright Amendment—named after Congressman Jim Wright, who, by no coincidence, represented a district centered on Fort Worth—which presumably got passed as a result of some horse trading with other congresspersons for whom the future of DFWI could not have been of the remotest consequence: something again typical of the American politics of development. But significantly it was also supported by the City of Dallas and by the major tenant at DFWI, American Airlines, also anxious about competition for its own reasons. The Wright Amendment limited service from Love Field to cities in Texas and in the four contiguous states of New Mexico, Oklahoma, Arkansas, and Louisiana, which meant that there could be no direct services from Love Field to major destinations like Los Angeles, Chicago, and New York. Southwest could provide service, but only if the plane landed first in Texas or in one of the four contiguous states before proceeding on. In that regard DFWI, and by reason of its dominant position there, American Airlines, would have a monopoly over direct long-distance flights. This agreement, however, would not endure.

First, there was the success of the Southwest Airlines business model. Offering low fares, it became a major challenger to the so-called legacy airlines. Airports across the country lobbied it to begin service there. It was not just that its low fares boosted traffic; Southwest could also be a challenge to airlines that enjoyed quasi monopolies stiffing the customer with hefty ticket prices, as in the case of TWA at St. Louis. So, and given the significance of Dallas as a major destination, there was pressure from a number of states to allow Southwest to start direct service beyond the limits defined by the Wright Amendment. Accordingly, in 1997 a law authored by Senator Richard Shelby of Alabama modified the Wright Amendment to allow flights to Alabama, Kansas, and Mississippi. In 2005, Senator Kit Bond of Missouri attached an amendment to a transportation spending bill to exempt his state from the Wright restrictions. After the bill's passage, Southwest began nonstop flights from Love Field to St. Louis and Kansas City.

Significantly, the City of Dallas supported the Shelby Amendment. This was because, with the growth of Southwest, it had begun to see the implications of Love Field for its own economic growth and demand for downtown real estate. Dallas, after all, was the headquarters city of Southwest Airlines and as such the recipient of all the taxes it paid on its airplanes. The airline also had a growing employment presence in the city: well over six thousand at its headquarters and maintenance facilities, which added to Dallas's tax income. And since Love Field belonged to the City of Dallas, Dallas got the rental income.

The City of Fort Worth was dismayed by the turn of events and sued, unsuccessfully, to prevent the Shelby Amendment coming into force. The fundamental problem was that its material stake in the proceedings was different from that of the City of Dallas. Its stake was in ensuring that the bonds in whose sale it participated, and which for an airport of the size of DFWI were huge, got paid off; in other words, Fort Worth faced a problem of investments of long life. Dallas also bore responsibility for the bonds, but in its case, and unlike Fort Worth, it had an alternative airport that would generate the necessary offsetting income. So while in the Dallas case growth interests lined up behind a liberalization of the rules allowing the use of Love Field, growth interests in Fort Worth were firmly opposed, not just because they did not stand to gain anything from opening up Love Field but also because they had stakes in the city's bonded debt. To the extent that there is concern that such debt will not be paid off according to schedule, a city's bond rating and hence its ability to raise money for other public works are affected. What seemed like a cozy idea between two cities, an opportunity to cooperate, now verged on the toxic.

All this of course, was without the entrenched resistance of American Airlines, which dominated service at DFWI and feared any competitive challenge. In fact the high fares that American was able to charge as a result of its monopoly—80 percent of all traffic—were one of the reasons used by those arguing for the dismantling of the Wright Amendment and indeed any restrictions on service from Dallas's Love Field. In its obdurate resistance, American had the support of its large number of employees and of all those other businesses, like the airport concessions, with some sort of stake in the future of DFWI.

Nevertheless, there would be change once again, but a compromise between all the contending forces. As of 2014 the Wright Amendment was completely repealed. In its place emerged something equally designed to help DFWI preserve its monopoly status: a limit on the number of gates at Love Field. In fact, the compromise lowered the number of gates from thirty-two to twenty, which certainly put a crimp on the ability of Southwest to take advantage of its access to the Dallas area market. In addition, there could be no nonstop flights to international destinations, which is not an issue for Southwest since it is not an international airline; but then at one point in this story it was not an interstate one either.

In review, several comments can be made about what turns out to be an extraordinarily rich case. The first relates to the competitive struggle between cities and the growth interests on which they depend for economic development or, more accurately, for rents from land and the improvements thereon; in this case, between Fort Worth and Dallas. Initially, they tried to cooperate so as to gain the advantages that would come in terms of service from an airport serving both cities. But the possibilities of Love Field as a money earner for Dallas, coupled with Fort Worth's concerns about bonded debt, eventually cast their marriage vows in a different light. This serves as an exquisite reminder of the significance of large investments of long life, like airports, in the politics of urban and regional development and the impulse they provide for guaranteeing what is in effect a spatial monopoly. And it was indeed anxieties about paying off the debt that initially led to attempts to limit service from the existing airports at Fort Worth and Dallas and to put pressure on the airlines serving those airports to abandon them in favor of DFWI.

With the creation of hubs dominated by major airlines, though, came a different set of anxieties, and this is the second point. Hubs give the airlines that dominate them some market power and were a response to the sharply more competitive context brought about by airline deregulation. Hub airlines have some leeway over the fares that they charge: something that can run afoul of local convention business and business more generally. The hub airline itself will try to defend its privilege. Another airport in the vicinity can be a challenge, which is why American Airlines has been so vigorous in its attempt to snuff out the use of Love Field by Southwest.[11] On the other hand, breaking the power of hub airlines

---

11. Other airlines have learned from the experience of American Airlines at DFWI. When the new Denver International Airport was proposed, one of two major hub airlines, United, refused to move from the existing Stapleton Airport unless there

elsewhere was one of the considerations behind Senator Kit Bond's intervention: to break the stranglehold that TWA had at that time at its major hub in St. Louis.

Third, the amendments introduced in an attempt to limit traffic from Love Field have important implications. The first is that, given the way in which they challenged the interstate commerce clause of the constitution, any action taken had to be through the federal government, which apparently does not give a damn about that clause if the local pressures are strong enough and various quid pro quos can be arranged. This is a politics, in short, that can quickly shift to arenas elsewhere: the locals engaging state or federal government to act on their behalf, and apparently, at least in cases like this one, succeeding. Second, note that sponsors of these amendments were all very local, underlining the way in which the American state is so open—even exceptionally so—to these sorts of pressures, but also recalling how the question of uneven development opened up by the emergence of Rust Belt anxieties rapidly became a federal one; just as indeed the question of the inner suburbs could not be confined to respective metropolitan areas.

Fourth, we should note the role that the deregulation of the airline industry played in all this. DFWI was already up and running in 1974, before deregulation was even on the federal radar screen.[12] It dates back, therefore, to a time when on interstate routes airline fares were regulated by the Civil Aeronautics Board, which also served as the arbitrator of all requests for new routes. Competition between airlines was therefore very limited indeed. Just what the consequences would be once deregulation occurred could not have been imagined, though Southwest Airlines was very quick to spot some of the possibilities. Yet nobody anticipated the emergence of hub-and-spoke patterns for airline routes and the tendency

---

was provision in the plans for its demolition. Demolition would prevent its use by any existing airline or any in the future for that matter: something that would have been attractive to the Denver flying public given the close proximity of Stapleton to downtown and the quite extraordinary distance of twenty-five miles between the downtown and the new airport.

12. Hearings would begin in 1975.

for airlines to try to create hub dominance, driving out rivals to seek hubs elsewhere. This, though, is an important part of the story since it then stiffened the interest of cities with hubs in attracting the likes of Southwest and so weakening the provisions of the Wright Amendment.

Finally, fiscal issues were inseparable from these conflicts. In fact, without them the conflicts would have been much less intense. Fort Worth worried about where the rents were to come from so as to pay off its share of the bonds that had been sold to build the airport. Dallas was less concerned because it was getting revenues from Love Field and from the taxes paid by all those working for Southwest Airlines, at least to the degree that they lived or shopped within city boundaries. Fiscal flows, therefore, are of huge importance in the American politics of local and regional development. Dallas and Fort Worth are major cities. But metropolitan areas in the United States are, as we have seen, made up of a tapestry of local governments—an important aspect of the country's specificity—and each of these is anxious to maximize its tax revenues while minimizing its expenditures.

Casino Controversies

In the November 2009 state elections in Ohio, an issue appeared on the ballot regarding casino gambling, which hitherto had not been permitted in that state. Passage of Issue 3 would allow an amendment to the constitution permitting the establishment of casinos in four of Ohio's major cities: Cincinnati, Cleveland, Columbus, and Toledo. The projected $600 million in state revenues would then be distributed to local governments and school districts. In the neighboring states of Indiana and Kentucky casino gambling *was* permitted, and had been attracting gamblers from Ohio. This meant, according to the arguments for casino gambling, that Ohio and the four cities in particular were losing out from the development gains that supposedly it would bring.

There was opposition to the issue. Some of this was based on moral grounds: casinos attracted those more vulnerable fractions of the population who could least afford it; they tended to be associated with criminal elements; and, quite simply, gambling was sinful (an idea always attractive in a country that still takes religion seriously). Some of the opposition was dependent on more local considerations. This was the case in Columbus. If Issue 3 passed, then the casino in Columbus would be built next to the Arena District (Figure 1): an area of new office developments, bars, and restaurants; home to major sports attractions, notably the Columbus Blue Jackets ice hockey team and the Columbus Clippers minor league baseball team; and, above all, an area of booming real estate values. It should come as no surprise, therefore, that the principal landlords in the Arena District—Nationwide Insurance and the *Columbus Dispatch*, the major daily newspaper in the city—were expressing concerns. In an article on March 14, 2009, the *Dispatch* averred: "The proposed site for central Ohio's first casino is a long-abandoned and pockmarked factory, but it's close to the thriving entertainment district surrounding Nationwide Arena. Although the casino—costing at least $250 million and providing table games and as many as 5,000 slot machines—would change the character of the neighborhood, its proponents did not vet the idea with the major landowner in the Arena District." The implication was, of course, that they should have done so, regardless of the fact that this is far from normal practice. In retrospect it seems that the *Dispatch* wanted to make it normal practice or imply to readers that it already was. In other words, this is a wonderful example of discourse at work in the American politics of local development.

In the end, Issue 3 passed by a margin of 53 percent to 47 percent, though not in Franklin County where Columbus is located. There it lost by a considerable margin of 58 to 42 percent, while in the City of Columbus it was 55 to 45 percent: "No" votes that the opposition in Columbus would later try to turn to its advantage. The fact that casino gambling was now scheduled to be coming to Columbus, and to a site next to the Arena District, heightened anxieties. Outrage took over the pages of the *Columbus Dispatch*, and the newspaper was happy to fan the flames if not to create the bonfire itself, despite its clear conflict of interest since it was itself 20 percent owner of the Arena District.[13]

13. Only later after there had been complaints did the newspaper start including in all its articles on the casino issue a disclosure regarding its ownership interest.

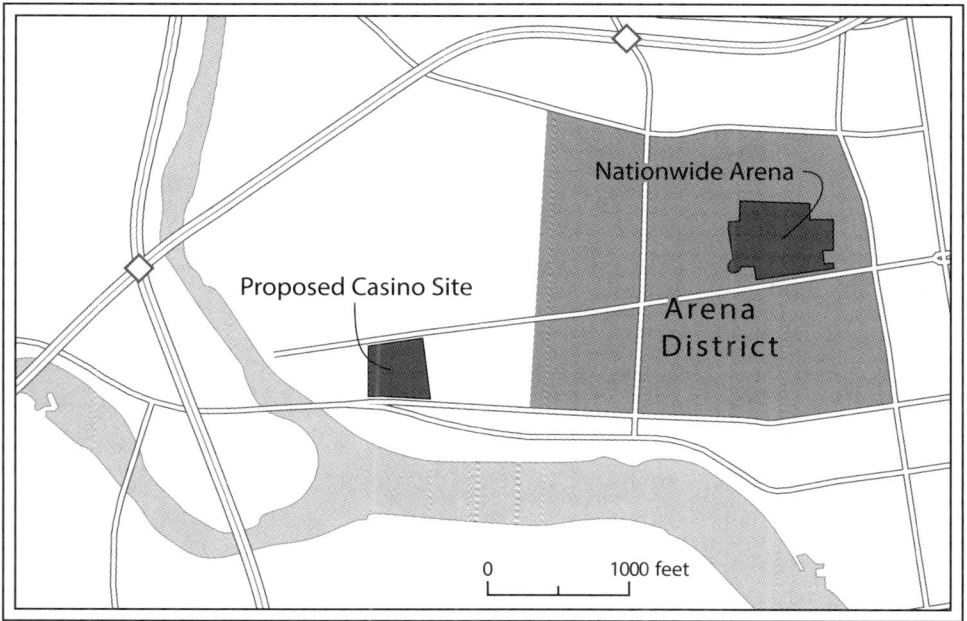

Fig. 1. The Arena district and the proposed casino site, Columbus, Ohio. Map by Jim DeGrand.

Several different forms of opposition were suggested, some of them in their sheer outrageousness, even puerility, hinting at desperation:

- That the city should make life difficult for the casino developers. The site to be occupied by the casino had previously been industrial. The owner of the site, before selling it to the casino company, had proposed housing there and had qualified for cleanup funds from the federal government, a qualification that remained with the site when it was sold. Columbus had been the recipient of those funds since it would carry out the cleanup. Now, the *Dispatch* argued, those funds should be withheld. Likewise the city should withhold all utilities and street improvements that the casino would require.[14]

14. "Whenever and however city leaders can block or slow the development of a casino in Columbus, they should do so. Where zoning changes, water and sewer lines

- That a constitutional amendment should be introduced into the state legislature to the effect that counties where Issue 3 did *not* pass should be exempt from its provisions; that is, if Franklin County said "No" then Columbus did not have to abide by the statewide vote.
- That if, nevertheless, Columbus had to abide by the decision of voters statewide, another site should be found for the casino. This would be the "solution" eventually adopted.

Meanwhile the *Dispatch* put out a series of editorials and articles on the horrors about to be unleashed on the City of Columbus and not least on what was defined as its crown jewel, the fabled Arena District. One of its major claims was that the casino was inappropriate in what it defined as a "family entertainment area," though the numerous watering holes and expensive restaurants that pepper the area hardly seem to be the place for young children. Some quotes from the newspaper's columns and editorials:

> Taxpayers have already paid to aid in the cleanup of the casino site, just west of Huntington Park, where a tool factory was once situated. A $750,000 grant from the Ohio Department of Development was used for the cleanup. The city applied for the grant and the state gladly complied, because the land was supposed to be redeveloped as a complex of condominiums, apartments and shops. Then, the casino people *swooped in*, bought the parcel and etched the site in ink into Issue 3. More than 1.67 million Ohio voters ostensibly green-lighted the location when they voted "yes" on the issue. Franklin County was outvoted. Columbus was outvoted. (Nov. 5, 2009)

> Franklin County Commissioner John O'Grady best summed up this sentiment. The Arena District, he said, represents the most *family-friendly* Downtown development in decades. Why would anyone want to jeopardize that? Why would anyone side with *an out-of-state gambling*

---

and access streets are needed, the city should not go along and should assert its constitutionally authorized home-rule rights to serve the best interests of its residents." (*Columbus Dispatch*, Dec. 21, 2009)

mogul over the express wishes of central Ohio's voters and its business community? (Nov. 15, 2009)

Penn National, *based in Wyomissing, Pa.*, did not consult with central Ohio leaders before *secretly negotiating* for the purchase of an 18.3-acre site just west of Huntington Park on Nationwide Boulevard. (Nov. 29, 2009)

A casino is like a black hole that swallows up the money that people otherwise would spend on restaurants, movies, concerts, ballgames and other *established businesses* in the area. At the same time, legalized gambling feeds *home-wrecking addictions*. (Dec. 21, 2009)

The italics are mine. They are meant to draw attention to some of the rhetorical flourishes indulged in by the *Dispatch* and its writers, but not untypical of cases elsewhere: "swooping in" like a predator, "secretly negotiating" like someone who has something to hide, and "gambling mogul," as in someone who amasses wealth irresponsibly. There are also some interesting assumptions in these statements that require comment. Why was the *Dispatch* underlining the out-of-state origins of the casino company, unless it believed that they reduced the legitimacy of its desire to establish a casino in Columbus?[15] The implication is that if the casino company had been home grown, then things would have been different, though clearly that has to be in doubt. The reference to "established businesses" is also interesting. Here the assumption seems to be that the desires of those already established should be given preference over those who have yet to establish themselves. Quite apart from the difficulty of knowing what it means to be "established," is that reasonable?

15. In reference to a group called "Stand Up Columbus!" which opposed the Arena District site, county commissioner Dewey Stokes "said in a news release that the group represents 'neighborhood leaders, soccer moms, doctors, accountants, coaches, lawyers, business owners, union workers, elected officials, retirees, independents, Democrats and Republicans. But all of us agree *it's not right that an out-of-town casino operator—without any community input—gets to decide where a casino will be built in our city*'" (Dec. 27, 2009; emphasis mine).

The newspaper also featured public interest stories designed to stir up public opinion against the casino and particularly the site next to the Arena District. People who had bought residential property in the area prior to passage of Issue 3 were interviewed and their sorrows, regrets, and frustrations put on public display. This was so even while the major concern of the *Dispatch* was its own investments. Meanwhile the biggest stakeholder of all, Nationwide Insurance, stood on the sidelines while the *Dispatch* did the dirty work.

The issue of location would eventually be resolved by finding an alternative site as far away from the Arena District as possible, and by persuading the casino company to buy it and sell the old one. The site eventually homed in on was on the far west side of the city and actually not in the city itself but in a township: Franklin Township. This was a part of the urban area that could defensibly (and patronizingly) be defined as "in need of economic development." Two of the specific sites (Figure 2) were defined as evidence of this need: one was the large, enclosed Westland Mall, which found itself in severe competitive difficulties with the opening of a more attractive mall to the north; the second was the former site of a large Delphi auto-parts plant. Likewise, with the closure of plants like Delphi, Franklin Township had been left scrambling for tax revenues to keep its fire and police services going. Yet either of the possible sites had major accessibility advantages since they were both close to interchanges on two major freeways. Much was also made in the pages of the *Dispatch* that in Franklin Township the vote in Issue 3 had been 55 percent in favor of having casino gambling.[16] Whatever site was chosen seemed to have a lot going for it. The problem was that the City of Columbus, despite having supported the campaign to prevent locating the casino next to the Arena District, wanted to annex the site so that it could claim the tax revenues from the casino. For reasons not clearly specified, the casino company, Penn National, after some resistance, decided that it also wanted the

16. What was not mentioned, of course, was that what people in Franklin Township were voting for in effect was a casino next to the Arena District and not one in Franklin Township, since the sites were widely publicized in advance of the statewide referendum.

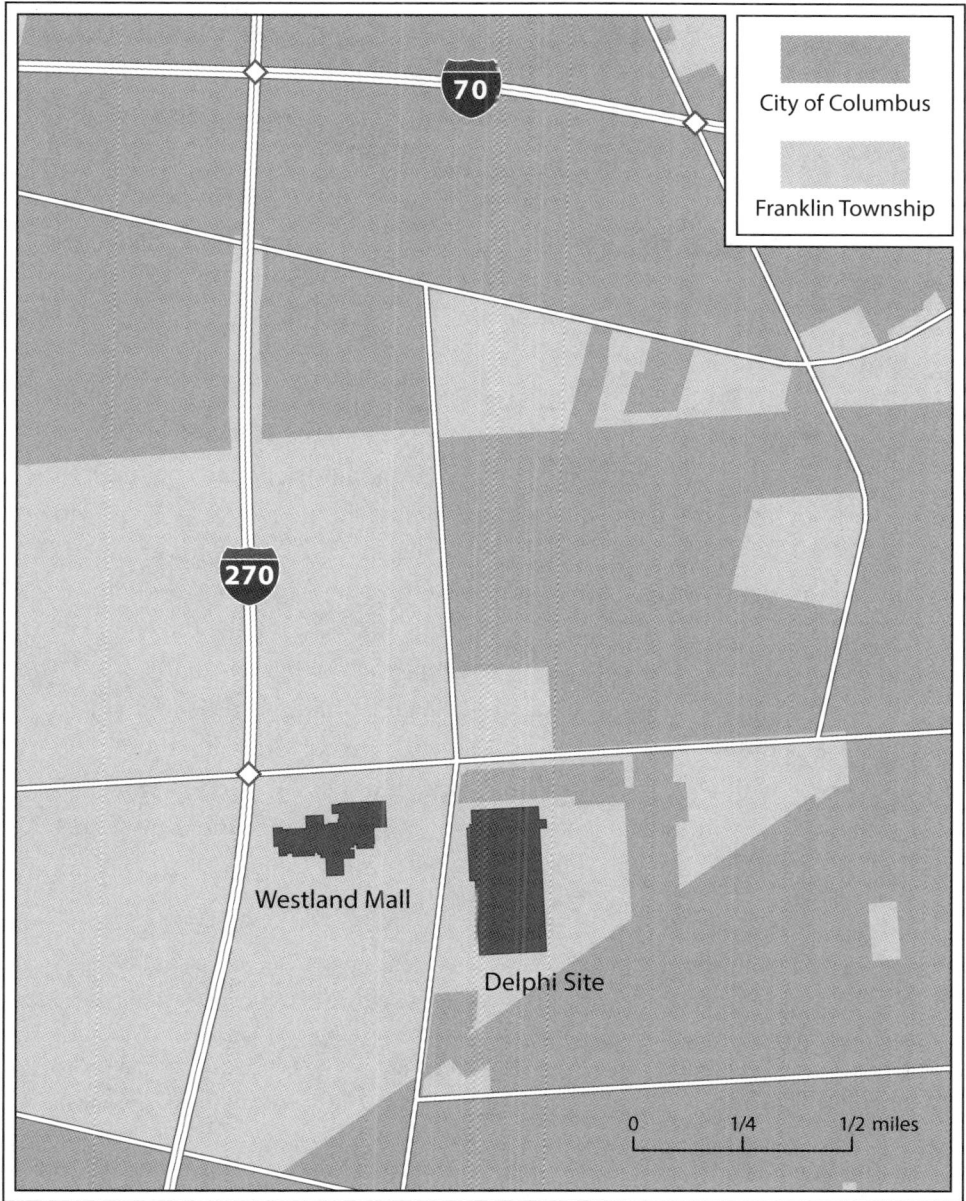

Fig. 2. The two proposed casino sites in Franklin Township, Ohio. Map by Jim DeGrand.

casino to be in the city.[17] Columbus's desire to bring something into the city that it had wanted at one time to see the end of would not be the final irony in this story.

What resolved the issue was the willingness of the Franklin Township trustees to allow annexation to Columbus in exchange for a revenue-sharing agreement. The agreement's most significant element is an approximate 75–25 percent split between city and township of income and property tax revenue. All other property taxes in the annexed area would continue to go to Franklin Township, and after fifty years it would get those from the casino site as well.

The interesting question then was what was going to happen to all the anticipated revenue flowing in the direction of the City of Columbus? There are no prizes for guessing that the Arena District once again raised its head, or rather its hand. The original claim when Issue 3 was "sold"[18] to the Ohio voting public was that the money would go to local governments and school districts. But what should the City of Columbus do with its share? There were lots of claimants, and one turned out to be the tenant of the ice hockey arena from which the Arena District takes its name.

Obtaining an ice hockey franchise for Columbus had been a key to the development of the area. The team is a major draw for those who spend money in area restaurants and bars, and who fill parking spaces in the numerous parking garages built there.[19] Once it was announced that the arena would have a resident, the *Columbus Dispatch* went to work

17. All I have been able to find on this is a statement from a representative of Penn National to the effect that "the company wants to build in the city because it wants to be part of the Columbus business community" (*Columbus Dispatch*, Jan. 12, 2010), which does not sound very convincing. Just why would they want to be part of the Columbus business community, particularly given the hostility displayed toward them by some of its prominent members?

18. A not inappropriate metaphor given the large amounts of money lavished on attracting support in the sort of referendum that opened this saga.

19. Outside of the season, of course, there was a problem, which is why the landlords of the Arena District (Nationwide Insurance and the *Columbus Dispatch*) went to so much trouble in getting the baseball arena relocated into the area: a summer market to complement the winter one provided by ice hockey.

once more, instructing—foregrounding—the delights of ice hockey to a readership that barely knew the difference between a puck and a golf ball. So ice hockey now has a constituency in Columbus, and that may be important for the rest of the story. Because the Blue Jackets had been losing money—lots of it. The majority owner, sensing pay dirt, threatened to relocate to some other city. A major problem had been the lease agreement between the team and the arena owners: that is, Nationwide Insurance and the *Columbus Dispatch*, who were also owners of the Arena District. Normally a team can gain revenue from arena naming rights and sky boxes. The Blue Jackets had none of these. So where would the money come from to make up the difference? No guesses there: Tax revenues that Columbus and Franklin County receive from the casino would be devoted to purchasing the arena, and the county would become its new owner; new contracts with the major tenant could then be made so as to ensure its continuing presence for the foreseeable future, which is what happened. This is money that could have been diverted to other, more defensible, public purposes.

We should, though, note who has *really* gained from all this: if the Bluejackets had indeed left town, then Nationwide Insurance and the *Columbus Dispatch* stood to lose a lot of money. The alternative to casino tax revenues to make up the team's deficit would have been to rewrite the contract with the Arena owners to whom the Blue Jackets were paying a rent. Nationwide owns the naming rights: hence it is called Nationwide Arena. The skybox revenues went 90 percent to Nationwide and 10 percent to the *Dispatch*. Nationwide and the *Dispatch* have also cashed in, and will continue to do so, from the parking garages where those attending games park their cars.

Finally, in this story we should note the huge part that has been played by the local newspaper. The *Columbus Dispatch* has continually taken the lead and promoted a particular point of view. One of the reasons it has had the power to do so is that it is the only newspaper in town and so has a monopoly on print information.[20] There is no other newspaper that

20. It also owns a television and radio station.

might advocate an alternative point of view or serve as a sounding board for those disenchanted with the view put out by the *Dispatch*. There *used to* be another newspaper, the *Columbus Citizen-Journal*, which closed down in 1985. Part of the reason it closed down—but only part—is decisions made by the *Dispatch*. The two newspapers had a contract whereby the *Dispatch* acted as the *Citizen-Journal*'s printer. Three years prior to the termination of the contract, the *Dispatch* informed the *Citizen-Journal* that it was no longer willing to print it.[21]

"It's the Environment, Stupid"

From the 1960s on, there was a new participant in struggles around urban and regional development: the environmental movement in its various guises, local and national, more transitory and more enduring, and pursuing various goals. The movement has embraced health issues and promoted the natural environment as something to be experienced. It has also explored what it means to be human, expressing anxieties about growth as an unmitigated good, a notion that began to emerge in the 1960s.

What it has to do with rents, of course, is the way it geographically differentiates, creating scarcities where they did not exist or enhancing them. The propensity of the environmental movement to work through a principle of separation—the creation of special preservation areas of various sorts—is an obvious instance. It not only provides the possibility of increased rents for those owning land outside the special areas; it also creates incentives for subverting the regulations, albeit in part, since if there is something to be preserved there, then creating a development in the

---

21. However, the *Dispatch* may not be the only source of the problem in this instance. The *Citizen-Journal* was owned by the Scripps-Howard media conglomerate. It was profitable for them and could conceivably have invested in printing presses of its own; but because it was in competition with the *Dispatch*, and Scripps-Howard preferred markets where it owned the sole newspaper, there was a decision not to make this investment. Nevertheless, the *Dispatch* gave them a nudge.

middle of it is obviously highly attractive to buyers.[22] But the legislation of special areas—national parks, nature reserves, even areas dominated by low density zoning—is not a necessary stepping stone to rent enhancement. The creation of scarcity and hence new possibilities of rent appropriation can also work through the way in which legislation that in its provisions is seemingly location-indifferent turns out to be anything but. Alternatively, there may be compromises in the creation of special areas: ideals of preservation are realized, but an area may remain a so-called working landscape in which farming and even some mineral exploitation can proceed. In this case the possibilities of rent extraction continue, but attention now turns to the relation between those using the land for some commercial purpose and the state agency regulating land use. In what follows, I explore through two instances how some of these possibilities have worked out in the United States and what they tell us about the peculiarities of the American politics of development, including its focus on rent and also the way it intersects with what is a federalism of an extreme sort.

How the 1993 Clean Air Act Changed the Geography of Coal Mining. Between 1973 and 2013 the American coal mining industry underwent a radical change in its geography: something that contributed in a distinctive way to the Cold Belt / Sun Belt opposition. In 1973 almost 64 percent of American coal production was concentrated in the Appalachian region, mainly in Pennsylvania and West Virginia, while only 10 percent was produced in the Mountain West. But forty years later the Appalachian contribution had sunk to just over a quarter of total production (27 percent) and the Mountain West, largely Wyoming but also Montana and Colorado, produced more than half (54 percent). There were certainly reasons other than environmental legislation; labor productivity in the surface mines of the West was vastly in excess of that in the adit and pit mines of

22. The same applies to nature reserves and national parks if the mining companies get even a sniff of serious money to be made. The ongoing saga of the Arctic National Wildlife Refuge and its supposed oil is an unhappy case in point.

Appalachia. But the Clean Air Act of 1993 bears some responsibility, along with the interstate competition that its implementation unleashed.

The issue was acid rain, something affecting the northeastern states in particular and with deleterious implications for ecosystems, timber growth, and sport fishing, but also for domestic plumbing systems. The acid in the rain was widely attributed to the emissions of power plants and some coal burning factories in the Midwest, carried eastward by the prevailing winds: in effect, high sulfur emissions transformed rain into a dilute sulfuric acid. This led to environmentalist pressure, aided by some development interests in the northeastern and mid-Atlantic states, to lobby for some sort of regulation of smokestack emissions in the Midwest. The initial approach was to get state environmental agencies to introduce legislation of their own. But the tradeoff with local economic bases was a major stumbling block. It was then that attention moved to the federal arena where the anti–acid rain forces would have more leverage. This would eventually culminate in the federal Clean Air Act of 1993.

The Clean Air Act calls on the major sources of high sulfur emissions—electric power companies—to simply reduce them. There were and remain two possible approaches. The first is for the electric utilities to install so-called scrubbers in their smokestacks. As the term suggests, these take most of the sulfurous particles out of the smoke prior to it leaving the smokestack. The second option is to substitute low-sulfur coal for the high-sulfur coal that had resulted in elevated sulfur emissions to begin with. For development interests in the states where some remedial action had to be taken, the choice has been a difficult one.

On the one hand, the scrubbers are expensive and would result in higher electricity prices in the states affected. This cost would have downstream impacts on the ability of state development departments to attract new businesses. In any case, major electricity consumers in particular, like the automobile industry, have been important sources of pressure for the power companies to adopt the low-sulfur coal solution. The problem, however, is that the high-sulfur coal that is burned comes in part from Appalachia but also from some of the Midwestern states in question: notably Illinois, Indiana, and Ohio. The upshot was that the coal mining companies, supported by the miners' unions, lobbied in favor of the scrubber solution and against low-sulfur coal.

Other territorialized interests would also play into the picture. Not least were the low-sulfur coal producers of the West who smelt a windfall of heroic proportions; in particular those in Colorado, Montana, and Wyoming, and all supported by respective state governments on account of the severance taxes that they collected. At the same time they opposed any policy that would increase the likelihood of the power companies installing scrubbers. For the Midwestern states affected, like Ohio, did indeed push for federal subsidies to defray the cost of the scrubbers: that is, a federalization of the cost of the legislation alongside a federalization of regulation. This was vigorously opposed not just by the low-sulfur coal producers but by some other western states, like California, many of which have relatively high electricity rates and which relished the prospect of the so-called "leveling of the playing field." For the high-sulfur coal burning states of the Midwest have historically enjoyed relatively low electricity rates, and this has redounded to the benefit of their economic development initiatives; all of which is seen as playing into the ability to attract new investment: the favored target of state development departments.

Another approach by the high-sulfur coal–producing states was to give financial incentives to the utilities if they continued to buy in-state (i.e., high-sulfur coal). This would not have meant that the utilities could ignore the Clean Air Act; only that the scrubber option would become financially more palatable. But this too was opposed by the coal producers and transporters of Colorado, Montana, Utah, and Wyoming operating through their lobbying association, the so-called Alliance for Clean Coal(!), and drawing on the same interstate commerce clause that in the DFWI case was so obviously shunted aside by the Wright Amendment. So much for the ideals of the founding fathers.

In this instance, environmental legislation had unintended consequences: changing the geography of coal production had not been the objective or even anticipated. In other cases, though, the separation of land uses, which has been a common objective of environmental groups, is fundamental to what has unfolded. This has been the case of the Sagebrush Rebellion.

The Sagebrush Rebellion. In the western United States (west, that is, of the Plains states, which stretch from the Dakotas in the north through Nebraska, Kansas and Oklahoma down to Texas), the federal government continues to own very large proportions of the land: aside from New Mexico and Washington, at least 40 percent, and in the states of Nevada, Utah, and Idaho over 60 percent of the land is so owned, and there are good reasons for this, including the failure or disinterest of settlers in the nineteenth century. Some of it is national forest land, some designated wilderness, some national parks, but a lot of it is just federally owned without any specific designation, and this is where much of the conflict originates. For the various federal agencies responsible for its management, like the Bureau of Land Management and the US Forest Service, do lease out land to private interests. These might be ranchers looking for pasture, timber companies or mining companies with permits to prospect and to extract. Any such use, though, is subject to regulation by the federal agency in charge, and rents and fees have to be paid, as in so much per animal grazed.

In consequence, and since the early 1900s, federal regulation has periodically become an issue. In the 1970s it took the form of the so-called Sagebrush Rebellion: a variety of state initiatives, with substantial popular backing, to have the federal government relinquish control of this land to the states and so reassert states' rights in land use regulation; and states' rights, of course, have always had a constituency in the United States, a nice rallying cry, even if the concrete cause behind their embrace has often been of a dubious nature. And indeed, what led to the efflorescence of anger that was the Sagebrush Rebellion was the interest shown by environmental groups in how federal land in the West was being managed. There were, in particular, concerns for land conservation and for the preservation of wildlife that ran counter to the interests of ranchers; and limits on mineral exploration and the imposition of land rehabilitation standards that were contrary to the interests of mining companies. Legislation like the 1971 Wild Horse and Burro Act, which ranchers believed led to a deterioration of the land on which their livestock grazed; and the Endangered Species Act of 1973, which put limits on land development, were like red rags. By the end of the 1970s indignation had grown into revolt.

The call for federal land to be relinquished to the states did not sit well with groups like the Sierra Club, the National Wildlife Federation, and the Audubon Society. State law requires that state-owned land (which is what the Sagebrush Rebellion wanted federally owned land to become) be managed on a revenue-maximizing basis; federal law, on the other hand, requires that *its* land be managed on a multiple-use basis, according to which all uses, including non-profitable ones, such as some recreational uses, must be weighted on an equal basis. But federal land was never handed over. Instead, regulation was relaxed under the Reagan administrations between 1982 and 1990. Efforts to disburse federal land, and there were some, actually foundered since the states did not want the responsibility. They also liked the federal subsidies provided in lieu of the property taxes that the land might otherwise have generated.

In the mid-1990s, and with a Democratic administration in office, as it was in the 1970s, there was a renewed outbreak of revolt in the West. The major issue was the attempt of the federal government to charge ranchers higher rents for the use of public land. These rents are commonly regarded as very low and even with the increases would have remained below those charged for private land. Even so, this was also opposed strenuously even while the increase was extremely modest. Environmental issues also continued to be a concern. The damage to public lands by grazing cattle has been considerable. They chew off the natural bunchgrass, which is replaced by fire-hazardous cheat grass. They also erode stream banks where they congregate. This in turn has led to attempts on the part of the Bureau of Land Management and the US Forest Service (which administers grazing on national forest lands) to limit the number of cattle allowed.

The major polarizations have been much as they were before: ranchers versus the federal government and environmental groups. A number of other local economic interests in the western states have been involved. This is because a threat to the economic viability of ranching in the areas is also a threat to them: local suppliers and local banks with loans extended to ranchers, for example. The overriding character of the Sagebrush rebellion, though, is the way it has brought together sets of locally dependent, *rent-seeking* interests in different places—ranchers, and those with stakes in the local economies for which the ranchers constitute the economic base—around a common agenda. The fact that it is the federal government from which redress is sought has dictated the national (or more accurately regional) nature of the alliance.

Summary Comments

In this first chapter, I have provided a set of windows on the American politics of urban and regional development. This is prefatory to drawing out how utterly singular it is. It certainly shares some features with that politics as it has emerged elsewhere in the advanced industrial societies. For a start, the logics of capitalist development are fundamental: we cannot begin to understand it without drawing on a language of class, of competition, of monopoly and contradiction. It is obviously a politics of space focusing on the way in which the contradictions of capitalist development have generated distinct urban and regional questions, even while the way they have been imbricated in the business of the state has been quite different—even, as we will see, startlingly so.

But while those contrasts must wait, the case studies do provide a basis for some interim conclusions. For a start, class has to be a central category in the discussion to follow. Its significance was evident in the American labor movement's involvement in the politics of development that ensued after the emergence of the Rust Belt, as well as in popular opposition to urban renewal. There are also the multiple meanings of class, and these will be drawn on in what follows. The sense of a capitalist class versus a working class was evident in the Rust Belt case, but in other cases class was viewed more from the standpoint of stratification: positions defined along an axis of both material and symbolic advantage. Residential exclusion has played a massive role in the American politics, filtering in certain forms of development and filtering out others. The Silicon Valley case suggested that this could be quite counterproductive from the standpoint of an area's economic base: a massive amount of wealth is produced, but to the degree that a large portion of it is siphoned off by exclusionary forces putting pressure on wages and salaries, so that wealth production can be compromised.

There is also a dialectic between class and territory. One way for those with stakes in rents to deal with a standoff with the masses is to enter into a coalition with them in defense not of particular class positions but rather of "our" city or region, and thereby position oneself against the challenge of other such territorial coalitions elsewhere. This dialectic was evident in the Rust Belt story. It is also the way in which the inner suburbs have tried to galvanize the support of the masses against the outer suburbs in a project that is more likely to redound to the advantage of interests in property development there than to those who live there. And in the wake of the Clean Air Act, it was one of the ways in which coal producing states in the Midwest tried to beat back the challenge of low-sulfur coal.

A second feature of the American politics that comes through loud and clear is its bottom-up nature: how it starts with initiatives in particular places designed to channel the flow of value through them or rather the real estate located there—in particular inner suburbs, particular developments like Columbus's Arena District, in parts of the West dependent on grazing on federal land, in distinct local economies like those of Akron, Buffalo, Gary, Scranton, and Youngstown, where the effects of the long downturn were felt particularly acutely, or indeed through the coal-bearing land of Wyoming and Montana. There is also the way in which these initiatives, while clearly rooted in very local concerns and conflicts, can then reach out beyond the local to draw in other places, forming what might be called cross-locality coalitions, as in the Northeast-Midwest Congressional Coalition or the First Suburbs Consortium or what, in the case of the fallout from the Clean Air Act, was a coalition of low-sulfur coal producers. Such coalitions then try to enroll state and federal governments in advancing their agenda. In the DFWI case there was no coalition of this form, but there were certainly connections with the federal government, putting in place conditions that would protect the massive investment there.[23]

The DFWI case also reminds us that at the center of the American politics is a tension between, to put it very abstractly, fixity and mobility.

23. The same applies to the Columbus Arena District case, since in order to get the casino moved there had to be a new state referendum allowing it. The original referendum had specifically identified not only four cities where casino gambling should be allowed, but even the sites themselves, which sounds like the state conniving in monopoly, but that is another story.

At stake was a massive infrastructural investment, financed by bonds of a long maturity. If the bondholders were to be paid, then DFWI had to generate the necessary revenues, and that in turn depended on the movement of passengers through it—something threatened by the re-emergence of Love Field as a serious competitor. In other cases fixity can assume less absolute forms. In principle, some set of locational arrangements might be portable elsewhere, but to transfer them, reconstituting them in some other location, would be extraordinarily difficult and costly. In virtue of the relations between its constituent firms, hardware and software, and auxiliary components of the division of labor there, like lenders and lawyers attuned to the needs of those firms, the computer industry of Silicon Valley has to make its money there; which is why the housing cost problem is such a challenge. Firms might indeed relocate but only if they could persuade their suppliers and client firms, the auxiliary parts of their divisions of labor like the banks with their expertise in the software industry, not to mention their skilled workers, to make the move at the same time. In the Columbus casino case, though, it was infrastructure in its physically fixed form that was at stake: money tied up in office, hospitality, and residential buildings, not to mention a massive investment in multistory parking garages. Here, as in the DFWI instance, the impulse was to seek out a monopoly: to ban anything that threatened the flow of rents through it.

At DFWI the challenge was to keep on attracting passengers. In the Arena District it was customers. These are very concrete ways in expressing the mobility that is the other side of the coin. Kit Bond wanted Southwest Airlines to fly directly to St. Louis to bring airline ticket prices down and so bring more conventions to the city, among other things. In contrast, later in the Arena District saga the ice hockey franchise provided its own challenge by threatening to move somewhere else. So when money is invested in fixed infrastructure of long life the bet is a speculative one regardless. The unanticipated—the failing financial fortunes of an ice hockey team, the deregulation of American commercial airlines—is going to happen, but its precise nature, and whether it will be adverse, cannot be foreseen. And when the unforeseen does happen, then new alliances have to be built, as was the case with DFWI.

The DFWI story also shows how state and federal branches get caught up in the American politics, even while it is driven by forces of a very local nature. The fact that the states are very different one from another also contributes to how this matrix of relations gets worked out. The United States is a federalism of a very radical sort: something of high significance for its politics of urban and regional development. But each of the states is *sui generis* and not merely because of state-specific issues and resolutions. California-specific legislation was certainly at work in Silicon Valley, where the fiscal implications of Proposition 13 have distorted land use policy. In the DFWI instance, though, part of what was at work was the sheer size of the state: without Texas's size and its widely spaced metropolitan areas of Austin, Dallas–Fort Worth, El Paso, Houston, and San Antonio, not to mention Amarillo and Corpus Christi, Southwest Airlines could never have grown to the point where, with airline deregulation, it was able to pose a threat to interstate routes.

We should also note the light these examples shed on power in the American politics. Power is obviously of the essence: how to ensure the future of an airport or an entertainment district, to revive the Rust Belt, to defend tax privileges, to defend the future of low-sulfur coal or grazing privileges in the West, or to protect the future of an industrial district like Silicon Valley. Power of a material sort is on display, but so too is that of a discursive variety, which is one of the reasons I included the Arena District instance, where it is so vividly on display. And in the Sagebrush instance, the "rebels" mobilized notions of rugged frontier individualism and anti-statism—all ideas that resonate with a wider American audience—in pursuit of their goals. The discursive has played a major role in the American politics. Even so, it is not independent of power of a more material sort. One might say it is subordinate to it. Operating a newspaper, driving out competitors as the *Columbus Dispatch* was able to do, requires lots of money; reminding us once more how central capitalism is to this politics. Material forms of power also work through networks; others have to be enrolled—congresspersons, state functionaries—if fixed investments are to be defended and, most important, bear fruit. And if you do not have power, then you get dumped on, which is what happened to the locality in which the casino ultimately landed up, even while the businesses there, at least, were happy to be so taken advantage of, dreaming of a neighborhood revival from which they might benefit.

Finally, and to set in relief the question this book addresses: It is hard to imagine any of these cases arriving with a return address from somewhere in the countries of Western Europe. There, local governments do not have the sort of control over land use policy to create local housing shortages, even while, as in contemporary Great Britain, national governments do. No Western European city is going to have the sort of discretion in building a new airport and creating congenial conditions for its success that Dallas and Fort Worth did, not least because infrastructures like that are not funded via a private bond market where places get labeled as good creditors or verging on deadbeats. Something like Vernon is hard to imagine. Exclusion certainly occurs but not on such a dramatic scale or with such an emphasis on the fiscal. The same applies to the other cases reviewed here. It was always a struggle to find cases of metropolitan fiscal disparities in Western Europe and the same applies to struggles around the uneven development between inner and outer suburbs. There are hints that some of these cases might be replicated in Western Europe—London has claimed a fiscal exploitation by the rest of the country redolent of the Rust Belt / fiscal balance case—but as yet they are only hints. Rather the Western European instance remains very different, as will become clearer. But initially the conditions under which "urban and regional development" emerged as preoccupations on the two sides of the Atlantic were actually quite similar, as we will see in the next chapter.

2

Prolegomenon to "Urban and Regional Development"

Context

Social scientists have often seen the end of the Second World War as something of a watershed. Before the war, the welfare state is more prospect than reality; only after can one seriously talk about Fordism; before the war empire is virtually unchallenged, but not so afterwards; the immediate postwar period is the golden age of labor, though also of capital; the Cold War takes off. And so on. These are of course, oversimplifications. There is more continuity than that. And that also applies to the emergence of an institutionalized interest in local and regional development. Its antecedents were certainly putting in an appearance prior to 1939. Most US states established what they called Departments of Development after 1945, but some Southern states had led the way some years earlier (Anton and Reynolds, n.d.). Likewise, in the early 1930s Great Britain was already experimenting with policies of aid to areas of high unemployment, as was the Netherlands, but it is only after the war that these policies became more than experiments and regional planning entered the scene in a serious way.

Even so, and important for the argument here, the institutional expression of that interest, including its institutional geography, its subsequent practices, and its ultimate goals, assumes starkly different forms in the United States. What emerges is a highly decentralized set of practices in which the individual states and particularly the localities assume primary roles. Formal responsibility inheres in the states and in local government, and their immediate goal is attracting inward investment in the form of new factories, offices, state facilities, and even major housing projects, typically through the offering of various financial incentives and regulatory concessions, but also, and over the longer term, through the provision of infrastructure like expanded airports, new freeway interchanges, and convention centers. But this responsibility is emphatically *formal*. Who takes the lead is typically very different, and while the much-vaunted American growth coalition hides a multiplicity of variation, more often than not it is local government that is pushed, led, and coopted—though typically, and in return, it imposes something of its own agenda.

In Western Europe a contrasting set of practices emerges, though with a similar, if not identical, concern. What takes shape is almost the mirror opposite of the American case. Instead of the initiating agencies working on behalf of particular localities or regions and reflecting the growth agendas of private interests, here it is the central governments and with a view to realizing some national view of the proper geography of development: in other words, urban and regional development as contributing to what is seen as a "good geography." The focus on inward investment on the part of firms looking for sites for branch plants or offices, along with the relocation of state agencies, remains. But in the Western European countries it is the central government that offers the incentives and decides where they will be made available. In some cases this is complemented by major infrastructural projects in the targeted areas, notably, though not exclusively, the creation of so-called New Towns.

This contrast lasted in its classic form until the early 1970s. In Western Europe a more self-consciously urban or regional engagement with the development function emerges; this goes along with some changes in the structure of the state of a facilitative sort. There has also been some cooptation of private interests as in the British notion of "partnerships." This new form still falls far short of the classic American practices, and central government orchestration remains much, much stronger. Local governments in Western Europe were always more reactive in their engagement with local economic development; this was entailed by their subordination to central government. That has changed somewhat in that they have acquired their own development agendas and brought private growth interests more into the picture. But at the same time, the proactivity of development interests in the United States, often organized into coalitions in which local and state government may play a part but still for the most part a subordinate one, has also increased. So quite categorically, and despite interesting changes that require attention, they remain very different animals.

They do, though, share a prehistory. In both instances, and to put it abstractly, the focus is the space economy as an object of state intervention, bracketing for the time being what branch—central or local—would be the major vehicle for intervention. Behind this is a story of how the space economy got to be defined as in some way problematic, creating in turn more specified notions of an urban and a regional problem. How indeed they got defined and who did the defining did ultimately vary, as I note above. Even the expression "urban and regional development" would acquire greater resonance in the United States than in Western Europe. Nevertheless, as one might reasonably expect, and regarding what was seen as significant, there was some degree of convergence.

The crucial starting point for any discussion of the coming of local and regional development is the uneven geographic character of the capitalist economy: differential rates of growth; inequalities in who gets what where; issues of over-use and under-use of shared facilities; and the unevenness that results from the fact that something that is very clearly capitalist in character lies alongside, and is actively dissolving, formations of a precapitalist nature. Accordingly, this chapter starts with the question: Just why and how does the capitalist mode of production generate uneven development over space? But if geographically uneven development is foundational for an institutionalized interest in urban and regional development, it has to be seen as somehow problematic: in other words, something that is generative of social tensions and that ultimately captures the attention of the state.

This brings us to the second major section of the chapter, which focuses on the *politics* of geographically uneven development and the various ways in which it did indeed become a public issue, beginning around the turn of the twentieth century and gathering pace through the 1920s and 1930s. Ultimately my point will be that this development is conditioned by the rise of the labor movement, of labor unions, social-ist parties and the revolutionary movements after the First World War. Without it and the crisis of confidence it entailed for the ruling classes, geographically uneven development would have been seen as not just a necessary aspect of the accumulation process but something that the state should stay clear of. In other words, it had to be pushed.

The idea of urban and regional development *policy*, though, emerges slowly. City and regional planning is an important change, legitimating state intervention into the geography of things. There are also private ini-tiatives in real estate development that become significant; the specialized industrial zone or trading estate, as in the case of Vernon, emerges along with the first planned shopping centers. Capital's division of labor changes in important ways. Not least industrial and commercial capital start to offload their real estate requirements to a more clearly defined property sector destined to play a central role in urban and regional development. And then clear models of the future start to take shape. Local initiatives aimed at attracting new industry appear not just in the United States but also in Western Europe, particularly in Great Britain. More central branches of the state also get drawn in. Something like the establishment of the Tennessee Valley Authority, aimed at bringing development to a significant chunk of the American South, finds a counterpart in attempts in 1930s Great Britain, if timid ones, to direct industry into areas of heavy unemployment.

After the war things become much clearer. In the United States, and the achievements of the Tennessee Valley Authority notwithstanding, the dominant emerging pattern is a highly decentralized approach to local and regional development with the localities and firms with interests in rents, organized collectively in various ways, taking the initiative. In West-ern Europe it is the reverse: the interventions of the central state and its orchestrating powers in terms of urban and regional planning come to dominate. Yet there remains a commonality: what emerges in terms of practice is a focus on, to put it quite simply, moving around things that promise a shift in the way value circulates geographically—factories, office and residential developments, and eventually shopping centers. Who orchestrates that movement differs, of course, as do the justifications. But in both cases movement is of the essence, as is the assumption that what is to be moved *can* be moved. From the late nineteenth century on, and increasing in scope through the advance of the twentieth century, is what I have called here a "new mobility": a new locational discretion, therefore, at both interregional and metropolitan scales, allowing a degree of structuring by agencies that had acquired some legitimacy to intervene. But how indeed this mobility would be structured would vary.

The Foundational Problematic: Uneven Development

Foundational for the politics of urban and regional development is the question of uneven development: an unevenness in material outcomes across space and at diverse geographic scales; as, indeed, in the older/ newer suburb instance or that of the Cold Belt / Sun Belt contrast. This is an unevenness that is constantly changing; a landscape of differential growth and decline as the geography of (value) production and distribution changes, as captured by stark contrasts of growth areas and rust belts, of slums and suburbs, of metropolitan growth and the decline of small towns; and a dialectic of concentration and dispersion.

This is to discuss uneven development in very descriptive terms. Analytically the crucial condition is the capitalist form of development and how, in the course of the accumulation process, it necessarily generates these various forms of unevenness. The accumulation process is central to the argument of the book: central to the creation of uneven development in its various forms and therefore to laying down the conditions for the politics of local economic development. But in addition, it is also what allows comparison between different cases, in this instance illuminating the peculiarities of the American one. Given, therefore, the centrality of the accumulation process to uneven development, why, nevertheless, is it also at the center of such radically different politics of local and regional development?

At the most fundamental level, the question of uneven development is one of production—differences in the development of the productive forces as signified by the ability of people to produce, and evident most clearly in differences in labor productivity. The socialization of production is key.

This typically occurs through the development of the division of labor around a particular product and the sharing of items of physical infrastructure. Geographically this generates strong clustering effects—what in more conventional terms are discussed under the heading of economies of agglomeration. The counterpoint to this is the tendency to dispersion, which is usually and correspondingly understood in terms of diseconomies of agglomeration, as in Myrdal's famous spread effects though periodically dusted off ever since and re-presented in slightly new forms. This emphasis on exchange relations, though, is to overlook the pressures of overaccumulation and the subsequent search for new markets and more profitable investment opportunities elsewhere. The search may, on the other hand, result in the development of new products. But that too is likely to entail changes in the geography of development as areas focused on the production of what is now obsolete go into decline while new raw materials and therefore source regions assume an enhanced prominence.

The assumption here is of a capitalist economy. It bears emphasis, however, that in Western Europe capitalism emerged within the context of social formations that can be called "capitalist" only by some stretch of the imagination. While in some countries, notably Great Britain and the Low Countries, the transition proceeded fairly quickly, in much of the continent agriculture still had a considerable precapitalist element to it. Peasant forms of agriculture, only slowly dwindling away, remained important in France, Germany, and much of Mediterranean Europe till after the Second World War. The result could be a fairly strong urban/rural contrast in ways of life, and this would play into the politics of local and regional development. The United States is different to the degree that it lacked a peasant sector only partially incorporated into the social formation. What the United States had, though, was the American South: a thoroughly contradictory area that in terms of the goal of production was part of the American capitalist economy, but in other ways was not. In particular, its labor markets were isolated from those of the rest of the country (Wright 1986). That would change, particularly after the Second World War, as African Americans moved to northern cities and as northern firms started to see a future for themselves in what was a low-wage region. Both trends would be important for the concrete trajectory of the American politics of urban and regional development.

This, however, is to discuss geographically uneven development only at the most fundamental level. In addition to the way production directly conditions that unevenness there is also the question of how the product, in value terms, gets distributed. For what is distributed in various forms— profits, rents, interest, salaries, wages, pensions, government subventions of various sorts—can end up in very different places: as, most graphically, in the case of those retirement communities for the wealthy scattered across the American Southwest and Southeast, the residents of which made their money in very different places.[1] Likewise, the idea that in a geographical division of labor those toiling away at the various branch plants appropriate a proportion of the firm's consumption fund for labor proportional to their production of value is clearly absurd; rather, the purpose of dispersing lower skill production jobs is to lower wages without forfeiting productivity and so to enhance profits (Clark 1981). Metropolitan areas taken individually can be considered unevenly developed, but this unevenness is more at the level of the distribution of rents and of incomes than at that of production. But if these questions of distribution are less fundamental to understanding geographically uneven development than variation in the development of the productive forces, they have certainly played into its politics and in very clear ways indeed.

The Politics of Geographically Uneven Development

During the first half of the twentieth century, uneven development in some of its more specific manifestations became a focus of public concern, both in North America and in Western Europe, and demands for state intervention were increasingly insistent. There were three different sorts of issue, and they came to the fore in distinctively imagined forms.

---

1. For a vigorous assertion of this fundamental point as it applies to France, see Davezies (2008) and Davezies and Pech (2014).

The first was the relative decline—and in some cases the absolute decline—of regions and cities that had developed during the first industrial revolution. The latter had been hugely dependent on the exploitation of coal and then the steam engine. Population geographies had changed dramatically as industry clustered on the coalfields or in areas accessible to coal in virtue of navigable water. The centrality of iron and steel making to the period accentuated the significance of the coalfields, or of easy access to them, and facilitated the emergence of heavy engineering in cities like Cleveland, Pittsburgh, St. Etienne, Middlesbrough, Sheffield, and Essen, and in Belgium's Borinage. In some instances this incorporated a geography of location inherited from preindustrial times. Along Glasgow's Clydeside and around Newcastle and Sunderland in northeastern England, craft traditions of ship building conjoined with access to iron and steel associated with nearby coalfields and the development of steel hulls to give further impetus to the industry, including upstream branches like the production of marine engines. This is not to deny the significance of the railroad in changing economic geographies. In some circumstances it played a major role in the assembly of raw materials, as in the rise of Chicago (Cronon 1992). Points where the railroads met navigable water were particularly attractive for the assembly of the necessary industrial inputs. Again the way in which the American iron and steel industry came to cluster around the Great Lakes, at least for a while, is a case in point.

But by the 1920s, the future of some of these areas was beginning to look increasingly qualified, marked as they were by growing and persistent unemployment. This tendency was aggravated by the fact that in many instances the new industries of the second industrial revolution—the chemical industry, the expanding array of consumer goods industries, including automobiles and electrical goods—were developing elsewhere. What was beginning to emerge was a geographic pattern in which areas dominated by the new growth industries were clearly separated from those where major employment sectors were in decline. This was modified by differences in rates of decline: employment in coal mining in England held up far longer in South Yorkshire and Nottinghamshire than it did in northeastern England; coal mining came later to the eastern end of the Campine coalfield around Maastricht in the Netherlands and continued longer than further west in Belgium; and the heyday of coal in southeastern Ohio was over by the turn of the century. But the pattern was clear and would become particularly apparent during the Depression years of the 1930s.

Obvious cases in the United States would include the textile towns of New England, badly hit by relocation to the South after the First World War; and Pennsylvania's anthracite belt focusing on Scranton, Wilkes-Barre, Hazleton, and Pottsville, where unemployment surged during the 1930s. Meanwhile the second industrial revolution led to growing employment in new places. The automobile industry centered on Detroit and component supplying cities like Akron and Toledo was a massive presence. But at the same time there was a relative shift away from the cities that had gained from access to navigable water—Buffalo, Cincinnati, Pittsburgh, and St. Louis are examples—toward new centers that had been disadvantaged in the age of the steam engine but which now expanded on the basis of electricity and assembly plants: cities like Columbus, Dayton, Indianapolis, and Kansas City.

In Great Britain and Belgium, on the other hand, the contrasts were more stark and were accentuated during the 1930s depression. The coal mining areas that had been such poles of attraction for industry in the nineteenth century were now clearly in decline, and some, like Northeast England, South Wales, and Central Scotland in the Lanarkshire coalfield southeast of Glasgow, more than others (Figure 3). The Midlands and South East England, including London, where the new consumer goods industries were concentrated, particularly the durable ones like automobiles and household equipment, were clearly affected to a much lesser degree. There were similar contrasts in Belgium, where a shift in the country's economic center of gravity from the French-speaking south to the Flemish-speaking north was already under way: a transition marked by the decline of the coal, iron, and steel of the Sambre-Meuse corridor, and by the rise of chemicals and the new light assembly industries in the north (Buyst 2009; Vandermotten 1998).

What is notable about these cases is the *change* in regional fortunes—changes tied to the decline of some industries and the emergence of others. What was also beginning to attract attention, though, was a

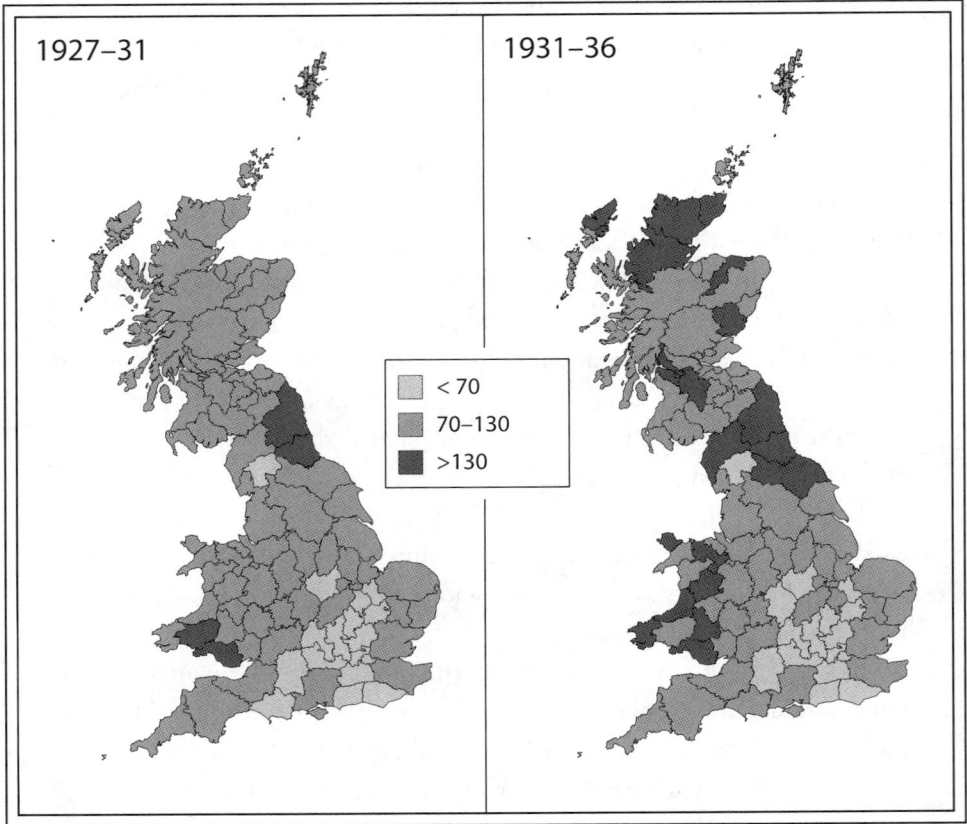

Fig. 3. Relative unemployment, in England, Wales, and Scotland, 1927–1936. The index is based on deviation around the national mean: county rates were divided by the national rate and multiplied by 100.

Based on: Team Britannia Hungary, "The Fires of Perfect Liberty: Labouring Men and Women of England, 1851–1951: Part Five," Oct. 2014, accessed June 29, 2015, https://chandlerozconsultants.wordpress.com/2014/10/29/the-fires-of-perfect-liberty-labouring-men-and-women-of-england-1851-1951-part-five/. Map by Jim DeGrand.

second and different expression of uneven development: that constituted by sharp regional contrasts of income. These sometimes coincided with the areas undergoing industrial decline, but not always. In the United States, and by the 1930s, the relative backwardness of the South and the poverty of the Appalachian coalfields were starting to attract public attention. The South had long been seen as wanting, but it was only after the First World War that this began to be defined as something worthy of federal intervention, laying the discursive foundation for the New Deal's Tennessee Valley Authority.

From the standpoint of some in the American West, though, the regional problem was defined somewhat differently since southern backwardness was paired in their imaginary with a supposed underdevelopment of their own region. The contrast in question was between the Manufacturing Belt on the one hand, concentrated in the Northeast and Midwest, and the South and West on the other. The former was seen as having the advantages of industry and the latter consigned to what was regarded as the subservient position of providers of minerals, foodstuffs, natural fibers and the like (Shermer 2013, 18, 20–22). The problem was supposedly eastern corporations, industrial and financial, which aimed at furthering their monopoly position through the stifling of western and southern industrial competition.[2] A particular gripe was the difference between railroad freight zones. Outside the zone corresponding to the Manufacturing Belt, rates were sharply higher on processed goods. Parenthetically, the fingering of monopoly here is significant: a dominant theme in American social imaginaries, and one to which we will have to return later.

---

2. See, for example, Berge (1946) and Mezerik (1946). Yet by the time they were writing, there is evidence that the investments of the War Production Board had significantly altered the industrial balance between the regions. Dallas–Fort Worth, Houston, San Diego, Los Angeles, San Jose, and Phoenix all benefited massively (Mollenkopf 1983, 104–7). According to Mollenkopf, "New military facilities were heavily placed in the South and West. World War II investments thus provided the basic, private capital stock for the postwar growth of Sunbelt cities" (105).

The third and final problem of uneven development that was attracting attention before the Second World War was the urban one, variably seen as a matter of congestion, poverty, and housing inadequacies, and of what would become known as degeneracy; the contrast here was with rural areas. Conditions in the cities led to critique of urbanization per se and a valorization of the rural. The details of the argument varied. In Western Europe a common view was that urban life was resulting in a biological degeneration of the poor. This was clearest in health and life expectancy; cities, it was argued, were eaters of people, unable to sustain themselves through the reproduction of their own inhabitants. In a period of national rivalries often bordering on war, stunted physical growth and susceptibility to disease fed anxieties about the ability of a country to defend itself.

Rural life was not just seen as healthier. From some points of view, at least, it was also considered more desirable—in its social life, in its supposed emphasis on community and on status and hierarchy—than an urban life built on contract, a social form that was seen from a ruling-class standpoint as divisive, particularly along class lines, and fomenting undesirable claims about democratic rights. Tönnies's gemeinschaft/gesellschaft, Weber's tradition/modernity, and Henry Maine's status/contract all tried to capture elements of this imaginary, without, of course, seeing it as in any way "imaginary." Significantly, the founding myth of Western and particularly Western European sociology would become the social dislocation brought about by urbanization.[3] Polanyi's highly influential *The Great Transformation* is a reflection of the same sort of understanding.

Everywhere in Western Europe during the 1920s and 1930s there was a valorization of the rural and a view of the urban as detrimental to what were defined as "national values." For sure this was in part a reaction to ruling-class anxieties induced by the Russian revolution and the abortive ones in Germany and Hungary, but the foundations for this sort of thinking

---

3. It has also been an important theme in literature. In Great Britain one thinks of George Eliot and Thomas Hardy and more recently Grassic Gibbon, but there are many other examples. See Raymond Williams (1973) for a development of this theme. In social thought more generally Oswald Spengler's *Decline of the West* was remarkably influential in its time.

went back much further. In Germany it had a long history (Dietz 2008) and would reach something of a climax under the Nazis (Mullin 1982b), for many of whom the industrial city was anathema. One argument was that cities should be limited to populations of no more than 100,000 and factories dispersed to small towns. The opposition of industrialists and preparations for war would put an end to this particular utopia, but the Nazi disdain for the urban had its precedents. Planning under the Weimar Republic had had emphases similar in character if not in degree (Mullin 1982a). Founded in 1902, the German Garden City Association was active in proposals for new urban forms that would, among other things, bring people back closer to the soil in the form of settlements that would mix industry and agriculture. It also emphasized the creation of satellite cities, nicely anticipating some aspects of post-war planning policy in certain of the Western European countries.

Germany was far from alone in these developments. In France the contributions of Jean-François Gravier, the deeply conservative writer who had enjoyed close associations with the Vichy government, came just a little later, and his book *Paris et le désert français* (1947), written during the war, would have a major impact on postwar French planning, even while his rationale would be rejected. As the title of his book might suggest, Gravier railed against the concentration of people and industry in Paris and advocated a radical decentralization.[4] His argument was inspired by a view of the big city as deeply injurious to the nation's moral fiber: it destroyed families, uprooted people from the communities that stabilized the social life of the country, and lowered the birth rate to the disadvantage of France as a great power. Gravier was not writing in a vacuum. Since

4. Marchand and Cavin (2007) have discussed Gravier's arguments, as well as outlining the similar views expressed by the influential Swiss planner Armin Meili. The *Plan Prost*, conceived during the five years before the war, also had the concentration of people in Paris in its sights, but it saw the answer less in a radical decentralization to the rest of France and more one of *deconcentration* into the wider metropolitan region (Cottour 2008, chapter 4). The plan provided for circumferential freeways at some distance from Paris in order to facilitate this process, along with limits to population density in the city of Paris itself. It was approved in 1939, but the war precluded its implementation.

the turn of the century there had been an ongoing critique, particularly from the French provinces, of the centralization of French life, *tout court*, in Paris. One product of this was something called la Fédération Française. Initially this was largely an intellectual movement advocating the virtues of local rootedness and a return to preindustrial values, but also, and significantly, a coalition of the employers and the employed against centralization (Thiesse 1992). After the Second World War, and until the 1960s, it would play a significant role in an emergent regional policy in France (Pasquier 2003).

Great Britain shared some similarities with these cases, particularly the German one (Dietz 2008). But lacking a peasantry and a Catholic Church with strong rural roots, it would also be different. From around the turn of the twentieth century, what particularly attracts attention is the influence of something called distributism. Associated in the public mind with the Catholic writers-cum-pundits Hilaire Belloc and G. K. Chesterton, responding to what they saw as the ills of economic and political centralization, distributism advocated a return to life in local, relatively self-sufficient, communities, based on a greater democratization of property ownership. Free trade capitalism and the destruction of small town life that it had caused were as much anathema as socialism.[5]

5. The British geographer Halford Mackinder was keenly aware—even persuaded—of these arguments simultaneously reflecting some of the demands of the Fédération Française; London was as much anathema to him as Paris was to the Fédération. As he wrote in 1919: "Centralization . . . is only one form of a more general process which I would call the segregation of social and economic functions . . . You have allowed industrial life to crowd certain districts and to leave other districts poor. I grant that in the past that was inevitable owing to the need of generating power near the collieries, but not to the extent that has occurred. By proper control you could have substituted a 'village region,' with a community dependent on each factory or group of small factories, wherein rich and poor, masters and men, might have been held together in a neighborly relationship; but you have allowed instead the East and West Ends to grow up in your great cities. Surely the essential characteristic of true statesmanship is foresight, the prevention of social disease; but our method for a century past has been to drift, and when things became bad, we applied palliative measures—factory legislation, housing legislation, and

For certain strands of British thought, though, the growth of large cities generated other concerns that would later factor into regional policy. Perhaps consistent with the fact that the peasantry and a distinctly rural way of life, and in contrast to France and Germany, had long since disappeared, the big bugaboo was what would emerge in the 1920s and 1930s as the hated "ribbon development": the extension of the city in a disorderly, unplanned way out from its edge into the countryside along major highways. The case was made by prominent planner Patrick Abercrombie, later to be significant in the planning of London and the creation of the Green Belt, in his 1926 book *The Preservation of Rural England*, a title that resonates in British planning circles down to the present day.[6] As David Matless (1993) has put it, Abercrombie's book was essentially the "founding manifesto" of the Council for the Preservation of Rural England, an organization that would prove to be very influential.

Of these different strands of anti-urbanism, all expressing a strong decentralizing sentiment, the one that was most apparent in the United States was distributism, even when that label was not explicitly adopted (Shapiro 1972).[7] A central goal for what was essentially an intellectual movement was a return to a Jeffersonian society of small property owners. This was seen as frustrated by two broad tendencies. One was the rise of big business, which was squeezing out the small businessperson as well as concentrating the ownership of property and reducing people to wage workers. The other was the rise of the city, where property was monopolized by big corporations while the dispossessed, sharing out their grievances, plotted a socialist future. On the other hand, anti-urbanism in the United States was suspicious of all concentrations of power, including that of the state. New Deal proposals like a national minimum wage and public housing would, in their view, make decentralization all the more

---

so forth. As things stand today, *the only organic remedy is at any cost to loosen out the town*" (249–50; emphasis mine)

6. See also Clough Williams-Ellis's polemic of 1928 with the title *England and the Octopus*.

7. See Woods (1939) for an example of this genre.

difficult. The minimum wage would take away the low-wage incentive that small towns had, while public housing would provide subsidies to the big employers of the major cities. There was, therefore, a more economistic edge to American anti-urbanism; something shorn, as one might have expected, of nostalgic yearnings for a world that had been lost, since, apart from diffused property ownership, it had never been there to lose. In this it connected with long-standing arguments about uneven development in the country, since it was believed that decentralization would work to the benefit of the South and West.

On the other hand, and crucially, that a particular geography should be defined as somehow problematic is not self-evident. Statistics and maps could be and were drawn on to justify the arguments that something needed to be done. There were government inquiries, as with the well-known Barlow Commission in Great Britain. There were polemics, like Jean-François Gravier's evocatively titled *Paris et le désert français* and Clough Williams-Ellis's equally evocative *England and the Octopus* deriding the ribbon development around major British cities, and there again Ralph Woods's (1939) plans for decentralizing industry in the United States. But this discursive construction of regions and places as problems of uneven development was not conjured out of thin air. It had its conditions, but ones about which we can only speculate.

I would suggest that the fundamental assumption that inequality of outcomes—distributional inequalities, including ones of a geographic nature—were a bad thing owes at least something to the advent of the welfare state and the thinking preceding it. This in turn was giving way to a recognition that state intervention of a mitigating sort was an entirely legitimate activity. Provision for unemployment insurance was well underway in the European countries by 1930, even if highly limited in what it provided. The idea that housing for the poor should be subsidized in various ways, including through government provision of the housing itself, had been realized in programs across much of Western Europe, including in France, Germany, Great Britain, and the Netherlands.

Battening on to this emergent world view was a genre of semi-popular character critically describing conditions in areas of severe poverty or unemployment. Without Harry Caudill's *Night Comes to the* Cumberlands

(1963), even while it came after the Second World War, it is unlikely that Appalachia would have become as salient in the American consciousness as it did. In Great Britain the classic is George Orwell's *Road to Wigan Pier* (1937), a piece of investigative journalism focusing on the lives of the poor during the depression in Northwest England. A more nuanced but still critical discussion was that of J. B. Priestley in his *English Journey* (1934): among other things, in addition to the poverty so clear in certain parts of Britain at that time, he was also keen to draw attention to the centralization of British life in London and the need to protect the vitality of the provinces. Works of fiction like Walter Greenwood's *Love on the Dole* or Zola's (much earlier) *Germinal* helped consolidate the image of the desperate life of working-class people in the one-industry towns that would be the ones most severely affected by periodic depression.

What this suggests, though, is that it is hard to separate the emergence of uneven development as a political issue from the rise of the labor movement, the moral claims it made, and the threat that it was seen to pose to the existing order. By the end of the nineteenth century, paternalism as a means of subordinating the working class to the accumulation process was in rapid retreat. With the advent of the joint-stock company and absentee ownership, the occupational communities of steel towns, colliery villages, textile mill towns, lumber mill settlements, and fishing ports could be mobilized by the emerging parties of the left. The push for state housing provision, recognition of labor unions, changes in labor law, and the beginnings of the welfare state was on.

Two decades into the twentieth century the shadows over the political landscape had lengthened. For the ruling class, the revolutionary upheavals between 1917 and 1923 created an unprecedented crisis of confidence. The divide between left and right seemed like a gulf. The depression of the 1930s and the rise of fascism then increased apprehensions about the future of the existing order. There had also been a sea change in how the working class was viewed: not so much a matter of moral failings, as argued by nineteenth-century critics, but rather one of the social conditions under which people lived, which in turn lent legitimacy to the demands of the organized working class. The emergent field of sociology lent its weight to what seemed to be giving history a new direction. These political anxieties would then endure into the postwar period and mark the emerging politics of urban and regional development, but to a greater degree and for a longer time in Western Europe than in the United States. For in Western Europe class tensions were superimposed on and even reinterpreted in terms of tensions between the urban and the rural, the centralizing and the decentralizing. The latter were particularly strong in France and to a lesser degree in Great Britain, while in Belgium, Germany, and Italy anxieties about urbanization in general tended to prevail. The countryside and the small town were seen as antidotes to the working class threat taking shape in the big cities. The growth of the metropolis was, it seemed, undermining class harmony.[8]

The Coming of Urban and Regional Development

The institutional forms that local and regional development policy would assume in the United States and in Western Europe would eventually be quite different, even remarkably so. But initially that was not very clear, and certainly the label "urban and regional development" was well in the future. What was clear, though, were various emergent practices and structures of relations that would eventually be brought together under that heading. Some of these would form the centerpieces of particular approaches to the question of local and regional development; the possibilities of both local initiatives and central state interventions were already apparent by the end of the inter-war period. There were also practices of a more complementary kind, like urban and regional planning, and new sorts of real estate development, like the industrial or trading estate, which would be mobilized regardless of the substantive form of what was to emerge. Finally a major, even crucial agent of urban and regional development—property capital—began to take more coherent shape.

8. The subtitle of Ebenezer Howard's (1898) manifesto for garden cities, *Tomorrow: A Peaceful Path to Real Reform*, is significant, although the book was later reprinted under the more anodyne title *Garden Cities of Tomorrow*.

Promoting Inward Investment

Although the idea of the growth coalition had yet to be articulated, the early years of the twentieth century bear eloquent witness to the sorts of relations and practices later to be assigned that label. Los Angeles is an early case in point. The movie *Chinatown*, set in early twentieth-century Los Angeles, describes some real events, but the interests of major speculator land owners did not stop at procuring water to quench their dreams. In their determination to establish the city as the major metropole of the West Coast and so usurp San Francisco, unions had been successfully suppressed by 1920 and the principle of the open shop established (Davis 1997). Working alongside the transcontinental railroads and the Los Angeles Department of Water and Power, the chamber of commerce then set about marketing the city as the location for the branch plants of eastern corporations. A Ford assembly plant and Goodyear tire factory were already in place in the 1920s, to be followed later by a Chrysler plant.[9]

There were initiatives at more regional levels. The movement of the textile industry to Southern states in the first two decades of the twentieth century created something of a regional crisis in New England (Koistinen 2013). This would lead in 1925 to the formation of the New England Council, a business organization with a view to changing the basis of the regional economy. The council had the backing of businesses with major stakes in the region, including banks, utilities and railroads: a *dramatis personae* typical of the growth coalitions that would become the standard for local development initiatives after 1945.

This sort of bottom-up approach was in sharp distinction to what would eventually unfold in Western Europe. But prior to the Second World War it could be hard to tell the difference. In Great Britain there

9. As Harvey Graff (2008, chapter 4) has shown, Dallas has a similar history of antagonism to labor organizers and of early success in attracting inward investment. Starting in 1928 an "Industrial Dallas" program focused on a $500,000 national marketing campaign attracting numerous new investments in the area on the part of major corporations. But there were many similar cases during that time scattered across the United States.

was a proliferation of this sort of activity, though typically led by local governments rather than by business organizations (Ward 1990). The spur to action was usually, as in the New England case, some local economic crisis. The fact that until 1937 local governments were largely responsible for unemployment assistance was a major incentive. Promotional efforts were stimulated by the fact that electricity and gas supply were often local government responsibilities. So in addition to the offer of cuts in local taxes, there could also be concessions on utility pricing. In some instances municipally owned land was offered at a concessionary rate. More regional, coordinating initiatives like the Lancashire and Scottish Development Councils also came into being. There were connections with more private interests. The railroads were particularly interested in increasing traffic in areas like northeastern England and Scotland that were badly hit by the depression of the 1930s. Some privately owned electric companies offered subsidies to new business customers. There was analogous practice in the Netherlands (Kaal 2009). During the interwar period cities contested the site of an international airport, and Amsterdam was to the forefront in efforts to attract in new industry.[10]

Even so, central governments did not necessarily approve of these initiatives. In Great Britain they were regarded as wasteful and not the proper function for local government. So lines were already being drawn that would have implications for the direction that local development policy would later take. There were also concerns in the United States. A 1937

10. On the whole, though, and in contrast to the United States, privately led initiatives were much less in evidence. A striking exception was the activity of a French railroad company in stimulating development that would redound to its advantage in terms of increased traffic (Bouneau 1990). This was the Compagnie du Midi, which served what was at the time one of the least developed of French regions: the area north of the Pyrenees, stretching from the Atlantic to the Mediterranean and taking in the cities of Bordeaux and Toulouse. In essence, it became a development agency for the southwest: electrifying its lines; investing in hydroelectric power in the Pyrenees for that purpose; using this availability of power as a basis for investments in electrical and electrochemical industries; and purchasing and developing real estate in forms that would generate traffic, including a summer resort on the Bay of Biscay and ski resorts in the Pyrenees. Earlier it had purchased land on either side of its tracks in the Landes and developed it for forestry.

report issued by the federal Research Committee on Urbanism with the title *Our Cities: Their Role in the National Economy* had come out with uneven development quite clearly in its sights. A central concern was the market in locations that was already taking shape in the 1930s thanks to the initiatives being taken at the local level. The problem was couched as one of "industrial structure":

> One of our specific economic problems is the lack of articulation among the various industries within our urban communities. Frequently the decision to locate an industry in one city or another is based upon the immediate opportunities of a particular enterprise or the desire of a community to increase the total amount of industrial activity, regardless of its effect upon the local industrial structure. Localities, by means of subsidies, tax exemption, and free sites, have indiscriminately attracted enterprises which did not mesh with the rest of the community's industries and which sooner or later helped to throw the entire industrial pattern out of gear. (Dykstra 1937, viii)

The federal government would have liked to have done something about it: the same report called for "planned industrial selection" by which development in the localities would be subordinated to national goals. Clearly it would not have its way, but like the British government of the time, it recognized that letting things take their course without some central intervention, in that case at the federal level, would be problematic.[11]

Central Government Interventions

If in Great Britain the central government had been ambivalent about the development initiatives of local governments, then the high unemployment of the 1930s necessarily increased the attention it gave to the issue. There was certainly a view among some, and despite the misgivings noted

---

11. Intriguingly it was part of a current of thought arguing that there should be a much greater degree of central planning in the United States, a goal that would be eventually frustrated. See Katznelson and Petrykowski (1991) for a discussion of this.

above, that the localized nature of the unemployment, concentrated in some of the coal mining and shipbuilding areas like the West of Scotland and northeastern England, was in fact best handled by local government action. What would eventually prevail, though, would be something that, while quite modest in its initial scope, to the point of being more symbolic than making a serious dent in local unemployment, would come to dominate approaches not just in postwar Great Britain but throughout Western Europe as a whole. Rather, policy would take the form of centrally orchestrated moves to influence the location of industry. In particular, there were inducements to industry to locate on the government-sponsored trading estates in the depressed areas, like those at Team Valley just outside Newcastle and at Treforest in South Wales. They had the power to rent out industrial property at cost. Firms locating there also qualified for certain tax incentives (McCrone 1969, chapter 3).

The only remotely comparable initiative in the United States was the creation of the Tennessee Valley Authority, designed to stimulate economic development in the upper South in response to the severe unemployment of the 1930s. Federal construction of dams would enhance navigation, produce electricity, and create opportunities for tourism. The electricity would then be sold to areas beyond the boundaries of the Tennessee River basin itself (Figure 4).

On the other hand, and during the 1930s, there was nothing to compare with the British initiative in the rest of Western Europe either. The French government had decentralization policies, but they were much more connected to rearmament and concerns about attack from the air than to anything involving local economic development (Dessus 1953, 4; Frankestein 1980, 758–59). Rather what attracts attention is less a response to localized unemployment and more one inspired by anti-urbanist sentiment. In Belgium policies designed to deter the concentration of workers in urban areas had a long history (De Decker 2008). Anxieties about public health and the moral state of the workers had led to early initiatives, supported in particular by the Catholic Church. For example, commuting from the countryside was facilitated by a dense network of railway and light rail connections and, from 1869 on, by subsidized workmen's fares. Second, and subsequent to deadly urban riots in 1886, the labor law

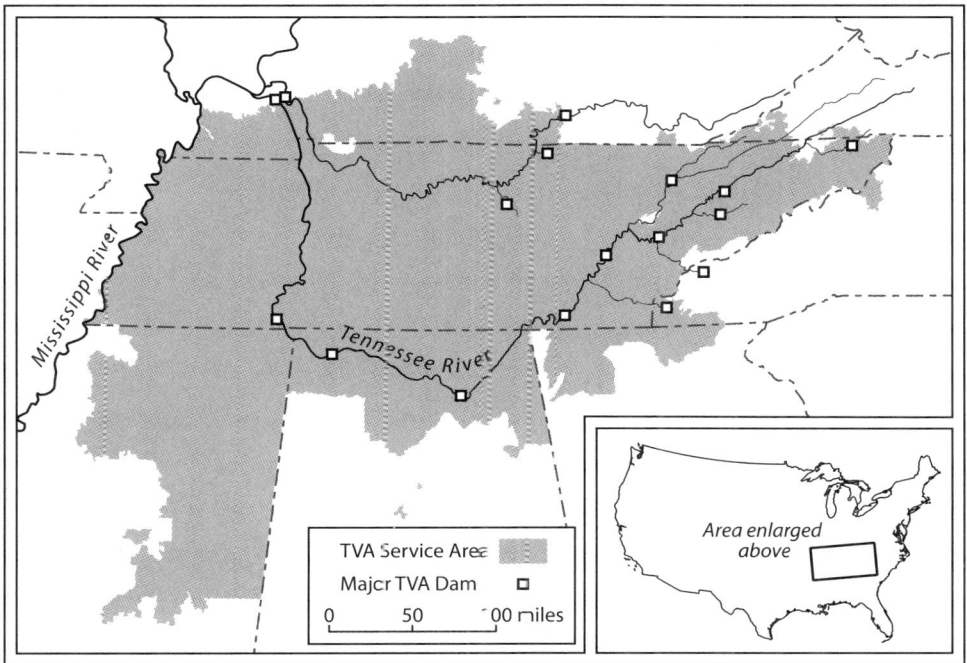

Fig. 4. The Tennessee Valley Authority project. Map by Jim DeGrand.

of 1889 included provision to encourage home ownership via tax exemptions, cheap loans, and even the offer of an extra vote. This, along with cheap rail transport, encouraged customized construction in the countryside, creating the pattern of sprawl for which Belgium is now famous, if not notorious.

Later, in the fascist countries of Germany and Italy, anti-urbanist policies would be taken up with vigor. As already noted, anti-urban feeling in Germany had a long history (Mullin 1982a), and even prior to 1914 there had been tensions between conservative national governments and big city governments dominated by the labor movement, for whom local home rule dating back to the early nineteenth century was both a norm and a weapon. Under the Nazis, the view that the cities were hotbeds of dangerous revolutionary potential would receive added impetus as their supposed cosmopolitanism and Jewishness were added to the list of evils (Mullin 1982b). The Third Reich had its "settlement" ideologists who, among other things, wanted to see cities limited to a size of no more than 100,000 and resettlement of the population in the rural areas. These would be trumped by recognition of the productive capacity of the big city, particularly in terms of preparation for war, but new towns were created, notably those of Salzgitter and Wolfsburg. In Italy under Mussolini there were similar sentiments about the baleful effects of cities (Caprotti 2007). The return to the countryside and to small towns was also seen, as in French claims, as a means to counter a declining birth rate. In practice most of the activity would focus on the creation of new but small towns in areas undergoing land reclamation, notably the Pontine Marshes.[12]

City and Regional Planning

Capitalist development requires a physical infrastructure that is other than the physical plant used directly in production: the premises, the pit-head gear and the mine shafts, the pottery kilns, the blast furnaces and the like. This additional infrastructure includes elements of the built environment like worker housing, water, sewerage, and highways. During the first industrial revolution of coal, steel, cotton textiles, and the steam engine, these were often provided by the employer himself. The company town was a standard feature of the time ranging all the way from the dreary provisions in mining areas across Appalachia and the American West, in the coalfields of Scotland, North East England, Belgium and Germany's Ruhr, and in lumber mill towns on the Pacific coast; to the more elaborate and paternalist arrangements of a Louis Schneider in the case of Le Creusot, Krupp's Zollverein mining-steel complex in Essen, or Titus Salt's Saltaire.

The larger cities that grew to service regional and national development of this sort—cities like Manchester, Pittsburgh, Boston, Leeds, Birmingham, Lille or Düsseldorf—were different. There was no single employer coordinating provision. Rather its different aspects were externalized to other agents who had their own objectives and constraints.

---

12. See also Ruth Lo's (2013) documentation of towns built in Sardinia.

Housing became a responsibility of the private builder and landlord. Providing for other needs, like water and sewerage and public transport to get workers to places of work, became a state responsibility. But this created very considerable problems of coordination and therefore of provision. Instead of private planning, the need for some sort of public planning surged to the fore. Growth was often chaotic, with little in the way of more centralized coordination of land uses.[13] The growing congestion created a need for land assembly and the widening of highways to cater to firm expansion; it also led to crises in the reproduction of labor power as a result of high rents, overcrowding, inadequate sewage disposal, and lack of access to pure water. These issues would become more geographically widespread with the second industrial revolution, the proliferation of factories in formerly nonindustrial towns, and the exploitation of economies of agglomeration.

These were what Edmond Preteceille (1976) has called the contradictions of capitalist urbanization: an urbanization that allowed firms to harness advantages of nearness to their goals of profitability but which at the same time, as firms expanded, threatened to undermine them. It would be the context within which new professions would arise—public health officer, municipal engineer, sanitary and housing inspectors, and sanitary engineer. Part of their briefs would then be appropriated by an emergent expertise targeting the geographic layout of things and drawing on utopian thinking about urban design. This would be city planning, with its goals of improving housing conditions, facilitating movement, and expanding the city itself through the anticipation of future needs. City planning's object of interest would be the physical arrangement of things in the city: of one land use relative to another, the location of housing,

---

13. There *was* private urban planning long before the public version as we know it, and, while targeted at a moneyed class, it could be effective where the extent of land being developed was on a suitably large scale. David Cannadine (1977) has shown what was possible in his discussion of the development of the Calthorpe estate on the edge of Birmingham during the nineteenth century. Many of the features of contemporary planning practice are clearly in evidence including the artful arrangement of land uses, the dedication of land for prestige uses, like universities, and residential exclusion.

highways, waterlines, city parks, new reservoirs, and sewage works.[14] The emerging profession in turn would justify itself in terms of a seemingly objective knowledge of managing problems defined as technical: serious social problems became externalities, the assembly of land was a matter of public purpose rather than a quite narrowly defined private interest.[15] The fundamentally capitalist nature of what was at stake would be defined by others. As the economist Robert Haig put it in 1927, metropolitan New York was "essentially a piece of productive economic machinery competing with other metropolitan machines. . . . The area of New York and its environs may be likened to the floor space of a factory. Regional Planning designates the best use of this floor space. . . . Unduly congested streets should be no more tolerated than the aisles of a factory impassably jammed by goods in process; factories scattered helter skelter should be no more tolerated than departments of a factory scattered helter skelter" (quote in Meyers 1998, 298).[16] Haig referred here to "the metropolis." After

14. Compare Harvey: "Professional planners find themselves confined, for the most part, to the task of defining and attempting to achieve a 'successful' ordering of the built environment. In the ultimate instance the planner is concerned with the 'proper' location, the appropriate mix of activities in space of all the diverse elements which make up the totality of physical structures—the houses, roads, factories, offices, water and sewage disposal facilities, hospitals, schools and the like—which comprise the built environment" (1979, 213).

15. In this way the class nature of what was at stake would be obscured. Social problems would become spatial ones to be resolved by interventions into spatial arrangements, as Harvey (1979) and Piven (1970) have made clear. Bad housing should be replaced by good housing but without giving the workers the increased wages that would allow them to pay the increased rents; so the slum got—and arguably continued to get—moved around.

16. According to Magri and Topalov, this was also European thinking:

A la fin de la guerre, cette idéologie américaine trouve un terrain favorable de développement en Europe, où l'industrialisme régnant s'applique à l'urbain comme à la production. "La ville, affirme Jaussely, par son organisation, doit donner le meilleur rendement possible tout en limitant l'effort des hommes (. . .). Il faut mieux produire pour mieux vivre et aussi mieux vivre pour mieux produire, tel est l'axiome du jour dont la réalisation est le problème de la société moderne; il domine entièrement la vie générale: c'est celui des sociétés et c'est celui des hommes comme des agglomérations." Et il poursuit:

the First World War, this view of the planner's function, essentially serving as handmaiden to capitalist development on an increasingly metropolitan scale, would become more and more common. The second industrial revolution, electricity, and the new assembly industries would produce the industrial suburb, initiating a long-term dispersion of employment that has continued down to the present day. Improvements in urban transportation—the tram, the trolley bus, and the rise of railroad commuting— then facilitated a lengthening of the journey to work so that those suburbs were not necessarily drawing on their immediate areas for workers. The railroads furthered the process through their real estate activities. Classic is the development of housing by the Metropolitan Railway in England on surplus land that had come into its possession to the northwest of London. The development of settlement along Philadelphia's Main Line and New York's Long Island Railroad has a similar history. The imbrication of transport and real estate development could also apply to the trolley bus, as Henry Huntington would demonstrate to highly profitable effect in Los Angeles (Friedricks 1987). In fact, in that particular instance, his trolley system was used as a loss leader to promote his real estate development activities. But the bottom line to all this is that the metropolitan area was beginning to take shape as a unified labor and housing market with all the issues of spatial externalities and coordination of land uses that were grist for the city planner's mill.

"On en est arrivé considérer l'organisation économique des cités comme une sorte de "taylorisation" en grand d'un très vaste atelier où, pour des raisons très précises, chaque chose doit avoir une place définie et ne peut-être qu'à cette place" (1987, 435).

[At the end of the war, this American view finds fertile ground in Europe, where the prevailing idea about industrialism is applied to the city in the same way as it is to production. "The city, argues Jaussely, must give through its organization the best possible yield while at the same time limiting the effort made by the worker (. . .) It is necessary to produce in order to live better and also to live better in order to produce, such is the axiom of today, the realization of which is the problem for modern society; it entirely dominates life in general; it is the problem of societies as it is of people as it is of agglomerations." And he continues: "One has reached the point of considering the economic organization of cities as a sort of scaled up 'taylorization' of a huge workshop where, for very precise reasons, everything must have a particular place and only that place."] (author's translation)

The acquisition of planning powers by the local governments making up metropolitan areas would then add to the problems since what was a reasonable plan for one was not necessarily the case for its neighbors (Hewitt 2011). With the 1920s and 1930s, therefore, planning on a metropolitan scale—or at least talking about it, as in the case of the New York Regional Plan Association, founded in 1922—would become au courant.[17] Alain Cotterau (1970) has described attempts as early as the 1920s to plan for the suburbanization of the population in the Greater Paris area. A major issue in the case of Paris, which gives concrete shape to the broader concerns of metropolitan planning at the time, was the provision of infrastructure to complement new industrial expansion in the suburbs. As the residential population increased around the new points of employment, infrastructural deficiencies had been accentuated by the practice of subdivision and the sale of lots to individuals without providing paved highways, sewerage, curbs, sidewalks, street lighting, and the like. The strategy, with major support from the big industrial employers, was to concentrate development along particular axes to be provided with improved public transport and in two new towns, Courneuve and Rungis, to be connected to central Paris by electric tramway. The plans were stillborn. The French government, under pressure from rural land owners, declined to provide the money requested, but the general concept was one that would eventually see the light of day after the war.

New Forms of Real Estate Product

The landscape of urban and regional development as we know it today is one of office parks, industrial parks, regional shopping centers, and so-called planned (residential) communities. Yet apart from the first, all of these were beginning to put in an appearance well before the onset of the Second World War and would be incorporated into urban and regional development policy as it took subsequent shape.

---

17. In the case of London it would be even earlier. See Hewitt (2011).

The specialized industrial district of Vernon, California, discussed in the first chapter of this book, is one such instance. As Mike Davis has indicated, it originated as a clone of something developed earlier in Chicago and known as the Central Manufacturing District. With railroad access and developer planning in terms of street layouts, setback requirements, and rights of way, by 1929 it had three hundred firms employing sixteen thousand workers (Davis 1997, 368–71).[18] There were similar developments in Great Britain, where they were more likely to be known as trading estates. The Slough Trading Estate west of London was created as early as 1920 and proved to be a major success attracting consumer goods firms like Citroën, Gillette, Johnson and Johnson, and later during the 1930s, Mars and Berlei. Trafford Park in Manchester was even earlier, going back to the turn of the century and attracting firms in the new industries of the time like electric turbines and aircraft engines but also consumption goods like packaged tea and even automobiles (P. Scott 2001). These were private ventures but local governments also created and marketed them. By 1939 Liverpool had developed an industrial park in its satellite town of Speke (Ward 1990, 110). Manchester would promote a similar development in *its* satellite town of Wythenshawe. As indicated earlier, the trading estate, with subsidized industrial sites, would be taken up in Great Britain in early government attempts to mitigate localized unemployment.

The contemporary shopping center also had its precursors. Perhaps the most well-known of these is Kansas City's Country Club Plaza, which was in operation by 1923 and geared to the shopper arriving by car. Something similar, if not quite so ambitious, was located in Main Line, a wealthy suburb of Philadelphia (Dyer 1998): Suburban Square was developed close to

18. In a discussion of "organized factory districts" Harris and Lewis point out how "these were planned privately by railway and real estate companies and supported by local government. Of small account before World War I, there were 122 such districts in 84 cities by mid-century (in North America). Places such as New York's Bush Terminal offered manufacturers cheap land, low taxes, direct freight car service, building design, financial assistance, and other external economies" (2001, 20).

a railroad station during the 1920s by a syndicate of local businesspeople, including ones with interests in real estate and banking. As in the case of Country Club Plaza, a notable feature was the way in which it managed to attract branches of department stores already well-established in the downtown, another portent for the future.

Novelty in real estate development also came in the form of the garden suburb. In its emergent stage, city planning had been greatly influenced by the garden city idea: a city at some remove from existing metropolitan areas, relatively self-sufficient in employment and allowing a much greater penetration of green space into the built environment and, by virtue of limited size, greater access to the countryside beyond.[19] By the end of the First World War, though, sentiment was beginning to turn against it in favor of towns much more closely linked to existing urban areas—what became known as satellite towns or alternatively as garden suburbs (Magri and Topalov 1987): developments on the edge of the city of freestanding or semidetached houses that enjoyed copious garden space and fronted onto tree-lined, curved streets, with the occasional apartment building that enjoyed access to the outside in the form of balconies. During the interwar period, and according to Kafkoula (2013, 172), this became the predominant form of urban extension for both public- and private-sector housing in Western Europe. Looking at housing developments from that same period, that conclusion also applied to the United States: for every Hampstead Garden Suburb there was a Radburn or a Forest Hills Gardens, and for every Suresnes, Gennevilliers, Römerstadt or Praunheim there was a Shaker Heights, a Glendale, or an Upper Arlington.[20] There

19. Ebenezer Howard should not get all the credit for this idea. It is not just that he owed much to the Arts and Crafts movement and William Morris's 1890 utopian tract *News from Nowhere*. A German contemporary, Theodor Fritsch had similar ideas published in a book with the title *Gartenstadt* (literally "garden city") but, and in contrast to Howard, found inspiration less in social reform and more in racism and anti-Semitism (Schubert 2004).

20. On the universality of this new urban form, compare Magri and Topalov in a discussion of France, Great Britain, Italy, and the United States:

Au lendemain de la guerre, apparemment, le modèle de la cité-jardin triomphe. Il s'impose partout, à la fois comme conception de la maison monofamiliale et comme

were also, though, important differences in how the idea of the garden suburb was implemented. In Western Europe, the state, both central and local, tended to play a much more important role than in the United States.

The Rise of Property Capital

The developers of the industrial district of Vernon, the Slough trading estate, Kansas City's Country Club Plaza, and Main Line's Suburban Square, as well as the community builders of the 1920s and 1930s (Weiss 1987), are forerunners of something that would be absolutely crucial to the politics of urban and regional development as it took shape in the

---

schéma d'opération urbanistique intégrée. Mais cette victoire du Garden city mouvement est peut-être amère pour ceux qui défendent toujours le projet initial de Ebenezer Howard (1898). En effet, en 1919, le consensus est clairement établi sur une conviction qui est aussi un renoncement: on ne réalisera pas l'unité spatiale de l'emploi et de la résidence dans le cadre de communautés autosuffisantes à l'écart des grandes cités. Le modèle abandonné s'inscrivait dans une perspective sinon anti-urbaine, du moins visant à arrêter la croissance indéfinie des métropoles et à redistribuer population et activités dans de nouveaux pôles urbains de taille limitée, ceintures de zones rurales. Désormais, il est clairement admis que les cités nouvelles seront situées dans les banlieues urbaines et conçues comme un élément d'une réorganisation de celles-ci et de la planification de leur extension future. L'urbanisme naît ainsi des cendres de l'utopie de Howard. (1987, 420)

[After the First World War, it seems that the garden-city model has triumphed. It appears everywhere both as a way of conceiving the single family home and as a form of integrated urban living. However, this victory of the Garden City movement might be a bitter one for the adherents of Ebenezer Howard's original idea (1898). In effect, in 1919 there is a clear consensus that is also a renunciation: the garden city is not going to take the form of a spatial unity of employment and residence in self-sufficient communities away from the big cities. This vision is a function of a view that, if not anti-urban, is at least aimed at stopping the indefinite expansion of the metropolitan areas and redistributing population and employment into new urban centers of limited size in surrounding rural areas. Rather there is now a clear admission that the new developments will be located in the suburbs and seen as part of the reorganization of metropolitan areas and the planning of their future extension. Thus is urbanism born of the ashes of Howard's utopia.] (author's translation)

aftermath of the Second World War. It seems not too farfetched to refer to them as early instances of what would come to be known later as property capital: that particular branch of capital which provides business premises in the form of office towers, office parks, industrial parks, modular factory units, warehouses, hotels, shopping centers, and, not least, housing, and whose subsequent claim on production takes the form of property rent. This rent is realized either as a continuing stream of revenue or as a one-time payment received from a buyer, as in home ownership which is, in effect, in exchange for the right to that rent. Writing in 1975 about Great Britain, Ambrose and Colenutt recognized the relative recency of this change, arguing that,

> Before the Second World War there were very few large property companies. Instead, redevelopment was undertaken by individual entrepreneurs, or by firms developing buildings for their own occupation. There were few speculative office blocks and the tendency was for firms to own freeholds to their premises rather than rent. Certainly there was no public awareness of "developers" as such. Few property companies were quoted on the Stock Exchange, there was virtually no property press dealing with commercial development, and there was no coherent organization lobbying for the developers. (Ambrose and Colenutt 1975, 37)

They were writing in particular about office buildings but the same could be said to have applied to retail premises, industrial property, and housing. Typically, retailers, even the chains, had owned their own premises, and the same applied to industrial firms. With respect to housing there was still a legacy of employer-owned property and, as Richard Harris (1991) has emphasized, a huge amount of self-build by working-class people. In Los Angeles, as Becky Nicolaides (1999) has described, whole suburbs could fall into this category. Land was subdivided by what the community builders referred to derogatorily as "curbstoners" (Weiss 1987), and the purchaser either supervised or did the building him or herself. Stovall (1989) has described the same process as it unfolded in what would become Paris's Red Belt to the north of the capital. As for rental property, and assuming that one was either not living with parents or in the boarding houses common at the turn of the century, this was a matter for capital of a petty bourgeois character: small shopkeepers looking to expand their incomes or to spread their risks, professionals anxious to provide an income for their anticipated widows, or, in American cities, co-ethnics who knew the people that they were renting to and for whom the relation was not simply one of arms-length market exchange.[21] The large apartment developments were well in the future; likewise the retirement communities, both big and small, that have become so common. The way in which the ultimate owner of premises took the initiative in their construction made a difference to the role of builders. Building had a strong custom element, as Ambrose and Colenutt emphasize with respect to office buildings. A business person bought the land, hired a builder, and took possession of the finished property.

In short, industrial and commercial capital have now to a very large degree externalized their needs for premises and for worker housing to that specialized branch that we know as property capital.[22] Property capital provides sites, developed or otherwise, in the right place and at an acceptable price, in exchange for a share of the surplus. In the first place this is a deduction from surplus value, so a deduction from capital's fund for accumulation. With the externalization of worker housing by employers it becomes a deduction from the working class's consumption fund; but given the way in which, as a component of the value of labor power, it gets translated into wage demands, it too is something that has to concern industrial capital, as we saw in the discussion of Silicon Valley in chapter 1.

As a separate branch of capital, property capitals enter into competition with one another, which turn gives their products a highly speculative

21. In Great Britain, municipal councils tended to be dominated by the small landlord class, intent on blunting the effects that public housing would have on its rents (Byrne 1980).

22. This has been an extremely uneven and protracted process. Provision of housing by employers entered a long-term decline subsequent to that of the one-industry town. Speculative housing coexisted with self-build or custom housing for a long time before the former was able to prevail after the Second World War. The shopping center and the marginalization of the nonrenting retailer would be even later.

character as they struggle to gain an advantage over each other: a continual process of purchasing land, subdividing it into separate lots, and building houses, shopping centers, office buildings with no certainty that there will be a buyer. The goal is rent from land and the improvements thereto, achieved in numerous, often complementary ways that were already taking shape prior to the war: artful land assembly to allow the inclusion of land that already has accessibility advantages; later the assembly of large contiguous areas of land to facilitate development on the sort of scale that makes it possible to internalize externalities (e.g., the apartment properties adjoining the shopping center, or even developments of single-family homes within the same perimeter; or the hospitality development that includes restaurants, hotels, and cinemas, and perhaps some offices). Size has meant scope for creating new geographic difference within the development so as to extract a premium price for some of the housing lots based, for example, on their proximity to a golf course or a lake.[23] Having secured all that, external access might still be a problem for the developer, but, in the United States at least, one that can be solved: a new freeway interchange in exchange for a contribution to a legislator's campaign finance fund or the promise of some community advantage like a park or a community center. The same applies to obtaining the permits or planning permission, though that is a matter not just of investing in people but of investing in the right connections and developing them in the first place.[24] Aside from the pursuit of rent through individual developments, property capital also comprises a class keenly aware of how more general conditions can facilitate rent appropriation. Squeezing out the curbstoners was an early agenda item pursued in the United States on a national level (Weiss 1987). More recently, impact fees have provided the necessary animus.

23. Lake St. Louis outside St Louis, Missouri, is a classic case: a lake, and not a small one—it covers over 600 acres—was created by the developers making the area highly attractive to buyers, particularly those with the money to buy lakeside lots. The fact that it was next to a major interstate allowing easy access to St. Louis, also helped.

24. This is one of the reasons that property capitals need local people with local connections working for them.

On the other hand, and as a class, property capital can only be under-stood in its relations with industrial and finance capital. Rent is ultimately a deduction from the total value produced; but without the laying out of money by industrial capital there is clearly no value from which to deduct it. There are two qualifiers that should be entered. First, property capital is hugely innovative in what it develops and sells. Shopping centers are noth-ing like they used to be, and the same goes for the single family home. Older office buildings are no longer up to scratch where the open plan has conquered all before it. Even if a local economy shows absolutely no tendency to expand, and even if it is contracting, property capital can still make money by attracting buyers away from what, by virtue of this inno-vation, starts to appear obsolete. Of course, without expansion someone will be left holding devalued property, and older parts of the city will then move down the path to redlining by banks and ultimately abandonment. But property capital continues to make money.

And second, some of this innovation clearly facilitates the develop-ment of the productive forces in various ways, and therefore the surplus from which rent is a deduction. As Harvey (1982, chapter 11) has made clear, land rent in its relation to property capital, and while a claim on industrial capital, should not be seen purely as a relation of distribution. The competition of property capitals one with another forces them to revolutionize spatial arrangement as a productive force: to change the use of particular sites in accord with the shifting demands of industrial and commercial capitals; and to provide new arrangements of complemen-tary uses that will enhance the speed with which industrial and commer-cial firms can rotate *their* capital and so increase the extraction of surplus value in a given time period. Through the way in which it promotes the retailing process, the shopping center helps speed up the rotation of capi-tal. Industrial parks, by bringing complementary uses together, enhance worker productivity, if only by allowing a reduction in the labor assigned to transport functions.

In its turn, finance capital is massively intertwined in its operations with the property companies. Real property represents an investment of very long life which, in terms of the revenues it generates, can only be amortized slowly. This means that property capitals need financing on a major scale: financing that is supplied largely by banks, insurance companies, and pension funds, but also by extremely wealthy individuals through the sale of limited partnerships in particular development projects. Payments in the form of interest or payouts to limited partners are then a deduction from rents received.

However, property capitals also need to sell, and this entails further reliance on finance capital. This is obvious in the case of single-family housing since purchase is typically through taking out a mortgage. So just what will pass muster with the banks and savings and loans becomes a consideration. Outside of single-family housing, though, the speed with which property companies rotate their capital can be increased by the sale of their shopping centers, apartment buildings, and office towers.[25] In turn, sale allows an acceleration of the accumulation process: money released to use as leverage for yet more loans to build even more shopping centers. Purchase of these properties is of particular interest to insurance companies and pension funds, which take in money from clients who expect a payoff continuing for a long time into the future. Just how attractive the terms are that insurance companies and pension funds offer to clients depends on expanding the money that they have under their control; which means investing it, and much of it will be invested in property. This is because rents from office and shopping center tenants provide a steady stream of revenues out of which to meet what is typically an equally steady stream of obligations. Of course, rents from any particular investment can deteriorate; which is why their owners tend to spread their risks by putting money into different projects across the country.[26]

25. Property companies may also retain some of their properties as a permanent source of revenue and as a way of handling downturns in the market for new properties.

26. It has also been suggested that there is a metropolitan bias to investment preferences. Those managing property portfolios prefer the big projects that will limit their management costs. The bigger, more diversified cities are also perceived as less risky because of the depth of their markets and greater ability to weather declines in demand (Halbert 2013b).

The New Mobility and the Difference It Made

By the end of the 1930s, all these preconditions for urban and regional development policy—new forms of real estate product, property capital, urban and regional planning—were clearly apparent. But how they would come together to be drawn on by an emergent practice of urban and regional development only became clear after the Second World War. In both American and Western European versions, they would be part of the mix but, and it bears emphasis, subordinated to very different overall approaches. The American version of local and regional development policy would be very bottom-up: driven by individual property capitals, including the developers, by the localities, particularly their growth coalitions, and to a lesser degree by the individual states, with the federal government playing a much more passive role. This would be in sharp contrast to Western Europe. Policies of a more highly centralized character would come to predominate and the discretion left to the localities far more circumscribed. Quite what tips the balance in either case from the more inchoate set of practices prior to the war can only be conjectured. Even then one might say that the future was preordained by conditions of a more structured sort; conditions that I will outline in the concluding chapter. But what they both share as a fundamental precondition is what I will call "the new mobility": something that would in its turn allow moving things and people around, attracting them in, and sometimes repelling them. This would then provide the keystone to policy on both sides of the Atlantic, albeit in very different ways.

The new mobility was experienced at both regional and more local scales and was in sharp contrast to what had prevailed in the nineteenth century. Above all, the range of locational choice for industry started to expand at the same time that firms found themselves with a new power to redistribute production from one facility to another: closing a plant here, opening a new one somewhere else. The growth and diversification of consumer goods industries, durable and nondurable, made a difference. The fact that they relied on semifinished inputs and electricity meant a widening of the locational calculus away from the sorts of demands associated with the heavy industry of the nineteenth century—notably away from coal for steam engines and estuarine access to raw materials—and toward conditions of labor and labor skills, market access, and ease of assembling the inputs. The invention of the internal combustion engine opened up new locational horizons, not just for the now-burgeoning light industry but also for residential development. There again, electricity helped to revolutionize urban transportation through the tram and then the trolley bus.

For industrial mobility, this widening of locational choice was not the only significant condition. The changing character of industrial organization and in particular how corporations managed their various operations across space (i.e., their spatial divisions of labor) was also important. This attracted little academic attention till the 1980s, but the changes were already underway at least a half-century earlier. In chapter 3 of her 1984 book, Massey identifies several different types of spatial division of labor, one of which she calls the spatially concentrated, in which all firm functions—administration, the different stages of the labor process—are located at the same site. During the nineteenth century, and certainly prior to the development of the joint-stock firm, this would have been the predominant form. Firms tended to be smaller. To the extent that they expanded, then it would be either on the same site or within the same urban area, retaining the same workers. Wholesale relocation, except within a tightly defined geographic area, would have been highly risky without the insurance provided by branches in other locations. What leads to change in this pattern is complex. In part it is a matter of horizontal and vertical integration of firms through buying out competitors or suppliers/customers elsewhere. The process therefore was part and parcel of a concentration of industry in fewer firms, something that also applied to banking and retailing.

The upshot was that firms acquired new spatial divisions of labor. The multilocational structure became standard, whether it was a matter of plants all producing the same thing or being connected through what Massey has called part-process relations. How this facilitated the creation of entirely new points of production bears further consideration. It was not just that the deep pockets resulting from firm size sheltered them from the risk of failure. Nor even was it one of buying up small firms in new areas and slowly building them up, important as that would be. Rather it was the attractions of colocation. In the new consumer goods industries, both durable and nondurable, firms were increasingly tied into relations with supplier and client firms, some of whom could be at a considerable distance, which would make the transfer of production facilities closer to them that much less risky; all part of the rationalization of locations made possible by the creation of new spatial divisions of labor. Later, as the creation of new branches became standard practice, the location consultants would help mediate new locations.[27]

Within urban areas an analogous new spatial division of consumption began to take shape. Improved urban transportation and a decline in the length of the workday allowed people to live further from their workplaces; it also created the possibility of more exclusive residential developments on the edge or even far edge of the city. The location of the new industries on the urban periphery then encouraged the creation of suburbs of a more working-class nature, adding to an emergent mosaic of residential areas that would later be regulated through land use zoning. In the United States the creation of mortgage markets on a metropolitan scale in place of the more localized, neighborhood-focused savings and loans would then facilitate the process further: the mobility of mortgage finance underwriting the mobility of people.

But the new mobility was also to some degree problematic. Not all firms or types of activity were mobile to the same degree. Those depending on urban rents, whether landlords or developers, could be particularly vulnerable to shifts in their market as major employers closed plants and opened them elsewhere. The same applied to locally owned and operated utility companies or banks that had failed to develop more extensive branching systems, not to mention the retailing sector.[28] Any decline

27. In the United States the economic development departments of the electric and gas utilities would also play this role, partly but not only as a result of their monopoly of site information.

28. To say that they depended on urban rents might appear strange. Profitability for these firms, though, has always been highly dependent on location, as retailers discover when they go from owning their own premises to renting them.

in land development would then impact the building trades where firms tended and still tend to be locked into very local sets of arrangements with subcontractors, banks, and suppliers: arrangements that are portable elsewhere only with difficulty (Buzzelli and Harris 2006; Wood 2004). This could be a dilemma shared by the local working class to the extent that people were, for whatever reason, locked into local labor markets undergoing a contraction as firms shifted operations elsewhere or simply went out of business. For the emergent professions, moved around from one bank branch or local government to another—Watson's (1964) "spiralists" or those Musgrove (1963) referred to as the migratory elite[29]—it might not be of such moment. But for those depending for their jobs on word of mouth and tied down by family considerations, it could be quite different. And to the extent that local government relied on locally generated tax revenues, there was no way it could retrieve its situation by following the tax base as it moved somewhere else.

It is this tension between mobility and a relative fixity that lies behind anxieties about local and regional economies and that is the *sine qua non* for any notion of local and regional development policy. Harvey outlined one solution: "The more corporations used their powers of dispersal . . . the less urban regions competed with each other on the basis of their industrial mix and the more they were forced to compete in terms of the attractions they had to offer to corporate investment as labor and commodity markets and as bundles of physical and social assets that corporations could exploit to their own advantage" (1985b, 203). But in fact this turns out to be an approach very specific to the United States. In Western Europe it would be different. The problem of mitigating local economic distress is taken in hand by central government: a much more top-down approach, therefore. But in both instances, and as Harvey implies, the new mobility would turn out to be not just a curse but also an opportunity.

Accordingly, the way in which this mobility would be exploited in development policy would vary very considerably. In the United States, the bits and pieces—parts of the divisions of labor of firms, and quickly

29. See also Stovel and Savage (2005).

defined as up for grabs—would become objects for local growth coalitions to attract or ignore depending on how they fit into a vision of local development. As per the concerns of the federal government noted above (Dykstra 1937), localities were using "subsidies, tax exemption, and free sites" in order to "indiscriminately attract enterprises." In Western Europe, on the other hand, the rise of the branch plant turned out to be something that could be used by central governments as they sought to alter the distribution of industry for their own purposes, which they did.

Indeed, in the second half of the century the opportunities for mobilizing the footloose for purposes of local economic development would expand significantly beyond the industrial branch plant. Large corporations with multiple branches would come to be a major feature of developed economies both in manufacturing and in the so-called service industries: bank branches, hotel chains, back offices, retail chains, and the shopping centers that serve as their characteristic locations. Retail chains then entailed the creation of warehouses and distribution centers, adding to the bits and pieces that could be the object of location policy in the Western European case or of policies of attracting inward investment in the American one. The expansion of the state increased the possibilities through its multiplication of military, air, and naval bases and the hiving off of routine office work from capital cities for relocation elsewhere. Eventually new residential developments, particularly the larger ones, would become objects of strategic planning for local and regional development.

But it bears repeating that how this mobility would be exploited for purposes of advancing development agendas would vary hugely between the United States and the Western European countries. In the United States the mobile would be the object of local, quite narrowly defined programs aimed at the enhancement of rents from property, which would then be subject to forces of a market-led nature and a competition: first between localities for the population growth and housing demand promised by investments in office or industrial employment; and then between the different local governments in a metropolitan area to land the housing developments that would result—a competition typically spearheaded by the land owners, the property companies, and local government itself. Planners would play a role, but they would be in the service of local government, and local government in turn would find itself subordinated to the pressures of local growth interests. Land use zoning might have been their idea, but property capitals would eagerly embrace it as a means to enhancing "their" city's ability to attract inward investment; something that was happening as early as the 1920s (Moskowitz 1998).

In Western Europe, it would be different. The various mobilities would be drawn on by central governments as part of creating what can only be described as the "good geography": a set of roughly interlocking goals reflecting national debates about growth, distribution, and landscape. There would be attention to questions of equity over space as we have already seen in discussion of policies aimed at redistributing employment. The national geography would also emerge as a consciously conceived and planned-for productive force as in specifically national port/airport/transport policies, ensuring that housing was located where it was most needed, and in attempts to create the compact city. Here the order of priorities would be reversed: central government rather than local, and planners, particularly those at the center, in a dominant position.

It is not just the meanings attaching to city and regional planning that are different as they get absorbed into two quite divergent approaches to local and regional development. The same applies to the various, specialized forms of real estate development that began to emerge in the 1930s and to property capital itself. Early forms of private industrial estate would be adapted in Western Europe to top-down development policies: government-owned and established specifically to cater to the needs of branch plant industrial investments. In the United States, of course, there would be no question of being subject in their construction to anything other than the market and the strategic thinking of private investors. And just as property capital would play a dominant role in local economic development policy in the United States, supporting—inciting—inward investment policies and subordinating local government to its will, so in Western Europe it would, *per necesita*, play a role more subordinate to some national vision of where things should go.

3

Local Economic Development and the Search for Monopoly Rent

Introduction

There are two ideas, albeit related, that tend to dominate academic discussion of urban and regional development in the United States: the growth coalition; and then the competition between growth coalitions for investments, typically seen as "inward." The objective of the growth coalition is, of course, growth, but growth of a local economy from which those participating in the coalition can benefit but for which they must compete with growth coalitions elsewhere. In all these regards, Harvey Molotch's 1976 paper "The City as a Growth Machine" is foundational. Aside from providing an initial conceptualization of these relations, both the idea of growth coalitions and their competition one with another, Molotch also placed an emphasis—crucial in my view and often missing in discussions of local economic development—on rent. He underlined the significance of interests in land and its development on the part of owners joined by what he called "land related interests." Insightful as this analysis was, and in my view it was hugely so, it is a framework that needs some qualification. For a start, it is not so much land owners as property capitals that need to be in focus. And once one admits that, then it is rent from all manner of real estate rather than just land rent that should be our concern. With this in mind, two major issues emerge.

The first concerns the various strategies through which property capitals try to channel value through their land so that it can be captured as rent. Molotch emphasized the formation of coalitions that would take steps, like promoting inward investment, to encourage population growth and so increase demand for their land. Strategies are quite a bit more diverse than this, though, and we need to place the formation of growth coalitions within a broader context of possibilities; at least, that is, if we are to understand local economic development and its politics rather than the simple growth of cities. And while for the most part those seeking rent do tend to engage with others to advance their interests, it is not necessarily in the classic growth coalition mode outlined by Molotch. In fact, I would argue that that is more the exception than the rule, even while the same discursive flimflam about "urban development" will be drawn on by those promoting different real estate projects. The organizational forms embraced are, in fact, quite varied.

The second concern is the emphasis on competition among growth coalitions. This is an idea that has become deeply embedded in the literature on urban and regional development and the policies promoting it. At a certain level it does have its uses. Growth coalitions and the property capitals that comprise them do indeed compete to attract into their cities new office developments, shopping centers, and the like from elsewhere; and in this process they come into competition with similar groupings and developers elsewhere, all with a view to circulating money through their real estate projects and so augmenting rents. Even so, the process could usefully be clarified. At a descriptive level it is a matter of deciding what sort of competition we are talking about. In discussing industrial capitals, Storper and Walker (1989, chapter 2) distinguished between what they called "weak" and "strong" competition. The literature on urban and regional development has never been clear on which sort is at stake and, as we will see, it can make a big difference. Descriptive categories are never innocent of underlying conditions, though. In this case, particular forms of competition have to be situated with respect to a more fundamental logic, which is that of the accumulation process. Competition of the capitalist sort turns out to be the way in which the drive to accumulate gets enforced.

There is a third point to be addressed in this chapter that also reflects these concerns. The focus of this book is on policy and the politics surrounding it, and of course it is hard to talk about the strategies of property capitals and the accumulation process without bringing the state in. The state is a crucial aspect of capital, and not some distant umpire for a game and outcome in which it has no interest of its own. Molotch focused on the role of local government, but local government that works in bottom-up fashion at the seeming behest of land owners and land-related interests. There are two elaborations that need to be emphasized here. First, other branches of the state, including federal and state governments also play a role and need to be factored into the discussion. An emphasis on the role of local government seems to me entirely apropos but not at the expense of the way in which federal and state governments enter the picture, some-times articulating with local governments and sometimes not. Second, while all these agencies of the state have their own interests in urban and regional development, local government is easily the most actively involved. This means that property capitals and the growth coalitions they so often form cannot have their way entirely. Policy has to be and is con-tested, as we will see.

The Market in Locations and Putting Competition in Its Place

The distinctive character of American urban and regional development policy—what separates it from its Western European cousins—lies in how, to put it at its most abstract, it seems to be constituted by something approx-imating a market in locations: a competition among localities to attract in firms, residents, government money in various forms, and conventions; and a competition among firms for sites in particular localities, among tenants for sites in particular shopping centers, and among residents for housing in developments. Localities, or rather those representing localities and even particular developments, function, in Robert Goodman's (1979) memora-ble words, as "the last entrepreneurs." Among these "entrepreneurs" local growth coalitions play a central role, but so too do more focused organiza-tions like visitors' bureaus or relatively short-term relations between a major land developer and a local government; in fact the local government may actually be created by the land developer, as in the case of Vernon. And there again there are the shopping center developers who will have their own connections with the chain stores that they assiduously cultivate. But in all these cases, it is those with an interest in real estate and the rents it generates who predominate. Meanwhile, busy fixing things are the various local economic development professionals attached to city planning offices, chambers of commerce, and state Departments of Development, as well as those working for the shopping center developers or the utilities. The "buyers" are massively diverse: various types of corporations—industrial firms, service companies, firms looking for a site for their headquarters, chain stores looking for locations in shopping centers—but also property developers, retirees buying houses in retirement communities, professional organizations seeking an annual convention site, and even the NFL as it scopes out sites for the Super Bowl.[1]

To say that locations are "sold," of course, requires an explanation. What is at stake is rent: obviously not just renting space in a shopping center or in an industrial park, or selling land to a major manufacturing firm. Rather it is also a matter of housing for those employed there along with the provision of gas and electricity.[2] Any new arrival will have development consequences for the locality or, more accurately, for money circulating through the local economy and that portion of it distributed as rent. Just how much will depend in part on the ability of (for example) an industrial firm to attract suppliers, which is one of the reasons that the Japanese auto transplants with their just-in-time production systems have been the targets of such furious competition on the part of state departments of development. And there again, local government is looking for a share of that rent in the form of property taxes.

As for the buying side, sites in different locations are being traded off one against another with a view to future revenue streams, and in the case of residents, to advantages of schools, amenities, and possibilities for home value appreciation. There is clearly a bargaining redolent of a marketplace. There are the incentive packages offered by localities that

---

1. For academic elaborations of the idea of local economic development as a market in locations, see Blair, Fichtenbaum, and Swaney (1984) and Feiock (2002).

2. It might seem odd to subsume the profits of utilities under the category of land rent but no odder than representing a significant part of the profit of a corner store as land rent: as that part of profit which reflects *its* favorable location.

get so much publicity in the media: the more they want to attract the buyer, the bigger the bait. And it is not just local governments that are in the incentives game; the utilities sometimes offer discount electricity and gas, particularly if the fish to be caught is going to be a big consumer. There is also the (variable) ability of firms to play one locality off against another. Less publicized are the lengths that the developers themselves believe they must go to in order to secure tenants: selling a site outright to an anchor store or even giving it part ownership in the shopping center, and rent holidays for new tenants. On the buyer side, there is the question of how much they are prepared to give up in terms of incentives to move into a particular city; and how much they are prepared to pay given that the price of the site can include a capitalization of the various externalities available there.

In other words, from the standpoint of the "buyers" it is not just physical sites that are sold with the usual physical attributes of size and access but sites in particular geographic contexts complete with various externalities that the firm can convert into enhanced profits and rents. This can include all the various contributors to a locality's "business climate": the willingness of a local government to cut red tape and to offer incentives, as well as the labor and tax laws in the state where the site happens to be located. Physical and social infrastructures can count in so many different ways: access to regional markets for distribution centers, airline service for corporations looking for a new place to put their headquarters, freeway interchanges for the shopping center developers. And so on.

To talk about markets, though, whether for locations or anything else, raises some quite tricky questions. A focus on price and how it is determined by market forces that are exogenous in their origin—a typical approach in urban and regional studies—can be quite misleading. Looking through the lens provided by the capital accumulation process, one gets a better sense of what is at stake and how it is expressed in the urban and regional development process. From this perspective, the market in locations has to be seen as entirely subordinated to and regulated by the accumulation process.

We should recall here the discussion about property capital in the last chapter and the role it has assumed in capital's division of labor. On the one hand it has become developer and landlord for much of capital as a whole.[3] By virtue of this it lays claim to a share of surplus value. And on the other it has replaced employers and self-build as two of the major alternatives in providing housing for the reproduction of the working class. It functions therefore so as to enhance space as a productive force for capital, putting the conditions of the labor process in those places where production costs, including those of moving things around, will be minimized. As such it assumes an essential role in the accumulation process.

Competition is clearly crucial to these processes. Developers keep housing costs down because they have to, on pain of losing business to others. Forced out of particular lines of real estate product, and if they are to avoid bankruptcy, they then need to look for new products that will give them an edge over the competition: think here of the shopping center and new leisure configurations like ski resorts, retirement complexes, golf club communities, and downtown hospitality areas with their bars, arenas, and restaurants—and of the Palm Springs and Sun Cities of this world. And as many others have pointed out, the low-density model of suburban development does wonders for energy consumption: a world of innovation, in other words, that revolutionizes space as a force of production and of consumption, both.

This is not the timid world of competition that is the received wisdom of introductory economics courses, where firms respond to demand drawing on a particular menu of products and technologies. Rather, and to paraphrase Storper and Walker, this is a world of "strong" competition: not one of firms passively responding to what is available, to already existing technological possibilities, therefore, but of firms that constantly revolutionize their own conditions of production and what they produce. As

---

3. Not all, though. While modular units rented from a property company serve the purposes of some firms, particularly in light assembly, it is hard to see oil refineries, chemical plants, or heavy engineering plants being rented out; on the one hand, firms develop and expand their premises according to need; and on the other the market for them is, to say the least, extremely thin. Offices with built-in specialized equipment like dental offices fall in the same category.

such, firms, including property capitals, and to paraphrase Marx,[4] work
at both ends at once, regulating both the supply of and demand for their
various products; and just as this works in the labor market through creating an industrial reserve army, so for property capital it is a matter of what
Richard Walker has called a "lumpen geography of places" (1978): abandoned housing, abandoned shopping centers, abandoned regions, even, as
one goes further back, abandoned towns. Property capital creates demand
through its imagining, fashioning and realization of new products and
representations. These include new sorts of housing and residential development from the old gridiron pattern to the garden suburb, from houses
with single-car garages to ones with two or even more, from the garden
suburb to the golf course community, and then from the golf course community to ones with lakes, jogging trails, bike trails, even horse trails. The
same pattern has been repeated in the case of shopping centers. From the
standpoint of first the shopping mall, then the *enclosed* shopping mall,
precursors like Kansas City's Country Club Plaza or Philadelphia's Main
Line, discussed in the last chapter, seem light years away. One could write
a similar history for office buildings and developments and indeed, with
the advent of modular units, for industry, too. And this is not to mention the quite massive variety of developments attuned to the life cycle,
not least Del Webb's hugely innovative retirement communities or leisure
complexes like Disneyworld and ski resorts.

There are also the innovative ways in which places have been imagined so as to tickle the fancy of buyers and intermediaries, all the way from

---

4. The reference is to the labor market and the implications of capital's tendency
to create an industrial reserve army through substituting machinery for workers in short
supply: "The demand for labor is not identical with increase of capital, nor is supply of
labor identical with increase of the working class. It is not a case of two independent
forces working on each other. *Les dés sont pipés* [The dice are loaded]. Capital acts on
both sides at once. If its accumulation on the one hand increases the demand for labor, it
increases on the other the supply of workers by 'setting them free,' while at the same time
the pressure of the unemployed compels those who are employed to furnish more labor,
and therefore makes the supply of labor to a certain extent independent of the supply of
workers" (1867, 793).

major industrial corporations to the location consultants and the realtors. Local schools were discovered as a selling point for new residential developments. Cities were always sold on the basis of their accessibility characteristics, and the idea of a hub city subsequent to the deregulation of the airline industry was just one incarnation of this. But the way in which Denver tried to sell itself, even promote the construction of a new airport, as midway between East Asia and Western Europe and so an ideal hub for international air cargo borders on genius.

On the other hand, the supply of new sorts of places, new sorts of real estate product, has tended to create its own demand—and regardless of whether people want it or not. The supply of new products puts downward pressure on the rents generated by older ones: on the older apartment developments that do not have tennis courts, swimming pools, and community centers; on the older office buildings that lack open-plan provision or off-street parking; on older types of shopping center; and last but not least on a lot of older central city housing. The result is predictable. The older shopping centers get abandoned[5] creating eyesores that can lower the value of other properties in the area. Areas of older housing get redlined. Earlier vintages of hotels are converted into accommodations for university students—if their owners are lucky. Older, inner suburbs struggle to compete for the lucrative tax-yielding land use with the newer ones. So people are pushed out to where they *can* obtain a mortgage, just as the chain stores follow the anchor stores in their search for a newer, more lucrative commercial paradise. Meanwhile in this crazy game of musical places, the developers have managed to push the losses on to others.

There is a limit of course. While in even the most depressed of urban areas, property capitals will add so-called "new concepts in living" and lavish new shopping centers on the periphery—to visit the suburbs surrounding Detroit can belie what has happened in Detroit itself—ultimately the ability of buyers to filter "up" into the new residential areas is limited by the difficulties that they will encounter in trickling down

5. Every metropolitan area of any size in the United States has its story to tell. For the St. Louis case, see Joe Huber's article "The Life and Death of Great St Louis Malls" (2012).

existing properties. So the vitality of the accumulation process more generally can be a challenge, which is why property capitals are often so keen on supporting attempts to bolster the local economic base. But despite their efforts to attract in new industry, and to sell sites on the back of labor through their support for lax labor law and the pursuit of a desirable business climate, a lumpen geography of places is an inevitable consequence of capital's tendency to uneven development.

It is possible that, to use Robert Goodman's (1979) evocative idea of a rotation of places, once the "fertility" of a city or a region for investment has been restored, once labor has learned its lesson not to push too hard, once the housing has been devalued and wage demands brought down commensurately, capital will return. Some places do eventually recover.[6] The same merry-go-round applies to the different districts making up metropolitan areas. Once there has been sufficient abandonment in the central parts of the city, once leases on commercial property have expired and industries moved out to the more expansive sites of the suburbs, then land can be assembled for newer more lucrative uses, as per Smith's (1979; 1987) rent gap theory. What impresses about the American instance, though, is how this process in its degree is so exaggerated. As we will see this sort of scorched earth effect—a landscape of abandoned central cities alongside burgeoning suburbs, of growing urban centers in the middle of rural hinterlands in a tailspin—is not nearly so evident in Western Europe. But before addressing that, we need to explore the various ways in which property capitals organize themselves in their search for enhanced rents.

Growth Coalitions in Question

In thinking about those who want, in fact may *need*, to "sell" locations, Molotch's 1976 paper "The City as a Growth Machine" is, as I said,

---

6. In some, though, unemployment has been extraordinarily stubborn over a very long period of time, like the old coal mining regions of northeastern Pennsylvania or of northeastern England. Larger regional centers have tended to reinvent themselves more easily, though in part by sucking the commercial life out of a deprived hinterland and centralizing it.

fundamental. Above all, he drew attention to the central interest of some businesses in land rent and what that meant for promoting urban growth. He was not very clear on who that included. I would argue that what is at issue is ownership of not just raw, developable land, and not just the land under shopping centers, apartment buildings, hotels, parking garages, office buildings, housing, airports, airport parking lots, and business parks, among others, but also the "improvements" themselves. In addition to land owners he also pointed to the significance of what he called those with land-based interests whose revenues depended on land development. I think that it is a bit more complex than that, but nevertheless Molotch captures much that is essential to understanding the passion for growth and how it gets represented as "urban development."

For a start, as Harvey has suggested in his discussion of monopoly rent (2012, 90–91), it is useful to distinguish between those cases where the source of rent is direct, as when land or a shopping center is sold or space is leased out; and those where it is indirect. In the latter, what is sold is not the land itself but some commodity (as in mining or agriculture) or service, like retail, a retirement center, or a hospital, which is produced through the use of the land. Retail profit is, to a very substantial degree, determined by the locational attributes of a site; what people buy when they buy the store is essentially the right to extract a rent. The same applies to the revenues of a utility from selling gas or electricity within its service area: as more people move in, sales increase.[7] The situation also holds true for local media.[8] And in the case of banks, the interest on mortgage loans is a form of rent.

7. What the utility is leasing out is the use of its improvements to the land within its service area in the form of gas lines or an electricity grid.

8. Compare Domhoff (2005): "There is one other important component of the local growth coalition: the daily newspaper. The newspaper is deeply committed to local growth so that its circulation and, even more important, its pages of advertising, will continue to rise. No better expression of this commitment can be found than a statement by the publisher of the *San Jose Mercury News* in the 1950s. When asked why he had consistently favored development on beautiful orchard lands that turned San Jose into one of the largest cities in California within a period of two decades, he replied, 'Trees do not read newspapers' (Downie 1974, 112)." There are some famous examples of newspaper

For property capitals, though, it is quite different: they specialize in land and its development, are in self-conscious pursuit of rent, and depend on a continuing stream of new projects. For them, the source of rent is direct. And as such, a major constraint on their calculations and choice of strategy has to be the fixity of the land, and that of the improvements to it. Money is mobile; it can buy real estate anywhere. But once bought, the land and the improvements thereon, by their very nature, cannot be moved around. This is why property capitals take such extraordinary steps to channel money through their investments: the lessee or buyer has to come to them; they cannot go to the customer. This fixity, though, is a little more complex than might at first appear. For sure, the land itself cannot be moved, but then neither can any improvements to it. Land can be bought speculatively with a view to selling it at a higher price, and some property capitals specialize in that. Developing it can then add to the possibilities of capturing still more rent: a particular internal arrangement of land uses or some innovative design. This, however, compounds the problems of fixity, as the developers of Columbus's Arena District realized when the possibility of a casino next door cropped up.[9]

---

involvement in development politics, including the role played by the *Los Angeles Times* in furthering the events depicted in the movie *Chinatown*. Harrison Otis, publisher of the *Times*, was part of the investment syndicate that had purchased large acreages in the San Fernando Valley and which stood to gain if its bet on an aqueduct bringing water from the Owens Valley paid off. In the battle to gain public support for the bonds that would be needed to pay for it, the *Times* was active in promoting a panic around future water shortages, even while the syndicate of which Otis was a part conspired with the Los Angeles Department of Water and Power to create a sense of drought by releasing water from public reservoirs under cover of darkness. Sometimes the masses just don't know what is good for them.

9. In practice property capitals do tend to hang on to some of their properties as revenue producing entities. Their raison d'être is indeed to expand by developing new projects, and that creates an impulse to sell to long-term owners like insurance companies, which is what in effect had happened to 80 percent by value of the Arena District. But when interest rates are high and new projects more expensive, then the revenues from existing properties provide a cushion. Once real estate markets recover, then they can be sold off to generate the cash necessary to leverage loan finance on a still greater scale.

There again, and even if development is particularly innovative, people have to want to be in that particular city or neighborhood: the question of demand attaches not just to a particular piece of property and the improvements to it but to a wider geographic area. So the prospects of a specific, geographically defined real estate market are a significant consideration, though not determinant; for even in a contracting market property capitals can and do take business away from each other. What all this means, though, is that life for a property capital can be, and typically is, a highly speculative business. Even when (for example) the local housing market is booming, nasty things can happen. This is particularly the case in "long stay" projects where the build-out period can be several years and perhaps longer. What you do not want is some unanticipated development of adjacent land that is going to degrade rather than enhance your rents. Land use zoning helps in hedging bets but is far from foolproof.

One way of countering risk is to spread it out. This distribution can be geographic, as in developing land in different cities on the assumption that unanticipated losses in some will be offset by gains, equally unanticipated, in others. Or, property capitals can and do shift their emphasis among different sorts of real estate development, assembling a mix of, for instance, office, retail, recreational, and apartment developments. The problem with the first option, though, is that property development, as the saying goes, is "very hands on" with the result that developers tend to stay in the same local real estate market and, furthermore, have trouble putting down roots elsewhere.

Developers need to know and they need to be known. All property markets, including those for new housing, are highly particular and geographically distinct. Familiarity is something that comes only with time, enabling developers to perceive trends, both geographic and otherwise, and to anticipate which areas are emerging and which are fading. There are contacts to be nurtured and then exploited: it is important to connect with local planners and planning commissions, gleaning insights into their criteria for acceptable development, and to know who the local fixers are—the zoning attorneys in particular but anyone else who has the ear of city council. Likewise, developers have to be known by local builders, since builders tend to follow particular developers. A developer can subdivide and draw up subdivision regulations, but then, particularly in more expensive developments, they need buy-in from individual builders who are the market for the lots. In order to have confidence that developments will indeed sell, builders must have some conviction that a housing developer knows the market and develops in the "right" place at the right level. And there again, development needs money and the banks need to know who they are lending to. Track records have to be built up. This takes time, and mistakes are costly.[10]

This is to confine our attention to the property capitals themselves and to their stakes in particular areas. There are also those others who, as Molotch described, "although not directly involved in land use, have their futures tied to growth of the metropolis as a whole" (1976, 314). Oddly he did not include construction interests under this heading. Yet they turn out to be hugely dependent on particular, local, construction markets and so a major participant in the growth coalitions whose significance he was so keen to emphasize. In a fascinating paper Buzzelli and Harris (2006) have likened the organization of house building in cities to that of an industrial district: a complex of vertically disintegrated builders, subcontractors, suppliers, architectural and legal firms, and real estate agencies in which relations of trust count for a great deal—relations of trust that are not portable elsewhere and which make the industry highly dependent on market conditions in a particular city or metropolitan area. A casual

10. Compare Charney in a discussion of property capitals: "Accumulating knowledge in a specific market, nurturing networks with local governments and businesses, and reaching a critical threshold of the market size, which enables the company to be a significant player in that specific market, are crucial considerations for real estate companies. These are major reasons for employing a strategy of spatial concentration and the spatial shifting of capital" (2001, 755). In large urban areas, this also results in a concentration in particular sub-areas. As Beauregard has argued: "Developers in large cities operate only in particular industrial districts or neighborhoods—not all. By doing so, they 'learn' the market and develop relations with government officials, bankers, real estate brokers, contractors, architects, appraisers, bank loan officers and others with whom they will have to work from one project to the next. Efficiency is increased through place-specific knowledge and uncertainty reduced" (2005, 2433). See Wood (2004) for further detail and corroboration.

glance at the names of the big construction firms in major cities, and how they vary across them, suggests that a similar point may apply to other forms of development. The big names in Denver—Mortenson, Haselden, Milender White—are different from those you will encounter in Pittsburgh—names like Mascaro, Stadelman, Martin, Sipes, and Benney.

But if his *dramatis personae* omitted construction interests, Molotch did make reference to how the utilities and media share certain interests with his land owners. The same applies to local governments and their interest in property taxes. Unlike property capitals and construction interests, though, the dependence of these on particular localities is more contingent than necessary. Local governments do not have to rely on locally generated revenues at all, as we will see when we turn to the Western European case. The dependence of gas and electric utilities on particular service areas goes back to antitrust legislation in the earlier decades of the twentieth century and the desire to prevent the emergence of national monopolies. Banks were subject to similar restrictions. Interstate branching was not allowed. Within states, banks were typically not allowed to branch across county lines. This put them in a similar position to the utilities: highly dependent on local deposits and loan business and so anxious to see the local economy grow. These restrictions have been relaxed over the last half century and, as banks have in effect been able to spread their spatial risks, their interest in "local economic development" has undergone a corresponding decline.

There are still other cases where an interest in real estate rents may intrude even where that is not the enduring purpose of a particular entity. A research institution, hospital, or small college can buy up housing in the immediate vicinity with a view to ultimately demolishing it so as to expand its operations (as in more office space or parking). But when plans are downsized, the object will be to sell the property off at an advantage: rehabbing the housing so as to sell to a better-heeled clientele. Still, necessary or not, a committal to rents entails a suite of distinct strategies, which raises the question of just what those strategies might be.

For a start, an interest in rent means competition with those who have a similar interest, and the more enduring that interest is—the more it is a firm's raison d'être—the more intense that competition will be, often driving each other out of business, even while it can involve strategic coalition with others, as we will see. Property capitals compete tooth and nail, and in the same property market. Cannibalization is the name of the game: the owners of older vintages of apartment development are driven out of the market by the owners of newer ones; the same applies to shopping center owners. Ideally property capitals and others dependent on the return to real estate would like to dominate a local property market, perhaps even establishing a monopoly. Most do not achieve that but some do. Once the monopoly is established, the problem becomes one of reproducing it; which is what is going on when the small retailers in small towns fight the arrival of a shopping center on the edge of town: an old story not just in the United States but also in Western Europe, of course.[11]

The growth coalition is the obverse of this: a coalition to expand the flow of rents rather than keeping the competition out so as to preserve what you have got, even while both can occur at the same time. But the thing is, when attention turns to the various ways in which property capitals have indeed organized among themselves and with others to achieve their goals, what strikes one is the multiplicity of forms assumed. This is already apparent from the cases discussed in the first chapter. The growth

---

11. Auto dealers as a distinct form of Molotch's "land related interests" provide a case in point. The plans of Tesla to sell its electric cars exclusively through its own dealerships and so challenge the dominant model for auto sales in the United States through franchised dealerships created an uproar among independent dealers. They have seen it as a possible precursor to the rest of the auto industry going the same way, which could provide stiff competition for them. The National Automobile Dealers' Association has spearheaded the drive to cut this challenge off at the pass and ban auto company–owned dealerships. Tesla is now banned from selling cars in a number of states, including Arizona, New Jersey, and Texas, and in others it runs up against earlier legislation introduced to preempt exactly this happening. This example is not out of place in a discussion of land rent, since that is exactly what much of the profit of an auto dealership amounts to, as in the case of other retailers. It is not irrelevant that they are to the fore in activities aimed at enhancing local markets. To recall the Ohio casino case discussed in chapter 1, the lead to welcome the casino to the west side of Columbus was taken by an auto dealership. They will also put their weight behind freeway interchange projects and new highway construction that enhances their accessibility.

coalition remains a useful point of comparison but does only limited justice to the complexity of the process of, what is essentially, organizing so as to capture rents.

I want to consider now, therefore, the huge variety of organizational forms through which property capitals go about their business. Some sense of this organizational variety was provided in the first chapter, but there are many other forms. They vary in purpose, the geographic scale at which they work (an individual city, the metropolitan area as a whole, even a neighborhood), and also in duration, as some have an institutional history of an ongoing nature while others are much more abbreviated (as a particular project is completed, the organization or network of connections through which it was achieved dissolves). The six cases presented below illustrate how property capitals interact and organize in a variety of forms that could be characterized as growth coalitions, but not in the classic sense. These examples serve as reference points for the critical discussion that follows, which is intended as a basis for deriving some more general conclusions.

First Suburbs Consortium

This case of Ohio's statewide First Suburbs Consortium was discussed in the first chapter. At first blush it seems quite remote from Harvey Molotch's idea of a growth coalition; it brings together not land dependent interests in a particular city or part of a city but across a number of different cities, all characterized, despite their very considerably diversity, by the dubious label "inner suburb." But there quite obviously *is* a relation. Through joining together with other local governments sharing the same interests and the same legislative agenda, the members pursue a common goal of turning state legislation to their particular advantage. The concrete interest is in the revitalization of local tax bases and rents or at least regenerating developer interest in assembling or redeveloping land with a view to that effect. The problem has been construed in terms of a competition with outer suburbs, which have had advantages of continuing access to large tracts of developable land through ongoing annexation, ripe for big innovative real estate projects, as well as being the beneficiaries of state money for physical infrastructure. The consortium's agenda then logically followed: Make annexation more difficult and divert some of the state money in their direction.

This sort of cross-locality coalition is quite common. We encountered it earlier in the form of the Northeast-Midwest Congressional Coalition, which came together to combat federal policies regarded as placing depressed local economies in the area, and therefore rents, at a disadvantage. The same applies to the Sagebrush Rebellion: lots of ranchers scattered across the West came together with those small communities dependent on them to get the federal government off their backs, as they saw it. There is a similar story of cross-local organization behind urban renewal legislation (Weiss 1980) and an interesting one about how community builders—very land dependent—managed to get federal legislation to protect their interests where local governments had turned them down, as we will see (Weiss 1987).

Silicon Valley Manufacturing Group

The case of the Silicon Valley Manufacturing Group, also discussed in chapter 1, is unusual in that it does not comprise land or land development interests in the way Molotch described. It does not consist of those firms, like developers and public utilities, anxious to expand local demand for their land, services, houses, and office buildings. Rather the group's members are, as their title conveys, manufacturers, and they organized for a very specific reason: to combat a serious housing problem threatening to make their own expansion more difficult. To compensate for high housing prices, they would have to offer higher salaries and wages, which is not something they have been keen on. This particular case also gives us some inkling of the struggles that emerge between different growth projects and policies in a metropolitan area. We got some sense of this in the discussion of inner and outer suburbs. In the Silicon Valley instance, it was the development priorities of the residential suburbs that were at issue: they made it easy to establish industrial parks but not to create the housing for those who will work there—housing that is supposed to go somewhere else.

Local Economic Development Networks

At whatever scale property capitals organize, bringing in money from "outside" is essential: this influx can be in the form of visitors spending money at a convention center or in Las Vegas, the money that home buyers exchange for a house, or some sort of commercial investment. Different forms of inward investment, though, get mediated in different ways. For office developments, city chambers of commerce can and do play the role of clearing house, directing inquiries to local office developers. Some office developers affiliate with national organizations through which they get referrals: a tenant in Denver is looking for an office building in some other city and gets referred by the Denver affiliate to one in the city in question. Developers of shopping centers work in a similar way: news of space in new shopping centers in new towns is circulated among their existing tenants elsewhere. They may also hire consultants to spread the word. None of this sounds much like a growth coalition, though that does not mean that the office and shopping center developers will not support initiatives aimed at bringing in new employment and expanding their market; such initiatives can translate into support, perhaps financial, for city bond levies aimed at raising money for an expansion of the airport or the convention center, or building a stadium to welcome a "major league" franchise.

In the case of industrial development, though, it is more clearly a coalition. This is what Andrew Wood and I christened the "local economic development network" (Cox and Wood 1997; see also Wood 1993a; 1993b): an enduring division of labor, supervised by the gas and electric utilities but including local chambers of commerce and local government. Gas and electric companies serve relatively large geographic areas, usually quite a bit more expansive than a single metropolitan area. Given the way in which sales expansion is so limited—antitrust legislation has made it hard to take over utilities elsewhere—along with very considerable investment in physical infrastructure, they have shown an interest for a very long time in what they call "local economic development" and invariably have departments dedicated to that purpose. It is with these departments that owners of industrial sites lodge their site information (e.g., number of acres adjacent to a railroad, distance from a specific town, proximity to an interstate highway). Firms seeking locations for branch plants or the consultants that they hire are well aware of this, so the utilities are almost invariably their first port of call. But the utilities need the help of local chambers of commerce and local government to swing a deal: the chambers to help market a particular city, and local government to provide the sweeteners in the form of financial inducements, zoning changes, and extensions of physical infrastructure. In short, there is no single growth coalition but a variety doing different sorts of work that may be complementary but is not necessarily so.

This particular division of labor is a vehicle of long standing, and from the utility standpoint, it embraces a very large target area. From the standpoint of the chambers and local government it does not, and that is where the coalition, such as it is, can begin to show signs of fraying at the edges. Whatever site the firm chooses in the utility's service area, assuming it does, the utility wins. Not so for particular chambers and local governments. For them it can be a crapshoot, so the intense motivation of the utilities is not necessarily shared. They have confronted what might be called a governance problem, one which they have managed to overcome in their own way (Cox and Wood 1997). The governance question applies to coalitions in general, but the limited partnership avoids it, and it is an overlooked vehicle through which local economic development, as their protagonists like to refer to their projects, comes about.

Limited Partnerships

Limited partnerships, especially those operating on the urban periphery, work on a large scale, both financially and in terms of acreage developed. Under such an arrangement, for example, a large amount of land might be assembled through front companies in order to limit price gouging by land owners. Given the magnitude of the area, a number of the functions that would otherwise be the responsibility of local government can be internalized. This can even include financing a new freeway interchange to give access to the development. All this, along with highways, a golf course-centered residential development, new office buildings and the like, can be financed by the sale of limited partnerships to local investors.[12] The contrast is with generating a unity among a set of land owners in an area with a view to sharing the infrastructural expenses that will spark the development of their land. The need to collaborate with other property capitals as in the classic growth coalition mode, and the subsequent risk of the free rider problem, can be avoided.[13] Local government may still be needed to provide water and sewer services but the sheer magnitude of the development means that the partnership operates from a position of strength. Local government is enrolled but on the latter's terms.

On the other hand, local government, for whatever reason, and particularly if we are talking about a large city with less dependence on particular development projects, may *not* be willing to cooperate. Developers each have their projects, the realization of which can depend on them taking their turn at the public spigot; some local government entity, like a metropolitan planning body, decides how state money will be spent on, say, the highway projects they all want. A morality of taking one's turn is adopted and accepted by the planners. But along comes a new development project cup in hand where the decisions of this planning body are not accepted as the final word. Rather this is a case where the developer has contacts at higher levels of the state: a case where campaign contributions to governors' races have given him some clout so pressure can be brought to bear on the state transportation department to ignore the usual

12. Not much is known about such local investors and how they operate, but in any metropolitan area there will be people of money willing to invest in local real estate projects as limited partners. Competition from other would-be investors can be restricted because the local real estate market is poorly known outside the area. As a result, the financial gains on offer can be highly attractive to those on the inside. But that commits them to the local real estate development market and makes them, like the utilities and the developers, dependent on it.

13. A set of land owners with property conveniently arranged in a contiguous fashion may come together, though, where it is a matter of requesting annexation by a city so as to make their land attractive from the standpoint of, among others, limited partnerships.

circuiting of money through the local planners.[14] But this does not sound like the classical growth coalition either: more an assemblage of useful connections put together ad hoc; which brings us to the adventures of one, now deceased, Earl Holding.

Organizing for Snowbasin

In 1998 the *Wall Street Journal* published a lengthy article on the imminent development of a "modest day-trip ski area" known as Snowbasin, located in Utah's Wasatch Mountains, into "a mammoth four-season resort."[15] Plans were for eight hundred condominiums, six hundred upscale houses, and several hotels. Much of it was to be on formerly federal forest land long denied to large scale development. The deal that brought it about involved an exchange of land with the US Forest Service and the waiving of numerous environmental laws. Only with this land transfer could the promoter of the development, Earl Holding, whose Sinclair Oil Corporation owned Sun Valley ski resort in Idaho and numerous hotels, build a resort of the magnitude he had in mind.

So the question that the *Wall Street Journal* posed was, why did the exchange take place? After all, the Forest Service had held out against similar requests in the past, and for very good reasons. These had to do with the history of land use in the area. Earlier in the century overgrazing had led to flooding, landslides, and water pollution affecting the downstream town of Ogden. Ogden had purchased the land in order to control the situation and then sold it to the US Forest Service, a federal agency. So, and to repeat, why? In brief, reported the *Journal*, "The formula he (Holding) has found to overcome that obstacle includes political generosity, a creative financial deal with Utah's Olympic Games boosters, and the aid of a Utah senator who may benefit from a bill he pushed through Congress forcing the Forest Service to relent."

14. For an interesting case of this in the Columbus area see Cox (2010, 224–25) and Newkirk (1995).

15. "Olympic Angle Helps Utah Ski Resort Gain U.S. Land to Expand," *Wall Street Journal*, July 9, 1998, p. A1.

The senator in question was Orrin Hatch, who represented and still represents, the State of Utah in which Snowbasin is located. Over the years Hatch had brought a variety of pressures to bear on the Forest Service on behalf of Holding, who apparently was a frequent financial contributor to his election campaigns. Furthermore, Hatch himself stood to gain from the development of Snowbasin since he was part owner of a 118-acre tract close to the ski area: a property that had gained greatly in value since the land swap and the imminent development by Holding.

The coalition of forces behind the swap, however, was quite a bit broader than Holding and Hatch. It also included the city of Ogden some twenty miles away, which, despite a history of environmental concerns regarding the land in question, saw itself to Snowbasin as Colorado's highly chic Aspen was to ski resorts in *its* vicinity.[16] The land exchange was also supported by the Salt Lake Organizing Committee for the 2002 Winter Olympic Games. The committee had previously stated that Snowbasin in its less developed state would suffice but now, as pressure built up for the deal, they were persuaded that this was not so after all. This, according to the *Journal*, was because the developer promised them that if the development went through he would pick up the bill for the extra facilities needed for the two races they wanted to see held there.

Given the resistance of the Forest Service, however, Hatch had to resort to legislation. In 1994 he introduced a bill in the Senate to force the agency to approve the land exchange. Simultaneously a companion bill was introduced into the House by a representative for Utah. Congress was also lobbied by Utah's governor as well as by the leaders of the state legislature: "All (apparently) recipients of Holding largess" (A10). But, "asked whether either his ownership of land in Ogden Canyon or the financial support from Holding interests had anything to do with his vigorous support for the land swap Mr. Holding sought, Senator Hatch [said] he backed the deal simply because of his long friendship with Mr. Holding and because it was a good deal for Utah" (A10).

16. For anyone who knows Ogden, you have to be a serious booster to be persuaded by this.

One of the things that attracts attention in this case is the sort of coalition that it exemplifies. The general sense of "coalition" is of a shared interest and of a spontaneous coming together. But in this case, the intensity of the interests varied. One can hazard a guess that Earl Holding's stake was considerably stronger than that of the Salt Lake Organizing Committee for the 2002 Olympic Games, which is why he had to provide a sweetener. Likewise, far from spontaneous this is a coalition of forces into the assembly of which Earl Holding had to put a lot of work; without him it obviously would not have happened.

The Snowbasin instance is also one of getting some decision from the federal government to favor a particular constituent, and such is the nature of the American state; it happens all the time, which is why people complain about "pork." Sometimes though, the "pork" can be spread far and wide by particular pieces of legislation, but favoring rent grabbers scattered throughout the United States; so many Earl Holdings, in other words. In this regard, the federal government can be said to have a very interesting history.

Mobilizing the Federal Government

When considering the problems of American metropolitan areas the finger is often pointed at the federal government: how it chases its tail by introducing policies that create an unevenness of development that then must be countered by new policies working in opposition to it. So it was that building freeways through cities—and launching Federal Housing Administration (FHA) programs that privileged peripheral development— emptied the cities out and required costly urban renewal programs to try to mitigate the effects, or at least to give the impression of mitigation. The underlying assumption, typically, is that these were policies generated by a wrong-headed government acting independently of local pressures; further fuel to add to the anti-statism so prevalent in the United States. In fact, when their histories are examined close up, local forces often were not just complicit but were implicated in either initiating the policies or giving them features that, while working to *their* advantage, worked contrary to the interests of others.

A major program of freeway construction did not occur till after the mid-1950s and the passage in 1956 of the Federal Aid Highway Act, but the idea of limited access highways connecting the central city to an expanding urban periphery had long been a gleam in the eye of downtown business interests dependent, in one way or another, on rents from real estate investments. As Robert Fogelson (2001) has outlined, as automobile use expanded, an increasing concern from the 1920s on was the congestion of downtown streets. The view was that ultimately this would drive customers away from the downtown and aid the growth of competing centers in the suburbs. Freeways, it was argued, would mitigate the problem. They would eliminate the lengthy delays at intersections as well as the problem of congestion caused by businesses on streets approaching the downtown. Adding their voices to this downtown property–owner lobby were the automakers, their component suppliers, and the oil companies, who all feared that a continuation of downtown congestion would stifle growth in demand for cars by encouraging people to use mass transit. It was certainly recognized that freeways would also stimulate the emptying out of the residential component of the central city, but this was regarded as a good thing since that too would reduce the congestion problem. A freeway system focused on the downtown would therefore be the answer. The problem, of course, was the huge expense involved: the purchase of properties along the right-of-way, their clearance, the construction of the highway itself and of interchanges. Local taxpayers would revolt at new fiscal impositions, not least by moving out of the central city into independent suburbs. Under the pressure of downtown business lobbies, though, an answer to the funding dilemma would emerge: responsibility for urban highways would be transferred from local government to the state and federal branches, the culmination of which would be the 1956 legislation that would fund freeway construction on the basis of a 90–10 federal-state funding split. But the point is, freeways would join up major cities and emphatically *through their centers*.

It needs to be emphasized that this particular configuration did not have to happen. In Western Europe the early freeway programs connected major cities but not *through* them; rather they went to one side. Later there would be offshoots toward central cities but taking them through completely is still unusual. And in the United States, too, the idea of pushing highways through central cities in the form of urban freeways did not go unchallenged (Mohl 2002, 21–23). This was on account of the huge cost of land acquisition that they would entail, not to mention the displacement of large numbers of a poor, dominantly African American, politically vulnerable population that happened to be in the way. But the downtown business groups aided and abetted by the automobile lobby would have their way.

And to some degree, clearing areas surrounding the downtown of their low income residents and releasing the land for redevelopment was part of the point—part of the overall goal of protecting downtown property values and coordinating with a growing chorus of demands for what would come to be defined as "urban renewal." As Marc Weiss (1980) has outlined, leading the charge was something called, in a deceptively anodyne way, the Urban Land Institute, a research organization established by the National Association of Real Estate Boards (NAREB, which later became the National Association of Realtors). NAREB was a crucial and intensely focused national coalition of real estate interests that, through the institute (Mohl 2002), had also pushed for urban freeways. What they wanted was a federal program that would first allow the use of the right of eminent domain to acquire the land to be "renewed," and would then have the federal government pay for it: so having your cake and eating it too. And in the provisions of the 1949 Housing Act, they would largely get their way, along with satisfaction on a few details that bothered them. Major concerns were the threat of public housing on the land so recently liberated from the poor; and who should own the land so cleared. On the latter point, planners wanted the land to remain public property and to be leased to developers: not a good idea from the perspective of a lobby that sucked off land rent. As for public housing, urban renewal would be the responsibility of a locally constituted authority, and responsibility for public housing would lie elsewhere.[17]

---

17. The only thing that NAREB did not get was flexibility on what the land should be used for. The 1949 legislation emphasized predominantly residential uses. But this

Regarding the FHA and Kenneth Jackson's (1987) *Crabgrass Frontier*, it is a very similar story. A lot of emphasis has been placed on the implications of the underwriting criteria used by the FHA in its mortgage insurance program—in particular, for a highly segregated residential form—but the interesting and more fundamental story lies elsewhere. Once again NAREB was in the thick of things, and even before the founding of the Urban Land Institute. As Marc Weiss has pointed out, the FHA, so crucial to the housing boom of the 1930s and postwar period, was "run to a large extent both by and for bankers, builders, and brokers" (1987, 142). Its creation in 1934 had been long in the making. During the 1920s the federal government had worked with NAREB on ways of promoting housing purchase (Hayden 2001). One result of this was the creation of something called Better Homes in America Inc., which, according to Hayden, had by 1930 established "over 7,000 local chapters composed of bankers, real estate brokers, builders, and manufacturers who lobbied for government support for private development of small homes to boost consumption." NAREB then lobbied hard for the creation of the FHA as a device for channeling low-cost loans to housing developers, stimulating demand and creating more conducive local environments for the so-called "community builders" (Weiss 1987). Most of the attention to the role of the FHA has focused on its mortgage insurance program and the way it persuaded banks and savings and loans to grant longer-term mortgages at lower interest rates. But, as Hayden points out, it also loosened up the spigot of loan finance for developers, since the FHA insured these too. This meant that developers could leverage their own funds to a quite massive degree, and as bankers shoveled out the mortgage money, virtually riskless, so they too would make hay.

There is also the role NAREB played in creating more conducive conditions for its members in their own local markets. Those builders investing more extensively in a physical infrastructure of highways, green spaces, sidewalks, and storm sewers, along with setback restrictions and

---

would subsequently be chipped away in favor of the commercial uses that had always been in the Urban Land Institute's sights.

uniform house-to-lot ratios—Weiss's "community builders"—wanted some way of protecting their investment against the hazards of spot zoning and the competitive threat of those who simply sold undeveloped lots and who had scant regard for land use regulation as a principle: the "curbstoners" (Weiss 1987, 5). Through the FHA's underwriting criteria—which NAREB wrote—they were able to achieve the goal of stiffening up the hitherto lax zoning and subdivision regulations that had stymied them. Henceforth, municipalities that did not introduce more rigorous land use legislation would risk the housing development that their land owners craved (Weiss 1987).

What is essential to grasp in this discussion is the role played by what has been essentially a coalition of very locally rooted interests in the defense, enhancement, and extraction of rents. They did not do it all on their own. They were aided and abetted by the banks that saw in the NAREB agenda a way of increasing their own lending activity and then siphoning off the rent enjoyed by home owners in the form of mortgage interest. To the extent that they were not developers, the builders too had major stakes in it all. From urban freeways, through urban renewal, to suburban home ownership, we are talking about a very bottom-up program that at various times would embrace the loaded term "urban and regional development." It is true that the federal government had its own interests in these programs. Promoting home ownership came to the fore in 1934 partly because of anxieties about the domestic market; the view that getting out of the depression would require stimulating demand, and part of that was stimulating demand for housing. This would continue into capital's golden postwar years, further boosted by the massive spending entailed by the construction of the interstate system. But the—literally as well as figuratively—concrete details of the Keynesian welfare state (Jessop 2002) city, to the extent that it applied to the United States, were clearly fashioned by a very narrow, locally rooted class interest.

▄▐▌▐▌▐ ▖

Thinking back across these different cases, there are several things that stand out. The first is the aptness of the idea of a coalition. As mentioned earlier, it has a sense of some spontaneous coming together. But in a number of the cases, neither the spontaneity nor the coming together is quite clear. In the Snowbasin case, and the ethics of Orrin Hatch aside, what is striking is the extended network of relations that were put together in order to make the project, at least as imagined by Earl Holding, happen. The Salt Lake Olympic organizing committee, the City of Ogden, a congressional delegation, the governor of Utah, a United States senator, and the national Forest Service all had to be enrolled in the project. This hardly sounds like a growth coalition, since most of the entities were only accessories to the fact. The network had a center, which was Earl Holding, and not a growth coalition, and it was from that center that the network was organized so as to channel value through Snowbasin: not too dissimilar from the center that the utilities provide in the local economic development network. But others had to be brought into the fold for that utility-driven project to be successful. The case is not unusual. It recalls the instance of DFWI and the Wright Amendment, courtesy of Senator Jim Wright, aimed at defending the huge fixed investments represented by the airport. And while in cases like Snowbasin and DFWI the networks are built upward and outward, they do not have to be. In the local economic development network, it is the utilities that take the lead in pressuring local chambers and local governments into cooperating with them. Many of these arrangements are clearly single purpose and will last only until that purpose is fulfilled. The time horizon of the partnership between Nationwide Insurance Company and the *Columbus Dispatch* is only as long as it takes to develop the raw land at their disposal and as long as, subsequently, they remain just landlords and have to fend off the dangers of casinos. On the other hand, something like the local economic development network has been there for a long time and will continue to function as such if the utilities have their way and can still make it work to their advantage. The same applies to the very different sort of coalition that is NAREB,[18] working at a much larger geographic scale, and seemingly without the power asymmetries of the local economic development network.

18. Known since 1974 as NAR, or the National Association of Realtors.

A second point is the variation in geographic scope of the areas through which value is to be channeled. For a utility it is its service area: this typically embraces a major metropolitan area and a very considerable hinterland of small towns and rural areas, and the metropolitan area can be quite ex-centrically located, or even divided by two competing utilities. The geographic focus of an inner suburb is obviously much more limited, and that of the Arena District discussed in the case of the Columbus casino even more so. The National Association of Realtors represents local real estate boards, and each of these enters into a coalition with others only to secure conditions in particular local property markets.

Third, it is useful to distinguish between those forms of organization that come into being around specific, dirt-moving, land-developing projects and those whose goal is laying down the broader legislative context that will make not just one project but many of them possible and enhance their land rent-producing possibilities. The various coalitions of inner suburbs—or rather of local governments and real estate interests there that have come into being to put limits on the expansion of their newer rivals on the urban periphery by getting states to change respective annexation laws—is one instance of taking the long view. The classic example of such an organization, though, and a hugely successful one at that, was NAREB (now NAR): without its lobbying of the federal government for FHA mortgage insurance and specific underwriting criteria, for urban renewal, the landscape of American cities would look very different indeed and, more significantly, so would the bottom lines of many developers working in very different places across the country.

Finally, in a number of these instances and those reviewed in the book's first chapter, there is also and quite clearly the fact of tension. To the extent that the inner suburbs achieve their goals of limiting the ability of outer suburbs to annex, then, and regardless of whether the investment is then directed toward them, the outer suburbs are likely to lose. Dallas and Fort Worth thought they were onto something when they joined together to sell the bonds to build DFWI, but when Love Field was resurrected it was a different story. NAREB, at least through to the 1950s, always had public housing and the threat it might pose to local housing markets in its sights. And in Silicon Valley there was a sense in which, through the Silicon Valley Manufacturing Group, the computer industry was fighting for its future against the residential suburbs. All of which brings us to the question of "policy" and the ways in which it is possible even to talk of urban or local development policy: the creation of particular marketing policies targeting particular sorts of business, along with, for example, the creation of policy-appropriate physical infrastructure. This, however, presupposes some understanding of the state, which is the topic we turn to next.

The Question of the State and Local Development Policy

In his 1976 paper Molotch laid heavy emphasis on the relation between land development interests and local government. But it is clear from the cases discussed above that the relation to the state is considerably broader than what he envisaged. Both state and federal governments are involved in what has been described as a politics of scale (Cox 1998). Growth interests in the older, inner suburbs look to state legislation for relief. To bring about Snowbasin, Earl Holding had to put together a network of forces that included both the state of Utah and the federal government. NAREB was a coalition of local real estate boards and worked wonders for itself as a result of its pressure on and even, some might argue, its incorporation into—or even *of*—the federal government.

It is true that state and federal governments have their own particular interests in urban and regional development, as indeed does local government. As Harvey (1974) pointed out, in its understandings of the depression of the 1930s, the federal government leaned toward a crisis of underconsumption: effective demand in the United States was insufficient to keep production going. Even then it did not have to go in the direction of stimulating the demand for housing, and private housing at that, as a major means of refloating the national economy. And of course the low-density suburbanization that it unleashed would be an important condition for the growth of the auto and oil industries as well as finance (Walker and Large 1975). As for the interest of the states, it is not just their reliance on income taxes and therefore on employment. So called "economic voting" also plays a part in gubernatorial elections, particularly in the more industrial states (Ebeid and Rodden 2006).

I am going to insist, though, that the interest in local and regional development diminishes as one ascends the state hierarchy; that local governments are more active, and that states are more passive and the federal government even more so—resources to be tapped by local growth interests, often in league with local government in their pursuit of rent from land and various real estate projects. The way local rent-seeking interests make themselves felt at the state level is similar to the way they work at the federal level: that is, via the committee system and the formation of bipartisan alliances around issues shared across different localities. To some degree the connections are more institutionalized. Every state has a department of development and these work in close coordination with state economic development councils or associations. What is interesting is the membership of the latter: an overwhelming presence of utilities, banks, railroads, and local development agencies, often organized at county levels. And when the latter are scrutinized what jumps out is again the prevalence of utilities and banks alongside insurance agencies, hospitals (as in renting out space to doctors and patients), and institutions of higher education keen to fill classrooms and student dorms.

Local government is therefore the most actively engaged and, contra Molotch, does not have to be pushed. In his original statement, the sense that Molotch provides of relations between, on the one hand, his land owners and other land-related interests, and on the other, local government, is a very bottom-up one. Local government responds to these pressures and, to the extent that they can, those with an interest in land make sure it does by performing as elected officials. One can certainly see why local government would be an attractive resource: something to be harnessed to their rent-seeking goals. In the United States it has powers that put it in sharp relief when compared with local governments in Western Europe: not least the ability to offer financial incentives to firms bringing the promise of employment, a zoning power virtually untrammeled by state oversight, the power to annex unincorporated land, and the ability to raise money for public works through the sale of bonds.

Local government, however, is not and cannot be purely an instrument of the rent seekers, even while a distinctive feature of the American case is how often they tend to take the lead. Not least, it has its own interests in rent as a result of its very considerable reliance on local property and sales taxes.[19] These are taxes that have to be raised locally from within its jurisdictional boundaries, which makes local government very dependent on a local accumulation process in which property capitals inevitably loom large. But they too are, in a sense, locked in, which limits the vulnerability of local government to their demands; their leverage is limited since they are not about to go anywhere. In short, local government has some discretion, and it is this which makes it possible to talk about "local development policy." Just what policy should be, though, is far from straightforward. The degrees of freedom can be quite limited.

For a start, while Molotch emphasized the growth of population as the goal of the rent seekers, this is not necessarily the goal of local government! Rather, it lies more in the growth of tax base and minimizing expenditures; in fact, as we will see, a growing population may be the last thing a local government wants. Local governments have increasing revenue needs: needs which have expanded way beyond the provision of police, fire safety, and schools to include parks and recreation, the expansion of family and children's services, libraries, senior centers, and community centers, in addition to a variety of "unfunded mandates" from state and federal government regarding the disabled and environmental protection. These demands occur in a context where, first, municipal employees are often organized, and in any case, where pensions and health care have added significantly to labor costs; and second, the services in question are subject to what Baumol and Bowen (1966) called "cost disease,"[20] which means that there are limited gains from worker productivity as service demands increase.[21]

---

19. Accordingly, as the sales from a particular rental property increase, so does the rent tenants are willing to pay for it.

20. Also known as the Baumol Effect.

21. Wages tend to increase despite minimal rates of productivity growth, since in order to attract workers they have to be competitive with those branches of production in the private economy where productivity growth is taken as normal.

All this tends to entail a bias toward land uses that are attractive on revenue grounds—high assessed values for property tax purposes and sales taxes in the case of retail uses—but which entail minimal local government expenditure. Retirement communities are desirable because provision for schools can be dispensed with. Shopping centers can generate a stream of sales tax revenues, but since no one lives there local government spending can again be limited apart from the occasional police visit to keep shoplifters in line. So for local governments everywhere cases like Vernon, where there are virtually no residents but a rich tax base, represent something of a gold standard; the problem is, not all local governments can possibly be like that.

On the other hand, this analysis might also suggest a local government unified in its interests, and this can be quite deceptive. In fact it is riddled with divisions that property companies and developers take advantage of. Not least, city councilors and mayors want to get re-elected, and elections in the United States, even local ones, are expensive matters; so donations are appreciated and even sought. Reports of corruption having to do with land use decisions are also common enough as to suggest that the iceberg is pretty huge, and there is no evidence that granting favors to developers regardless of the substance of their demands contributes to coherence in a city's development trajectory. And there again there are the city bureaucracies: what "water and sewer" wants is not necessarily what "public safety" wants. The water and sewer department almost invariably supports annexation so as to expand its revenue base and make sure that the bonds funding a speculative expansion of its infrastructure get paid off. The police and fire departments, though, know that annexation does not necessarily work to their advantage, since although they have to cover more ground city councils are notoriously stingy in giving them the money to expand.

Beyond its own revenue needs and budget balancing, and in determining policy, local government is subject to demands from different property interests that can be, and typically are, highly conflicting and even countervailing in their effects. This can undermine the local tax base that local government is so interested not just in preserving but in expanding. How to impose coherence in the form of "policy" is the challenge. For a start, it does not help that many of those dependent on land rent in some form or another have some monopoly power. They can be interested in seeing local demand increase, but the exploitative prices they charge can make that less likely. This can be true of the gas and electric utilities. It can also apply to water and sewer and to the hub airline, if indeed the city can boast of one, since hub status is eagerly sought for the connections that it brings.

To some degree monopoly power can work to the advantage of the development projects of others. It puts the electric and gas providers in a position where they can grant price concessions to new developments as incentives. Existing high-density development is used to subsidize, in effect, new, lower-density projects on the urban periphery (Gaffney 1962): "in effect" because given the infrastructural costs per customer at lower densities the service is costlier to provide but everyone pays the same price per kilowatt, per cubic foot, per gallon, or whatever.[22] But market power can also become an issue and run afoul of what has been determined should be "the" or "a" route to enhanced "development." Hub airlines, while they might help attract corporate headquarters where the extravagant fares often charged can be passed on to customers, can work the other way for the local hotel industry and possibly for the city, to the extent that it has invested in a convention center. The Missouri senator Kit Bond wanted to breach the Wright Amendment so that Southwest Airlines could enter the St. Louis market with a view to curbing the monopoly power of the airline dominant there at that time, TWA.[23]

22. A subsidy to continuing peripheral expansion, therefore: this is a case of what has been called "postage stamp pricing" and which Marion Clawson (1971) identified as a factor in low-density development in the United States.

23. There have been similar conflicts elsewhere. The plans of the city of Denver to construct a major new airport, much bigger than the old one, were part of a broader strategy to turn the city into a corporate hub of continental proportions: not too farfetched given the city's location. But the new airport was opposed by the operators of hubs at the existing one, United and Continental. Although the public reason given was one of cost, since they would be asked to help pay for the new facility through increased landing fees, it was darkly hinted that the real reason was the desire not to see additional gates created because of the potential that would have for competition from other airlines. This did indeed materialize in 2003 as United Airlines got locked in a battle with a growing

Implicitly, and quite crucially, though, this is to accede to a particular vision of local development policy. This is one that thrives on one new project after another: shopping centers, distribution centers, a new assembly plant or office park, and so on. The function of local government is then to counter the cannibalization of the local market resulting from this understanding of development policy so that the local economy can grow and provide it with the increasing tax base that is its goal. It is also a fact that the growth of the local market does not necessarily follow on from a succession of particular real estate developments, even while they might indeed promise new employment and an increased demand for housing in the area.

This is because the local economy expands not just through bringing in new investments but also through the growth of existing firms, existing state agencies, and existing regional shopping centers. The planners and utilities do not entirely neglect the existing economic base.[24] The economic development departments of the utilities are active in what is called "retention." Chambers of commerce will try to broker agreements between a firm, its employees, and local government in an attempt to persuade against plant closure. City officials will add their weight to the uproar if it looks as if a massive federal contract will escape a local employer. But defense is not their métier.

Developers depend on a succession of projects. This is how they accumulate: developing, selling on to a corporation looking for a long-term revenue source in the form of rents, using the money to leverage yet bigger and more loans for bigger and more projects, and so on. Instead of the relatively slow, steady growth of an existing economic base, possibly though not inevitably subject to reduced employment needs as productivity develops (and

---

low-cost airline over the distribution of gates ("Denver's Idle Gates Draw Covetous Eyes," *New York Times*, Aug. 5, 2003). What the city and the airlines *could* agree on, as discussed in chapter 1, was the closure and demolition of the old airport, foreclosing the possibility of competition for the new airport and a repeat of the DFWI saga.

24. In some instances there are strong forces impelling their attention, such as a major local employer that does indeed promise growth. This is the case in Rochester Minnesota, dominated by the Mayo Clinic (see Miszczyk 2013).

which in many cases could suddenly go totally south), new investments from the outside promise quantum leaps in demand for new housing, office developments, shopping centers and the like, and at the very least a substitute for an economic base that is no longer generating employment.

The local economic development professionals and local government officials have their own reasons for supporting this agenda. What attracts them is the glamor of big media announcements, of notches on the belt that come with the coup of landing a Japanese transplant, of the photo in the suburban newspaper showing the mayor against the backdrop of a new shopping center or, if it is a very small town, a Walmart. This commitment to new projects, though, opens up the possibility of conflict with those existing firms who do not share these priorities.

As a slogan, "local economic development" has been taken over by the developers and by the professionals in the utilities and city planning departments who are keen on attracting new investment from the outside, corporate or otherwise. Yet as we saw in the Silicon Valley case, what these local economic development professionals may be doing in this regard— filtering in industrial and commercial land uses while keeping out the workers—does not always fit well with the plans of firms whose expansion prospects are more than promising and capable of providing a demand for housing that property capitals in many other parts of the country would slather over. The computer and software firms need workers, and limiting the availability of housing through zoning policies makes it harder for them to hire, particularly at wages they are comfortable with.

At this point three interim conclusions emerge. The first is that the relation between property capital on the one hand and industrial and commercial capital on the other can be quite severely contradictory. Recall here that the splitting off of property capital was in part premised on the promise of an expertise in the organization of capital's spatial arrangements. Property capital, albeit with the support of the planners, would apply its understanding of what was complementary to what, and of what juxtapositions were problematic to the development of space as a productive force. But through the pursuit of land rent as a thing in itself, it could actually work contrary to that end.

This suggests, though, that part of the problem is that the land use planners can also exist in some contradiction not just with industrial capital but with property capital, too. Local government has its own agenda and it is not necessarily that of creating a geography that will contribute to the efficiency and growth of industrial capital. The effects of this are hugely magnified by the characteristic fragmentation of metropolitan areas in the United States into numerous local governments. As in Silicon Valley, they can recognize the problem while looking to neighboring local governments to take the initiative, which they are not likely to do since that would mean a cost-revenue penalty. In a more territorially coherent metropolitan area, the effects of failure to attend to the needs of the economic base would be more obvious and therefore more likely to generate some mitigating action.

The final point, of course, is that the discussion puts in question the idea of any coherent local development policy. Just how can these contradictions be resolved, if only fleetingly? In part the answer can be found in the way in which the competition for locations gets structured, and structured in a stratified way. As the city's economic base changes, for whatever reason, wages and salaries and housing costs may increase to make it decreasingly attractive for industry, which gets pushed out, perhaps into a penumbra of smaller towns in the immediate hinterland—something to be looked on with favor by those viewing the city's future as "postindustrial."

What tends to emerge is a landscape of very uneven development: outcomes distributed across cities and urban regions but with some that are clearly more desirable than others. Not just a matter of inner and outer suburbs, but of branch plant towns liable to periodic layoffs and even plant closures as firms succumb to the siren song of lower—much lower—wage bills outside North America. On the other hand, there are the postindustrial cities, which base their futures more on growth sectors in services. Still other localities have been able to carve out a niche in national, even international, divisions of labor as centers for skilled, even high-tech manufacturing. And of course some of these sources of growth may come together: Seattle and Minneapolis remain major centers of skilled manufacturing while also aspiring with some success to the status of postindustrial city.

This is a hierarchy that makes sense to the local economic development professionals and to the property companies. The rent per square foot returned by a shopping center serving an exclusive suburb is likely to be considerably more attractive than that generated by one catering to a more middle-market clientele. Retail and residential rents in general in a city tending to the postindustrial are likely to be higher than in a branch plant town. In consequence, to the extent that there is a "policy" debate it tends to focus on what local government can do to push the city or metropolitan area up the rankings: If your future seems to consist of no more than that of hosting a branch of the state prison, then the offer of a major branch plant will certainly be attractive, and if you are already a branch plant town, then attracting some research and development is a welcome, if unlikely, insurance. For others, looking to become "a major league city," then a convention center, an arena to attract a sports franchise, and airline service to international destinations are all seen as logical targets.

One way of thinking about this is in terms of a competition for positions in the geographic division of production: for the more mental rather than the more manual parts of the labor process. Given the way in which manufacturing has tended to shift in the direction of the technically more demanding, this also means a preference for the growth industries of biotech and software over the older industries mourned in rust belt stories. Something similar occurs in metropolitan areas. In part this replicates what happens at a larger geographic scale: major urban areas also have their rust belts of declining heavy industries alongside new shiny industrial parks on the urban periphery.[25]

In addition there is a competition among clusters of interests—typically including both local government and classic growth coalition elements—for positions not so much in a geographic division of production but in one of consumption. What is on offer is not simply variations in the housing

25. On the other hand, while this is to emphasize competition between growth interests for positions in spatial divisions of labor, those positions are in a dialectical relation with one another as Gough has emphasized (2012, 102–4).

stock but also in elements of *collective* consumption: schools certainly but also the aesthetic of places that tends to go along with the more expensive of residential developments—a social class aesthetic (Werthman, Mandel, and Dienstfrey 1965) of winding, tree-lined streets and cul-de-sacs. This is something that can be observed in a way that is orthogonal to jurisdictional boundaries, most notably in the form of gentrifying areas and the sorts of landscapes that they try to offer: the brick streets, tree plantings, and closing off to the rest of the world through barriers to through traffic. This sort of competition can also extend to retail offerings. To be an exclusive suburb means not just who lives there but also who sets up shop; so Nordstrom and Whole Foods rather than Walmart or Target. The market typically works consistent with this vision but not necessarily.

One result is a certain segmentation in the competition for inward investments. The local economic development "communities" in particular cities—to the extent that some consensus emerges—know what they want and do not want, what they will have to struggle for, and also what they might have to put up with if they are to get any growth at all. In terms of incentives, what they are willing to concede to a firm considering a location there—what they *have* to offer—is a variable. The city of Chicago does not have to offer incentives to airlines to establish hubs there, but in other cases, as in St. Louis and Pittsburgh, hubs have come and gone and generated a lot of local angst.[26] Airlines seek out some cities as points of origin for trans-Atlantic flights, but Nashville had to offer a subsidy. Simply by virtue of their location, cities like St. Louis, Louisville, Memphis, or Chicago are "naturals" for major distribution centers, but places like Buffalo, Miami, or Portland, Oregon, are clearly a bit more iffy.

In the same way, growth interests in cities expanding on the backs of sunrise industries are unlikely to fight hard to keep a metal bashing plant open. But in a Warren, Ohio, or Hammond, Indiana, which has little apart

26. In St. Louis, the effect of the loss of hub status was dramatic. In 2000 there were over 31 million passenger embarkations; by 2004, and with the decision of American Airlines to scratch its hub there—a legacy of its takeover of TWA—that had dropped to 13 million. With the withdrawal of Delta's hub. Cincinnati has undergone an even more drastic decline, even collapse: from almost 23 million in 2005 to 5.7 million in 2013.

from that plant, and where the loss of employment would be unlikely to be made up for by the expansion of other firms, the story is likely to be very different. And as Mike Davis (1992, chapter 7) has shown, with the closure of the steel mill at Fontana, California, local growth interests were willing to sell the farm in order to rebuild the locality's economic base around a role as dormitory suburb; and given a location on the extreme edge of the Los Angeles metropolitan area beyond which lay the nothingness of the Mojave Desert, they probably *had* to.

Growth interests in particular places develop a sense of what is feasible for them and what is not, what is within their reach and what is outside it, what is worth competing for and what is not, what has to be competed for because other, more attractive investments are so unlikely: a state or federal prison instead of a branch plant, a branch plant instead of a research and design center. At the same time there is some sense of what has to be retained and what can be let go. Minimal resistance may be offered to the closure of an assembly plant, but the case of a software company may be very different. Cities with postindustrial status are unlikely to pursue a major assembly plant or even try to dissuade a firm from closing a plant, though for appearances' sake with the locals, some sort of minimal effort may be required.[27]

27. Just what is feasible is often very project-specific. Columbus is a major office center but failed in a bid for a 450-employee operations center that the brokerage firm Salomon Brothers was relocating from New York. Salomon Brothers was planning to relocate over one hundred key workers at considerable expense, and retaining those workers was an important priority. The—eventually successful—competition was Tampa, Florida. As the then-mayor of Columbus, Dana Rinehart, ruefully commented: "We cannot out-civic-arena them, we cannot out-major-league them, and we cannot out-ocean them. That's just the way it is. Columbus has to fight twice as hard" (*Columbus Dispatch*, Feb. 20, 1991, 1G). Rinehart's comment is also interesting because it signifies certain subtleties of Columbus's position that do in fact make it a struggle to attract in certain types of activity. Columbus does indeed lack the airline services and the major league franchises that Tampa has to offer. But this is partly owing to a regional context in which the hubs and franchises went to the larger (regional) cities of Cincinnati, Detroit, Pittsburgh, and Cleveland. And any attempt by the city to acquire sports franchises of its own invariably meets with opposition from the existing holders in Cleveland and Cincinnati, which

Concluding Remarks

As we saw in the last chapter, the idea of local economic development would have been inconceivable in the nineteenth century. Only after the Second World War would it become a serious concern for local and state governments. Certainly there were boosters keen to attract a railroad stop with a view to bringing in those who would buy land and perhaps expand the local economy through additional rent-seeking investments, but something organized under the heading of "local economic development" along with its own "professionals" adept at attracting in branch plants and the like was well in the future. What makes a difference, what is a necessary if not sufficient condition for the construction of the idea, is the enhanced mobility of capitals: an enhanced mobility that is a result of sectoral changes in the composition of manufacturing along with changes in the ways firms have organized themselves over space.

The big sectoral shift is the expansion of durable consumer goods industries, particularly assembly industries of which the automobile is emblematic: industries that were more reliant on the assembly of raw materials and finished components, and on fluid forms of energy than on locations on coalfields, at break of bulk points or accessible to tidewater.[28] Even then it took the emergence of multilocational firms with concerns about locating branch plants and then headquarters to make what would become known as local economic development—attracting in investments in these industries—a serious objective for agents that lacked that mobility. These agents would be the property capitals and local government

---

helps account for the fact that, as discussed in chapter one, they had to resign themselves to the less attractive ice hockey franchise.

28. These were already appearing round about the turn of the century. Examples include sewing machines, the bicycle and the radio. Later there would be gas and electric cookers, refrigerators, and household appliances, notably the vacuum sweeper and bathroom equipment. The big one, of course, would be the automobile. Even while technically they were capital goods industries, given their orientation to personal consumption one should probably include under this heading other transportation equipment, notably airplanes and buses.

providing the necessary infrastructure, those constructing housing for the workers and providing retail services for them; those in other words, who had a stake in attracting these firms into their vicinity, onto their land or into their jurisdictions or service areas, so as to extract rents from them in some form or another, because their own necessary fixity prohibited any movement to markets elsewhere.

It is this combination of circumstances—abstractly put, the mobility of some and the immobility of others—that creates the humus for the emergence of "local economic development," a nice euphemistic term that gives a public-interest gloss to the profit-seeking activities of the developers and the utilities, not to mention the tax chasing ones of local governments. What then comes about as a result of their activities is, in effect, a market in locations but one emphatically subordinated to the logic of accumulation: a market therefore that would be dynamic in what was being offered by property capitals and their rent seeking allies; but also dynamic in their market as spatial divisions of labor changed and new objects of desire like call centers emerged.

A major stimulus to thinking about these relations was undoubtedly Harvey Molotch's 1976 paper on the city as a growth machine. He captured both the stakes of those with interests in land rent in attracting money through their land (in his view it would be subsequent to the growth in a city's population) and the competition among clusters of rent seeking interests and, indeed, among individual rent seekers themselves. His statement needed refining, for sure, and that has been a major purpose of this chapter. A focus on competition rather than accumulation had its limits, and "the growth coalition" is a rather narrow way of capturing the different forms of organization into which the competitors—for they are still that—enter in order to make land sprout money. Likewise, the rents being pursued cannot be reduced to those from land. Nevertheless, Molotch's statement has been hugely influential and rightly so.

In some ways the statement was overdue, since the sorts of interventions that local governments started making into the space economy to satisfy both their own interests in rent and that of their clients in the property development fraternity had been increasingly evident since the end of the Second World War. In Western Europe too, the state was intervening in the geographic arrangement of the same branch plants, office parks, and residential developments that were the object of developer and local government interest in the United States. In order to understand what was happening there some tried to draw on Molotch's claims, but the importation would fail (Harding 1991). The experience of the Western European countries, how urban and regional development were imagined and carried out, would be very different. Instead of it being a matter for local branches of the state, the central state took the initiative. This was a world in which central planners held pole position and in which specifically local impulses toward local economic development, not to mention property capitals, were far less in evidence: a crucial foil for understanding the specificity of the American case, therefore. It is to that world that we turn in the next chapter.

4

Planning the "Good Geography"

Planning Locations

In Western Europe, the priority accorded to the state's role in the planning of locations has been quite other than in the American case. This immediately makes questions of urban and regional development more complex, because to plan locations means with respect to some understanding of what a "proper" geography of development should look like. The planning process is open to debate in a way that allocation via the market cannot possibly be. Of course, as we just saw, and over and above the insertion of infrastructure in response to private development, there has always been a degree of planning even in the United States: a preference for particular sorts of development to the exclusion of others. But within that constraint local governments and their developer allies compete with those targeting similar sorts of activity.

Planning in the Western European sense—planning from the center—has been different. The arrangement of activities relative to each other, and their relation to some conception of the good geography, has always been subject to debate at a national level, even if more so in the past than now. This, along with the inputs of special commissions of inquiry and the reports of consultants, government-appointed committees, and government-financed research organizations, has generated particular sorts of presumption. Emphatically, though, to refer to debate does not mean endless change. There has been a fairly stable compromise around certain criteria of what good urban and regional planning means and a remarkable convergence between countries. The relative priority accorded the criteria has tended to change over time, and again in a fairly repetitive pattern, creating a history quite other than that of the American case. Some of those standards have definitely become less significant as market forms of allocation have gained in appeal, but they have had, nevertheless, a continuing presence so that the difference between American and Western European approaches continues, if not quite as stark as it used to be.

Among other things, in the Western European case there is a history of interventions designed to counter uneven development. This was very evident in the policies of employment redistribution after the Second World War. But despite some shift in the direction of a market in locations American style, this goal persists both materially and as something to be drawn on discursively when arguing in favor of certain policies. There have been clear limits to this in the American case, where mitigating uneven development is an inadvertent consequence of the market in locations and barely features in any intervention on the part of the federal or state governments.

Redistribution is often seen by mainstream economics as running counter to the pursuit of growth. A common argument is that state attempts to counter uneven development typically result in a misallocation of resources. Areas that cannot benefit from investment to the same degree as others, areas where the marginal product of an investment will be less, nevertheless get it. But at least until the early 1970s, the view of the central planners in Western Europe was that there was no inconsistency; that guiding new industrial development into areas of labor surplus could reduce the pressure on labor and housing markets in major industrial agglomerations and so allow the price competitiveness of exports to be maintained. At the same time, by trying to make employment conform more to the existing distribution of population, investment in new housing could be restrained; something important in the aftermath of the Second World War and the overwhelming demands of reconstruction, particularly in the larger cities. Since then, national growth as an objective of central planning policy has undoubtedly gained in emphasis relative to that of mitigating geographically uneven development seen simply in redistributional terms. This is in part where increasing reliance on market mechanisms comes from and the belief that through the market "winning" regions will emerge. The job of the state is then to support them through appropriate infrastructural policies.

A major feature of local development has been, of course, the development of cities, including their physical form. What has been notable about the Western European case, and in stark contrast to the American one, has been the conscious attempt to create cities that are geographically compact; that is, cities that are relatively dense residentially, and with clear geographic limits rather than the sorts of dispersed, sprawling settlement characteristic of urban areas in the United States. This has entailed other priorities including brownfield over greenfield development; public transport over private; the development of light rail-cum-subway systems in secondary cities like Newcastle in England, Rennes, Lyon and Toulouse in France and in German cities like Nuremberg and Hamburg; the introduction of park-and-ride schemes; and the preservation of central city shopping through limits to the development of new shopping centers on the edge of the city. The contrast with what has occurred in the United States should be clear and, in fact, it is drawn on by those defending the compact city.

To some degree this interest corresponds to an enhanced attention to conservation goals. In the United States the idea of the "new" has a positive resonance that is not always echoed in Western Europe. Rather, the national heritage, rural landscapes, old buildings seen as having some architectural merit must be preserved, and limits on the height of new buildings imposed so as to preserve a particular aesthetic. This tends to complement the objective of the compact city by limiting peripheral expansion; though combining this with limits on vertical expansion can make it a highly contradictory policy (Chester and Hilber 2008) and even a contested one as in the ongoing battle in Paris over whether or not to relax very severe limits on the construction of skyscrapers.

The compact city also expresses, in part, a preference for redistribution. In the Western European countries planning was always seen as an aspect of the welfare state. Through its ability to sustain public transport, the compact city was and continues to be viewed as widening the accessibility alternatives of those too poor to own a car, too young to have a driver's license, or too old to have ever learned to drive. Limits on the development of suburban shopping centers protect the historic downtown and serve the same purpose. But in addition, housing policy has also had a marked redistributional component. In France there is currently a law enjoining every commune above a certain population threshold to aim for a housing stock in which 20 percent of the units are available at a *loyer modéré*, or moderate rent. In Great Britain, local governments typically negotiate with housing developers before giving permission to develop, and a major aim is to obtain some portion of what is called "planning gain": the increase in the value of the land subsequent to planning permission. This share has typically taken the form of developer intent to make some of the units affordable to those of moderate income.

The Golden Years and the Redistribution of Employment

After the Second World War, with some immediate prewar antecedents, as we have seen, there were strong tendencies toward central intervention into national space economies. This occurred in diverse ways. There were programs designed to shift investment away from major urban centers to areas vulnerable to unemployment: what have been known in the British case as the "depressed areas." These programs employed both carrots and sticks. Limits were placed on investment in certain regions or metropolitan areas where labor supply was judged to be tight. For a long time these limits applied to the construction of offices within a certain radius of both London and Paris. In Great Britain a large swathe of the Midlands and southern England was off limits to industrial expansion above a certain maximum floor space.[1] At the same time, financial incentives were offered to firms to locate in areas of declining employment, like the

---

1. Though in practice, as Pickvance (1977) has shown, making exceptions was not that unusual. See also Rosevear (1998). They were particularly likely where sites for the expansion of major exporting firms were at stake. In a discussion of how these policies applied to office employment, Pickvance (1981) has shown how, as far as London itself was concerned, expansion limits were much more likely to be enforced for routine functions as opposed to those connected to headquarter or major bank expansion, which were seen as contributing to the development of the city as a major international center.

coalfield areas stretching from northern France through Belgium into the Netherlands' Limburg province and into areas of long-standing economic stagnation like southern Italy or western France, or to places, such as Merseyside in Britain, that were the victims of locational shift within the country itself.[2] In West Germany areas close to the border with East Germany were shunned by private firms, and the federal government again provided financial incentives to them to counter this tendency.[3]

A second set of policies, somewhat complementary, revolved around the creation of new or expanded towns.[4] Not all Western European countries had these; they were especially prominent in France (Tuppen 1983), Great Britain, the Netherlands (Nozeman 1990), and Sweden.[5] New town construction was intended in part to reduce the populations of the major cities with a view to mitigating congestion. This redistribution was to be accomplished through the offer of housing to those on public housing waiting lists in major cities and through the relocation of firms along with their labor forces. New towns also facilitated processes of population concentration and the concentration of labor reserves in parts of the country, like the coalfields that were beginning to shed employment, and where populations had been dispersed in relatively small mining

2. However, questions have been raised about just how important these incentives were in the location of branch plants in small towns in areas with labor reserves. See, for example, Veltz (1996).

3. It was *not*, therefore, as Brenner has claimed, a matter of "spreading urban growth as evenly as possible across the entire surface of each national territory" (2004, 115).

4. As with policies of interregional employment redistribution, there were antecedents for these that undoubtedly influenced the thinking of planners: not just the model communities of towns like Bournville and Saltaire in England, but also the Garden Cities of Letchworth and Welwyn, products of the Garden City movement.

5. Germany did not have them, though Wolfsburg is an interesting antecedent, founded in 1938 to house the workers of the Volkswagen plant established under the auspices of the National Socialist state. Salzgitter, greatly expanded in the 1930s to accommodate the workforce for a massive iron and steel works, is another. On the other hand, on reunification in 1990, Germany inherited some, like Halle-Neustadt, created by the East German government.

villages (Hudson 1982).[6] In addition, central government infrastructural investment was concentrated in a preferential manner in particular, long-standing cities. This was done with a view to reducing market pressures elsewhere while providing favorable conditions for the concentration of labor, achieving economies of scale in the provision of public services, and so on. In some understandings of these policies, these cities were defined as growth poles.[7] The French *metropoles d'équilibre*, designed to reduce the dominance of Paris in the French space economy, are a case in point.

A different sort of state-promoted real estate development comprised the new tourist areas in France where the state would assemble the land and then sell at cut-market rates to private developers, as well as providing the necessary physical infrastructure. This is the story behind the development of La Grande Motte (Furlough and Wakeman 2004) on the Languedoc coast, intended in part to bring new employment to a depressed area, to take the pressure off the Côte d'Azur and to promote France as a tourism destination. Between 1964 and 1975, the French state was also active in the development of new ski resorts in the French Alps. This was the so-called "Plan Neige": less a matter of bringing development

---

6. In County Durham, this was also facilitated by controlling the construction of public housing. People were "encouraged" to move to the new town of Washington since that was where the public housing was being constructed. At the same time, the county council introduced a policy of contracting some of the smaller settlements by forbidding the construction of new housing there and limiting investment in public infrastructure in accordance with what was projected as the remaining life of existing housing. See Barr (1969).

7. Despite the recent enthusiasm for neoliberal policies, for privatization and the retreat from public ownership this sort of central government orchestration of local economic development initiatives continues. A case in point has been the Canary Wharf project in London, bringing together a variety of government powers and subsidies for land acquisition, the provision of infrastructure, and developers. Again, this had a more global, public planning, intent, the original inspiration being that the redevelopment of the London Docklands in this way would take the pressure off the City—home to much of the financial services industry so crucial to the British economy—where rents have reached very high levels.

to a backward region than of cementing France's position as a major tourist destination.

The fact that public ownership played such a considerable role in the Western European economies in the thirty or so years after the war afforded other forms of leverage. Where the industries in question were in declining sectors, as was the case with coal, then public ownership could mean a hefty regional subsidy, maintaining employment at levels that would otherwise have been hard to achieve. It also meant new possibilities of collaboration between different industries simply by virtue of government fiat. In Britain, and until the Thatcher privatizations of the 1980s, both coal and iron and steel were in public ownership. These were the necessary conditions for a 1970s plan to greatly expand output in the Teesside steel industry with a view to stimulating demand for coking coal from the nearby Durham coalfield: an area with relatively high unemployment rates (Beynon, Hudson, and Sadler 1986). When allied to a national spatial strategy, public ownership could be a major instrument for achieving national goals of redistributing employment. This was the case in France, where all infrastructure industries were controlled by the state, along with parts of industry, including automobiles, defense industries, electronics and many banks (T. Marshall 2011).

There is also the fact that central governments were and continue to be major employers. In a number of Western European countries, including France, Great Britain, Ireland, and the Netherlands, this was and remains the basis for additional policies aimed at reducing regional disparities. All have programs aimed at relocating government employment where it is logistically feasible, from capital cities to provincial centers. This was usually with the goal of reducing regional disparities by pumping value through local economies suffering from relatively high unemployment. These are programs that continue down to the present day (J. Marshall 2007).[8]

Even where government did not have control of employment, the willingness of the state to use public funds to achieve national purposes

8. On the Netherlands case, see Grit and Korteweg (1976).

brought about developments that would otherwise have proven elusive. Sidney Tarrow (1978) has documented the interventions of the French state into the steel industry during the 1960s. A major goal was the modernization of the French steel industry to be achieved in part by a massive relocation to coastal plants at Dunkirk and Fos-sur-Mer, next to Marseilles. But in order to bring this about huge subsidies were required, albeit in exchange for a decision on the part of the industry not just to relocate but also to close down old plants and concentrate ownership.

In the case of new town policy, public ownership of large amounts of housing during the 1950s and 1960s—about a third in the British and Dutch cases and about a quarter in France and Sweden—was an important condition for "persuading" people to relocate: housing would be allocated sooner to people who were willing to go where the government wanted them to go. But even with private housing, a fairly tight central control over location was and continues to be exercised. In the British case, and until very recently, national projections of housing requirements were broken down regionally. Within particular regions local authorities then had to negotiate over where the housing would go, and within local authorities the same procedures were repeated among the minor authorities of which they are comprised.[9] France and Germany have had similar policies.

A final and more implicit form of regional policy operated, and continues to operate, through the welfare state. Increasing taxes of a progressive sort and expanding state employment in schools, hospitals, local government, public transport, and diverse social services—all paid according to national salary scales—as well as support for the unemployed have meant some redistributional effect between regions. Assuming geographically uneven development, declines in economic activity within some regions are cushioned by public employment and various forms of income support, notably unemployment compensation, while, at the same time, the

9. For a discussion of the procedures involved, see Cowell and Murdoch (1999). Regional housing targets have now been abolished. However, local governments must plan to set aside enough land to meet local housing demand. These are then scrutinized and approved by the government department charged with land use planning matters, the Department for Communities and Local Government.

tax take goes down. It works otherwise in regions experiencing increases in economic activity (see Mackay 2001). To the extent that wages and salaries in the public service are negotiated nationally, which is typically the case, this effect is reinforced: it puts a floor under payrolls in areas experiencing contraction while holding them steady in those undergoing increased expansion. So while in areas of declining employment wages in the private sector may well be reduced, either explicitly or more implicitly as a result of reduced work time, public sector wages are unaffected; which has multiplier effects for other parts of a regional economy.[10]

In all these regards, the American case was and remains almost as different as it could possibly be. I say "almost" because the sorts of regionally redistributive policies that were central to policy in Western Europe were not entirely absent. There were some notable initiatives, significantly in the 1930s, a period when the balance of public opinion was more in favor of federal intervention than would prove to be the case after the Second World War. These included (1) the Tennessee Valley Authority which, as noted earlier, was imagined as a spur to regional development in a relatively backward part of the United States, through the improvement of river navigation, flood control, and the generation of electricity; (2) legislation enabling electricity cooperatives for the rural areas deemed uneconomic by the private electricity companies; and (3) the planning of the national freeway system. This was enunciated in a federal document in 1939 with the telling title *Toll Roads and Free Roads* (Fishman 1999) and came in the wake of the construction of the Pennsylvania Turnpike in 1937. The conclusion was that while limited access highways were the future of the country, to rely on toll roads would reinforce existing population patterns in the United States and so deprive less densely populated areas of the advantages of development. All of these

---

10. Nevertheless, this can be and often is a problem for the recruitment of public service workers in boom areas where prices can put housing beyond the reach of workers on nationally uniform salary scales.

programs—the electrification of large parts of the South, bringing electricity to small towns and later even access to a freeway—would help lay the basis for branch plant industrialization after the war, and particularly as the 1960s turned into the 1970s and people started talking of the "rural turnaround." In short, they were initiatives whose significance should not be downplayed.

In contrast to Western Europe, though, programs aimed at mitigating localized unemployment through the direction of industry were never introduced. There have been a number of programs designed to subsidize infrastructure construction in areas so affected. But the tendencies to horse trading and log rolling, to which in virtue of its structure the American state is highly susceptible, have resulted in the spreading of monies into areas that were only marginally deserving, if at all: a diluting effect that severely qualified the success of the programs.

If there had been a new town policy in the United States, one can imagine that the same would have occurred. But despite quite heated debate around the topic in the 1960s, it did not happen. The closest one has got to new towns were private creations like the much vaunted Reston, Virginia, and Irvine in California, and these made no pretense of working against the drift of population concentration as had been the intent in a number of Western European instances. Many of the new towns were, to be sure, relatively close to metropolitan centers; one thinks in particular of those around London and Paris. But the goal of central planners was always to locate them sufficiently far away so that they could be free-standing, with their own economic bases, rather than multiplying the numbers of commuters. The view in Western Europe was to reduce the diseconomies of agglomeration in a major metropolitan center even though in the course of time commuting has become more important, including commuting *out* to the new towns. In the United States instance, and in the absence of strong top-down pressures working against the drift of development, this would have been impossible. Accordingly, while there have been new towns in the sense of rapid expansion around a small settlement on the urban fringe, they have been the speculative creations of private developers working hand-in-glove with a small village or town, and typically of the dormitory type.[11] One of the purposes of the new town program in Western Europe was to reduce the uncertainty for developers, and this enticed them beyond limits that they would not have been willing to go in the American instance.

Finally, we should note the limitations of any countercyclical regional policy working through the welfare state. This is not just because the United States lacks a welfare state of the scope typical of the Western European countries. Notably there was, until very recently, no national health care provision, and this is certainly important. The main point, though, is its geographic form: its federal component is so limited. One might even argue that the United States does not *have* a welfare state; rather it has fifty of them. The rules governing unemployment compensation are determined at the state level, albeit within federal guidelines. Apart from some federal subsidies that have no countercyclical intent, education is entirely a state responsibility and salaries are negotiated at local levels.

These contrasts, it should be emphasized, are tendential rather than absolute. As we saw above, there have been top-down initiatives in the American case. It is just that for the most part they have not gone under the label of local and regional development policy. Agricultural subsidies have pumped money into rural areas since the 1930s. Their original goal was to support agricultural incomes, but they have, in effect, nourished the business districts of many a small town throughout the South and the Great Plains. Likewise, the huge swathes of private housing developments on the periphery of American cities, realizing the ambitions of numerous large land owners and small retailing nuclei that formerly served agricultural populations, are absolutely inconceivable without the massive federal subsidies discussed in the previous chapter. Mortgage interest payments come off the top of income before federal income taxes

11. Highlands Ranch, south of Denver and developed in a planned fashion over a large area by the Mission Viejo Company, is a classic instance. The dormitory function did not apply to the case of Irvine, though. Irvine was the brainchild of legatees of a very large piece of land accumulated over the decades. There is a good deal of local employment, including that provided by a campus of the state university.

are calculated, as do property tax payments. The effects, of course, are thoroughly regressive, even among those supposedly gaining, since those buying more expensive housing in, say, golf course "communities" get a much bigger tax break.

By the same token the sorts of growth coalition activity so characteristic of the United States have not been entirely absent from the Western European scene. Pickvance (1985) has made reference to the presence of what he calls "spatial coalitions" in Great Britain. He has also used the case of seaside resorts there to show how local government invested in facilities that would attract visitors and so enhance the receipts of the local hotels, guest houses, and retailers (1990, 169), a pattern repeated elsewhere in Western Europe.[12] There is other evidence from Great Britain that further substantiates his claims (Bassett and Hoare 1984; Axford and Pinch 1994). Local governments have also engaged in the same sort of bottom-up scalar practices as in the United States. In France the *cumul des mandats* has worked for a very long time in this way. This is a practice of multiple office holding that allows big city mayors or regional councilors to also function as deputies in the National Assembly or even as cabinet ministers, so putting them in a strong position to divert resources to their home bases.[13] Nevertheless, this sort of practice has been a decidedly minor theme in the policies affecting local economic development, particularly in other Western European countries.[14]

12. The municipal establishment of casinos in seaside resorts in France and Italy is a case in point; likewise the promotion of annual events like the film festival in Cannes and the Nice flower parade.

13. There is, among others, a fascinating story around the decision to locate a major node in the Trains à Grande Vitesse (TGV) network at Lille, including the spur to London through the Channel Tunnel (Newman and Thornley 1995).

14. Just what role bottom-upward pressures played in the formulation of central government policy in Western Europe is something that has not received the attention that it deserves. Cooke (1983) has written persuasively on the importance of what he calls a labor-led territorial coalition in South Wales in the immediate postwar period calling for the nationalization of the coal and steel industries and for industrial diversification. In his critical discussion of the top-down nature of French policy, seemingly in the absence

On the other hand, even without the sorts of top-down policies aimed at redistributing employment and raising living standards in depressed, marginalized, or relatively undeveloped areas, the American record bears some scrutiny. Table 1 compares per capita incomes as percentages of the national average for the nine regional divisions of the American census over the period 1929–2010. Aside from their general interregional convergence, and putting aside for a moment the fact that there has recently been a modest *div*ergence, what strikes one is the experience of the South, within which the pertinent divisions are South Atlantic, East South Central, and West South Central. Incomes per capita are still lower there but the change over an eighty-year period is noticeable, even remarkable. Meanwhile the wealthiest areas—the Middle Atlantic division in the Northeast, and the Pacific division in the West—have become relatively less so, and this has also contributed to the decline in the coefficient of variation in the last row of the table.

Just what is behind the relative increase in per capita incomes in the South is unclear. Conceivably crop support programs have been important as I suggested above; likewise the introduction of a state pension scheme through the Social Security Act of 1935, even while very significant proportions of the southern workforce, notably agricultural workers and domestic servants, were excluded. It was also in Southern states (Cobb 1982) that development departments first made their appearance, with a view to attracting branch plants by using financial incentives and exploiting the lure of relatively low wages; and there are certainly stories testifying to their success, ranging from the movement of rubber tire manufacture to small towns in Alabama, Mississippi, Oklahoma, and Tennessee in the 1960s, all the way to the arrival of the transnational auto plants in the 1980s. This then raises the comparative question of just how important was the Western European approach to mitigating the poverty and low

---

of any demands from the regions, Pasquier (2003) likewise raises doubts. Nevertheless, it needs to be emphasized that subsequent central government policies were applied to all regions facing similar problematic futures and in a way that could be defensibly referred to ideas of the "good geography."

Table 1

Income per Capita for US Census Divisions, 1929–2010, as Percentages of the National Average

	1929	1940	1950	1960	1970	1980	1990	2000	2010
New England	125	127	109	111	109	106	119	121	122
Middle Atlantic	139	132	118	117	114	106	116	112	115
East North Central	114	112	111	107	104	103	98	98	94
West North Central	81	81	94	93	95	98	94	96	97
South Atlantic	66	77	81	83	93	92	98	97	97
East South Central	50	49	60	65	75	78	80	81	83
West South Central	62	64	80	81	85	95	85	89	95
Mountain	83	87	93	94	92	94	92	92	91
Pacific	130	132	120	113	111	113	108	108	105
Coefficient of Variation	0.36	0.32	0.21	0.19	0.13	0.10	0.13	0.12	0.12

incomes of certain areas. Or would the branch plants have moved to North East England, South Wales, western France and southern Italy anyway?[15]

The Compact City

The cities of Western Europe are typically more compact than American ones. The built-up areas have sharper boundaries; you know when you have finally left the city. The leapfrogging so characteristic of suburban

15. This question of just how important incentives were, and regardless of whether it was the more local or central branches of the state that were offering them, has been raised in the French case (Veltz 1996, chapter 1) and in still other contexts (Bell 1986).

development around US cities—the creation of new built-up areas surrounded by fields to be filled in later, if at all—is quite rare. And population densities tend to be much higher. Cross-national comparisons are notoriously difficult, but this is one point about which there seems to be consensus.

Compactness is now widely touted as a policy goal: it enhances the economic viability of public transport, reduces the consumption of agricultural land, and, most of all today, it reduces carbon footprints. It has become a sought-after goal, and European cities find themselves advantageously positioned. Public policy has been crucial. But how intentional it has all been, rather than the combined outcome of diverse policies with highly specific goals having little to do with achieving compactness, is debatable. It is now a national planning goal and drawn on to justify particular initiatives, but its origins seem to lie elsewhere; serendipity has ruled. In addition, and with some exceptions, the concrete nature of these different policies has tended to vary from one country to another. So while the result has been very similar, the different policies playing into it have often been quite varied.

In some countries, limits on the expansion of urban areas have been a by-product of attempts to preserve the surrounding countryside. The most well-known has been the so-called British "green belt" policy that in turn generated claims of "urban containment." This idea, initially advanced in not very positive terms, originated in the work that the British geographer Peter Hall did in the mid-1970s, first on England (Hall et al. 1973; Hall 1974) and then in a book written with the American planner Marion Clawson (Hall and Clawson 1973), which tried to capture some of the quite strong contrasts with the American case; in other words, urban growth in the two countries was generating very different sorts of patterns. In England, something also applicable to the rest of Great Britain, the geographic expansion of urban land uses was being limited by central government fiat, symbolized by the institution of green belts surrounding major urban areas and in which new development of any sort was to be strictly limited. Hall's point was that this was creating a distinctive form of urbanization in which housing densities in cities would be higher, in which public housing would tend to assume, necessarily and more and more, a multistory character but with very clear boundaries between urban and rural uses. Hall and Clawson then contrasted this with the much lower density American city with its greater degree of dispersion, not to mention sprawl.

Hall's containment has continued down to the present day and, if anything, the barriers to further geographic expansion of urban uses have increased. Since the introduction of green belt legislation after 1945, rural areas have changed a great deal. The small villages have acquired a residential cachet that was entirely lacking before. What were essentially settlements of agricultural workers and very small and cheap dormitories for workers in neighboring towns have been transformed. Not to put too fine a point on it, they have been gentrified and have become *the* desirable places to live for anyone with money, either as a first home or as a weekend retreat. The last thing people living there want now is additional residential development cluttering up "their" landscape and amenities, and the green belt has become an extraordinarily powerful weapon in their exclusionary struggles; and the fact that many of these residents are not only rich but also famous can give their resistance a publicity, even plausibility it might not otherwise receive.[16] Fortifying their power in this is the fact that the boundary between them and neighboring towns is often an administrative one.[17]

Something similar to the green belt has operated in the Netherlands under the label "Green Heart" (Figure 5). This is not so much a peripheral zone but, as its label suggests, a relatively rural area separating the major urban areas in the west and south of the country—cities like Amsterdam, Rotterdam, and The Hague—from those further east, like Hilversum and Utrecht. There is a national plan to protect the Green Heart from further development. Municipalities adopt plans in accord with this and then implement it through building permit policy (Eickmann 2009). If necessary, the central government can enforce its vision by withholding

16. For some examples of celebrities stepping up: "Eco-towns Will Ruin Our Heritage, Warns Actor," *Daily Telegraph*, May 5, 2008, http://www.telegraph.co.uk/news/uk news/1929826/John-Nettles-Eco-towns-will-ruin-our-heritage.html.

17. See While, Jonas, and Gibbs (2004) for an example of how this has worked in the case of a city—Cambridge—experiencing very severe housing market pressures.

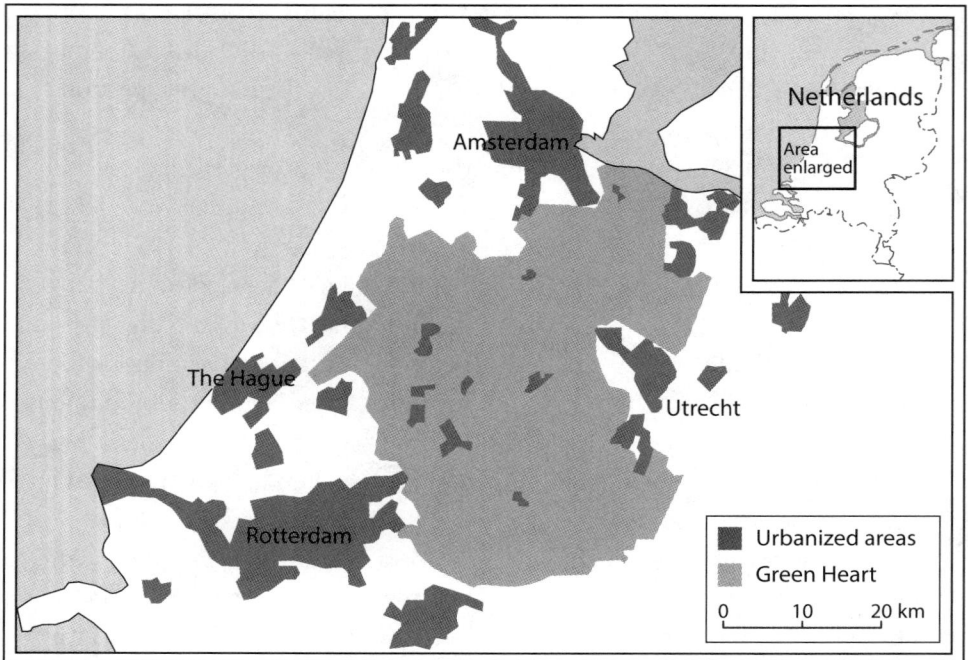

Fig. 5. The Netherlands' Green Heart. Map by Jim DeGrand.

money for public works. Given the dependence of local government on these transfers, this approach is highly effective. To prevent encroachment on the Green Heart, the central government can also veto local plans, although this is rarely done and the need to do so is regarded as a failure in concertation.

In Denmark and Sweden there is a related idea of "green fingers" or "green wedges." In the case of Copenhagen, a policy of channeling urban expansion along major transport arteries and declaring interstitial areas off limits to development goes back to a 1947 land use plan for the area. Closer to the city a good deal of the green finger space is taken up with allotment gardens, parks, and sports fields, giving way to agriculture further out. Stockholm has a similar system of green wedges dating back to the 1930s.[18]

18. Green belts, green hearts, and green fingers are government policy. However, France and Germany have nothing comparable. In Germany, peripheral expansion has

The significance of urban containment is how it has contributed to the formation of the compact city; an important policy goal of Western European governments even while green belts, green hearts, green fingers and rural opposition to new housing developments were not conceived with that end in view. In this regard, mention should also be made of policies regarding suburban shopping centers, which tend to be far less favorable than in the United States. According to Clifford Guy, "control over off-center retail development has been applied, with varying degrees of rigor, in virtually all parts of Western Europe since the 1960s. There has been a huge volume of such development, but town centers still dominate retailing in a manner unknown in the US since the 1940s" (Guy 1998, 975). Again, this was not originally inspired by ideas of the compact city. Rather it was a matter of the protectionist concerns of retailers in historic downtowns, but sustainability goals have recently given them new life.

The same applies to the relative encouragement given to public as opposed to private transport. Cars are expensive to operate, since gasoline costs greatly exceed what is common in the United States. They are also more expensive to begin with, which seems an unlikely condition for the low-density, sprawling form characteristic of the American city. One result is that public transport can be economically more viable in Western Europe, and it is. At the same time, the increased population densities subsequent to the various policies, implicit or otherwise, of urban containment, enhance this effect.

---

been much more rapid than in Great Britain (Baing 2010), but significantly this is almost entirely development that, unlike in the American instance, is contiguous to the city's built-up area. France also lacks a green belt policy, but the tendency has been for *ceintures vertes*, as they are called, to emerge de facto (Charmes 2010a; 2010b). While there has been residential growth in peri-urban communes, the tendency has been for the newcomers to then take over local councils and implement highly exclusionary land use policies. Mayors have the final say in granting construction permits and are extremely wary of the dangers, particularly as election times approach. According to Vincent Renard (2015), "le slogan "maire bâtisseur, maire battu" continue à avoir assez bonne presse chez les élus" [the slogan "a mayor who builds is a mayor who won't be re-elected" continues to resonate among the elected officials] (author's translation).

Adding to the attractiveness of public transport has been the way in which national policies have encouraged the linkup of their different forms. Mass transit systems, including local subway and light rail, invariably connect with mainline railroad stations. Major airports in turn are connected to the railroad system and/or to subway and light rail: something still to be approached in the case of some major US airports, most notoriously those in New York and Los Angeles.

Yet while compactness and its desirable implications for the public/ private balance in transport tends to set the cities of Western Europe apart, there are other effects that might be judged less desirable. As a result in part of demand for housing that has to be built within much smaller areas, housing costs tend to be much higher and housing units noticeably smaller

Table 2

Price Elasticity of Housing Supply and Square Footage of New Houses for Selected Countries, 2011

	Price Elasticity	Average Square Footage of New Houses	Price to Income Ratio 2015
United States	2.014	2204	3.39
Belgium	0.315	1293	6.46
Denmark	1.206	1489	5.18
Finland	0.988	880	6.78
France	0.363	1228	9.11
Germany	0.428	1185	7.07
Great Britain	0.395	826	8.25
Netherlands	0.186	1261	5.43
Spain	0.452	1054	8.52
Sweden	1.381	902	8.40

Sources: Price elasticity of supply: Sanchez C., and A. Johansson. 2011. "The Price Responsiveness of Housing Supply in OECD Countries," *OECD Economics Department Working Papers*, no. 837, OECD Publishing, p. 21.

Square footage for new houses: Demographia. n.d. *International House Sizes*. Accessed May 17, 2016. http://www.demographia.com/db-intlhouse.htm.

Price to income ratio: Numbeo. 2011. "Property Prices Index by Country." http://www.numbeo.com /property-investment/rankings_by_country.jsp.

(Table 2). Limits to expansion into green belts, fingers or whatever, tend, in the context of increasing population numbers, to give a strong speculative impulse to land markets. Given the circumstances, the price of land will increase, and the longer it is kept off the market, the bigger the gain is likely to be. This adds to the scarcity of land for new construction and so puts upward pressure on housing costs. It also means that housing markets are much less responsive to increased demand so that the standard measure of responsiveness—the price elasticity of supply—is markedly lower in Western Europe.

All of this, of course, is very different from American practice. As Walker and Large (1975) pointed out long ago, the American city is far from compact: low density, covering vast areas, and continually expanding at the edge seemingly effortlessly. These are tendencies that are hard to reverse, even if the political will was present. Low densities make competition between the private automobile and mass transit a nonstarter. The tendency is hard to rein in, in part because decisions have been made and money has been committed to sustaining this form and, indeed, for further expansion. Walker and Large pointed to the stakes of major corporate interests: the automobile companies, the oil firms, the banks with mortgages extended. To those one can add the investments that have been made in land beyond the urban periphery free of the sorts of statutory discouragement implicit in green belts or green fingers.

The fragmented form of the American metropolitan area adds to the pressures. It is the basis for new waves of suburbanization. Farmers keen to get out of the business as the city expands, but on terms that will be to their advantage, make common cause with land speculators and local officials—township trustees, village councilors and mayors, often deeply implicated in land ownership themselves—to promote the area as the next development frontier. Developers searching for ever larger areas on which to locate their likewise ever larger subdivisions, golf course communities, gigantesque shopping centers, and mixed use developments eagerly answer the call. To the competition of ever more local governments for development is added the competition of developers one with another for the buyer's attention.

Stemming the tide is therefore far from easy. There are clearly some exceptions. A few cities like Portland, Oregon, and Boulder, Colorado, have instituted urban growth boundaries and vigorously promoted denser forms of residential development while generating massive hostility from development interests—a hostility that is wholly at one with a dominant discourse of freedom of choice for the customer, as if the low density form of the city had ever offered them anything different. Once a household has two cars, it is unlikely to vote for mass transit levies. And residents who have invested in a single family home on a large lot are unlikely to sympathize with city-supported rezonings of neighboring lots to allow higher densities.

The Fair City

Despite the higher housing prices that it seemingly entails, compactness is often defended as fairer: more "socially just" to those who lack the money to afford a car and also to often-neglected groups like children, the aged, and the disabled. Fairness is also invoked in arguing for some of the other policies typically associated with the countries of Western Europe and in contrast to the American case. These include social housing policies aimed at subsidizing the housing costs of poorer people, including the public ownership of housing.

This aspect of urban development in Western Europe needs to be situated with respect to the question of land rent. The relatively low rents of public housing are a challenge to alternative, private-sector tenures.[19] When privately owned houses change hands it will typically be at an increased price, in line with the more general inflation of housing costs, including the cost of new units. When apartment developments are sold, rents are likely to increase to reflect the new price. But public housing never changes hands, which, and allowing for maintenance costs, puts some limit on rent increases. Meanwhile the private rental sector has had

19. In Great Britain, rents were also held down by virtue of a pooling of historic costs. Public housing built earlier tended to be cheaper, in part because of lower land prices. This lower cost was then used to offset the higher cost of later vintages of public housing so that rents could be held at lower levels than might otherwise be possible.

to be mindful of the competition, while the private housing developer has looked enviously at the potential market locked up, in his mind at least, in public housing.

In still other regards, the question of land rent looms large over urban policy. Henry George may have been American, but his arguments about the essentially social character of land rent—its nature as unearned and reflecting accessibility and proximity arrangements created for the most part by others and at their expense—have been taken much more seriously there. This is the justification for attempts to rein in land speculation and the capital gains available to an owner when permission is given to develop. Rather the view is that given the social costs that any new development imposes in the form of new highways, schools, parks, and the like, it is the increased land rent that should be drawn on to pay for these. This is the issue of what is referred to as "value capture" and sometimes as "planning gain."

As far as social housing is concerned, its image as an essential part of the Western European welfare state—overly generous in a common American view—is slightly deceptive. In its prevalence, social housing actually varies quite dramatically across the countries of Western Europe. With the odd exception of Germany, its center of gravity has lain in northwestern Europe. This has included, above all, France, Great Britain, the Netherlands, and the Nordic countries. Currently it accounts for at least a fifth of all the housing units in those countries.[20] In the southern periphery— Italy, Portugal, and Spain—it has always been very small: closer to the American case, though not quite as derisory or, for that matter, derided.

The heyday of social housing was undoubtedly in the 1950s and 1960s. Since then it has undergone some retreat. The most dramatic instance was the highly publicized and effective drive of the Thatcher governments in Great Britain to sell off public housing units to existing tenants. At the other end of the spectrum, though, is the recent commitment of the French government through the Solidarity and Urban Renewal Act of 2003 to impose a 20 percent affordable housing standard

20. Also Austria.

on all communes of ten thousand people or more, using fines to enforce compliance. But the fact that it has in general been in some decline as a share of the housing stock is significant, especially when taken alongside other aspects of the "fair city."

There is also a history of attempts to rein in land speculation, which would give American developers, not to mention land owners looking for the right time to sell, a total fit. Permission to construct, whether it is housing, shopping centers, or office parks, usually results in a dramatic increase in land value. At the same time, new development will generate a need for public investments in highways, schools, parks, and sewer and waterline extensions. This raises the question of whether or not that additional value should be "captured" by the state in order to pay for the public infrastructure that the development will entail. Sometimes these two separate questions of social housing and value capture have been linked: how to capture some of that value in the form of additions to "affordable" housing, whether publicly or privately owned. Again, approaches to this tend to have been much bolder in the Western European case. On the other hand, as with the location of employment, government intervention, the planning of location in these regards, has diminished since the 1970s; the decommodification of housing and land, the investment of both with serious public purpose, have been in retreat. (See Appendix A at the end of this chapter.)

The United States has also had techniques of value capture, but they are quite different in form and in effect. With so-called impact fees, the argument is that new development can generate a need for public infrastructure and therefore spending that has typically not been the developer's immediate responsibility: new schools, expanded highways, and parks. By imposing a fee per house sold or, in the case of commercial developments, per square foot, some of the enhanced value accruing to the developer can be drawn on and at the same time provide the local tax payer with some relief.[21] At present there is enabling legislation for impact

---

21. On the other hand, who foots the bill for impact fees depends on market circumstances. Where demand for housing is intense, it will be passed on to the home buyer.

fees in twenty-six US states, but others allow it through what are called home rule provisions so that impact fees can be levied in a clear majority of them. This does not mean that they are always made use of though. Remarkably, the vast majority, including some of the larger, expanding cities, like Columbus, Dallas, Denver, Houston, Indianapolis, Minneapolis, Portland (Oregon), San Jose, and Seattle, do not. Likewise allowing impact fees to go toward the provision of new schools—a major burden on existing residents and a critical issue in development fights—is allowed in only seven states (Evans-Cowley 2006) remarkable.

Tax increment financing (TIF) districts provide a second form of value capture and are typically used to help fund the common physical infrastructure shared by a cluster of different shopping centers: highways and new freeway interchanges, in particular. The idea is to capture the increased value resulting from the development of the land through taxation: taxes on the value additional to that prior to development are ring-fenced for investment within the boundaries of the TIF district.

Linkage fees are even less common than impact fees and are almost entirely confined to areas of very high housing costs in California and Massachusetts. The assumption is that in such areas high land rents can generate an under-provision of housing and particularly of housing for the lower waged. For a long time, San Francisco has had a policy of making permission for the construction of new office towers conditional on the provision of some proportional number of housing units or money in lieu. In other cases there, the fee has gone to the provision of day care facilities.

In short, it would seem that, historically at least, the issue of value capture has been taken quite a bit more seriously in Western Europe than in the American case. Local governments and development corporations have been given the power in various instances to appropriate land compulsorily: the British new towns and the French "grands ensembles" come to mind but are by no means the only cases. There have also been

---

Only where demand is relatively slack does the developer have to eat the cost; which explains why, in those circumstances, resistance to the very idea of impact fees can be intense.

provisions for the purchase of land at existing use value rather than the value that the land would assume once development permission had been granted. In Great Britain betterment levies have always been part of the legislative debate and have been applied.

In contrast, the United States has never had any serious pretensions to the idea of the fair city. Hopes were raised during the New Deal that public housing would play a much bigger role in the American future, but the lobbying of the real estate industry and the exploitation of Cold War panics about "socialist" programs put paid to it.[22] Inevitably this goes back in substantial part to the weakness of the federal government in city planning and reliance on local initiatives, and also to a weaker vision and public acceptance of the American state as a welfare state. Even then individual states have simply enabled rather than enforced. In this way impact fees, TIFs, and linkage fees have become incorporated into the market in locations. TIFs are used as a way of sweetening the pot, supposedly tipping the balance of developer calculations.[23] Impact fees and linkage fees come into play only when demand for housing, offices, retail space, or whatever is so intense that developers can push the costs onto someone else, including the home buyer or the office tenant—which undermines the idea that they have been more "popular" in areas like California or Massachusetts; rather they have been politically more feasible. As for compulsory purchase, aside from urban renewal, where it was conceived as a federal subsidy to developers, anxieties over the "takings clause" have long made this a rare and hazardous route, as the Kelo case discussed in chapter 1 underlines.

꜀꜀꜀꜀꜀

Development policy as it emerged in the Western European countries after the Second World War was clearly quite different from what took shape in the United States. It was more coordinated from the center, more planned and more inspired by the sorts of social purpose one thinks of

22. See Don Parson (2005) for the Los Angeles case.

23. "Supposedly" because the evidence that investment would *not* occur without the TIF is notoriously hard to establish.

in the context of the welfare state. The goal was the "good geography": employment redistributed to areas of relatively high unemployment, more compact cities, cities where housing costs were restrained by a significant public housing commitment. Extensive public ownership was used to the same purpose. Welfare states that operated at a national scale and more generously then worked to buffer the impact of localized unemployment. This is to emphasize the redistributional effects of development policy. Interventions also had in mind the national geography as a productive force. A good example is the role played by the French government in stimulating the national tourism industry as well as in the geographic reorganization of France's iron and steel industry. In Great Britain in the 1960s, regional policy was seen as a way of dampening down the inflationary pressures on labor and housing markets in major metropolitan areas so as to enhance the country's export competitiveness.

The contrast with development policy as it emerged in the United States, described in chapter 3, is therefore stark. Instead of the bottom-up, developer-led initiatives and the creation of a market in locations, with limited state oversight, the state has been much more proactive, and within the state central government particularly so. This compares with an American instance, in which the state is seen as more of a resource for property capitals, and the higher one goes in the state hierarchy, the more that seems to be the case. At least at the local government level there is the strong incentive of local tax revenue enhancement. Ideas of regional redistribution, of evening out geographically uneven development, which would logically be implemented from the center, have been barely visible. There is interest in compact city policies, but the centrifugal forces of development in American metropolitan areas remain a very serious challenge. The idea of creating a good geography is low on the policy agenda. The pursuit of rents, something that the state has supported in so many different ways, has been the primary motivation.

This is all the more interesting for the fact that during the 1930s these different outcomes in the form of development policy would have been hard to anticipate. The conditions for some sort of explicit urban and regional development policy were present on both sides of the Atlantic: the emergence of city and regional planning, new real estate products like the industrial estate, practices of both stimulating inward investment and central state intervention into areas of high unemployment—for North East England read the Tennessee Valley—as well as a new mobility of firms and of people that could be drawn on in formulating policy. It is certainly possible at this early stage in the argument to proffer some suggestions as to why the bifurcation in policy occurred. The more expansive welfare state pushed by strong labor movements in the Western European countries must have made a major difference: regional redistribution, the fair city, and other elements of the "good geography." But this raises questions about respective social formations. If the welfare state was important, why was it stronger in Western Europe? As we will see, the answer is more complex than simply referring to the strength of respective labor movements and the presence of social democratic parties.

Furthermore, by the late 1970s, welfare state thinking was clearly in question, and with it the future of the "good geography." Central planning of locations was to some degree in retreat, and greater responsibilities for development were being delegated to local governments. There was even talk and some instances of competing for inward investment. The deepening of geographically uneven development lent impetus to these changes. It seemed as though development policy in Western Europe was moving more in an American direction. But, as we will see in the next chapter, the changes were quite modest and hardly justified the hype that they generated.

Appendix A: Land Value Capture in Western Europe

In the Netherlands land for development was typically bought by municipal land companies at its value under agriculture. They installed the necessary physical infrastructure and then subdivided it and sold it to private developers and social housing associations, recovering the cost of the infrastructural provision in the process. Land for social housing was sold at a lower price, which was in turn subsidized by the higher prices at which it was made available to private developers. This is tending to break down to some degree as developers have purchased the agricultural land ahead of the municipal land companies.

In France there is a history of compulsory purchase of land for development and the taxation of developers to pay for the necessary infrastructure. There has been a sequence of various legislative tools, each trying to improve on its predecessors, going back to the ZUPs (Zones à Urbaniser en Priorité) introduced in 1958, which were used to construct what would be known as the "grands ensembles" of social housing; through to ZACs (Zones d'Aménagement Concerté) designed to shift infrastructural costs to developers; to the more recent EPFs (Établissements Publics Fonciers) and EPAs (Établissements Publics d'Aménagement). The goal of EPFs is to limit land banking and so mitigate the problem of speculation. EPAs have powers of compulsory purchase and preempting purchase by private developers.

Historically municipalities in Germany have been centrally involved in housing development, buying land ahead of development to create their own land banks (Schmidt and Buehler 2007) and through compulsory purchase of land at existing use value (Baing 2010). Once a developer purchases a site, it is the municipality's responsibility to provide the physical infrastructure, but this can then be charged to the developer to a maximum of 90 percent of the total cost. Municipal responsibility puts the city in a strong bargaining position, since without agreement on costs there can be no development.

A fourth and final example is Great Britain. As in the case of France, there is a long history of trying to appropriate development value so as to limit speculation and to fund the infrastructural investment that development necessitates. The legislation surrounding the new towns initiative was exemplary. At the center of their construction were development corporations, which had the right to purchase land compulsorily at current use values; the increase in value resulting from development was then captured for community purposes. The latter reflected a more general policy governing betterment, but this subsequently became something of a political football. The taxation of the increased land values was abolished by the Conservatives in 1954. The Labour Party then introduced a betterment levy which was subsequently abolished by the Conservatives. On their return to power, Labour then introduced a development land tax set at 80 percent of the increased land value. Although initially retained at a lower rate by the Thatcher government, it was, like the earlier betterment levy, dropped. What took its place in 1990 was something called Section 106[24] agreements, according to which local authorities could withhold planning permission until an agreement had been reached with a developer regarding not just for physical infrastructure but also for some "affordable" housing. In 2007 the subsequent Labour government then introduced something called the Community Infrastructure Levy. This is at the discretion of a local authority and imposes a set charge on developers.

24. Section 106 of the 1990 Town and Country Planning Act.

5

Moving in Tandem, but Still Far Apart

In identifying the specificities of the Western European approach to local and regional development, I have focused so far on what might be called the "classical period". This was marked by a general acceptance of central planning and redistribution from wealthier and more developed areas to poorer and less developed ones and lasted from just after the Second World War until sometime in the 1970s. From then on mutations set in. Even while there have been changes in the American instance also, most of the attention here has been directed at Western Europe and in a way that might seem to challenge American distinctiveness.[1] In some respects it might indeed be argued that there has been some convergence toward the American model: an increased decentralization of policy responsibilities and some displacement of the old administrative fiat by forms of local governance that include civil society participation. I think, though, that the changes have been exaggerated. There has been change in the United States, too, and this has been in the direction of a deepening of the tendencies that marked it out as distinctive from the start. So the convergence of the respective politics seems a long way off (Cox 2009).

There has also been some shift in policy goals, again in a direction that is more "American." As local governments have acquired more competencies and responsibilities, so the focus has been much more on encouraging

1. One such case for this has been set out by Brenner (2004).

specifically *local* economic growth;[2] and less on the achievement of national goals of spatial equity[3] or the national space as a force of production working to the advantage of the country as a whole: less emphasis, in other words, on the "good geography." The competition of one local government with another has become a way of understanding policy that would be more familiar to American local economic development professionals. Even so, the raison d'être remains quite different: emphatically it is much more a matter of jobs than rents and, accordingly, it is local government that has tended to take the initiative. As Preteceille put it, while pointing to some of the context within which these changes have occurred:

> The rapid growth of unemployment has introduced another factor, quite different politically but very pressing. No local politician or party can hope to maintain a position of power locally without stressing that preoccupation with economic growth, without promoting some spectacular action in the field, and eventually without getting some results that could be widely advertised. Whatever the political orientation, to do something for the economy, oriented towards the creation of jobs, has become a hegemonic obligation. It is pushed forward by a strong, explicit social demand, eventually by the pressure of social movements. (1990, 39–40)

This interpretation suggests a different balance between the demands of the property companies and the planners. But even then, national spatial

---

2. "[A] common fact should be acknowledged. Local governments have become openly preoccupied with economic development almost everywhere, and most will say it is their first priority. It is certainly the case in France . . . but also in Great Britain, Italy, Spain and the United States" (Preteceille 1990, 37).

3. Compare Harvey: "Since the mid-1980s, neoliberal urban policy (applied, for example, across the European Union) concluded that redistributing wealth to less advantaged neighborhoods, cities and regions was futile and that resources should instead be channeled to dynamic 'entrepreneurial' growth poles. A spatial version of 'trickle down' would then in the proverbial long run (which never comes) take care of all those pesky regional, spatial and urban inequalities. Turning the city over to the developers and speculative financiers redounds to the benefit of all!" (2012, 29).

strategies are still developed and referred to (Zepf and Andres 2011), and what is called "territorial solidarity" or "territorial cohesion" remains important, particularly in EU rhetoric.

There has also been some change in the focus of development policy. The old emphasis on inward investment and the different parts of the firm's technical division of labor—branch plants, headquarters, research and development—as targets of development policy on both sides of the Atlantic has undergone some eclipse. Stimulated by the loss of many assembly style industries to the Newly Industrializing Countries and the surge of interest in high tech during the 1980s, talk from the 1990s on was of the knowledge economy and how best to capture its advantages for purposes of local and regional development. Clusters became another buzzword among the local economic development professionals, and this was reflected in academic work as in Michael Porter's arguments about clusters, Philippe Aydalot's (1986) *milieux innovateurs*, and Allen Scott's (1988) "new industrial spaces." Once again, care needs to be exercised. The academic focus on new forms of development risks a hyping of what is actually happening on the ground.

In the first section of this chapter, I review the changes that have occurred before turning to examine how we might understand what has happened. The conclusion will be that, despite these changes, American institutions and practice remain as distinctive, if mutated in their details, as they ever were. So while there have indeed been some moves toward more decentralized forms in Western Europe, common claims of some trans-Atlantic convergence—and they are very common (Cox 2009)—are thoroughly exaggerated. The decentralizing tendencies in the American case are of an intensity that cannot be matched and for very good reasons that we will explore in the rest of the book. In Western Europe, more central branches of the state still remain an important presence in local and regional development policy as a result, in large part, of a state structure that resists radical change. Logically, what is being claimed by some observers in terms of a dramatic change in the Western European politics simply cannot be sustained, since the conditions that would allow it are just not present and to implement them would be politically a highly fraught process.

Mutations

> The reply (to the question of knowing if the metropolitan area must continue to develop or if it is necessary to allow a pause) appears to me simple. The reply is that a pause cannot be. There are only two possibilities: development or decline. There is no third. Competition between metropolitan areas is European and global. Pause, and that allows other metropolitan areas of comparable size to take over from you and with respect to production and investment and therefore to increase their employment and revenues. To pause is to be less attractive with respect to people and capital and therefore to reduce our means of responding to new needs. (Prefect for the département of Loire-Atlantique, June 10, 2005, quoted in Pinson 2009, 319; author's translation)[4]

> Even if the competition between cities and, as an oblique result of this, the entrepreneurial strategies of cities are greater than before, European cities are not American cities. (Le Galès and Harding 1998)

Nine years separate these two quotations but I believe that the second and earlier one is closer to the truth. It remains the case that in Western Europe, there have indeed been changes in the institutional forms and practices assumed by the state in local and regional development. Among other things, there are local initiatives designed to enhance the flow of value through a particular locality or region. These can range from the subsidies offered by smaller cities in Belgium, France, Germany, Italy, and Spain, among others, to secure low-fare airline services, all the way to the provision of cut-rate sites to firms by French and German cities.

4. "La réponse [à la question de savoir si la métropole doit continuer à se développer ou il faut se décréter une pause] me paraît simple. La réponse est que la pause n'existe pas. Il n'y en a que deux hypothèses: le développement ou le déclin. Il n'y en a pas de troisième. La concurrence entre les métropoles est européenne et mondiale. Faire la pause, c'est laisser d'autres métropoles de taille comparable occuper l'espace de la production et de l'investissement et donc accroître leurs emplois et leurs revenus. Faire la pause, c'est être moins attractif à l'égard des hommes et des capitaux donc réduire nos moyens pour répondre à de nouveaux besoins."

Philippe Subra (2007, chapter 3) has described other forms of competition between French cities, including mobilizing the joint political office holding referred to as *cumul des mandats* in order to attract a station on the TGV network. From the 1970s on in Great Britain, there was an upsurge of interest on the part of local governments in developing their land holdings so as to attract in new investment. From a figure of 5 percent in 1972, by 1978 well over half of all local governments were operating new factory schemes (Baker 1995, 360).[5] In short, cities of diverse size are competing with one another today in ways that would have been very unusual during the classical period of development policy, and there have been some notable struggles to land employment.[6] But there are still important differences.

First, it is local government rather than any local business interest that tends to take the lead.[7] There is evidence that this was already happening before any decentralization of state competences got underway. The

5. See also Tickell and Dicken (1993) on the growth of local government interest in development.

6. A well-publicized case, at least in Germany, was the struggle between Hamburg and Rostock to land the Airbus contract to construct the Superbus A-380. The assembly plant at Hamburg had been the obvious choice but the site would have to be expanded, and that raised serious environmental issues; notably the partial filling of a wetland known as the Mühlenberg Loch. There was also some pressure from the German government in favor of the Rostock site since it would bring employment to part of the still-depressed former East Germany. Meanwhile the *land* government of Hamburg had made a quite massive loan of 1.3 billion marks (over 600 million euros) to persuade Airbus of its serious intentions: part of the effort to reconstruct Hamburg as a center of technology-intensive industry as well as to bring two thousand new jobs and perhaps the same number in local supply industries. This effort received the support of both local industry and labor unions redolent of the sort of cross-class coalitions typical of the American case. Eventually the decision was made in favor of Hamburg but only after a judgment in a *land* court reversing an earlier one that would have made expansion of the site difficult.

7. Italy seems to have been an important exception. As Galimberti (2015) shows in her study of Milan, business organizations were dominant, though without constituting a growth coalition of the American sort (Vicari and Molotch 1990).

British case referred to above is an example.[8] In a discussion of the emergence of an interest in local economic development in Lyon, Galimberti (2015) makes a similar point even while the early running there had been made by a grouping of larger firms with a strong presence in the city.[9] The situation is quite other than in the United States where it is typically property companies and growth coalitions that have mobilized local government to their purposes around what has come to be called "local development policy."

Second, they have been more circumscribed in what they can do: they lack the sort of unilateral land use discretion of local governments in the United States; the ability to grant tax abatements is typically very limited; municipal expansion through annexation so as to incorporate new, greenfield sites is difficult; they do not have the same capacity as American local governments to raise money for infrastructure through the sale of bonds; and they lack the sort of privileged access to more central branches of the state that has been a hallmark of the American case. On the other hand, they *are* the ones with the information on industrial and commercial sites. This is in contrast to the American case, where it has always been the utilities for the former and the chambers of commerce for the latter (Cox

8. There were variations though. In a fascinating study, Le Galès (1991) shows how the British city of Coventry lagged in institutionalizing some local development capacity. A city council dominated by Labour Party councilors with strong roots in a highly unionized milieu refused to believe that the problems affecting the locally dominant auto industry would be enduring. Rather they saw them as a result of the business cycle and of Thatcherite economic policies that would be quickly reversed once the Labour Party was returned to power, which they expected to be soon. Quite how general responses of this sort were in other cities with strong union presences, like Luton or Nottingham, would be worth examining.

9. This was Aderly (Association pour le développement économique de l'agglomération lyonnaise), which originally emerged in the early 1970s in resistance to central state initiatives aimed at relocating the polluting metallurgical and chemical industries out of the city to the periphery; though it would also soon embrace policies aimed at attracting new investment from outside.

and Townsend 2005).[10] Municipal land ownership has tended to be more extensive across Western Europe (Eskilsson 1997) and this has facilitated development initiatives, including science and technology parks (Clark, Notay, and Evans 2010). It has also made it possible to offer subsidies to firms considering investments by offering land at below market rates: a different form of financial incentive, therefore. In addition, and a major function of the Development Departments which sprang up in Western European cities in the last three or so decades, marketing has assumed a much greater prominence; something attested to by the attention given to it in the academic literature under the heading "place marketing."

Third, and perhaps reflecting these limits on the powers of local or regional governments and agencies, the balance between strategies emphasizing the attraction of inward investment and stimulating the development of a locality's existing firms has been different: one reason why property firms have tended to be less prominent in local development. In Germany this was always so; *land* governments were always active in the training of workers and, through the *land* banks, lending to small firms. As a local government capacity, increased attention to labor upgrading and to the support of smaller businesses has now become generalized in Western Europe. Local governments have also been active in the establishment of science and technology parks, often in collaboration with local universities, though the uptake has sometimes been disappointing.[11] But the point is, local development policy has tended to have a different focus with less emphasis on inward investment.

Yet in the case of major investments it has sometimes been different, as national governments have also entered the fray to attract investment onto

10. There has, however, been the occasional sighting of classic, Molotch-type growth coalitions: property-led in the case of Roubaix (Rousseau 2010) and to a lesser degree in Lyon (Galimberti 2013), and bringing pressure to bear on local government to pursue policies enhancing to their interests: attracting in gentrifiers in the first case and corporate investment in the second.

11. Galimberti (2015) provides a useful case study in Lyon. On science parks in England, see Massey and Wield (1991).

the national territory or in support of some particular locality. The competition for Euro Disney and the massive subsidies given by the French government to attract it to the Paris region come to mind.[12] The promise of a Toyota plant at locations in France and Great Britain led to a bidding war reminiscent of those between American states for similar transplants. When General Motors was considering selling their European factories to a Canadian consortium, the German government offered it a large sum of money in an attempt to ensure that any plant closures should occur elsewhere in Europe and not in Germany. Foreign takeovers that might result in plant closures and unemployment can become national issues.[13]

In the literature, much has also been made of a decentralization of regulatory functions to more local levels; a decentralization that has been heralded as inducing a more territorialized form of development politics as local and regional governments obtain powers that can facilitate, and that may even enjoin, competition for new investment. Reference is often made to the devolutionary reforms in France and to those in Great Britain, for example. Even so, I think that there is a real danger of exaggerating the significance of these changes.

In the first place, old forms of regional policy persist, if in a scaled down form. Second, and most significant of all, the central state remains crucial to what happens in the localities. There has certainly been a change in the division of labor between central state agencies and the localities and regions but in no way approaching that in the United States, where the localities clearly have the advantage. Rather, in Western Europe the idea of a national interest, of contributing to creating a good geography when

12. These included tax advantages to write off construction costs; the large area of land required sold (in 1987) at 1971 agricultural prices; and perhaps most significant of all, a station on the TGV high-speed rail network linking it to major markets in England, Germany, and the Low Countries, as well as to elsewhere in France. The major competitor had been Barcelona.

13. A recent instance was the takeover of a famous British brand, Cadbury by Kraft Foods, in 2010. This was hugely controversial generating not just questions in the House of Commons but investigations by a joint-party select committee. Kraft might have got away with it, but the subsequent closure of a plant that had employed four hundred after commitments that no plants would be closed simply fanned the flames further.

it comes to decisions about allowing particular developments, still counts for something.

The way in which the land use planning function works is absolutely crucial. Local discretion has always been circumscribed by more central branches of the state, and this continues. In Germany, municipalities plan within regional plans and regions within *länder* plans, with greater detail allowed as one descends the territorial hierarchy, and this within a general set of spatial planning guidelines set out by the federal government (Schmidt and Buehler 2007). *Länder* can and do override regional plans and regional plans can override municipal ones. How they plan is also important owing to criteria of spatial equity defined by the federal government and accepted by the *länder*, which form the crucial nexus of land use planning. As of 1994 there has been some weakening of the constitutional guarantee of "equal living conditions": now it is a matter of "similar living conditions." Likewise *länder* policies have tended to increase the powers of regional governments so as to facilitate international competition:[14] in other words, a more general devolution of responsibilities and a weakening of central oversight. Emphatically, though, this does not amount to the elimination of the latter.

For many years, France was the prototype of centrally orchestrated local and regional development policy. Starting in the 1980s, this has changed, but again the effects should not be exaggerated. The threads of the Napoleonic state may have become a little longer but they are far from frayed. The aim of the reforms after 1982 was supposed to be a compromise between the centralizing and the decentralizing. Regional governments[15] would have the prime role in economic development and would in turn negotiate with central government via a revived plan that would serve as a vehicle for intergovernment negotiation. Regional plans, subsequent to

14. "It can be said, with some exaggeration, that all *Land* governments now behave like the management of a business, attempting to direct their entire policy at the needs and requirements of the *Land* as an industrial location in postfordist world capitalism" (Esser and Hirsch 1989, 430).

15. The regional councils have been directly elected since 1986 and now have their own executives.

inputs from departments and communes, were to be produced alongside a national plan and views on priorities then exchanged. Planning contracts would then be signed. Since most state aid is tied to national priorities, regions tend to emphasize these (e.g., sectoral emphases) in their plans.

The twenty-two regions have responsibilities with respect to education and vocational training, economic development, and land use planning, which sounds promising but is actually much less than it might seem. This is because of continuing and strong central government control. For each four-year period each regional council has to complete a contract with the central government regarding a broad land use plan for the region and for major infrastructural projects. As Subra (2007) has pointed out, the state tries to impose its wishes on the regions and has the power to do so.[16] And

16. Galimberti's 2015 study of the emergence of an interest in local economic development in Lyon reinforces this conclusion: "Cela dit, dans ce chapitre, nous montrerons que les réseaux d'acteurs patronaux qui se structurent à l'échelle locale sont largement conditionnés par le contexte institutionnel et plus particulièrement par la présence d'un État fort en France. Malgré la crise du projet hégémonique de planification nationale, l'État continue à exercer une influence structurante sur les projets locaux de développement" (27). [That said, in this chapter we will show that the business networks that emerge at the local level are largely conditioned by the institutional context and more particularly by the fact of a strong French state] (author's translation). And later she adds, "Nous verrons que les compétences dévolués aux gouvernements locaux—communes et régions—sont toutefois assez limitées. Les conseils régionaux agissent en stricte collaboration avec les services étatiques, qui continuent à exercer un rôle majeur d'orientation. De surcroît, les communautés urbaines ne sont que marginalement touchées par les lois de décentralisation" (172). [We will see that the capacities devolved to local governments—to the communes and the regions—are indeed quite limited. The regional councils act in strict collaboration with the central state which continues to exercise a major orienting role. In addition, the urban communities (which are for the most part the major cities—KRC) are only affected marginally by the decentralization laws] (author's translation).

On the other hand, in a personal communication (Oct. 27, 2015), she has also emphasized that the larger agglomerations have developed a technical capacity in local development that has allowed them to bargain with the regions and the central state for conditions under their patronage that would further local development; something that has been more difficult for smaller French cities. See also Schmidt (1988, 1990).

as Schmidt concludes, "national level *dirigisme* has not disappeared with official decentralization" (1990, 290).[17]

Schmidt was writing in 1990, but it is corroborated in a more recent assessment by Baudelle (2008). Decentralization *is* a reality, but the central government still plays a very important role. Local and regional development have become "co-constructions" and this has introduced new elements of complexity into the process. Now the central state has to collaborate on local and regional development with the regions, the departments, and the agglomerations.[18] Competition is the new watchword—the central development agency has changed its name and this has involved a shift from an emphasis on territorial development to one shared with territorial competitivity[19]—but competition is still orchestrated in a top-down manner and, one might add, according to old criteria of regional fairness. So while territorial policy now targets the reinforcement of clusters through the identification and support of what have been called poles of competitivity, Figure 6 shows their distribution by the year 2007 and suggests some attempt at targeting places across the entirety of the country.

17. Likewise Keating: "A powerful and cohesive state continues to exert a major influence on the pattern of urban development. It restricts, with varying degrees of success, the concessions which local governments can make to investors. It protects local finances and the ability of local governments to incur debt. Local governments in France rarely have to worry about their rating in the bond markets as do their American counterparts. Fiscal equalization also reduces but does not eliminate local government dependence on business taxes" 1991, 457).

18. "Plus que jamais, l'aménagement, aujourd'hui compétence partagée par l'Etat avec les Régions, les Départements et même les agglomérations, est donc un processus inévitablement conduit à plusieurs qui fait des réalisations élaborées et mises en œuvre en commun des coproductions dans le cadre d'une *"politique cogérée et contractualisée""* (Baudelle 2008). [More than ever, development today is a competence shared by the state with the regions, the departments and even the agglomerations, and is therefore a process inevitably carried out by several which makes outcomes developed and put to work together, co-productions within the framework of a "policy that is co-managed and contractualized"] (author's translation).

19. From DATAR, or Delegation for Territorial Development and Regional Action, to DIACT, or Interministerial Delegation for Territorial Development and Competitivity.

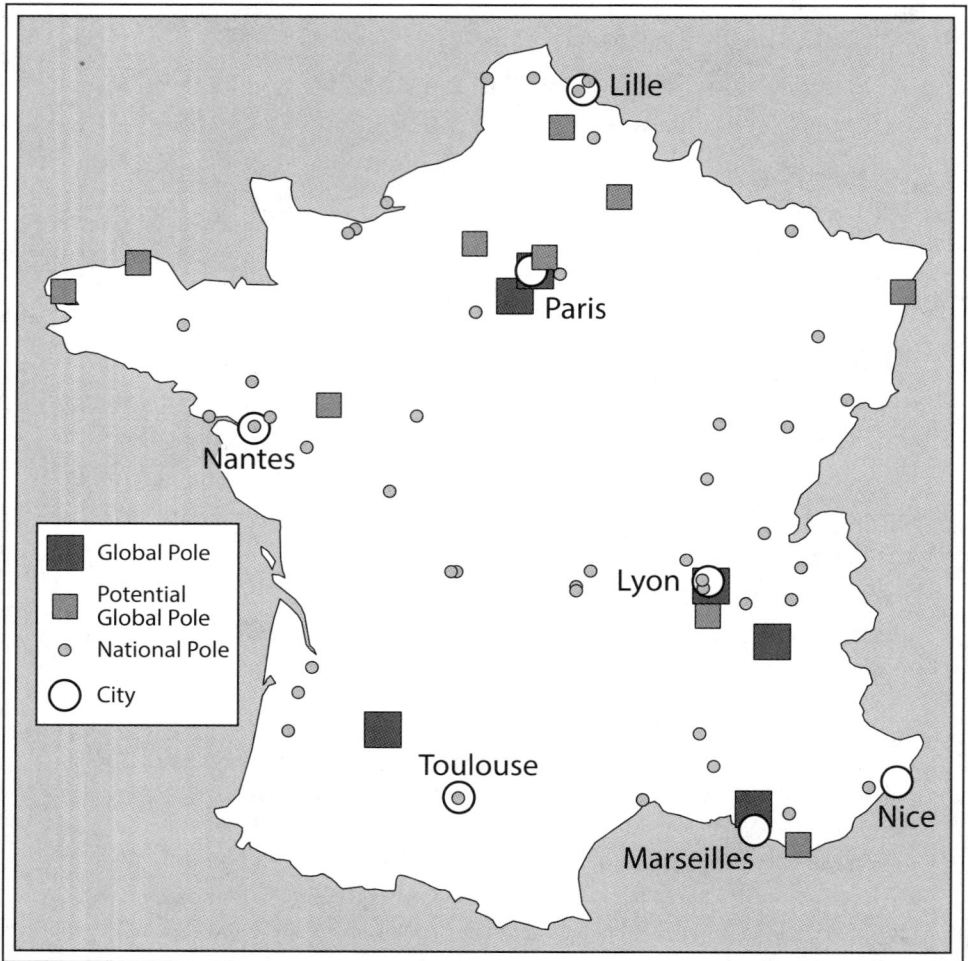

Fig. 6. The French poles of competitivity. Map by Jim DeGrand.

A third and final case of changing institutional frameworks is the British one. This is probably the weakest case to choose in demonstrating the reality of a decentralization of responsibilities. Devolution got off to a late start. During the period in which France was beginning to engage with devolution, Great Britain was seemingly moving in the opposite direction. During the Thatcherite period local government was, for the most part, a problem rather than an opportunity. If local economic development was to be achieved, then it had to be through the initiatives of the central government: primarily through the creation of enterprise zones and through what were called urban development corporations (Anderson 1990).

Only from the late 1990s on is there serious reversal of this. Since then there have been two attempts at devolving responsibility for local and regional economic development. The first was that of the regional development agencies, of which there were eight. Their powers, however, were severely circumscribed (Dees and Ward 2000); personnel and policies were subject to close central government scrutiny, and their funding was risible (Morgan 2001). Since 2010 these have been abandoned in favor of local enterprise partnerships, each one supposedly formed with some rationale in terms of journey-to-work areas (and so more numerous than the regional development agencies that they have replaced). The "partnership" envisaged in each case is between local governments within a particular area and business representatives. The evidence so far is that the government is still not committed to granting them the resources and powers necessary to make a difference: "The removal of the regional tier of economic development policy means that many economic development functions, such as inward investment, SME development, sectors and cluster policy, tourism, and European policy, will be passed back up to the national level and will leave a capacity gap. The new localism is not localism at all but recentralization in disguise" (Bentley, Bailey, and Shutt 2010, 537).

This "new localism" also includes measures for a greater devolution of local planning, but it is not a devolution aimed at facilitating or providing incentives for local development initiatives. Historically, local land use plans had to be consistent with regional strategic plans; the latter were subject to central government approval. One of the goals of the government was to assure that sufficient land would be made available for new housing.

As mentioned, targets were assigned to different regions based on projections and regions then had to divvy them up among constituent local governments. These targets have been a continual aggravation for many local governments, or more accurately their residents, anxious to exclude rather than make way for new housing. Accordingly, the regional level has been abolished along with the housing targets. This, however, is quite dangerous from a national standpoint, something that the government recognizes. As a result, centralization has assumed new forms. On the one hand, local governments are to be offered financial incentives for granting permission for every new home constructed; on the other, each local government has to—repeat *has to*—make provision in its plans for sites for new construction in accord with central government–approved forecasts of how much housing will be required there. Again, it does not sound much like the United States.

Moreover, alongside the hosannas of those who look forward to a new age of decentralized government in Western Europe has been an enthusiastic embrace of what they see as a new age of governance. In the discourse of development policy governance is indeed a new watchword in at least some of the Western European countries.[20] The English local enterprise partnerships, embracing local government and business, are an example. Pinson's 2009 book on major urban projects in five cities— two in France, two in Italy, and one in England—also underlines this change, drawing attention to the displacement of state hierarchy by local networks that bring together state agents and private interests. These include not just businesses but universities, hospitals, labor unions, public and semi-public enterprises, and civic organizations. What is interesting in Pinson's treatment, though, is the emphasis he gives to how the central government has engineered the shift from government to governance: by offering state aid as an incentive for the creation of some local public-private organization around a major urban project. This recalls Peck's work (1995) on the emergence of "movers and shakers" in Manchester: something orchestrated from the top rather than testimony to any strong, local, grassroots

---

20. Note, though, the qualification of Le Galès and Harding: "As far as urban governance is concerned . . . this evolution in urban government toward urban governance may have some relevance for France and for Great Britain. The argument seems equally valid for some large German and Dutch cities. However, the stability of the traditional forms of bureaucratic, hierarchical local authorities still seems to be dominant in Portugal, Ireland, Sweden, Norway and Belgium" (1998, 133).

impulse.[21] And this suggests, of course, the continuing significance of the central state in whatever is "new" in the institutions through which local economic development gets delivered in Western Europe.

There has undoubtedly been change, therefore, but it is more a new balance between centralizing and decentralizing forces than the sort of radical decentralization that one associates with the United States both past and present: central government remains in control and both a crucial source of local funding and a proc for new local development initiatives.[22] The old institutional framework of planned locations, while diminished, is by no means eliminated. There are still areas of persistent unemployment that qualify for government aid, even as EU rules drastically curtail the areas so qualifying. Central governments are still relocating government employees from capital cities to provincial cities (J. Marshall 2007). New towns are out, but the British government has embarked on a new policy of establishing so-called eco-towns, even while the program has been drastically downscaled in the wake of rural resistance. The French government has a similar program of what it calls "villes durables" but as yet with less to show for it.[23] It also tries to orchestrate its high-tech geography through poles of competitivity, something that would be totally alien

21. Compare Cochrane: "In the case of the U.K. it has been necessary to construct business involvement from above. It has not simply been generated as a result of local pressure from existing business groups. Instead, national and local states have taken the lead in creating the institutional space for a local politics of business. In some cases national government has gone so far as to set up agencies (such as Training and Enterprise Councils in England) whose boards are explicitly required to have representatives of local business as members" (1999, 115). This is a conclusion echoed by Harding (1991).

22. In some of the Western European countries, attempts to decentralize functions to local government ran aground on the resistance of either provincial-level politicians who feared the creation of stronger local governments (Italy), or the opposition of civil society groups to the entrepreneurial turn that the reforms might imply (the Netherlands) (Jouve 2005, 182–83).

23. Both of these programs incorporate ideas central to the new urbanism, something that is likewise gaining in favor, though encountering similar headwinds as the British eco-towns. See MacLeod (2013) for an example.

to the way things are done in the United States and which would certainly elicit cries of outrage at the state "picking winners." And in contrast to the American case, where local governments have essentially carte blanche in land use planning, in Western Europe the central state (or in the federal state of Germany, the *länder*) retains a very significant structuring and regulatory presence. The central branches of the state also retain important discretionary funding power that can be and is used to advance their own priorities. So while the leash has been made a little longer, it has not been withdrawn, and local governments get reined in.

There are two other differentiating features. The first is that local economic development in Western Europe is still far from being the preoccupation that it is in the United States; something in accord with the more general idea of the "good geography." There is, rather, a different balance regarding questions of residential amenity, preventing encroachment by industrial uses, preserving open space, and the provision of social housing. And second, there are reservations about territorial competition. Its virtues are more likely to be counterposed to those of maintaining some degree of national solidarity and of regulation for a greater good.[24] This sounds rather pious but it has an explanation that underlines something quite fundamental when comparing policy and politics in the United States and in Western Europe: in most of the countries of the latter, and certainly the larger ones, there is a strong left-radical tradition. Quite aside from the difference this makes to national discourse about development issues, Labor parties, and Social Democratic parties—and sometimes Communist parties—are represented in local government. Their priorities regarding local policy are different from anything imaginable in the more monochrome picture of representation in American local government and in state government for that matter, too. It should not be surprising, therefore, if the

24. Significantly, and according to Deas and Ward (2000), the powers of England's regional development agencies did not extend to control over Regional Selective Assistance through which subsidies were given to firms opting to locate in the so-called Assisted Areas. This power was retained by the Department of Technology and Industry in London in order to put a limit on competition between those regional development agencies that included Assisted Areas.

policy framework for local economic development in Western Europe is still quite different from that in the United States. The United States remains very particular, and in light of the exaggerated claims made about change in Western Europe, that needs to be underscored.

Local Development in a Changing World

In trying to understand the changes that *have* taken place, we should recall at the outset how the classical politics of urban and regional development unfolded with respect to a very specific set of conditions. In both the American and Western European instances, the point of departure for policy was the mobility of the different and separable parts of the spatial divisions of labor of firms and of state agencies: branch plants, research and development facilities, corporate headquarters, back offices, branches of state universities, federal offices, perhaps even whole ministries. In the United States local governments were preoccupied with attracting these in so as to boost local economic growth. In Western Europe it was more a matter of moving employment around in accordance with a plan designed either to enhance national economic growth or to mitigate localized unemployment, or both. The important facilitating condition, though, was that there were things to attract in or move around. During this classical period firms were eager to spin off the less skilled aspects of production in the form of branch plants to smaller towns, often into regions with some sort of labor cost advantage. Yet the buoyancy of the overall global economy was such as to raise all boats. Local economic development had yet to become the zero-sum game that it has often appeared in more recent years.

The changes started to set in from the early 1970s on. There was talk of rust belts on both sides of the Atlantic as areas of heavy industry and mining experienced an attrition of employment. Later still, the branch plants established in small towns started to experience the pressure and to close down. What Robert Brenner (1998) has called the long downturn reduced demand but also resulted in a search for new bases of profitability that would alter the map of geographically uneven development and change the spacing of its contours. There are at least five, albeit related, transformations that need to be signaled.

1. The first transformation was the emergence of what has been called the *New International Division of Labor*. This was particularly associated with the rise of the Newly Industrializing Countries as producers of labor intensive, less skills-intensive products. In part this was a matter of insertion into the geographic divisions of labor of multinational corporations, decanting some component production to sites in developing countries and then reimporting the parts for final assembly in the United States and Western Europe. The division is not clear-cut though since the NICs also included countries, notably South Korea and Taiwan, that managed to ascend the skills hierarchy and make entries into sectors which firms in the developed world had once thought safe: products like consumer electronics and ships. This obviously involved changes in the geography of development in North America and Western Europe, but aside from plant closures, firm bankruptcies, or takeovers by other firms, there have also been expansions in the more skills-intensive sectors. As the economies of developing countries expand, not to mention those of the developed ones, so too does the demand for things like airplanes, computers, water purification plants, heavy construction services, pharmaceuticals, financial services, automobiles, medical equipment, earth moving machinery, and the like. Even when local industries collapse there is often a residue of skills of considerable sophistication that can form the basis for a new tissue of smaller firms collaborating in engineering and design services for branches of the economy whose center of gravity has shifted elsewhere—the "phoenix industries" (Christopherson 2009). As a wealthy stratum has started to emerge in the NICs, so this has created demand for the sorts of branded luxury goods whose production remains in the more developed countries, from Jaguar cars to Scotch whiskey, Italian clothing, French wine and cheese, Waterford crystal, and Swiss watches.[25] This means that certain localities and regions have actually experienced growth during this period.

25. Growing inequality in the United States and many of the countries of Western Europe has been accompanied by notable increases in purchasing power at the upper end of the stratification system with similar implications for the expansion in production of these luxury goods: what Mike Davis (1984) referred to quite early on as "overconsumptionism."

2. The second transformation has been a shift in economic policy known as the *neoliberal turn*: the pullback of state intervention and involvement in national economies entailing privatization, deregulation and a macroeconomic austerity designed to purge national economies of the inflation that had replaced unemployment as the big bugaboo.[26] This shift has been ongoing since the age of Thatcher and Reagan and has been hugely implicated in intensifying uneven development. Not least, macroeconomic austerity, lasting at least until the mid-1990s, meant an increase in business closures and unemployment in those regions that would inevitably be more vulnerable to downturns in the business climate by virtue of location, skills-mix, product composition, and so on.

The neoliberal turn also meant deregulation and privatization, and these had their own implications for uneven development. The loss of rail-line connections and of air services among small towns in the rural areas of the United States made no sense outside of the deregulation of the railroad and aviation industries. This unleashed price competition among providers in exchange for dropping services to less viable destinations. The other side of that coin was the emergence of airports as hubs concentrating civil aviation employment in a few places as well as giving the hub cities major advantages in the ability to attract new employment: another component of the quite rapidly changing geography of uneven development, therefore.

In Western Europe deregulation had an additional face. This was the dismantling of significant portions of the regional planning legislation. Limits on development in certain areas facing congestion and pressure on labor and housing markets and aimed at diverting employment into areas of severe need were eliminated. Henceforth there would be no restrictions on office expansion in the London and Paris areas. The areas eligible for assistance in attracting new investment underwent a dramatic diminution. Regional policy in Western Europe had also worked through the public ownership of industry; iron and steel, shipbuilding, and coal mining

---

26. Though in retrospect this pullback is something that has contributed to the quite massive reassertion of income inequality and the corralling of ever-growing proportions of national wealth by the so-called one percent. See Harvey (2005).

were typically concentrated in areas more susceptible to unemployment and certainly lagging in terms of incomes, so the subsidies that had been accorded them were of very, very considerable importance in mitigating uneven development. All that changed with the neoliberal turn. The goal of governments across Western Europe has been to divest themselves of this responsibility by selling to private business. But in order to make them marketable the scale of production had to be dramatically reduced, pruning out uneconomical mines, the less profitable iron and steel plants and the like. This had a striking effect on the map of unemployment, as Ray Hudson (1986; 1989) has pointed out for the British case.[27]

Closely associated with neoliberalism, and certainly facilitated by it, has been the tendency to financialization of the economy and the growth in power of finance relative to industrial capital. The increasing power of shareholders relative to management, and the emphasis on short-term profitability and equity value under the threat of hostile merger and leveraged buyout, has had important implications for the role of property firms, as Halbert (2013b) has described. Not least it has put further pressure on other firms to externalize their real estate needs; as the clamor for favorable stock market figures has intensified, so firms have been persuaded that they should be concentrating on their "core activities" rather than managing real estate and on increasing the speed at which they are able to rotate capital by renting rather than owning. But as property capitals look to make hay out of this, they are constrained by the preferences of those, like the insurance companies and pension funds, who are the immediate market for their office developments, distribution centers, and industrial parks. Portfolio managers like bigger projects because that reduces the costs of management. They also prefer developments in deeper, more liquid markets where property can be sold more easily if the occasion arises. Frankfurt, London, and Paris get the nod, therefore, where Aachen, St. Etienne, and Hull are a harder sell.

27. We should also note the way in which the denationalization of industry affected strategic planning. This was of particular importance in France (T. Marshall 2011). The prospects of those areas once dominated by coal mining and heavy industry are especially dismal. The analysis of a particular case by Dawley et al. (2014) is particularly instructive.

3. Accordingly, and for reasons that go beyond the investment preferences of the pension funds and insurance companies, another element in the new map of geographically uneven development has been the *increasing significance of the major urban centers*. John Mollenkopf was one of the first to notice the importance of this in his discussion of what he called postindustrial cities (1983, chapter 1). The growth of larger cities is indeed closely related to the expansion of service industries, particularly finance, insurance, and real estate (collectively defined by the acronym FIRE), but also the health industries, higher education, and distribution. Distribution centers have accompanied the rise of the retail chains and tend to be located in, or in close proximity to, larger cities and in virtue of their accessibility advantages. In the case of health care, there has been a similar concentration. The expansion of service industries has been a crucial condition for the restructuring of the central city and has provided a new focus for the development activities of property capitals. This has included the expansion of office space, of hospitals and universities, but also of leisure complexes centered around sports stadia: a spinoff of the attempts of growth coalitions to attract new corporate headquarters and retain those they already have. There are also the so-called "mega projects" like Canary Wharf in London, Plaine St. Denis in Paris, Santa Giulia planned for Milan, and the huge Copley Place hotel-retail-office complex in Boston. These changes have been a crucial precondition for the emergence of gentrification: quite unknown before the early 1960s, and something that gave a further boost to downtown redevelopment.

In addition, the larger cities have become major centers of employment for export beyond the metropolitan area or even the country itself. This is in part to do with the fact of the New International Division of Labor and the loss of price advantage in developing countries that many products enjoyed. But in developing new products, Veltz (1996) has argued, larger cities have major advantages. They often have a more differentiated division of labor facilitating combinations and hybridizations that can form the basis for new products. In larger cities, uncertainty is reduced since there is likely to be more than one producer firm to choose from as a collaborator or source of inputs. At the same time, the resultant growth of firms facilitates the vertical disintegration of labor processes and the advantages of deepening specialization, as Allen Scott has emphasized.[28]

The expansion of larger cities and their morphing into polynuclear forms with employment concentrations on the periphery has encouraged expanded commuter fields and given new life to small towns there as dormitory suburbs. These are also the places likely to hang onto an industrial role: far enough from the city to take advantage of lower labor costs but close enough to enjoy its accessibility advantages and, from the standpoint of the managerial strata, its residential advantages as well. Accordingly, the larger cities have been the major beneficiaries of development, both in the United States and in Western Europe, and this has been accompanied by new foci for growth coalitions, as well as increasing frustrations—even desperation—for those in the less advantaged smaller towns.

Major agglomerations are now seen as drivers of national economies, though interestingly more so in Western Europe than in the United States, even while their significance has been enhanced in both. This has had implications for economic development policy and further underlines the continuing role of the central state in the latter. As Le Galès and

28. Regarding the increased significance of major metropolitan areas in national economies and their distinctive economic bases, see Krätke (2007) on the Western European case, and Markusen and Schrock (2003) on the American one. Allen Scott has also written at length and illuminatingly on the topic (Scott 2008a; 2008b). Halbert (2010) has added some important wrinkles to the argument, emphasizing the way in which the multiscalar connections of the major metropolitan centers and their enhanced cosmopolitanism lay the foundations for a market in ideas, contributing to the sorts of random juxtapositions that Massey (2005) has emphasized, and so the likelihood of innovation. Gough (1996) has pointed out the ironies of a neoliberal policy emphasizing competition, which has tended to encourage, nevertheless, an enhanced interest in the socialization of the productive forces at the local level: this so as to compete more effectively at wider geographic scales. It is in this way that one can make additional sense of the emphasis on clusters as well as the enhanced significance of the major metropolitan areas. On the other hand, as Gough also argues, this socialization has added to the tendencies toward increased geographically uneven development under the neoliberal dispensation since they tend to privilege certain sorts of places—like the major metropolitan areas—over others.

Harding (1998) have argued, capital cities in Western Europe have always been treated as *sui generis* from a national planning standpoint, calling for central government interventions that would be unusual elsewhere. In the past this might have been a result of their symbolic significance, but now their importance for national economic growth provides additional impetus, as Crouch and Le Galès (2012) have pointed out.[29] This is especially clear in Great Britain, where London and its surrounding area have been showered with major infrastructural investments, mainly to facilitate transportation. There has also been national legislation aimed at providing the Greater London Authority with planning powers that would allow it to work toward mitigating the area's chronic housing shortage and therefore something that impedes its ability to continue to attract the necessary skilled workers, including those in the public service (Ancien 2012). In France likewise there has been an ongoing debate about the future expansion of Paris—the creation of a so-called Grand Paris explicitly targeted at reinforcing the city's competitive position on a global stage—which is now giving birth to a number of nationally funded and highly expensive infrastructural initiatives, particularly an expansion of rail transport in the wider metropolitan area designed to counter the current Paris-centric nature of the network.[30]

4. Lending further impetus to the growth of the major metropolitan areas has been a *shift in the substantive focus of local economic development policy*. There has clearly been some move away from attracting

---

29. But not necessarily just capital cities. For German policy interest in the larger urban agglomerations of the country, see Hoyler, Freytag, and Mager (2006).

30. This project is by no means funded entirely by the national government, though. Of the 19 billion euros anticipated, the central government will contribute 4 billion as an outright grant and 7 billion euros in loans. There will be new taxes on retail and real estate in the greater Paris region (Ile-de-France). Intriguingly, though, the central government will use its right of eminent domain to redevelop land around the new stations and use rents to help pay off the debt. Again the possibility of this happening in the United States just boggles the mind. Crouch and Le Galès (2012) also refer to the government-sponsored Paris-Saclay research and higher education complex to the southeast of Paris, designed to provide French firms with an additional pipeline of ideas and technologies for their own research and development activities.

inward investment in favor of encouraging the growth of clusters of activity. This reflects changes in the international division of labor and the loss of advantage of the more developed economies in the production of relatively low-skill, labor-intensive products. There are simply fewer branch plants to attract in. Attention has tended to shift to the development of new products and to improving process-technologies, though I would argue more in the Western European than in the American case, at least as far as local policy is concerned. This should not be exaggerated. There are still many labor processes which have resisted de-skilling and which can be off-shored to developing countries only with difficulty. In some cases where labor is in fact de-skilled, there are important reasons for keeping these activities in North America and Western Europe. The tendency in development policy focus is observable, however, as anybody who checks out *European Planning Studies* can readily affirm.[31] The success of Silicon Valley made a huge impression and sparked a much wider interest in high tech and how to go about creating the conditions for it (Saxenian 1985). This then received a more theoretical, academic elaboration through the work of people like Michael Porter.

For the sort of technical development and upgrading envisaged, clusters offer important advantages. Partly it is a question of firm size. Smaller, more entrepreneurial, less bureaucratic firms are seen as having advantages in the development of new products and technical breakthroughs. In so doing, though, they need the external support of other firms that can collaborate in, for example, developing a custom-made part, solving particular technical problems, or providing finance and marketing advice. Likewise, in developing new technologies, firms, regardless of their size, need to be located close to their potential corporate customers, not just to obtain a sense of what the technical problems are for these clients but to consult on possible solutions. Accordingly clusters tend to be specialized in some particular sector.

---

31. An example of a national program along these lines is the Dutch "Peaks in the Delta" program. For a synoptic view of the Belgian case which has wider applicability see Vanthillo and Verhetsel (2012).

This brings us back to the enhanced significance of major urban centers for development policy. Larger cities provide advantages to small firms whose business is product or process research and development. The big city is a risk-minimizing location. The presence of a vertically disintegrated business structure is a common feature, though not universal, as cases like Detroit or Pittsburgh make clear. This business structure reduces the risks for firms that, in their search for new products or technologies, need to have available a variety of possible partners: suppliers with highly specialized knowledges and experiences as well as a diversity of clients. Benjamin Chinitz (1961) was talking about these sorts of relationships many years ago, but they have become the new wisdom, and this conception has lent further impetus to emphasizing major cities as the drivers of the economies of the developed countries.[32]

It is within this context that Richard Florida's (2002) arguments about the creative class have attracted the interest of the development professionals. Product development and new technologies require knowledgeable people: the creative class. This applies to both "hard" products like machine tools and to "soft" ones like computer games or any number of "apps." Make a city attractive to the engineers and chemists, to computer geeks, and to those MBAs who know how to put it all together, and you lay an important foundation for getting small firms and clusters off the ground.

The role of major cities in cluster development should not be overstated. There is an inherent unpredictability to the emergence of new

---

32. In a fascinating article Nicholas Phelps (2009) has asked why it took so long for the planners to come round to the idea of stimulating the development of interrelated firms as the basis of recapitalizing lagging regional economies. In the wake of the closures of those branch plants so eagerly sought, it does look odd. In fact, concern about relieving congestion in the major cities was contrary to exploiting economies of agglomeration and promoting cluster forms of development. Yet, as Phelps points out, the issue at the time was one of countering regional dependence on particular lines by promoting industrial diversity; and one can add that the sorts of changes in the global economy that have led to those branch plant closures could not have been anticipated. There were dissident voices at the time, as he indicates. But what this story suggests is the significance for regional development theory of the circumstances of time and place.

sectors or subsectors, including their locations, which recalls the leapfrog-ging phenomenon that Storper and Walker (1989) wrote about. Just how clustering starts is something of a mystery: the initial nucleation, the verti-cal disintegration of labor processes emphasized by Scott, then attracting the attention of major corporations who need an ear to the ground. No one could have anticipated Silicon Valley, or Silicon Fen for that matter. In this regard the French poles of competitivity approach may underline the sheer obsolescence of the old approaches of relocating employment through the use of carrots and sticks, and regardless of their expense at a time of fiscal constraint. The new forms of economic development are inherently harder to anticipate, and some of the poles will inevitably do much better than others. Better, therefore, to allow for all contingencies.[33] And given the significance of a highly skilled technical elite that has a sharp eye on its leisure and a desire to go where there are not just the jobs but the countryside, the mountains, and the ocean, there is an additional reason why trying to direct the new developments into the old rust belts would be a futile activity.

5. In combination one with another—the New International Division of Labor, neoliberalism, increasing concentration in major metropolitan areas, and shifts in the substantive focus of development policy—the ten-dency has been to create, even encourage, an unevenness of development that is in sharp contrast with the contours of national economic geog-raphies in what I have called the golden years. More recently this has received still further impetus with the shift of investment out of industry into real estate, and by no means necessarily into new construction; rather

---

33. This inherent unpredictability can also apply to firms of the classical Fordist sort as they have tried to adapt to the challenges of globalization. No one would have predicted the emergence of what Hancké (2003) has referred to as "autarchic regional production systems" in France. But in a context of widespread adoption of just-in-time production by major firms, their interventions into the labor processes of suppliers, and the use of newly decentralized technology and training systems, along with the newfound capacity of the regions to provide funds, this is exactly what has happened. Citroen, Peu-geot, Aérospatiale, and Michelin developed in similar ways, giving a highly contingent turn to local development in respective regions in the Rennes area, Franche Comté, the South West, and Auvergne respectively.

and significantly, much of the money has gone into the purchase of exist-ing real estate assets, creating speculative bubbles particularly in housing prices and in major metropolitan areas (Tables 3 and 4). Western Euro-pean countries, with the notable exception of Germany, appear to have been more affected than the United States, but within the latter there are some important geographic variations: not just the metropolitan tendency but also the disproportionately high price-income ratios on the West Coast and in the area stretching from Washington, DC, to Boston and corre-sponding to Gottmann's megalopolis (Figure 7).

The connection to the long downturn initiating change in the poli-tics of development is once again through the search for a new basis for profitability and recalls Harvey's arguments (1989b, chapter 2) about over-accumulation and the shift of investment from the primary circuit of industry to the secondary, property, one. The effect was delayed as a result of the early stagflationary form assumed by the crisis in the 1970s. High

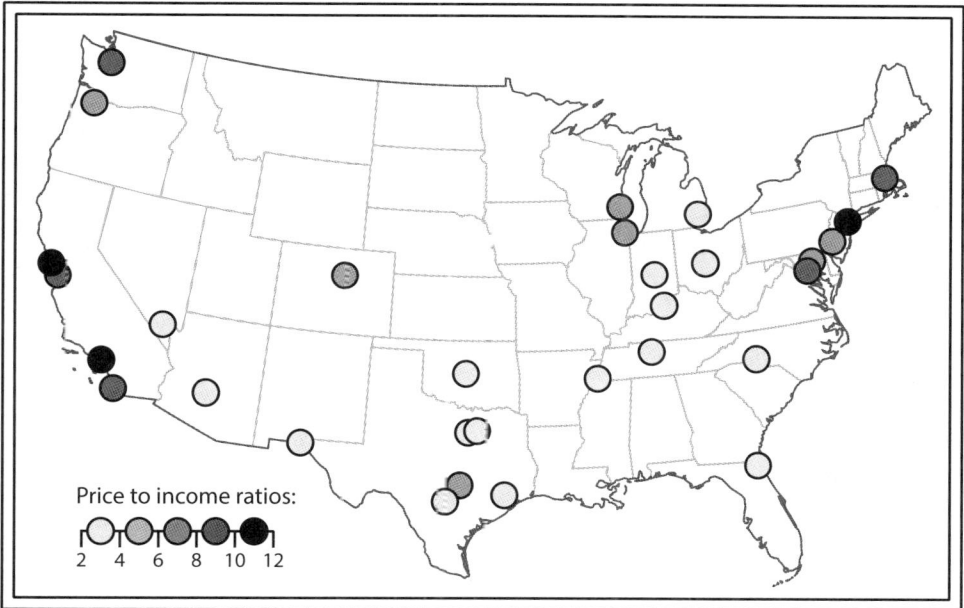

Fig. 7. Housing price-income ratios for American cities. Source: Numbeo, "Price to Income Ratio," http://www.numbeo.com/property-investment/gmaps_rankings.jsp. Map by Jim DeGrand.

Table 3

Housing Price-Income Ratios for Selected Countries

	1981	1986	1991	1996	2001	2006	2011
Belgium	3.20	2.55	3.00	2.90	3.50	5.00	4.50
Denmark	2.75	3.65	2.50	2.85	3.90	5.95	4.70
France	1.65	2.10	2.50	2.50	2.70	4.50	4.85
Germany	3.65	3.60	3.10	3.00	3.00	3.20	3.50
Great Britain	3.00	3.15	3.60	2.65	2.60	5.00	4.20
Ireland	2.50	2.20	2.30	2.40	3.60	3.40	4.50
Italy	1.90	1.25	1.80	2.50	2.50	3.25	3.60
Netherlands	3.00	2.50	3.10	3.40	4.90	5.60	5.30
Norway	2.30	3.15	1.80	2.50	2.95	3.30	3.60
Spain	2.10	2.20	3.90	2.50	2.75	4.50	4.20
United States	1.80	1.90	1.80	1.70	2.00	2.55	1.55

Source: Fox, Ryan, and Richard Finlay. 2012. "Dwelling Prices and Household Income." *Bulletin* (December quarter). Sidney: Reserve Bank of Australia. Accessed Dec. 29, 2015. http://www.rba.gov.au /publications/bulletin/2012/dec/2.html.

inflation was to be reined in by high interest rates. But once austerity had done its dirty work, the pretensions of labor suppressed, while profitability remained elusive, interest rates could be lowered as a stimulus to investment and to refloat national economies; or that at least was the thought. There was some improvement in production, particularly in consumption goods, soaking up some of the overcapacity, but it came on the back of a real estate boom (R. Brenner 2004). Shortages of housing, due to supply failures as in Great Britain and to a lesser degree in parts of France, stimulated speculative frenzies. Increasing prices encouraged turnover of housing at still higher prices, creating crises of housing affordability that are ongoing. There was and remains a rash of buying of second homes, buying-to-let, and the purchase of pieds-à-terre in cities like London, Paris, and New York. Increasing real estate values then created the collateral for still larger loans. Through so-called wealth effects, increasing home values facilitated increased consumption, as Allen, Massey, and Cochrane (1998) noted in their discussion of the boom in South East England.

Table 4

Housing Price-Income Ratios for Selected Cities, 2015

City	P-I Ratio	For Rest of Country
London	30.53	8.25
Paris	20.56	9.11
Amsterdam	7.83	5.43
Brussels	6.95	6.46
Berlin	8.51	7.14
Frankfurt	7.52	7.14
Munich	11.02	7.14
Stockholm	14.13	8.42
Barcelona	9.90	8.52
Madrid	10.07	8.52
Milan	18.04	10.59
Rome	22.09	10.59
Helsinki	10.04	6.78
Boston	7.09	3.39
Chicago	4.15	3.39
Los Angeles	8.85	3.39
New York	21.49	3.39
San Francisco	13.22	3.39

Sources: Numbeo. 2015. "Property Price Index by Country 2015." http://www
.numbeo.com/property-investment/-ankings_by_country.jsp.
Numbeo. "Price to Income Ratio." http://www.numbeo.com/property-investment
/gmaps_rankings.jsp.

Geographically, therefore, the effects have been very uneven. The crisis of housing affordability has been highly concentrated in major metropolitan areas and their surrounding regions, as in Southeast England, Ile-de-France, or indeed megalopolis and Southern California. They have, accordingly, added to the tendencies to uneven geographic development. High housing values create, through wealth effects, increased local demand for services. They can be at the root of crises in public provision as those on national pay scales in teaching, social services, and public safety are forced out of housing markets: something particularly clear in parts of Western Europe. They also check internal movement in the direction of the boom areas, especially among home owners who are reluctant to sell in what are relatively stagnant property markets so as to find themselves short of the money to buy into the booming ones.

It is clearly not just cheap money that has made the difference. The search for new niches in the international division of labor, the rise of the postindustrial city, and the liberalization of international finance have all been significant. Crises of housing affordability are crises of the major financial hubs and high-tech centers. Currency convertibility has opened up the real estate markets of New York, Los Angeles, London, and Paris to tsunamis of money from East Asia, Russia, and the Gulf. Some local scarcity in supply, typically of a planning sort, has then fed the expectations of future increases in property values and created the self-fulfilling prophecy of still further increases, which is why the Western European countries have been so much more affected than the United States. But without cheap money the wild landscape of variation in real estate values and its implications for uneven development elsewhere in the space economy would not have been nearly as intense.

▄▄▌▐▌▐▌▐▐

A common way in which at least some of the changes in development practice have been imagined, particularly by European observers, has been through regulation theory. This merits some comment. The contrast has been between the implications of a Fordist economy and something that seems to have followed it but which has been hard to specify. There have been references to post-Fordism and flexible accumulation, although as Peck and Tickell (1994) pointed out, regulation theory is about an institutional fix harmonizing production and consumption whereas flexible accumulation and the world of "new industrial spaces" were more about the organization of production. The attempt to hang on to an institutional interpretation of changes has, rather, been expressed through a contrast in the geography of institutions as it has applied to local development: an earlier, more centralized one and a later more decentralized one. These have then been tied to changing national priorities: earlier those of redistribution; and later those of focusing on winning cities and regions, to be facilitated by the structures of a more decentralized state.[34]

The reference to regulation theory seems more gestural than significant in any explanatory way. Spatializing regulation theory is a useful goal, but it has to remain faithful to the idea of coordinating consumption with production. There have been glimpses of what might be. There is some fascinating work on Italy: redistributional policies working through the welfare state lifted incomes in the southern part of the country increasing the market for the mass production consumption industries that grew rapidly in the North. Meanwhile, the migration of southerners northward facilitated wage discipline in the factories there (Trigilia 1992, 14–15, cited in Galimberti 2015, 61–62; Vercellone 2006). But this sort of approach is foreign to most of the discussions of spatial Keynesianism or other attempts to characterize the world of local and regional development as it emerged in Western Europe in the postwar years.

Above and beyond this, there is the question of the merits of regulation theory anyway. There have been some powerful, even devastating critiques (Brenner and Glick 1991; Clarke 1988) but with seemingly limited influence. The fundamental problem is the overriding significance assigned to institutional forms in the course of capitalist development. For Brenner and Glick, what is crucial is what they term "the broader system of capitalist social-property relations that form the backdrop to their (i.e., the regulationists) succession of institutionally defined phases" (1991, 105).[35]

34. Breathnach provided a summary statement of this viewpoint: "The transition, in the 1970s and 1980s, from the Fordist regime of accumulation built around the mass-producing welfare state to a post-Fordist regime of flexible neoliberalism is widely associated with a profound restructuring of state spatialities throughout western Europe, whereby the centralized Fordist welfare state, oriented to the spatial equalization of living standards and employment opportunities within its borders, was replaced by a decentralized neoliberal state wherein regional economies pursued their own economic interests through direct participation in the global economy" (2010, 1181).

35. "Paths of capital accumulation . . . are simply incomprehensible apart from a specification of the broader system of social-property relations in which they are embedded. This is not only because those systems will define the range of economic strategies that individual economic actors can find it sensible to adopt; it is also because those

For Clarke it is more about institutions as institutionalizations of particular balances of class forces, which recalls Harvey's (2005) arguments about neoliberalism as a class project. The circumstances of the time were ripe: Keynesianism seemed bereft of answers to the crisis of the 1970s; the New International Division of Labor opened up possibilities of driving a wedge between the less skilled of the working class and the more skilled; the creation of a global market in currencies provided new opportunities for financialization; and a shift in the thinking of economists provided the discursive ammunition for Harvey's reassertion of class power, of which the changes in development policy toward more of an American model, and however much hyped they have been, were one expression.

The European Union

Exercising congruent effects has been the European Union and its progressive transformation into a single market that includes the former Soviet satellites of Eastern Europe. On the one hand it has assumed a developmental role; and on the other it has placed pressures on member states, explicit and implicit, that have nudged them toward policies more similar to those one associates with the American states; specifically ones of competing for the inward investments that are still up for grabs, particularly for the very large ones that can bring large numbers of jobs and, where successful, that can be touted in election campaigns. On the other hand, these policies need to be set beside the EU commitment to policies of what it calls "territorial cohesion"—something quite un-American.

In the first place, therefore, the European Union has put in place policies aimed, rather ambitiously, at eliminating spatial disparities among the member states. These were always very considerable and were the target, historically, of the development policies of the Western European members of the union: how to improve incomes in relatively poor areas,

---

systems constitute a field of natural selection for the adoption of institutions and heavily determine the effect of given institutions, once adopted, on capital accumulation" (Brenner and Glick 1991, 110).

therefore, like southern Italy or southwestern France as it would have been before French policy got to work on it; how to restructure declining industrial areas like the Nord-Pas de Calais area of northeastern France or Belgium's Borinage. Currently one-third of the EU budget goes to this purpose, primarily in the form of money for physical infrastructure, including transport and energy, and for the upgrading of labor skills.[36] The enlargement of the EU since 2007 to include the former communist states of Eastern Europe has greatly magnified this task: how to cope with the challenge without taking money away from existing members? The response to this has been to increase overall regional fund spending by 50 percent, and grants to existing members were to be phased out by 2013. This has created some opposition from the wealthier members, including Great Britain, Germany, and the Netherlands, who tend to be net donors to rather than beneficiaries of EU expenditures. There is, of course, no such redistributional program courtesy of the federal government in the United States.

Second, however, and in the interests of creating a so-called level playing field, in the eyes of the European Union all national subsidies are now suspect. These include the financial incentives once offered by national governments to persuade firms to locate in certain designated areas, typically ones of relatively high unemployment. These can still be offered in the form of what is called "regional aid" but are strictly limited. For areas to be so designated, regional GDP per capita must be no more than 75 percent of the EU average. Allowable aid then increases with relative disadvantage. But with the expansion of the EU into areas of relatively low income, this has clearly put severe limits on the areas that can be so

36. MacLeod (1999), drawing on the case of the Strathclyde European Partnership, has shown how local development initiatives can make use of funding that the EU has put together for disadvantaged regions. Another instance where EU funds were drawn on was the—ultimately unsuccessful—restructuring of the former Limburg coalfield in Belgium (Baeten, Swyngedouw, and Albrechts 1999). MacLeod suggests how relations between regions and the EU can be a challenge to the long-time centralized character of states in Western Europe. Mark Boyle (2000; 2003), writing about the Irish case, has explored the various ways in which these tensions can come about.

designated in the wealthier countries. This is what is allowable. Other location aids aimed at keeping a particular plant open are strictly taboo and this can be important.

Even so, national variations in labor legislation, in how taxes are levied, and indeed in levels of corporate taxation, continue to vary so that national governments can now compete for investments in terms of "business climate," and they do. This is the aspect of the new dispensation that has made local and regional development practice in Western Europe come a little closer, at least, to that in the United States. For as in the US case, there are now no restrictions on the movement of goods, capital, and, to an increasing degree, labor between the member states of the EU. This means that firms now locate with respect to the EU as a whole rather than with respect to the space economies of individual members. Location patterns likewise get rationalized with respect to the geography of the EU taken in toto.[37]

Even before the advent of the low-wage areas of Eastern Europe in the form of new members like Poland and Hungary, this was an issue. The much-publicized and controversial movement of a Hoover factory from Dijon to Cambuslang in Scotland in 1993 is a case in point. The decision to relocate was secured in large part by the Scottish workforce agreeing to accept limited period contracts for new workers, constraints on the right to strike, cuts in overtime, a year-long freeze in wages, flexible working time and practices, and the introduction of video cameras on the factory floor. And to be sure, British unwillingness to sign on to the so-called social chapter of the EU was prompted by concerns that it would otherwise lose its present preponderant advantage in the EU; its advantage, that is, as a production platform for American and Japanese companies serving the EU as a whole.[38] This is something therefore, that, given the current insti-

37. As Dunford has written: "The removal of non-tariff barriers makes it easier to supply the whole of the European market from a smaller number of locations and reduces further the incentive to locate inside of national markets" (1994, 109).

38. The EU social chapter covers employment rights, holiday entitlements and pay rates, social benefits, and employee participation in workplace decision-making. The British government initially negotiated a partial opt-out. But after the Labour victory of

tutional framework of local and regional development policy, cannot be addressed short of homogenizing social policies at the level of the EU as a whole, which is something that the wealthier members would prefer so long as the homogenization is upward.

A Balance Sheet

Since the 1970s geographically uneven development in both the United States and Western Europe has markedly increased. In the wake of the New International Division of Labor, rust belts have emerged with a vengeance across the old American Manufacturing Belt, northeastern France, southern Belgium, the Ruhr and Saarland areas of Germany, and large parts of northern England and central Scotland, as they have found themselves saddled with declining sectors of production. The revivified and sunrise sectors, concentrating on more technology- and knowledge-intensive products, have emerged elsewhere: parts of Texas, parts of the West Coast of the United States, in and around major metropolitan areas like Minneapolis, Charlotte in North Carolina, Seattle, Salt Lake City, and Denver. In Western Europe, northern Belgium, southeastern England, Bavaria, Hessen and Württemberg in southern Germany, and northern Italy are examples.

One effect of this has been to widen the fiscal gap between regions: supplicants are now more "supplicant" than ever, while those who make up the difference through interregional fiscal flows are beginning to complain, particularly in Western Europe where the flows have been institutionalized. As a result the older solidarities that underpinned redistribution are coming under strain, though more is certainly at stake than this. At the same time, frustrations in the areas of decline or relative stagnation have led to demands for greater central government attention, either in

---

1997, the new government accepted its provisions. Anxieties about business climate have persisted, however, with a continuing sensitivity to employers' concerns about the regulatory burden on businesses, particularly the impact of EU legislation—something that factored into the Brexit vote of June 2016.

the form of increased funds,[39] which is one of the demands of the British Core Cities Group,[40] to demands for increased powers in development policy.[41] On the other hand, they are not about to do away with the old welfare state ideals and structures as they play out over space, since they have been, remain, or could be net beneficiaries.[42] But until they do, the

39. The demands of Germany's Left Party, with its representation in rust belt areas, and particularly in the old East Germany, from where it gets the bulk of its support, are symptomatic.

40. The Core Cities group comprises the cities of Birmingham, Bristol, Leeds, Liverpool, Manchester, Newcastle, Nottingham, and Sheffield. According to their mission statement, the group's goal is "to work in partnership with Government and other key stakeholders to promote and strengthen Core Cities as drivers of regional and national competitiveness and prosperity with the aim of creating internationally competitive regions." In addition, there is now a group of smaller cities in England and Wales calling themselves the Key Cities Group. There are currently twenty-six of them, and they are asking for similar devolution of budgets for employment, housing, transport, and business development of the sort that the government is now offering larger entities like Manchester and Birmingham.

41. Something less organized has emerged in Germany, where numerous city mayors in depressed areas like the Ruhr are pressing for an end to the transfer payments introduced in order to build up the infrastructure in East Germany subsequent to reunification (see "Mayors Attack Solidarity Pact: Poor Western Cities Fed Up with Funding East," *Spiegel International,* Mar. 20, 2012, http://www.spiegel.de/international/germany/west -german-cities-call-for-end-to-east-german-subsidies-a-822473.html). This has played out differently in Finland, where it is the "successful" cities that have organized against what are seen as state attempts to counter uneven development. What has been particularly at stake is the redistribution of the corporate tax across municipalities (Haila and Le Galès 2005). This has been withheld from the more rapidly growing cities; subsequently six of these cities, including Helsinki, came together with a view to negotiating directly with the state as well as developing common positions on other urban issues.

42. Also observable is some reassertion of regional demands. This of course is at the heart of the more radical separatist strategies observable in cases like Flanders and Scotland. Within Great Britain, though, and separatisms aside, new regional identities are forming around ideas of central government neglect. As a response to this, and from 2014 on, the government has broached a set of measures designed to promote what it calls the "Northern Powerhouse," though so far it has gone little further than promising transport improvements that will facilitate the exploitation of economies of agglomeration on a

Western European model of local and regional development is likely to remain quite different from that of the United States.

Regional planning during the classical era of development policy in the countries of Western Europe was always inspired by the idea of leveling up material outcomes in the most marginalized of areas: nationalized industries there would be subsidized, and employment displaced from more favored regions. This was in sharp contrast to the United States, where neither federal nor state governments have ever been moved by ideals of equality of outcomes over space. Rather, material outcomes should be left up to the supposedly benign hand of market forces. This might have worked in the case of the South as a result largely of branch plant industrialization, although government programs like crop supports almost certainly factored into the equation, as did southern business climates; so one might say that there were regional policies, but that they were not formulated as such and inspired by the ideals of the welfare state. But in Western Europe, courtesy of social democratic parties, and however much drained of the old passions as they might be, the memories are sustained and continue to affect the politics of local and regional development in distinctive ways.

Likewise, and despite some decentralization of powers, in Western Europe the structures of a centralized state remain largely intact. Their normative basis is for sure partly a matter of social protection; but it is also the idea that all citizens should be treated the same and given the same opportunities and state support wherever they are located. So while there have indeed been so-called reforms, they are not especially profound; they cannot seriously dislodge the existing framework of development policy. In order to do so they require intervention into a much more basic set of incentive structures: so basic that it is hard to envisage change in the politics of local and regional development in the direction of the American model. Under current arrangements local governments lack the incentive

---

larger geographic scale. This is also seen as part of a regional rebalancing of the economy to reduce the inflationary pressures emanating from London: so the idea of planning for the national space as a force of production endures.

to get involved in local economic development in a way that is taken for granted in the United States.

The French case is illuminating. Police, fire service, and schools (apart from the provision of buildings) are all national responsibilities, which means revenue needs of the sort that haunt American local governments—and which incite them to embrace the cause of local economic development and the generation of rents—are just not there. As noted previously, a feature of French devolution has been the encouragement given to the formation of new intercommunal structures particularly in the urban areas. Significantly, these have new responsibilities for economic development and planning. This sounds promising, but on closer examination is less so. Plans have to conform with regional priorities, and fiscal powers are limited to something called the professional tax levied on businesses and previously levied by the constituent communes individually.

With respect to the British case, *The Economist* for April 12, 2004, included a leader with the provocative title "Does Britain Want to Be Rich?" Like most of their leaders it linked up with a news article in the body of the magazine, in this case a discussion of planning for growth in the Cambridge area ("Silicon Fen Strains to Grow") and the discouragement that the entrepreneurial element there was experiencing as a result of adverse planning decisions. As the article went on to argue there: "Many of the companies (in the Cambridge area) say it is a struggle to grow . . . They say that the main reason they cannot grow is the planning system. Applications to erect a new building grind slowly through the system; appeals, if an application is turned down, take years. High-tech businesses do not have years to waste." The underlying problem, according to the leader, was that "while councils have so much power to determine the level of growth in their area they have little interest in fostering it." The reason for this was that their worries about revenues, in contrast to the United States case, were minor ("The state of the local economy . . . makes little difference to local government coffers"). A central feature of British local government finance is the centrally provided revenue support grant. This doles out by far the larger proportion of local government revenue—75 percent on average—through a formula that takes into account both local resources, including the rate base, and local needs; so holding needs constant, increasing the resource base will simply result in a lowering of the revenue support grant that local government receives.

It is not difficult to see the difficulties of engineering a radical change in the sources of local government and regional funding. In practice it would certainly challenge widely held ideals regarding equality in provision of public services. It would also, and inevitably, threaten the system of national wage bargaining for schoolteachers and municipal workers, and invite, in consequence, not just their opposition but that of the whole labor movement.[43] Most significantly, proposals in 2006 for a far-reaching decentralization of functions to the Italian provinces that actually went to a national referendum but were defeated, resulted in sharp labor union opposition.[44]

This is not to say that there is not demand in some cases for a radical change in the allocation of revenue raising powers. In some instances the tensions are very sharp. Demands for greater autonomy, even separatism, come from the wealthier regions of Belgium and Italy. In Germany there have been disputes over federal equalization policies between the more rapidly growing *länder* in the south and the rustbelt ones in the north and east (Jeffrey 1999). This suggests that the old interregional redistribution mechanisms are under threat. It also sheds light on just why these demands have emerged now.

43. Significantly, in the United States wages and salaries are determined at the local level with individual municipalities and school districts.

44. "A more federal structure is also seen as jeopardizing the collective bargaining policies of the trade unions. The Italian bargaining structure currently privileges the national level over the regional or local level. The proposed new institutional structure might imply, for public sector workers, the abolition of national collective agreements and the establishment of regional-level agreements. If this occurred, the trade unions would have to question their structures, which are largely based on national sectoral organizations. Unions would have to undertake a difficult review of the relations between their central and regional organizations, which would entail a redistribution of powers and resources in favor of the latter. There would be scant possibilities of coordinating wage and bargaining policies and the gap between Northern and Southern workers would continue to widen" (Paparella and Rino fi 2003).

6

Locations in Question

Context

In trying to understand the American politics of local and regional development, a major theme in this book is its relation to the accumulation process. The driving force for this is industrial capital. But capital's division of labor has changed. Industrial capital has increasingly assigned its financial, commercial, and real estate needs to specialized sectors. Industrial capital produces value, but that value is in part shared with these three other branches in the respective forms of interest, profits on sales, and rents. Accordingly, their revenues depend on the ability of industrial capital to extract a surplus from its employees. In effect, and in return, financial, commercial, and property capital perform crucial functions and are not idle in discovering new ways of facilitating the growth of that surplus. At the same time, each has its own logic, which, equally, can undermine the capacity of industrial capital to accumulate.

Property capital's function with respect to the rest of capital is both direct and indirect. On the one hand, it provides premises: shopping centers, distribution centers, industrial parks, and office towers. On the other hand, it provides housing for employees. Its ability to provide both in the right places and at minimum cost is crucial to the accumulation process as a whole, and its contribution is facilitated by its innovative products and cost-cutting practices; a result of the competition of property capitals one with another. This has consequences for the vast majority of the population: for while costs are cut and innovations introduced, by and large this happens regardless of the social costs incurred. Provision remains on property capital's own terms, rather than, say, on the terms of an employer offering company housing; and the temptations of monopolistic exploitation, whether on the part of the land owner or the developer, are hard to resist.

The resultant tensions are of a class sort: pressures on wages as growth coalitions in which developers are a prominent presence try to mediate worker givebacks; pressures on housing costs and home values. Some, particularly the more moneyed and the more skilled, are able to adapt to the shifting geography of the space economy. Others are more or less trapped, even while for the more privileged they may be trapped in a place they otherwise want to be, and it is among these that resistance is most likely to emerge. How that resistance gets expressed is by no means straightforward. Sometimes the conflict clearly pits more popular forces against the local growth coalition, or particular developers, or even, in some instances, the financial interests underwriting the process. At other times the changing map of development looks more like a backdrop to struggles not between those popular forces and property capital, but between different fractions of the working class—notably between those better off (more endowed in terms of both social and cultural capital) and those less so. The shifting geography of labor and housing markets then seems to be something that the more affluent, whether in the labor force or retired from it, exploit for their own purposes.

Paradoxically, these struggles. whether between popular forces and property interests or within the working class itself, create degrees of freedom for property capitals in countering, co-opting, and exploiting for their own benefit. The way in which development issues—plant arrivals and closures, rezonings and annexations, particular development projects like shopping centers and residential developments—get represented is central to this struggle. The problem is that resistance is typically understood and acted out in territorial terms: a politics of turf, as in NIMBYism. This creates a space for property capitals to play one territorially defined set of interests off against another.

The chapter starts by outlining the nature of the class oppressions dealt out by property capital, typically in alliance with different branches of the state, in its pursuit of rent. The way in which these are experienced is often highly variable. More affluent segments of the working class are often able to cope and adapt to subsequent changes in the space economy. In other instances there is resistance and conflict, sometimes directed against property capital and sometimes directed against those seen to be the beneficiaries of its projects and, particularly, their geography. Attention finally turns to just how and why, in the midst of all these struggles, property capital not only survives but manages to thrive.

Local Economic Development and the Popular Classes

As we have seen, the competitive pursuit by property companies, land owners, developers, and the coalitions they form of rent from real estate is central to the American politics of urban and regional development. Necessary to that end is some demand from industrial, finance, and commercial capitals, and the residential developments that typically follow in the wake of their location decisions. What growth interests provide in order to attract those investments are the necessary physical and social infrastructures. This is a process characterized by strong inter-scalar properties. The arrival of a major employment-creating investment can spark competition among developers and property firms not just for that investment but also for the numerous externalities it will provide—notably, new residential developments and shopping centers. The subsequent urban growth can have further knock-on effects. The achievement of new thresholds for other developments can alter a locality's position in a scalar division of labor (with respect to distribution centers, or health care provision, for example), and this too sparks further competition within the urban area.

Competitive struggles among the property interests, their rent-seeking allies in local government and the utilities, and the growth coalitions that they form in order to pursue their ends are primarily distributional ones; that is, they revolve around how the loot will be shared out among different capitalist contenders.[1] More fundamental as a source of tension and conflict is the class relation. This should come as no surprise, even if the

---

1. However, the activities of property capitals can also make a contribution to production by facilitating a rationalization of capitalist geography.

way in which the tensions are apprehended is not always in class terms. Conflicts around "business climate" underscore the struggles around labor law and what the outcomes imply for the ability of capital to extract a surplus from labor. Others involve capital and particular fractions of the working class, with capitalist projects engineering, in effect, a redistribution from labor's consumption fund to its fund for accumulation. We can identify four major sources of tension, often overlapping one with another.

1. The first of these is related to what has come to be known in development circles as business climate, where the location question, in effect, gets incorporated into the struggle between capital and labor over the extraction of surplus value. In their competitive attempts to attract new investment—whether a branch plant seeking a low-wage location in the South or a Walmart trying to enter a big-city market—growth coalitions and property interests are, in effect, in league with capital in general in the drive to increase the exploitation of the working class. They act as battering rams to clear away resistance to the changes in labor law and conditions of work that they believe will be attractive to those inward investors they are so keen to attract.[2]

This also works at very local levels. Local governments raise money for public works on bond markets. Just what rate of interest a local government will have to pay can vary considerably. It depends first on how the bonds are rated by agencies like Standard and Poors, which decide what factors are taken into account. Anything smacking of fiscal imprudence will be punished. But often it is precisely that "imprudence" which protects the working class in its living places. Municipal pensions have been a recent battleground. During the good years, local governments often negotiated pension agreements that they failed to fund adequately. When they did fund them, they borrowed against them, which is meat for the grinder as far as the rating agencies are concerned; hence, the claims that the municipal unions were greedy, that they have to tighten their belts, and that pensions have to be renegotiated.[3] The pressures are particularly

2. See Goodman (1979) for a particularly good exposition of these tendencies.
3. See Matt Taibbi "Looting the Pension Funds," *Rolling Stone*, Sept. 2013.

intense in cases where a city has had to declare bankruptcy, as in Detroit and San Bernardino.

It might also be a question of some coalition of growth interests, the local business chamber and local government perhaps, mediating a "deal" aimed at keeping a plant in the city but through worker "give-backs" (i.e., a renegotiation of hard-won gains in wages and work conditions). To this end pressure is brought to bear on union locals; a pressure applied through local media trumpeting the irrationality of not doing a deal, explaining how the world has changed, and so on. States are also the targets of local lobbying, although often they can be thoroughly complicit, particularly in those with relatively weak union movements. This is because the individual states are responsible for major elements in American labor law, including workers' compensation law and right-to-work legislation. States have their own development agenda, of course, and may quickly embrace workers compensation reform or right-to-work, egged on by local firms that have no ability to move elsewhere but are more than happy to join in the chorus. All this can be hugely controversial, particularly in states where unions are still relatively well organized and membership is higher, and when an economic downturn persuades growth advocates that conditions might be conducive to a successful assault on wages and conditions.

2. The second source of tension arises from the fact that *any* capitalist development depends on the provision of shared items of physical infrastructure. The physical fabric of cities—the highways, the housing, the water and sewer systems, the airport—all function as crucial means of production and reproduction. They are a shared means: firms share the highways, the airport, and the housing for their workers; and these means are shared with workers who use them for their own reproduction and consumption. This raises the question of who should pay for it all. In some cases the answer is clear; as developments have become larger, there are privatizing tendencies, at least in the original provision of something like the highways, the subsurface improvements, and for very large developments, sometimes even a freeway interchange. But for the most part it is a matter for local agencies of the state—municipalities, school districts,

counties, special districts—so that who is going to pay for what will be fought out locally through referenda, zoning fights, and pressures on city councils.

The absence of planning, the failure to direct growth to where there is existing capacity, aggravates the problem. The private sector leads. New commercial and residential developments are inserted, new growth frontiers materialize, and then the expansion of highway capacity, the reinforcement of bridges to take the weight of appropriate fire equipment, the provision of public schools, public libraries, parks, and the like, have to catch up. Meanwhile, the land speculation subsequent to new growth inflates the value of the land that has to be purchased to accommodate the expanded public facilities, all adding insult to injury by increasing the claim on the public purse.

Tax-increment financing has been one of the ways in which local governments have, in effect, financed some of the physical infrastructure. Cities sell bonds to pay for the construction, using as collateral the (putative) increase in values generated by the development. The alternative, of course, would be for the developers themselves to pay for it directly out of the values created by strokes of the city council's pen as it changes the zoning, rather than divert the increased property taxes into financing the project's public infrastructural needs—an odd rebuke to the claim that the development will increase city revenues to the advantage of all.

A major flashpoint has been the provision of new schools. This is a matter for local school districts. As new residential developments appear at the suburban frontier, existing schools inevitably get crowded and the cry goes up to provide new ones. Given the timid approaches to value capture that tend to prevail among American local governments, new schools will be paid for by bonds issued by the school district. But who will be responsible for paying the bonds off? Certainly the school district—but all residents, or just the newcomers? Resentments among existing residents can run high as they question why they should pay when they were not responsible for the overcrowding.

This is one of the major sources of battles over new development, its density, and the value of the homes, since more expensive housing will contribute proportionally more to the school district's tax base. A common demand has been for impact fees, which are payable by the developer for each housing unit constructed, with the money then used to defray the cost of new schools. Typically, and in housing markets where demand is such that the developers will have to eat them, impact fees will be bitterly contested, not just by the developers themselves but also by the building suppliers and local land owners who want to smooth the way for further land sales and rents and who could not care less about the school district's problems, which are not theirs provided the costs are footed by someone, and the development bandwagon continues to roll.

But while the developers can shove off the schools question into a future when they will have moved on, in other cases the infrastructure has to be in place. Attracting a major employer can involve the provision of highway, water and sewer line extensions, or even new freeway interchanges, although the latter are rarely that contentious given that most of the money will come from the state. More controversial has been the provision of new downtown infrastructure to support a city's hotel and hospitality industry. Convention centers have to be funded along with sports arenas. These can then generate more demands, such as subsidies to professional sports franchises, as in the Columbus case reviewed in chapter 1, or incentives to hotel chains to expand so that the convention center can make money. All of these are the object of popular resistance, as bond levies and increases in county sales taxes to cover the costs can be hotly contested.

3. Acquiring the space required for new development is a third source of tension. If growth coalitions succeed and new investment comes in, then not only do the industrial and office parks require sites, so too does the supporting infrastructure of shopping centers, housing developments, wider highways, bigger airports, and the like. If the public infrastructure lags, as it typically does (see above) then there will be congestion. As new infrastructure is introduced, physical displacement will be the inevitable consequence, along with all the externality effects that go along with increased densities. Of course, the shopping centers and the new residential developments can be turned down. But such is the fragmentation of the American metropolis that they are likely to be displaced only a short

distance away into a neighboring jurisdiction;[4] so there will be traffic issues to be confronted anyway and ones over which other local governments will have absolutely no control at all.

4. Fourth, and finally, the place competition that is the hallmark of the American development process brings in its wake extraordinarily uneven development, and at all manner of scales, creating a mess that imposes costs on publics who did not ask for it. Just as growth can be dramatic in some regions, in some towns, and on urban peripheries, so too can be the decline: the sinking fortunes of Rust Belt cities has led to the collapse of numerous central city economies, including places like St. Louis, Buffalo, Cleveland and, more recently, Detroit, as well as lesser ones like Youngstown, Ohio, Flint, Michigan, and Camden, New Jersey.[5] Public facilities designed for larger populations now have to be run on a lower customer base, which can be a challenge, particularly if there are bonds outstanding. Unfunded public-sector pension funds now look as if they will never be viable. Home values decline, and areas are redlined and then abandoned; not a nice prospect if you happen to be a home owner. The rot then spreads to some of the older, inner suburbs with a housing stock that just cannot compete with what is going up on the urban periphery.[6]

Meanwhile, in numerous small towns, not just across the South and West but also in the Midwest, the golden years of the so-called "rural

4. This is a common threat of about-to-be thwarted developers: If you do not allow us to put in a shopping center here, then another local government close by will be more than happy to accommodate and you'll be affected by the resulting traffic regardless, and without the offsetting property and sales taxes.

5. The Sun Belt has not been exempt. Stockton and San Bernardino in California are recent cases and Reno, Nevada, was looking pretty sick until Tesla decided to build a huge factory for the manufacture of batteries for electric cars there (see Hull 2015).

6. The sources of the problem can be quite random, reinforcing one another in a wholly unexpected manner and generating local effects of a devastating intensity. Economic bases can be diverse without any assurance that that will protect the local economy. Such has been the story of San Bernardino, where the closure of three major local employers—the steel mill in nearby Fontana, a US air force base, and then a major depot on the Santa Fe railroad—brought skyrocketing unemployment and rapidly deteriorating housing values.

turnaround" are now but a memory. Competition from the NICs has taken a toll of the branch plants set up there not so long ago. The fact that the plants were often the single major employer in town adds to the effect. More advantaged have been the small towns in the vicinity of major cities, which can take the industrial employment that a postindustrial city is no longer interested in or provide a base from which to commute to some industrial suburb.

Within the metropolitan areas, property capital's speculative nature has generated the rolling carpet or scorched earth effect: one new wave of development after another on the city edge, "bigger and better," undermining demand for older housing and the retailing establishments that go with it—rolling the carpet of opportunity out on the edge while it is rolled up further in. New sorts of housing have emerged in quick succession: single-car-garage homes, two-car-garage homes, homes on cul-de-sacs; and then new "designs for living" like golf course communities or lakeside ones with jogging trails and copious open space. The result has been a low-density city that has progressively encouraged home ownership and, by virtue of its economics, squeezed mass transit out, as discussed in chapter 4.

Once again, the property development firms and the growth coalitions have been crucial agents in imposing this particular model, though as we saw in chapter 3, with very, very considerable help from the federal government. As the city expands at its edge, as the urban frontier gets closer, new, freestanding suburbs sprout up: land owners, speculators who have bought land in anticipation of appreciating values, township trustees, villages, and developers looking for ever bigger chunks of land on which to develop their new models for shopping centers and residential neighborhoods come together around plans to incorporate, zone, subdivide, shift the cost of the physical infrastructure onto the existing residents, and so on. These then compete with older suburbs closer in, putting pressure on them if land owners and landlords there are to extract rent, and on the residents who will be called on to pay the bill for whatever enticements they can offer to new investors.

All this is to confine our attention to material interests and to say nothing about people's identities and the effect that plant closures can have on them, particularly in small towns. A plant with "roots" in the town can be important to how people define themselves— a point of reference for relatives, even for generations of relatives who worked there—and, to the extent that it is locally owned and operated, acts as and is seen as part of the community. This is a reason why the arrival of Walmart in many small towns across the United States is greeted with such ambivalence: on the one hand, it may indeed mean lower prices; on the other, it devastates local retailers who have been part of the warp and weft of the place, connected through kinship, bonds of familiarity, and the like.

What aggravates these tensions is the way in which they tend to get concentrated, to accumulate and build on one another spatially. In Western Europe, the strongly redistributional form—emphatically *national* in character—works to counteract the geographic unevenness and, therefore, the uneven social impacts that go with it, which are the necessary concomitants of capitalist development. In growth areas the progressiveness of the national tax system means that more revenue will be skimmed off there, while in areas experiencing disinvestment the consequences for local economies will be mitigated by the way the drop in local consumption is limited by decreasing taxes. Meanwhile, the national welfare state delivers income supplements and unemployment compensation to areas experiencing job losses and declining income levels. National pay scales for the public service, including teachers, local government officials, and the police, put a further floor under local consumption. Some of this applies to the United States, but in a very qualified form. Federal taxation exists alongside state taxation, which tends to bottle up and sequester the gains from unusual regional growth. The American welfare state is highly fragmented. Unemployment compensation is only in part a federal program. The same applies to other income-supplement programs, like Temporary Assistance for Needy Families.

At the national level, therefore, the mechanisms for socializing the local impacts of capitalist development are very limited. Within metropolitan areas, this bleak picture gets repeated. Apart from the central city, jurisdictions tend to be small. The cost of building new schools on the development frontier is borne almost entirely (depending on state legislation) by the newcomers and the existing residents and not shared out over a wider population, which is one reason it generates such anger, since the effects on property tax bills can be dramatic, particularly in hitherto sparsely populated suburbs. As suburbanization has occurred, so too has the tax base migrated, reducing the resources that central cities can draw on. It seems unlikely that Detroit, had it embraced jurisdictionally its surrounding suburbs, would have gone bankrupt, with all the tensions that has generated around issues like public-sector union pensions. Some jurisdictional arrangements quite clearly come into existence in order to frustrate the sort of socialization of cost that is common on the other side of the Atlantic and which serves to blunt resident anger there, however questionable that blunting might be from the standpoint of making developers responsible for the mess they make.

Uneven Development, Uneven Experience

If the effects are uneven geographically, so too is it the case socially. How people are affected by the decline of a local economy varies hugely. The children from the more advantaged backgrounds are clearly more likely to go to college and obtain some formal qualification. If they attend college in a big city, then they may well stay there, particularly if they move in with a fellow undergraduate and get inducted into what is still a very common middle-class trajectory of home ownership, children, and a destination in a suburban school district. Children aside, the highly qualified are going to move to where the jobs are. The managers and engineers at some assembly plant due to close will be transferred. And if they are not then they will be reading the job ads in the trade journals and entering the interview circuit, all costs paid by the hiring firm (a national labor market, therefore). Meanwhile, some of the more skilled workers might be offered positions at another plant elsewhere, but the broader mass of the semi-skilled and unskilled who typically find jobs through the local newspaper or word of mouth are out of luck: no trade journals for them, no paid-for interviews in some distant city—just the sheer uncertainty that if one does make the move it might not work out, and the financial reserves to buffer the boldness do not exist. All that is left is cheaper shelter as the housing market goes south, early—very early—retirement, or the prospect of a lengthy commute to a job elsewhere. But even within the major metropolitan areas, job markets are highly differentiated. While many of them can boast clusters of the technically intensive industries, emphasizing work skills and experience on the job, the older assembly-style industries that provided the "good blue-collar jobs" once occupied by those without a high school diploma are in terminal decline—one reason for high levels of unemployment in central cities, particularly among African Americans (Wilson 1987; 1996).

Meanwhile, in metropolitan areas as a whole the social power of money both protects and enables: it protects from the worst implications of the rolling carpet effect at the same time it allows people to take advantage of the new cornucopia of consumer delights on the edge of the city, the golf course or lakeside communities, not to mention the school districts of the privileged. Not for them the threat of falling home values or even inability to sell at all as a result of redlining; nor the forced removals as universities or hospitals expand, or as housing is cleared for a downtown arena; nor yet the displacements that gentrification entails. In short, dumping on the working class bears down much more intensely on the poor and on those with fewer workplace skills, and this will be reflected in the topography of conflict that surrounds geographically uneven development.

The cleavages that emerge are accordingly complex and far from a simple antagonism of the more popular forces to the projects of property capitals and to the sort of trends that they set in motion both within and across urban areas. What people resist and how they resist turns out to be quite mixed, albeit with some crucial commonalities. A sense of class can sometimes be detected, and it would be strange if it were otherwise in a country where labor unionism has not been entirely put to sleep. But it exists in uneasy cohabitation with other cleavages. The stratification of the population by income and occupation plays into the picture, deflecting attention from the provocations of property developers and growth coalitions to struggles around divvying up labor's consumption fund. To some degree this overlaps with a very American politics of difference, substantially defined along racial lines and still—civil rights notwithstanding—far from irrelevant. Finally, and overlapping with all of these is the fact of territory; defending not just an interest in home values or jobs but home values and jobs in particular places, and, often enough, against those, including the property development industry, with interests, again diverse, in other places. As we will see this territorialization of conflict plays a crucial role in strengthening the hand of the development industry at the same time as it weakens that of its antagonists.

Resisting Property Capital

While the social costs of land development have been unevenly spread, affecting in particular the poor, the African American, and the Hispanic, there has obviously been resistance both at the point of production and where people live. As far as plant closures are concerned, and the way they have been used by growth coalitions as a reason for renewed attack on labor rights deemed an obstacle to recapitalization, attention obviously turns to the role of the labor unions. As we saw in chapter 1, up to the early 1970s unemployment in the Manufacturing Belt was not a severe problem. Firms closed down, and some even relocated. There were even major changes like the hollowing out of Akron's rubber tire industry and the movement of meat packing away from major centers like Chicago, Fort Worth, and St. Louis in the direction of smaller towns to the west. But for the most part local economies enjoyed a buoyancy of historic proportions: capital's golden years. Even when conditions changed and American manufacturing's shifting center of gravity became an issue, labor unions, with their membership heavily concentrated in the Cold/Snow Belt or Rust Belt, were able to resist the attempts of employers to use the occasion to "reform" state labor laws. There were legislative initiatives aimed at impeding the plant closure process, and the attempt to unionize workers in the South, the Plains, and the Mountain West has continued to the present day.[7]

7. A recent example was the attempt in 2014 to unionize the new Volkswagen plant in Alabama; something, interestingly, preferred by VW but not by some of the local politicos, including Alabama senator Bob Corker, who in an effort to sway the vote away from the union, spread the nice bit of misinformation that unionization would mean that an auto model planned for the future would be produced elsewhere.

Nevertheless, under the neoliberal onslaught—and compounded by a shift to service occupations, which have seemed harder to organize—the tide has turned against the union movement and it has experienced quite precipitous decline in its membership. Its distinctive geography, with a concentration in the old Manufacturing Belt and on the West Coast, remains and is still exploited by growth-coalition rhetoric. Moreover, the right-to-work movement has enjoyed a resurgence, recording successes within the last five years in Michigan and Wisconsin: testimony in itself to the drop in membership, since the union movement was always in the frontline of opposition to the flag bearers of Taft-Hartley.

The new frontier of labor organizing has to be service workers: the myriad cleaners, security personnel, food workers, parking attendants, hospital orderlies, and care workers who are a major presence in the postindustrial city with its hotels, office buildings, big airports, and hospitals, and who, of course, help to give the big cities their characteristically massive income inequality. And *their* organization represents a direct threat to the rent extractors rather than to the profits of industrial capital.[8] From the organizing standpoint, they are a different sort of challenge. In the case of industrial workers, a cross-regional approach is imperative to organizing those in regions where low wages fuel the relocation tactics of employers. For service industries, organizing workers within a particular metropolitan labor market has been of equal if not greater importance: eliminating the cut-throat competition between the subcontractors who provide hotel workers and parking services, and who are not going to threaten exit (Gough 2012, 98). And this has been all the more feasible given the monopoly nature of the rents available in the major metropolitan centers: something that does not necessarily come out of the pockets of the building owners, therefore.

8. Compare Howley (1990, 64): "When rental revenues decline, building managers have limited options for cutting costs. Financing costs, which eat up about half of an office building's revenues, are fixed; so are property taxes, utility rates and insurance charges. So despite the fact that the cost of cleaning typically accounts for less than a nickel out of every dollar of office rent, it became a prime target of cost cutting."

The organizing success of the Justice for Janitors movement (Howley 1990; Savage 2006) is well known. Less so is what has unfolded in Las Vegas, now one of the most unionized cities in the United States. In a fascinating article Gray and DeFilippis (2015) have underlined the role played by the Culinary Workers Union in organizing workers employed in the city's hotels, casinos, and resorts: porters, housekeepers, cooks, waiters and waitresses, doormen; all the more remarkable in that groups historically harder to organize—ethnic minorities and women—comprise a majority. The result has been considerably improved wages and work conditions, as well as an illustration of what is possible in a right-to-work state like Nevada.[9] The authors make clear, though, that one of the conditions enabling this is the empowerment entailed by the place-dependent nature of the Las Vegas casino industry. "Las Vegas" is a nonportable brand with very considerable allure; imitation is hard. Nevertheless, in a context where casino gambling has spread to numerous other states, it is still a brand that needs promoting. The result is that the Culinary Workers Union has given strong and active support to Las Vegas's growth coalition, always centered on promoting the gaming industry; suggesting that, while effective resistance is possible, it leaves in place the basic structure of a territorialized competition and the pressures that means for workers.

On the other hand, and to judge from the media, resistance in the living place is dominated by the better-off, particularly the home owners: the usual cast of characters who will show up at rezoning hearings or the unveiling of plans for whatever is projected to go on that nearby, still-vacant piece of land. The very wealthy can relax. Any resident organization that they subscribe to will retain a lawyer who does the work for them, including anything behind the scenes. Poorer neighborhoods have their own challenges: not so much the greenfield sites eagerly sought by the developers as the brownfield ones with their history of contamination, or simply those necessary but undesirable land uses, like a juvenile detention center or a municipal incinerator, that just tend to come their way.

9. Wages are about 25 percent higher than in Nevada's other major casino destination, Reno, where there is no similar organization.

So opposition is not to be excluded particularly when a string of cancer deaths arouses suspicion and some nurse living in the neighborhood starts to pay attention. But on the whole, people in poorer neighborhoods are less likely to have the stake of home ownership, and those in the very poorest are looking to escape anyway. And when gentrification comes knocking, those who do own their own homes see it as an opportunity to get rid of those who, in their eyes, dragged the neighborhood down.

In other words, resistance to the often scattershot depredations of the developers and their local government allies takes the form of a very parochial, turf-oriented politics, whereas some citywide coalition of resident organizations might be much more effective in the struggle with the development industry. This needs qualifying. There *have* been broader based alliances, usually targeting particular forms of imposition dealt out by property capitals and their allies in finance. Redlining, a result of the continuous addition of new housing at the urban periphery, became the target of one such alliance in the early 1970s. This was National People's Action, a coalition of community[10] groups across the country, pushing for federal intervention. One result would be the Community Reinvestment Act of 1977, designed to discourage redlining—not to ban it—within the limits of prudential lending.[11] The act did have some serious teeth though: leverage came as a result of bank requests to merge, common at a time when the barriers to interstate banking were being dismantled. Since federal permission was required this provided an opportunity to examine lending records and impose some sort of community restitution where past lending patterns were found wanting.

---

10. "Community" is a loaded word in the literature on the American city, implying some organization rooted in poorer parts of the city. Middle-class suburbanites, in contrast, have "resident," "neighborhood" or "home owner" rather than "community" organizations.

11. In other words, lending institutions should not be required to offset their losses in lending in some parts of the city by higher mortgage rates elsewhere. This is an ironic confirmation of a broader tendency, given the way in which the flat rate pricing practices of utilities entail a subsidy from the denser, older parts of a city to the less dense outer areas where costs of service are necessarily elevated.

A final case of something approximating a class politics of local economic development is more difficult to classify. These are the initiatives
of the various urban-centered organizations around the country that
emerged in the 1990s, funded by labor and foundations, with an agenda
focusing on local labor and development issues. Some of them contained
"new economy" in their titles as in the Los Angeles Alliance for a New
Economy (LAANE) and the Connecticut Center for a New Economy
(CCNE), and very loosely one might say that, to a degree, they were
responding to problems thrown up by a period of rapid economic transformation: in particular the emergence of a bipolar income distribution,
a related growth of low-paying service jobs, the erosion of the minimum
wage and a continued decline of union membership.[12] They continue to
exist and have an agenda that includes a living wage and resisting the erosion of national labor law that makes unionization so much more difficult
than it was. The contracting out of city services is also a target of opposition, since it typically means consigning their provision to low-wage, non-
unionized firms.

These initiatives have been distinguished therefore by strong antagonism to what Stone (1987) has called corporate development policies, and
a desire to shift them to the opposite, more progressive, pole. They have
sponsored studies of the "trickle-down" effects of state-subsidized development and the effects, beneficial or otherwise, of devices like tax increment
finance districts. They have also pressed local governments to use the
leverage they enjoy through their discretionary power over tax abatements
and land use permits to extract concessions on the employment of locals,
the provision of new parks, youth centers, and even day care centers; in
other words, what was referred to in chapter 4 as "linkage."[13]

12. Others included the East Bay Alliance for a Sustainable Economy (Oakland
area), the Center on Policy Initiatives (San Diego), and the Neighborhood Capital Budget
Group (Chicago).

13. This is not exhaustive. In New Haven, Yale University has been a particular
target of the CCNE. It is, after all, a huge employer in the local economy with implications for the circulation of value through it, and also, through its hospital, a major service
provider. But the fact that it is subsidized as a result of its tax-exempt status was regarded

Stratum Struggles

In the late 1960s and into the 1970s, there was something of a furor in the media and then in policy circles around what was termed "exclusionary zoning." It was certainly "zoning" and it was certainly "exclusionary." What was exciting attention was the emphasis in many independent suburbs on zoning for single-family housing rather than rental; and on zoning for low-density housing—perhaps a maximum of four houses per acre, or even in some cases, one. The argument was that these zoning designations were being used as a social filter: renters, it was claimed, were being excluded because they typically earned less money and dragged an area down, both materially and symbolically, and their per capita contribution to the property tax base was lower than that for the single family house. On the other hand, some home owners were better off than others, and on the scale of desirability as neighbors by those doing the ranking, preferable. Density restrictions would mean that the land price component of the house increased, and that kept out the less worthy, the ones whose children, by virtue of their trifling contribution to the tax base, would have to be subsidized in the local schools by other home owners. It was not just the independent suburbs that were exclusionary; even in the central city, home owners in wealthier neighborhoods might try to gain property value advantages by making sure that the vacant land next door kept its zoning as single-family. But in the independent suburbs there were the additional capacities to fence off the school district and prevent dilution of the tax base. In fact, of course, the zoning tool was just one of several drawn on with exclusionary intent. It was rare indeed for an independent suburb to agree to a public housing project; and building code requirements, house setback provisions, and other subdivision rules could add cost to a house and keep it out of the hands of "them."

---

as a major reason why New Haven schools were not funded as well as they might be. The Yale–New Haven Hospital was also a target as a result of its practice of treating charity patients as "bad debtors" and pursuing payment through the garnishing of wages and placing liens on property.

It was not journalists or academics rummaging through zoning maps and doing some investigative reporting into the conniving schemes of suburban planners who first drew attention to this. In fact, in its original intent, much of the restrictive zoning had not been exclusionary in the current sense, but a legacy of the historical reliance on well water and septic tanks: health concerns led to state legislation of high minimum densities, and these earlier rules were grandfathered into later zoning plans. Instead, it was the publicity given to the sporadic rezoning fight that attracted public interest: the attempt of suburban home owners to maintain the earlier low density zoning in the face of developer attempts to get the land rezoned. Suburbia became the land par excellence of the resident or neighborhood organization, packed with home owners and parents, and paranoid about preserving their privileges. And given those privileges, it was inevitable that developers would spot the money to be made by rezoning to a higher density and selling to the masses.

Exclusionary zoning was represented largely in terms of its distributional implications for the less well off, though these were always defined in relative terms. Just about every independent suburb was and remains exclusionary to some degree; it is just that, as per the struggle for positions in the geographic division of consumption referred to in chapter 3, some are more exclusionary than others. The tone was a moralizing one: the nasty things some people did to others and typically subsequent to a rejection for downzoning by a developer: part of the developer's case would be that "he was trying to provide housing for the less well off." Meanwhile, the hay that property capitals could nevertheless make out of it and were in the habit of doing so was left out of the picture.

More recently, media and academic attention has turned to a different set of conflicts: those associated with gentrification. Here again the issue is one of exclusion of those who cannot afford to pay, though in this case the chagrin is intensified because they are being excluded by displacement, and perhaps from a neighborhood which provided them with relatively low rents and within easy reach—perhaps walking distance—of work downtown. Once again, as in the suburbs, there have been fights, particularly where large swathes of housing have been rehabbed by a single owner so that the impact has been shared by many. How to frustrate what is happening then becomes important. One can anticipate opposition to the sorts of city "improvements" that are part of the property owner's scheme, like the rezoning that would allow a small neighborhood shopping center; or simply symbolic acts of youth peeing on the newcomers' doorsteps (Cybriwsky 1978); or there again, vandalizing the trees planted by the city to prettify the neighborhood. Meanwhile the newcomers organize in order to promote the further gentrification of the neighborhood and speed the original residents on their way.

The social power of money is once more to the fore though often fortified by changes in zoning.[14] Gentrification has placed central city governments in something of a dilemma, but one resolved, again, by the seductions of money. So while they have historically been antagonistic to the zoning practices of the independent suburbs, seemingly siding with the frustrated ambitions of those residents who are less well-off, they have been perfectly at ease with and even encouraged gentrification. For from their standpoint it makes perfect sense to see their poor moving into the (usually older) suburbs and being replaced by those who would be able to invest in their property and so enhance the property tax base: a solution of sorts to their fiscal problems.

Analytically, what strikes one about these representations of development politics in cities—and I use the term "representation" deliberately—is the way in which the landlords, the developers, and the growth coalitions play such an oddly passive role. Markets certainly enter into the common understandings, but it is the demands and politically inflected strategies of the better-off consumers that predominate and to which property capitals

14. Particularly in the older cities of the Northeast and Midwest, it was not uncommon for areas zoned for rental to be largely inhabited by resident home owners. Land use zoning assumes a hierarchy of land uses: in areas zoned as single-family, that is all that is permissible; but in areas zoned for rental, single-family homes can be built. Just why they were zoned for rental while most of the houses built were single-family is unclear, although it may have been a sort of insurance against a downturn in family fortunes; if incomes faltered then one could always rent out the house or subdivide it. But gentrification often occurs in exactly those areas, and to make sure that the process is fortified, resident organizations commonly ask for a blanket rezoning to single-family.

seemingly and meekly adapt by building according to the zoning prescriptions of the independent suburbs; or, alternatively, they discover a new market in gentrifying areas, purchasing speculatively and rehabilitating, perhaps even holding for rent, but simply reinforcing market forces already in play. It is, in short, an understanding that sidelines the role of property development interests and it turns out to be not so much entirely wrong as incomplete.

One can certainly accept the fact of these sorts of divisions within the working class,[15] but they need to be set in the context of the particular pressures and incentives that come from living in a society where capitalism dictates the way of life. This is a life full of uncertainty, both material and having to do with identity and social recognition. Housing markets and investments in home ownership factor into this. Where one can afford to live is widely understood as an expression of success or failure. Buying a house in some areas provides more secure and, even better, returns to investment than buying elsewhere. On top of that the vicissitudes of job markets—the different opportunities that they present and the significance of formal educational qualifications—has made parents extremely sensitive to schools and to the need to gain access to the "better" school districts. Clearly the projects of the developers—where they build housing and the sorts of housing that they build—are far from irrelevant to mitigating these insecurities, and they have been happy to help in alleviating them, or, alternatively, and as circumstances demand, heightening them.

What might seem somewhat irrelevant to the developers is the quite massive gulf observable in the living conditions, housing, and neighborhoods of rich and poor in the United States. An often overlooked factor in all this though is the lopsided, even perverse, nature of housing

15. Although the idea of "working class" here is blurred at its upper margins. In referring to the working class, I mean all those who are employed for a wage or salary. The problem is, of course, that as one moves up the ladder defined by wages and salaries, so household revenues tend to get more diversified and, most importantly, include elements that are claims on profits and rents, as in the ownership of stocks and bonds. There are also the self-employed, including doctors, dentists, and lawyers, who can be very wealthy indeed.

subsidies. A little-known fact about housing in the United States is that the wealthy take the lion's share of the subsidies; what public housing and programs like housing vouchers for the poor get is, by comparison, miniscule.[16] What gives the wealthy the advantage is the federal tax deduction for mortgage interest: you buy a house and deduct the interest on your mortgage payments before calculating that adjusted gross income, which is what the tax rate is applied to. This is a subsidy that goes overwhelmingly to the wealthy, in part because they are more likely to be aware of and to make the deduction; but also because they buy big houses with correspondingly bigger mortgages. So the higher the price of the house, the bigger the subsidy; and for those at the upper end of the progressive income tax scale, that interest deduction can put you in a lower tax bracket as well. Nice work if you can get it! But bottom line, there is an incentive to buying bigger houses on bigger lots; long live the low-density suburb. Yet, and interestingly, anxieties about federal budget balance periodically crop up and, as attention turns to eliminating the tax subsidy, the first in line to defend it is the onetime NAREB (now the National Association of Realtors), the National Association of Home Builders, and the Mortgage Bankers' Association. And why not? They are in the business of selling bigger homes and making money from heftier mortgages.[17]

This is one condition for the exclusive American suburb and for the possibilities of siphoning some of that spending power off in terms of rent, but not the only condition. The form of the American state is the other. The sort of geographic separation that the struggle for distributional advantage has encouraged and which has been a major source of what Harvey (1974) has called "class monopoly rents" ultimately depends on the highly decentralized form of the American state: not just the right of local governments to control land use virtually untrammeled by state oversight, but also the power to provide for schooling, to fund that schooling, and

16. By one estimate the amount spent on tax subsidies in the form of the mortgage interest deduction for home owners exceeds the amount spent on affordable housing, the vast majority of which goes to means tested programs, by a margin of over four. See Florida (2015).

17. See Ulam (2014) and Liberto (2012).

then to establish new local governments to do the same further out from the urban edge. This has created the conditions for ever more exclusive suburbs and hence the possibilities for corralling the rents of the wealthy, and not just through the school districts they offer. The ability to form new municipalities means that you can exclude the children by law, eliminate the need for schools, and so allow the subsequent (low) taxes to be capitalized into rents, as indeed has happened in places like Sun City West next to Phoenix, Arizona. But again, only the wealthy need apply.[18]

The Politics of Difference

Material privilege is clearly spread very unevenly across the city. It is not just, to express it in rather antiseptic terms, a matter of the spatial division of consumption, since this marginalizes the disruption in housing and neighborhood to which poorer people are typically most subject. A location toward the center of the city was always going to mean that the poor would be more affected by the construction of downtown-focused freeways, the subsequent air pollution, and the urban renewal that NAREB pushed for so vigorously. In addition, they have been the ones on the thin end of the wedge of the scorched earth policy: the endless expansion at the periphery, battening on the increasing revenues of the salariat and the stock and bond holders, and stoked by waves of development around new sorts of, usually bigger, housing and new riffs on the garden suburb; but leaving an oversupply of housing toward the center. These are the older, now socially obsolete units, which apart from those attractive to the gentrifiers, get devalued, their neighborhoods redlined, then purchased by

18. As the publicity material for this development boasts: "Sun City West is unincorporated and Maricopa County maintains the streets, provides police protection and other services. The cost of these is a part of the property tax paid by each home owner. Local school taxes can often be a major part of property taxes but most of Sun City West was removed years ago from the surrounding school district. As a result, a typical property tax on a $150,000 home is less than $575 annually" (http://www.suncitywest.org /index.php?page=feestaxes.inc&greeting=Fees%20%7Band%7D%20Taxes, accessed May 5, 2016).

small landlords[19] (who milk them of their value to the detriment of their tenants), and then abandoned.

Property companies, developers, and growth coalitions, particularly those in the suburbs, have clearly played an important role in this, supporting generously subsidized housing for the wealthy while opposing that for the poor, and pursuing class monopoly rents through the creation of ever more exclusive, ever more distinctive residential enclaves. But by virtue of the power of money, they have obviously been supported in this by the more well-to-do strata. They have been the big gainers, and the disparities in what Harvey (1973, chapter 2) called "real income" appropriately huge. The question is: How on earth do they justify their privileges of housing, neighborhood, and school district? And conversely, since their presence is hard to ignore, how do they justify the consignment of the less moneyed to areas that are so obviously less privileged and across so many different dimensions?

The answer has been through ideas of difference: a politics of difference, therefore, in which the privileged are privileged because they deserve to be and in contrast to the incorrigible losers at the bottom of the social order. The sense of privilege earned is a common refrain in letters to the editor; how "we worked for it" while, implicitly, others did not. The contrast is between those who did not put forth the effort and those who did, those who couldn't care less about their children and those who do, the work shy and the diligent. These claims are sometimes embellished by resort to ideas about the Other as innately wanting, whether by virtue of some deeply embedded cultural imprint as a cracker or a hillbilly, or racially as a black or a Hispanic or—equally racially—as "white trash." All the arguments about difference and how life chances are determined by attributes of personal character in which others are wanting is, of course, sheer fantasy. Inherited wealth is of central importance in putting people, literally, where they are, not to mention the benefits from being brought up in a household plugged more substantially into the circulation of value.

---

19. Using properties owned free and clear elsewhere as their collateral in order to obviate the redlining restriction and taking advantage of the low prices that existing home owners are willing to accept given the way that redlining affects them.

The big losers from this have been the African Americans, typically concentrated and to a disproportional degree in the older housing of the central city. African Americans have historically been defined by the majority as in various ways lacking, inferior, and undesirable, in turn justifying a self-serving discrimination: discrimination in the workplace, particularly by labor unions (Frymer 2004), as well as in the housing market, even while low incomes made it hard to move out of the ghetto anyway. Historically, the state legitimated this notion of irreducible difference and the federal government was central to what happened. This was more than a matter of neglect; failing to consolidate the gains of the Civil War against Southern intransigence and then to intervene in their Jim Crow institutions; or, indeed, a more enduring refusal to regulate the more informal practices of realtors and school boards. Rather, there is a record of discrimination in federal practice and legislation itself. FHA mortgage insurance, introduced in 1934, was a bonanza for property developers, which is why NAREB was so keen to bring it about for the new armies of white home owners who could then benefit from generous federal tax subsidies—but not for African Americans. Restrictive covenants tended to bar them from the newer housing of the suburbs.[20] FHA underwriting rules, put together by our friends at NAREB, favored newer over older housing, which then made it hard for African Americans to buy even what had hitherto been rental property in the central city. There was also explicit underwriter bias against mortgage insurance for African Americans.

There was always resistance to the identity that whites foisted on them and to institutional exclusion. But as Piven and Cloward (1971) have shown, it was the massive urbanization of African Americans that would be a crucial condition for bringing about change.[21] The results of the civil rights revolution and the formal dismantling of discrimination in housing,

20. Levittown, the posterchild for the mass-produced suburb, was a notorious instance.

21. The civil rights movement was something to which the Democratic administrations of the 1960s responded with alacrity, but increasingly for quite transparent reasons of electoral advantage: countering the Republican takeover of the Deep South subsequent to the concessions that were being made.

employment, and education have been varied. On the one hand, a much larger African American middle class has taken shape. The suburbs have become more racially mixed. It has, however, left a large mass of poor African Americans in inner cities, with deteriorating job prospects as manufacturing jobs contract, leaving a very large proportion dependent on state assistance: what has become known as the black underclass. This and high levels of crime have kept the politics of difference alive, so that the contrast now drawn is between a largely white population that flatters itself on its relative independence and success and a black population defined as state-dependent failures (though in an interesting twist, some conservatives argue that state intervention came first and failure second).

All this has had important implications for property firms and their projects going back at least to the 1940s. The assumption of African Americans as undeserving, as an unwelcome presence combined with political impotence, made them a line of least resistance for the urban renewers and the highway builders. In subsequent criticism, urban renewal acquired the sobriquet "Negro removal" and the association between areas of African American settlement and compulsory purchase and demolition was certainly a striking one. This would eventually help stoke the fires of African American resistance, adding to the grievances that led to the riots of the 1960s (see Duhl and Steetle 1968 for an example).

Strong tendencies to racial segregation on the part of whites in both housing and schools created different sorts of windfall for the housing developers, and long after the civil rights revolution. A rash of so-called "neighborhood change" studies during the late 1960s and 1970s[22] documented the flight of whites as the black ghetto expanded. In many cities, busing for racial balance, which was almost entirely confined to central city school districts, created a bonanza for suburban developers in the late 1970s and early 1980s, lending further impetus to the island-like structures that Harvey (1974) had identified earlier as the source of class monopoly rents.

---

22. Some examples among many include Wolf and Lebeaux (1969, chapter 3); Molotch (1973); Ginsberg (1975); and Leven et al. (1976).

More recently still African Americans have been sucked into some of the standard growth coalition logics. In numerous major metropolitan areas,[23] white flight has resulted in a central city with a black majority, but the result has been disappointing from the standpoint of any resistance to further impositions on the part of property capital. Structural limits to financing local government have encouraged an absorption into dominant practices of competition for inward investment and the honing of the local business climate.[24] Meanwhile, central cities, still home to most African Americans trapped historically by discriminatory structures in both living and work place, have been revalorized via redevelopment and gentrification, including around universities and hospitals, with consequences that recall a history of displacement in the wake of the hunt for new sources of rent.[25]

If there are winners aside from the developers and others pursuing rent in its various guises—and even if "winning" is sometimes relative to the broad mass of the working class—they are the largely white, higher income salariat: the so-called "technical and managerial" class, the professionals in both public and private employment along with a sizeable group of wealthy retirees fueled by generous pension plans and their stock holdings. For them, issues of business climate, right-to-work, and workers' compensation are largely irrelevant, except from a narrow ideological standpoint of sticking it to those whom they believe to be only worthy of contempt. They live in the more exclusive suburbs in tree-shaded neighborhoods in large

23. Including Atlanta, Baltimore, Cleveland, Detroit, Memphis, Newark, New Orleans, and St Louis. In other cases where African Americans have had a significant presence but not a majority, African American politicians of an accommodationist bent have been favorites of parties anxious to guarantee success in a mayoral election.

24. On the Detroit case, see Hill (1983); and on Oakland, Self (2003).

25. Emphatically, though, racial divisions as not something that capital necessarily fosters, but it will take advantage of these divisions when and where they emerge (Meiksins Wood 1988). In this instance, the reproduction of the American politics of difference owes much more to the efforts of the white working class than those of capital: a sorry history that connects with class struggle in only highly mediated ways.

houses on big lots and, for those with children at least, in the prized school districts. Meanwhile increasing numbers of retirees live in elaborate care homes where the admission fee can be in the tens of thousands of dollars and the rent quite staggering, or in so-called "senior living" communities. To some degree the exclusive suburb is often the product of an alliance between developers and residents, in the sense that it is the residents, the houses they live in, their winding tree-lined streets with the occasional view across a lake, that give an area its cachet. And if there should be a challenge of some sort, they are moderately well equipped through their lawyers and connections to deal with it. Meanwhile, at the other end of the social spectrum, it is the poor who bear the brunt of plant closures, the war on unionization, demolition, and gentrification; so no prizes for guessing that this is where class responses are most likely. And in between the effects are more mixed.

Territorialization and the Politics of Development

Regardless of the complexity of the cleavages and their role as representations of development politics and as framings of concrete issues, what is striking, and what is so crucial to how the property sector and its logics get reproduced, is their territorial aspect. When describing the social cleavages that emerge, whether in class, stratum or racial terms, territory, the defense of turf, the pursuit of local advantage is never, it would appear far away. So often, it seems, the politics of development tends to get played out as a series of battles about particular places and the policies to be adopted in their defense: a litany of fights around encroachments on residential neighborhoods; fights led by those who, through the labels they adopt—"The Clintonville Residents' Association" or "Cahoga Heights United Neighbors" or the seemingly de rigueur, even aggressive, acronym, as in WHAM (Worthington Heights Against Malls) or STAMP (Save Our Town Against Mad Planners)—announce their parochial goals.

Even where one might expect class to be the more obvious experience, conflict and its representation seem nevertheless to get absorbed into territorialized logics. Through organizing the hotel, casino, and resort workers in Las Vegas, the Culinary Workers Union was able to make more than trivial gains in wages and conditions of work. But as a local initiative, in defense of the gains made, the union provided support for the casino industry in its competitive struggles with casino interests elsewhere in the United States. In the same way, achievement of African American majorities in local governments, including those in sizeable cities like Oakland (Self 2003), seemed to promise a new local welfare state. But the victory has been deceptive as the suburbanization that emptied central cities of their white residents also took with it much of the city's employment base and, in consequence, its taxable wealth. How to replace it has been a major issue, and the solution embraced has been to join in the competition for inward investment.

In other words, it seems that more often than not territory trumps class. In part the territorial imaginary appears to emerge spontaneously, and it certainly has a logic that, in its own terms, is defensible. Residents organize because they believe that there is some threat to the neighborhood, to their living conditions, home values, and schools. This threat is a result of some private development project, often a rezoning request, or some change in the local public infrastructure designed to facilitate that development: a new highway or an expanded airport. In the same way, unionized workers will organize against a plant closure or, as in the case of Las Vegas, join with the hotel industry in marketing the city and its casinos. In all these instances, people are working to ensure that value continues to flow through their neighborhoods, places of work, or cities because they are somehow trapped there, at least over the short to medium term, and therefore dependent on that flow. Home owners with children in local schools, workers with their family ties and reliance on local labor markets, and perhaps housing markets for their homes are in an important sense dependent on local fortunes.

In part, though, the territorialization of local development and its politics is less a result of some independent citizen or worker initiative and more a construction by the property sector. Again, one can understand the way in which their interests too are dependent on what ensues in particular localities or cities and regions. The ultimate goal is the appropriation of rent, but that means attracting investment into a particular area, shooing off other development projects that might threaten that appropriation, as in the Columbus casino case, or mitigating the damage they might cause as with Love Field and the DFW. And again this is because of *their* local dependence. Fixity is a central constraint on their modi operandi, whether it is the fixity of property and its improvements or some (local) network of relations and understandings with others who are vital to achieving that appropriation. Developers, as we saw earlier, typically have a broad set of connections to local lenders and construction companies, as well as a knowledge of local market conditions built up over a long period of time: a serious opportunity cost to be weighed when considering abandoning a particular market in favor of a new one elsewhere. The utilities that are so crucial in the inward investment process have historically had their own fixities in the form of highly limited service areas, investments of long life embedded in the ground, and, therefore, stakes in facilitating new industrial investments. A territorialized view of their business, it would seem, is genetically encoded.

There is also a discursive aspect to this. Property capitals, through their projects, incite resistance. Some of it is quite clearly of a class sort, and that is not what the developers and the growth coalitions want. Class, or any cross-local or regional solidarity for that matter, is more dangerous and difficult to deal with than people relying on their resident associations or union locals in single, one-off fights. This is because it introduces the threat of state or federal legislation that would narrow opportunities (rather than open them up), bogging them down in rules and regulations and so increasing the time for getting everything in order—permits, financing, architectural design, environmental clearance, public infrastructure—before a project can begin. The challenge of some solidarity among those who stand to be affected at some time, just not altogether at the same time, can also emerge within particular municipalities: proposals to make it easier to get referenda on development issues on the ballot or—heaven forbid—a city ordinance that would delegate decisions on rezoning issues to the neighborhood level.

Developers and their rent-seeking allies like the utilities do not want this, nor do they want any other sort of challenge to their bottom lines like impact fees or an impediment to their operations, such as (for the industrial prospecting of the utilities) an increase in workers' compensation rates. So sometimes workers and residents have to be "educated." Territory is the ground on which property capitals prefer to fight. They need allies, coalitions with the masses, particularly when legislation is at stake or a referendum on some development issue is in the offing. They can usually rely on the support of the media and local government, but democracy still counts for something. The trick is to play one area off against another, holding out the possibility of jobs, housing, or tax base lost to others elsewhere if they should not prevail. The NIMBY stigma is emblematic: a small, selfish group protecting their turf at the expense of a wider, deserving public. Developers, keen to get the permissions necessary for a new shopping center but faced with opposition from local residents whose neighborhood abuts the site, will point to the tax revenues, inevitably exaggerated, likely accruing to a larger local school district should permission be granted. Imposing impact fees on shopping centers becomes a "bad" idea, forcing developers to look elsewhere and so deprive "us" of an addition to "our" tax base. Other places have experienced decline, they observe, and a major reason for that is that they allowed labor unions to get too powerful; a warning for "all of us" who live here in Ohio or wherever, they will point out (Cox and Mair 1988, 318–19).

So what might seem to be issues of class—ones dividing business from people either in the workplace or living place—get conjured into ones of territory. Struggles around workers' compensation get transformed into struggles between states for inward investment. Struggles between residents and developers suffer a similar fate: impact fees, it is claimed, will simply drive the investment elsewhere along with all the juicy jobs and tax revenues that would otherwise ensue. Bond referenda to fund new schools can be highly controversial and, if rejected, can put new residential development in question. Those without children in local schools will be the first to ask questions. This is the moment at which realty interests[26] move in to flatter the voter, making it a matter not of a subsidy to developers

---

26. Not necessarily the developer but perhaps realtors who have taken the trouble to cultivate a particular suburb and participate in local community activities, and so have some name recognition, and who see additional housing in the area as working to their advantage.

who fail to pick up the costs they are imposing on the school district but of "support for education by a district noted for that support," albeit suitably seasoned with reference to how improving the local schools will boost the home values of all, regardless of whether they have children in them. In other words, the dominant tendency for the property companies and the growth coalitions, driven by their own place-dependence and the need to deflect opposition, is toward a discourse of a highly territorialized nature.

What it is about, of course, when it is not a matter of flattering people on the quality of the local schools, is "local and regional development," with the implication that this is something from which all will gain if they are in a particular "region" or "locality," regardless of what can otherwise divide a population, like class, status, or even race. To use the standard metaphor it promises to "raise all boats." But different regions and localities want the same things, and it is assumed that these are in short supply. Accordingly, so the common argument goes, "places" must "compete" with each other. Territorial competition becomes a leitmotif of the local and regional development discourse, as indeed does the exploitation of one place by another—an extraordinary claim if one stops and thinks about it. But it follows on from the idea of places competing with one another. Competition is not necessarily "fair." Places exploit each other through the interregional redistributions that are at least implicit in government spending, as in the claims about federal favoritism toward Sun Belt states. State-wide legislation that is indifferent to local variations, like a minimum wage law, can have the same effect. This in turn creates an uneven geography of competitive advantage so that "the playing field has to be leveled."

These claims are endlessly communicated through the public statements of politicians and through the media. In newspapers, it may be in the form of the synthetic, more abstract statements of the editorial and op-ed pages. The reports on individual rezonings, city council hearings on infrastructural initiatives, and on pending state legislation are replete with references to implications for "development" or "business climate" and "creating a city we can be proud of."

A product of this discourse that is of special interest and which feeds back to further fan the flames is the creation of a set of imaginary geographies that then circulate through the pages of the newspapers and news magazines. These may include maps of performance showing how "our" state is doing relative to others—always compared to the "competitors"—in population growth, a typical sort of news commentary when census or interim-census counts are announced. A particularly insidious form of this is the publication in local newspapers of tables ranking school districts in terms of how the children have done in statewide proficiency tests; not necessarily good for all developers, but if class monopoly rent in the suburbs is your target, manna sent from heaven. There are also geographies, perhaps mapped and perhaps not, which deal in a simplified world of oppositions: Cold Belt / Sun Belt, the "other" Ohio,[27] central city / suburbs, and also inner suburbs / outer suburbs.

Central to the creation of many of these imaginative geographies are the various agencies representing the development interests of particular states, but also the consultants who thrive on the intense desire of local governments and growth coalitions to "develop." In some cases, states or the growth interests located in them have come together in order to push agendas that are more regional in character, sponsoring "research" organizations to provide them with the necessary lobbying ammunition: organizations like the Northeast-Midwest Institute, which is sponsored by the Northeast-Midwest Congressional Coalition, a bipartisan group that, as discussed in chapter 1, lobbies for the so-called Cold Belt states; or something like the Center for the New West, which has a strong conservative edge. There are also the consultants and they can be extraordinarily influential. The person whose name springs readily to mind is Richard Florida and his thesis of "the creative class" as a tool in local development. There are numerous others, though, including Joel Kotkin, a strong advocate of traditional suburban development, and Myron Orfield, who has helped inscribe the inner/outer suburb opposition in the consciousness of development interests in many an older suburb in the country.

From a class standpoint, this is a conception of the world that is utterly upside down, which, of course, is partly the point. It is one in which class

---

27. The Other Ohio was a grouping of the larger cities, including Dayton and Toledo, that argued for a more even geographic distribution of state employment as opposed to the monopoly excised by Columbus, the capital city.

differences and antagonisms are erased as employers and workers come together to march behind the banner of jobs for "our" city or region. Capital does not exploit labor; rather it is places that exploit one another—suburbs that exploit central cities, major metropolitan areas which, through the state taxation apparatus and its redistributions, suck off the rest of the state; or outer suburbs that grow courtesy of an uneven playing field and at the expense of the older suburbs closer to the urban core. This is not to argue that territorialization cannot be contested on its own terms, that there are not different forms that can work better for the broad mass of the population. There can be territorializations for the people, as well as for property capital. The siren song of the local realtors about "pride in our local schools" when pushing for a bond levy to expand the school accommodations necessitated by new, large-scale residential developments does not have to seduce. Nor did the diagnosis of local growth coalitions when unemployment started to affect local economies in the emergent Rust Belt in the 1970s. Union resistance to the medicine of burnishing local business climates through the introduction of right-to-work laws and "reformed" workers' compensation lent impetus to the very different approach of arguing with the federal government for a redistribution of federal spending that would work to their advantage, rather than that of the burgeoning West and South.

But the susceptibility of the masses to a territorializing argument, even when it is conceived defensively, betrays more than a dependence on local job and housing markets or on maintaining home values in particular neighborhoods. There *are* alternative forms of understanding, as we have seen, that might help people resist the extreme territorialization of reactions. So exactly *why* are people so susceptible?

The efflorescence of a turf politics centering on the defensive tactics of resident organizations seems to have been a postwar phenomenon (Cox 1984, 289–92) and there are ways in which that might be understood. Zoning raised expectations about neighborhood futures that were bound to be challenged. Home ownership increased remarkably after the 1930s, stimulated by the availability of longer mortgages with lower deposits and interest rates that resulted from the introduction of federal mortgage insurance in 1934. This is important because home ownership gives people a stake in the future of "their" neighborhood, partly through a concern for preserving the value of the house, and partly through the obstacles to moving imposed by the transaction costs of involvement in buying and selling houses (Cox 1985). I would suggest, though, that home ownership is part of something much bigger—a privatization of households around consumption that Habermas termed family-vocational privatism: "a family orientation with developed interests in consumption and leisure on the one hand, and in a career orientation suitable to status competition on the other. This privatism thus corresponds to the structures of educational and occupational systems that are regulated by competition through achievement" (1973, 75). This in turn was linked by Habermas to what he called "civil privatism"—high output orientation and low input" and the experience of packed rezoning hearings with a few giving vent to neighborhood fury certainly rings a bell; spasmodic awakenings separated by lengthy periods of metaphoric slumber.

The time at which Habermas was writing is significant. It was subsequent to a period of ten years or more in which a major theme in community studies, in the United States, France, and particularly in Great Britain, had been exactly the privatism of which he spoke, and also in the wake of the disintegration of social formations that had been the basis of strong radical identities. Very similar themes were in play, whether it was John Alt (1976) writing about "the passage in the US from the primacy of labor in daily life under competitive capitalism to that of consumerism under 'monopoly capitalism'"; or Rosser and Harris (1965) on the transition from what they called the coherent to the mobile society in South Wales; or the work of Young and Willmott (1957) on the implications of the move from a kin-focused Bethnal Green to a more anonymous suburban environment; or that of Henri Coing (1966) on housing clearance and urban renewal in Paris. Face-to-face communities united in and across both living place and workplace, and often kin- or ethnically mediated, were giving way to more atomized forms of social life, typically in some lower-density suburb of single-family houses: a world of slimmed-down, nuclear families, protective of their children and their education against meddling grandparents and focused on "getting on" in life, acquiring the new status symbols of a car, an address in the "right" neighborhood, and the appliances to go with it. Some hinted at its political implications. In the United States, political sociologists wondered if suburbanization meant an unshakeable Republican majority. In Great Britain, the question became in the light of this changing geography *Must Labor Lose?* (Abrams, Rose, and Hiden 1960). Neighborhood as community seemed to be giving way to neighborhood as commodity: something organic was being replaced by something more provisional, to be exchanged for something else as circumstances determined, but until that time arrived, to be defended as a bundle of valued and quantifiable assets (Cox 1981).[28]

The nature of the ties to neighborhood seemed to have changed and, with it, people's politics, which became more conservative in both the broader sense of the word and in the narrower one as the "great moving right show" got under way, and on both sides of the Atlantic, even starting from different positions. My hypothesis is that this has been a significant condition for a territorialization of the politics of development, both in the workplace and in the living place. This in turn has endowed property capitals, the utilities, and the growth coalitions in which they often participate with formidable powers when confronting the opposition. It is not determinant since it is often a case of one set of territorial interests against another. Just why they nevertheless tend to prevail is the final question to which we turn in this chapter.

Getting Your Way in Practice

To the extent that workers or residents draw on territorialized conceptions of their dilemmas, the question becomes one of resolving a conflict between *their* territorial dependences and claims and those of the property companies, developers, and their allies. This usually turns out to be an unequal fight. The bargaining process is one in which, inevitably, the latter hold key advantages. The disparity in resources is huge. Overcoming roadblocks is something in which developers and local economic

---

28. Tiebout's (1956) image of people "voting with their feet" and Wingo's (1973) later idea of people forming and reforming clubs is part of the same framework of understanding, but without the historical context.

development professionals have acquired a wealth of experience. They have fashioned the connections, they know the sorts of challenges they will get from resident and other protest organizations, and they have learnt how to deal with them. They know which buttons to press and which to avoid. They often have massive financial resources that they can draw on in hiring the right public relations people, zoning lawyers, even civil engineers and planning consultants.

There is also the strategic way in which they make their demands. The golden rule appears to be to ask for too much, on the assumption that one can then "retreat" to the position actually desired and so give the opposition a (false) sense of victory—the so-called "win-win" solutions that get such publicity in the United States. Meanwhile neighborhood groups face relatively rare situations that they are ill-equipped to confront, in part because they have limited if any experience to draw on. They also lack the financial resources, unless they receive help from some other developer who, for competitive reasons, wants to see this particular project fail. The neighborhoods of the more affluent are likely to be a good deal better off. They may have organizations to which residents contribute in order to finance common services like the maintenance of a pond or snow ploughing, and many retain a lawyer. If they are on the development frontier then they can probably rely on the challenge coming from developers of similar housing, who see their presence as providing a condition for their own class monopoly rents: a case of fortifying Harvey's (1974) island structure. The vast majority of people living in more modest neighborhoods, though, are very, very vulnerable indeed.

Nevertheless, there are what seem to be victories, and quite aside from developer "concessions" of a strategic nature. The assault of big-box stores is repelled (Mitchell 2006). Proposals for new residential development are rejected through referendum.[29] Unions manage to organize workplaces in the South or resist demands for a right-to-work law. Increases in local sales taxes to fund a new convention center get rejected. And living wage

---

29. In practice this is much more feasible in a smaller suburb where the number of names required to petition for a referendum is reduced in proportion to its population.

ordinances are passed. Sometimes the victories are deceptive. Developers may yield on the question of impact cr linkage fees because they know that in the circumstances of a particular urban housing market they can pass them on to the buyer or tenant. Developers will complain about impact fees but they are much more likely to dig in their heels where housing markets are relatively slack. In areas with tighter markets, like Massachusetts, New Jersey, or Southern California and the Bay Area, these costs can be passed on to the buyer with relative ease. San Francisco is the example usually given when talking about linkage policies and the ability to extract affordable housing, or money in lieu of it, from the developers of high-rise office buildings. But the point is, demand for office space in San Francisco, and prestigious space at that, is not likely to go away soon. Tenants are willing to pay a premium, and if that premium has to include something extra demanded by the city, so be it. In Indianapolis or even St. Louis, it would not be that easy; and that also helps to explain why organizations like LAANE in Los Angeles or CCNE in Connecticut are doing what they do there and not in those other two cities.

In other cases, though, local citizens' groups can do serious damage, sometimes by using strategies that ape those of their antagonists. Del Webb or Target have been through it all before and have accumulated a massive amount of experience that they can draw on as well as retaining savvy lawyers. The trick for a local citizens' group is to tie in with a national organization that can draw on an analogous pool of information, legal know-how, and experience. A not uncommon pattern where there is even a sniff of an environmental issue—ecological diversity, air pollution implications—is to involve the local chapter of the Sierra Club or Audubon Society, which may be able to provide advice, both legal and otherwise, and clarify how a local issue can be constructed as "metropolitan" so as to build a broader coalition, while the group itself advocates for what is seen as something of environmental significance. And then, through a succession of legal interventions and requests, the groups manage to delay: developers hate delay since it costs.[30] This, of course, is the pattern

30. For an excellent case study of how this can work in practice see Smith, Guagnano, and Posehn (1989).

long followed by workers seeking to organize a plant, drawing on the help of a union local and the union's central office. A myriad of national organizations fulfill analogous functions in other local fights. Jobs with Justice has been a thorn in Walmart's side as it has tried to enter new markets, joining up with local activists and sharing its expertise.

And if there is no national organization, then some ongoing one at a citywide level can do the trick, particularly if it can take over local government. In Santa Cruz, California, local property interests had long sought a branch campus of the state university as a boost to the demand for real estate in the city; but when it arrived in 1965 it turned out to be a poisoned chalice (Gendron and Domhoff 2009). Allying with neighborhood groups, faculty and students[31] were able to defeat a succession of projects held dear by the local growth coalition: highway widenings, new housing projects, a convention center, and an expanded central business district were all stymied. From 1981 on, for an eight-year period the more progressive elements that had emerged subsequent to the creation of UC Santa Cruz then came to dominate the city council, adding to developer frustrations.[32]

Even so, property companies have a habit of learning from their defeats and adjusting their strategies. The Walmart case is instructive. Walmart is a lightning rod for a diversity of issues affecting lower paid working-class people because of its low wages, union busting, and lack of health care provision for most of its workers, as well as the way in which its massive imports from low-wage countries, particularly China, have lent further impetus to deindustrialization in the United States. As a result, it has been a target of more progressive forces, which have tried to frustrate its entry into new markets. Making common cause with existing owner-operated stores fearing the competition, drawing financial support from unionized

31. Significant for this is that for students, even only temporary residence allowed them the right to vote in local elections.

32. Santa Monica in the early 1980s is another interesting case. The Santa Monicans for Renter Rights numerically dominated the city council: a result of the fact that the city had a majority of renters. This allowed them to implement rent control as well as extracting concessions from developers. See Clavel (1986, chapter 5).

grocery chains, and fortified by a national organization "Making Change at Walmart," they have managed to orchestrate a number of successful campaigns to keep Walmart out. Despite the huge disparity in resources typically brought to bear and to their disadvantage, they have been able to prevail in rezoning disputes, and, where city council has passed an accommodating ordinance anyway, through local referenda.

Walmart, though, has learned and, throwing massive amounts of money into the campaign, has found ways to turn the tables. In California the opposition often drew strength from the California Environmental Quality Act of 1970. This required developers to submit a review of the environmental and traffic impacts of what they were proposing to local governments. Lawyers would then argue that Walmart had not gone far enough in its statement. Nevertheless Walmart has discovered a way out: if it sponsors a local ballot initiative and prevails there, then the law does not apply. And the same applies to other measures to keep big-box stores out, like limits on store floor space. Using a company specializing in putting together petitions (National Petition Management) the target is a relatively modest 15 percent of eligible voters requesting a referendum.[33] The problem is—and Walmart knows it—that such special elections are expensive, and cities would prefer to avoid them. So they cave in. Bingo.

There are, though, broader structural issues which mean that property capitals, in general and despite the occasional reverse, are going to prevail: rents will still get appropriated and at a rate of return that compares with other financial assets. They "Keep On, Keepin' On," and it is not the Woody Herman band doing a chart. There must be land for industry, commerce, housing, schools, and airports. To the extent that limits are imposed on land development via the local planning mechanism, then countervailing tendencies will come into play, the particular combination depending on circumstances; but somewhere and somehow rents will be appropriated.

33. "Relatively modest" in the smaller jurisdictions, that is. In a large city putting together the necessary number of signatures can be more difficult though just the threat of a referendum led San Diego to go back on a decision to limit big box stores.

In part, land development moves elsewhere. Some property capitals in some places may be discomfited, but others will gain. The owners of land that remains undeveloped as the suburban frontier advances are more than likely going to face opposition from the new residents as they seek the necessary permits and rezonings. But those who have bought up land just beyond the haphazard pattern of developed and undeveloped land on the urban periphery can expect to cash in. Employers resisting the incorporation of high housing prices into wage demands will, to the extent possible, decant the less skilled parts of their labor processes to less stressed housing markets elsewhere.

Rising real estate values encourage speculation, particularly in land that is zoned for the uses in short supply. Retention in the interest of a bigger payoff becomes the name of the game. High land costs then encourage more intensive forms of development so as to bring the land rent per square foot of commercial or residential space within the limits of what people are prepared to pay. But high land prices also encourage purchase of land that is over-zoned and in relative surplus—the land zoned for commercial and industrial uses that local government sees as a boon in its cost-revenue calculations. The trick then is to seek the rezoning that will make the value of the land soar overnight; a trick that invites corruption and for which the land use permitting process in the United States is notorious (for example, Kushner 2014).

7

Contesting the "Good Geography"

Introduction

In the capitalist societies of the West, the policy and practice of urban and regional development is inevitably marked by contradiction and social tension: questions of finding space for new physical infrastructure and paying for it, and of managing the unevenness of development at scales both metropolitan and interregional. But how these conflicts have been expressed, their apparent forms and the ways in which they have been represented, has been different between the United States and the countries of Western Europe.

In the United States it is the localness of conflict that impresses: how the politics of urban and regional development has seemingly been fought out as a series of isolated, one-off fights around plant closures, changes in the built environment, alterations in state labor law, gentrification, the construction of new shopping centers and the like. Some sort of trans-local coordination has by and large been lacking, though with some exceptions like anti-Walmart campaigns, the attempts of national unions to organize the South or in some states, the united pressures of the inner suburbs. Conditions defined by a highly fragmented state (notably fifty welfare states), high levels of jurisdictional fragmentation in metropolitan areas, and relatively weak senses of class interest have laid the foundation for interpretations of a highly territorialized sort: something that, as we saw in the previous chapter, has tended to play into the hands of those dominant agents of the American development agenda, the property companies and the growth coalitions.

The Western European case has been otherwise. The tensions are similar but are now filtered through a quite different institutional and social context: notably states that are far more centralized, and a stronger sense of class interest. The property companies, the developers, and their rent-seeking allies are far less significant as agents. Rather, central planning and the ideals of the welfare state, if now somewhat frayed, assume much greater significance: so questions of interregional equity or what is sometimes referred to as "solidarity," of employment, of a physical amenity accessible to all, have occupied the foreground—what I referred to earlier as the "good geography." It has been, moreover, a *national* foreground so that territorialized responses have been much less in evidence, at least in an explicit form. This framework has tended to weaken since the 1970s as a result of the neoliberal turn and the growth and institutional development of the European Union, but it still bears weight.

This chapter starts out with six vignettes designed to provide windows through which to view the distinctive character of the Western European politics. These examples are followed by a more abstracted discussion of the major forms of conflict in Western Europe and their distinct forms of representation. A final section then explores the way in which changes have occurred over the last forty years, raising the question of whether the Western European politics of local and regional development is becoming more similar to that of its trans-Atlantic cousin.

Six Vignettes

1. The Politics of Plant Closures: General Motors Europe for Sale

General Motors, the producer of cars and their components, has long had a major presence in Western Europe (see Figure 8). But in 2009, in the wake of the global financial crisis, it experienced very severe economic difficulties and had to be bailed out by the US government. GM Europe was then put up for sale. This was part of the company's deal for help from the US government in emerging in a restructured form from bankruptcy. The view was that bits of GM had to be hived off in order to make it a

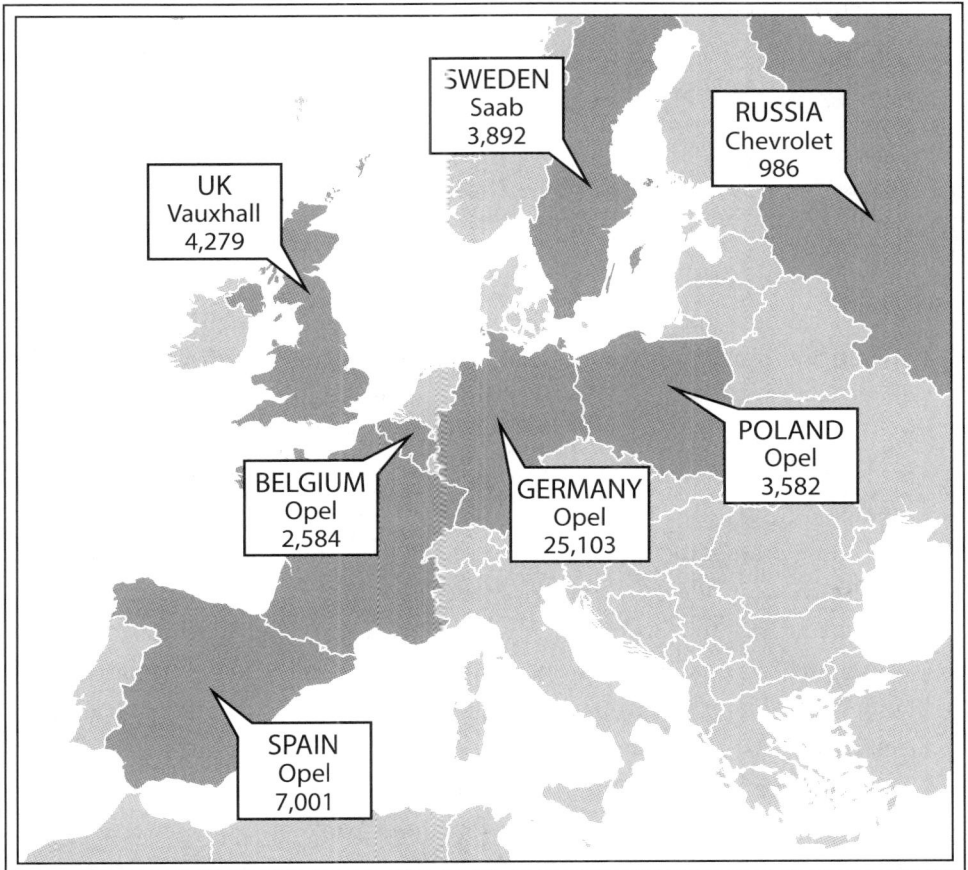

Fig. 8. General Motors Europe, 2009. Numbers represent respective employment numbers. Map by Jim DeGrand.

more viable corporation. Because of the concern that US taxpayers would not give money to support GM's foreign operations, in addition to that already laid out to help it emerge from Chapter 11, it was GM Europe that was put up for sale.

Several companies entered the fray in order to negotiate a deal, but the one that emerged as the preferred choice was a consortium put together by a Canadian firm called Magna. The German government played an important role in the negotiations because it had by far the largest number of employees of any country where GM Europe had plants (over 50 percent of all employees of GM Europe); these were employees of the GM brand, Opel. Under the terms of the Magna bid, the consortium would take a 55 percent stake, with GM continuing to hold 35 percent and Opel workers 10 percent. Part of the attraction for Magna in making this offer was that the German government agreed to provide transitional credit equivalent to $2.1 billion.

The background to the German government's offer was twofold. First, Magna had already stated that it would reduce the production capacity of GM Europe, and this meant closing plants; the German government offered the money on the understanding that plant closures would not affect plants in Germany. Second, this understanding was significant in part because of the prospect of a German election in fall 2009, which created anxieties that plant closures would affect the popularity of the government and hence the outcome.

These arrangements were the source of great angst among GM workers elsewhere in Europe, since they increased the chances that it would be their factory that would be closed. This in turn led to serious splits among the workers of the various GM plants around Europe, in particular between Unite, the British union, and German counterparts. German unions were accused of trying to railroad Unite, which represented the workers of Vauxhall, another GM brand, into agreeing to Magna's business plan, for obvious reasons. The Opel and Vauxhall unions were represented on something called the European Works Council, which had to arrive at a position on the Magna proposal. Union representatives from the UK, as well as from Belgium, Poland, and Spain, which also have Opel plants, were vehemently opposed. They were, though, in a minority on the council and so unable to veto an agreement.

Crucially, the European Commission was raising questions that threatened to torpedo the deal. This was in response to concerns raised by the Belgian government, representing the interests of the GM (Opel) workers there and the possibility of a major jump in unemployment in the city of Ghent. The problem was that the Magna deal violated EU competition rules. According to these rules, member countries cannot use subsidies to firms to protect employment in plants owned by a corporation that has plants in other member countries of the European Union, and this was clearly what Germany was doing in this instance. However, in November 2009 all these plans, resistance, and questions became moot when GM, basking in something of a business turnaround, decided that it was not going to sell GM Europe after all.

What strikes one about this instance is, first, the role the EU played. The very rough equivalent of the federal government in the United States exercised power over the competitive strategies of member governments, in this instance the German one. The content of the particular rule being applied is also interesting. It is not so much a matter of limiting territorial competition *tout court* (though as we will see it is not held in such awe as on the other side of the Atlantic), but rather certain aspects of it that would be the usual way of doing business there: laying out money to preempt a plant closure. The role of labor unions should also be noted. They were territorially divided, for sure, but without their pressure the Belgian government would not have acted.

2. The Politics of Plant Closures: The Case of Florange

Arcelor-Mittal is one of the world's major steel producers, with large operations employing twenty thousand at numerous sites in France. One of these has been at Florange in the Lorraine region in the northeast of the country (see Figure 9). Florange was the site of both a blast furnace and a rolling mill.

In 2012 amid pressing and extensive overcapacity in steel making in Western Europe and also a desire to cut costs by concentrating its ore reduction operations at its coastal plants, Arcelor Mittal declared its intention to close the blast furnace at Florange while maintaining the rolling mill there and supplying it with steel slab from its blast furnaces at Dunkirk on the English Channel. This would result in the loss of over 600 employees out of a total of 2,700: not inconsiderable in a town of only about 11,000 people. The government's response was to threaten nationalization with a view to then selling the facilities to a third party.

For Arcelor Mittal, state purchase of the two blast furnaces at Florange, statutorily enforced, was not a problem. It was happy to get rid of them. But the French government recognized that without the rolling

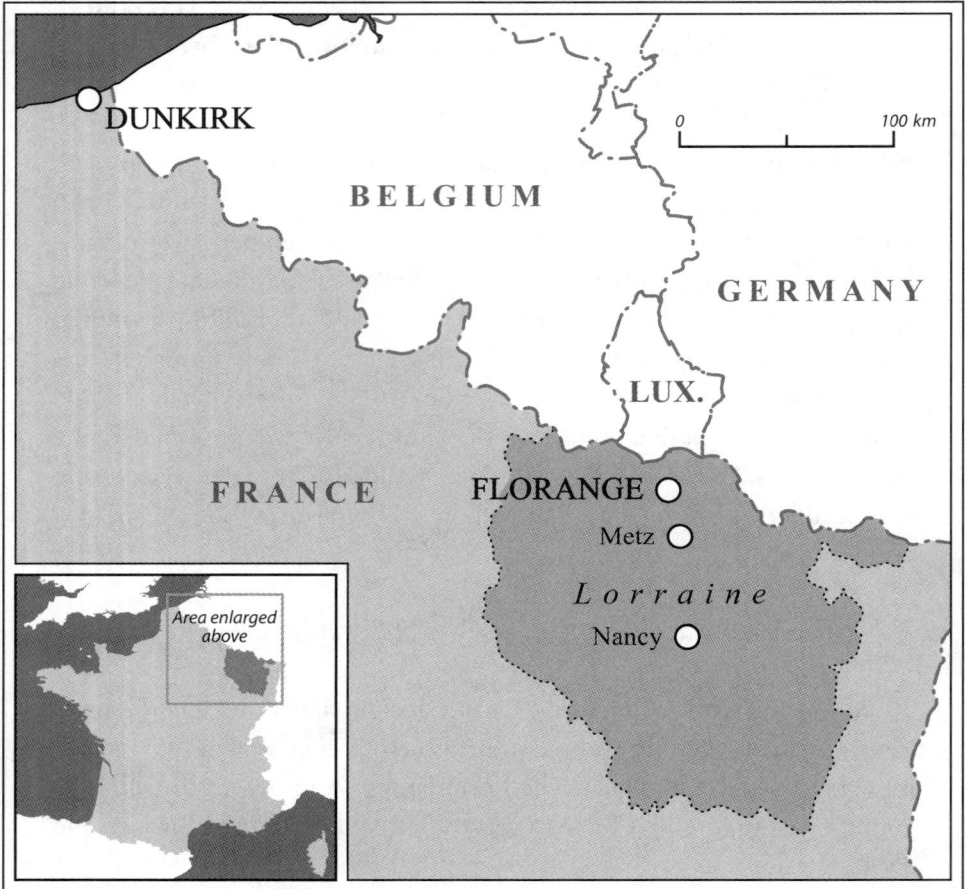

Fig. 9. Florange in regional context. Map by Jim DeGrand.

mill as part of the nationalization, the blast furnaces would be white ele-phants. So both the blast furnaces *and* the rolling mill were to be part of the state takeover unless Arcelor Mittal reneged on its closure plan.

An initial reaction in the French business press and the government's conservative opposition was to decry the maneuver as a poke in the eye of any attempt to burnish the country's "business climate": why, after all, would firms want to invest in France if they risked this sort of arbitrary action? But over and above these anxieties there were other problems. Not the least was that the transfer of ownership of the blast furnaces *and* the rolling mill at Florange simply shifted the problem elsewhere. For without the Florange rolling mill as an outlet, production of steel slab at Dunkirk was in doubt. In other words, the unemployment would simply be moved around, something of which the unions at Dunkirk became quickly aware. An answer to that, of course, would be for the French government to nationalize the Dunkirk production facilities as well.

The second problem from the government's standpoint was that taking the nationalization card out of the drawer threatened it with popular demands to make it a more general policy. Employees of a shipyard in St. Nazaire facing an empty order book requested a state buyout of its South Korean ownership. Employees of a bankrupt Swiss-owned oil refinery in Rouen also called for state ownership. So the option of *any* state ownership, whether at Florange or elsewhere, was rapidly removed from the table.

Even so, what is interesting about this case, as in the German government's concerns about the sale of GM Europe, is the way in which, in the first place, the unions and the affected communities looked to the central government for a solution—something in deep contrast with the American case. Second, nobody in the United States used the dreaded nationalization word when talking about helping GM get out of bankruptcy. But in Western Europe, extensive public ownership of industry remains a recent historical memory, and national governments can still retain minority ownership in major corporations. In France the value of state-owned firms amounts to over 10 percent of GDP; in Sweden the figure is 30 percent and in Norway a massive 58 percent.[1] And in all the larger economies with the exception of Great Britain[2]—France, Germany, Italy, Spain—the railways are publicly owned. Public ownership still has a legitimacy that is lacking in the United States.

1. See "Setting Out the Store," *The Economist*, Jan. 11, 2004, accessed Sept. 25, 2015, http://www.economist.com/news/briefing/21593458-advanced-countries-have-been-slow-sell-or-make-better-use-of-their-assets-they-are-missing.

2. Rail services are the responsibility of private companies, but the infrastructure is owned by Network Rail, which describes itself as "an arms-length central government body."

Third, and finally, even while not universally shared in the government of the time,[3] there are the French anxieties about "business climate" as a reason for not taking a private firm that refused to do the government's bidding into public ownership, if only temporarily. This seems to be very much of the time. I would argue that prior to globalization and the neoliberalization of economies—certainly prior to 1975—such anxieties would not have arisen. Since then, the private has been valorized over the public. This also says something very specific to globalization in Western Europe, which is the single market. Any member country can in principle be regarded as the location for investment since market access is no longer an issue; so aspects of labor law, national taxation, and state-business relations become much more important than they were in the past as a crucial feature of the politics of local and regional development. This is a theme to be pursued at greater length later in the chapter.

3. Airports and the Limits to Territorial Competition

Since 1992 and the deregulation of airline service within the European Union, civil aviation in Western Europe has been utterly transformed. This change has been brought about not just by the arrival of the low-cost airlines. The transformation is also noticeable in the fact that destinations now typically include locations unknown to those without a detailed knowledge of European geography—places like Bergerac, Angouleme or Pau in southwestern France, Bydgoszcz in Poland, Enontekio in Finland, Robin Hood (Doncaster and Sheffield, in case you were wondering)—but also places that, while recognizable, would not have had air service some twenty-five years ago—Avignon, Grenoble, Katowice, Monaco, Montpellier, Almeria, La Rochelle, Kaunas. More secondary centers like Lyon, Nurnberg, Strasbourg, Bremen, Lille, and Salonika have also been targeted.

Most of these airports are publicly owned and have been happy to provide gate subsidies and lower landing fees as a means of attracting business.

---

3. The government was, in fact, deeply divided on the issue of public ownership.

As the number of low-cost airlines expanded, so the availability of these sorts of enticements became part of their business model. Initially they tended to provide access to major metropolitan areas alternative to the larger international airports with their worldwide network of destinations: so Beauvais instead of Paris, Charleroi instead of Brussels,[4] and Luton enjoying access to London. The European Union smiled upon this, as it was seen as a way of taking pressure off airports that were already struggling with under-capacity. In fact, for many years the European Union has subsidized "second-tier airports" as a way to reduce the congestion at the major hubs like Frankfurt, London, Paris, and Brussels. But the airlines then extended themselves to prime tourist destinations, particularly around the Mediterranean, to areas favored by retirees from northern Europe, and to those towns, particularly in eastern Europe, that have become part of the grid of places serving recent migrants to other countries and the migratory labor market. Some of these destinations, though, have also been on the radar screens of the major carriers who have been vastly put out by the low-cost airlines as it is.

What they have tried to take advantage of is EU law. This bans state aid if it seriously distorts markets, whatever that means in practice. Once complaints were received from the major airlines, investigations of subsidy practices at smaller airports were set in motion. The outcome of this has been a new set of regulations designed to limit the subsidies being granted and so to put a cap on the competition between airports, but also, it should be added, between the local economies that have struggled to attract investment in tourism or retirement industries or more generally by expanding air service. Airports with less than three million passengers a year can continue to receive state aid for a transitional period of ten years. During this time they are supposed to adjust to a subsidy-free existence.

Again, there would be nothing extraordinary about offering subsidies of this nature in the American case. It happens all the time: subsidies to airlines to make an airport their hub, subsidies to provide new routes,

---

4. Cheekily, Charleroi airport dubs itself "Brussels South" even though Brussels is some 34 miles away.

particularly international ones. But if competition has to be limited, then, judging from the DFWI case, the initiative will be a local one. In Western Europe, by contrast, at least when it comes to local economic development (and certainly where local governments or chambers have offered subsidies to the low-cost airlines to include them as a destination), competition does not seem to enjoy the same cachet.[5] Much more intoxicating has been the idea of "solidarity" as we will now see.

4. The New Regional Question in Western Europe

With neoliberalism and the globalization which is one of its expressions, a very distinct politics of regional development has taken shape in Western Europe; a politics that would be almost unimaginable in the United States. In the first place, as explained in chapter 4, a distinctive feature of the Western European case has been centrally orchestrated efforts through the national treasury to mitigate the inequalities brought about by geographically uneven development: notably via shifts in the geography of government revenues and of social expenditures, which help to put a floor under incomes in depressed areas and a ceiling on them in areas of growth. Interregional migration has reinforced these effects by evening out the geography of unemployment. But with neoliberalism and globalization, geographically uneven development has tended to intensify, and this has brought serious regional tensions in its wake.

A case in point is Germany. In addition to the interregional redistribution of income occurring through the federal treasury and labor market effects resulting from interregional migration, there has long been provision for so-called regional solidarity payments; payments, that is, from the more prosperous *länder* to the less so. Prior to 1990 these were primarily from the booming south, particularly Bavaria and Baden-Württemberg,

---

5. On the British case, compare Meyer: "The US metaphor for efficient government—the successful for-profit firm—is not accepted in the British context. Local policies of 'beggar they neighbor' in competition for new investments are considered appropriate in the United States. By contrast, inter-location competition is deemed wasteful and is actively opposed in policies at both the national and the local level in Britain" (1991, 388).

to the rust belt regions of the north. But after reunification in 1990, the *länder* of the former East Germany have become major recipients (see Figure 10).

When reunification occurred, it was recognized that worker productivity in East Germany and concomitant material standards of living were quite inferior to those in West Germany, but market forces were supposed

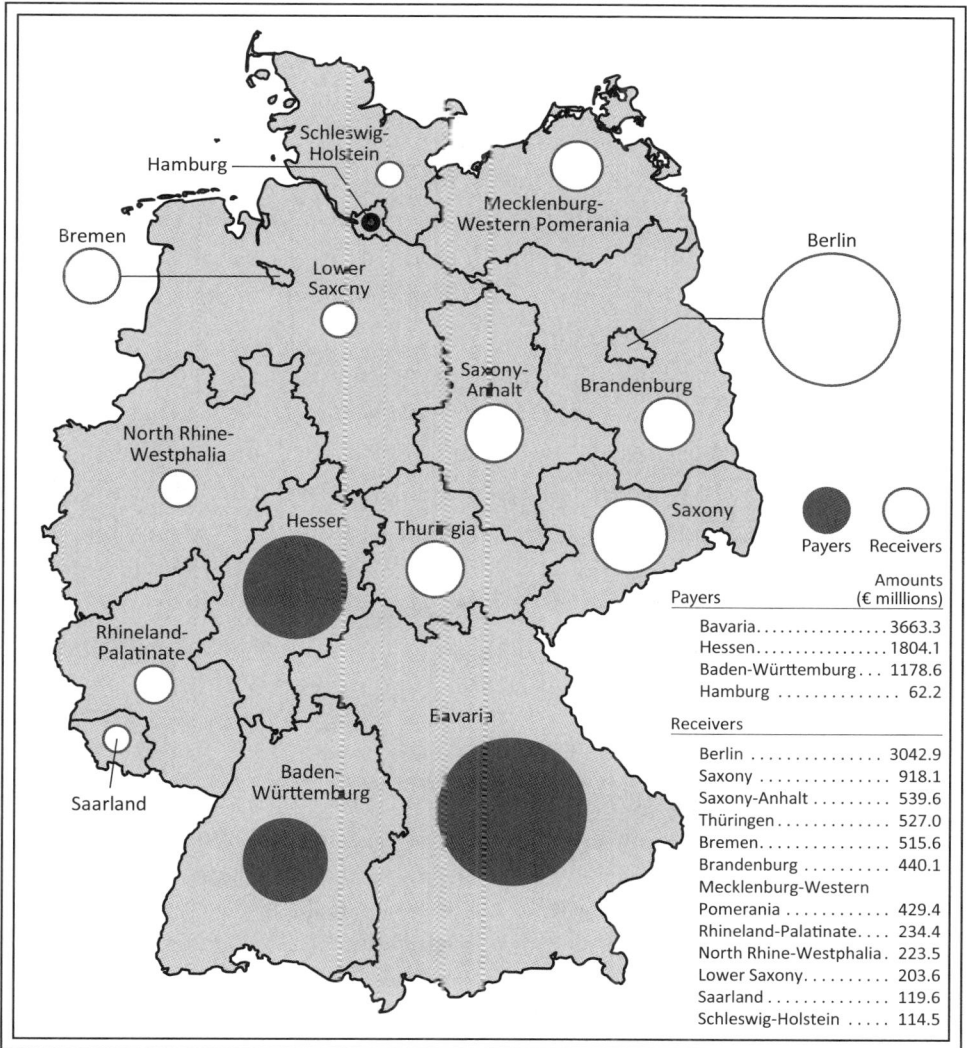

Payers	Amounts (€ millions)
Bavaria	3663.3
Hessen	1804.1
Baden-Württemburg	1178.6
Hamburg	62.2

Receivers	
Berlin	3042.9
Saxony	918.1
Saxony-Anhalt	539.6
Thüringen	527.0
Bremen	515.6
Brandenburg	440.1
Mecklenburg-Western Pomerania	429.4
Rhineland-Palatinate	234.4
North Rhine-Westphalia	223.5
Lower Saxony	203.6
Saarland	119.6
Schleswig-Holstein	114.5

Fig. 10. Fiscal equalization in Germany, 2011. Map by Jim DeGrand.

to remedy this. This approach has worked to some degree, but serious disparities still remain. Despite some convergence, production per worker remains markedly lower in the former East Germany and unemployment rates higher. Without significant government transfers from the rest of the country, income per capita would be increasing at a much, much slower rate than in the west.

In hindsight the reunification process was botched. Salaries, wages, savings, and pensions in East German marks were exchanged at a ratio of one to one for the West German currency—which was a good deal for East Germans at the time. But inferior productivity meant that the newly privatized firms in East Germany would struggle, which they did. Equally if not more significant, and certainly more interesting, was the transfer of West German wage negotiation practices to the east. This led to wage settlements vastly out of proportion to productivity gains, something supported both by West German labor unions and corporations fearful of low-wage competition from the east.[6]

The long-term political fallout has been impressive. Without the failure to lower unemployment rates in the east (Figure 11)—rates that would be much higher without the outmigration of about 2 million East Germans to the rest of Germany—it seems unlikely that the Left Party would have emerged. Certainly its base is in the east (Figure 12), even while it is now making gains in some of the rust belt areas of the west like the Saarland. This is a party that regularly polls between 8 and 10 percent of the total vote in federal elections and situates itself to the far left of the political spectrum, calling for drastic redistribution of both income

6. As Hefeker and Wunner explain: "[T]he wage policies pursued in East Germany were a very defective means of preventing low-wage competition for West German workers emerging in their own country. For West German enterprises, these wage increases and the real appreciation faced by East German producers also had the beneficial side-effect that there was no real danger of new, independent competitors arising in the East. Besides, given the precarious situation of most East German firms, West German enterprises were in many cases able to buy up these firms at highly favorable conditions and to negotiate large subsidies" (2003, 102).

and wealth through the federal government. It is not a regional party, in that it is not separatist or even calling for a more radical federalism. It is, rather, a party of the poor whose social base is regionalized, as was to some degree that of the British Labour Party during the Thatcher years (Savage 1987). On the other hand, resistance of a more clearly territorial sort has emerged in southern Germany, notably in Bavaria and to a lesser degree in Hesse: *Länder* which see themselves as exploited by the rest of the country through the federal government's fiscal equalization program. Calls for reform have been persistent, and the idea of an independent Bavaria has even been mooted though it is not yet taken seriously.[7]

Something similar has emerged in Italy. The separatist ambitions of the Northern League and its support base in the northern part of the country are well known (Agnew 1995); likewise their antipathy to the long-standing mechanisms through which the Italian state has tried to alleviate the country's uneven development. But also, as in Germany, wage-setting mechanisms designed to protect northern workers have been seen as part of the problem. Since 1968 national collective bargaining has been the rule. And while this has meant higher wages in the southern part of the country, lower levels of productivity there created problems of firm viability. The government response was then to make cuts in the social security payments that firms in the south had to pay. This clearly has not been sufficient: while the interregional wage gap has narrowed, the corresponding gap in the rate of unemployment has increased (Lucifora and Origo 1999).

What is also interesting, however, is that migration from south to north has greatly declined. Cannari, Nucci, and Sestito (2000) have suggested that this is owing to substantial interregional differences in housing costs, though they do not comment on why these differences exist. For Italy as a whole, the responsiveness of housing supply to demand is comparatively very weak indeed, and this is related to the lengthy time it takes to acquire building permits (Caldera Sánchez and Johansson 2011).

---

7. For example, Wilfried Schnargl (2012) *Bayern kann es auch allein.*

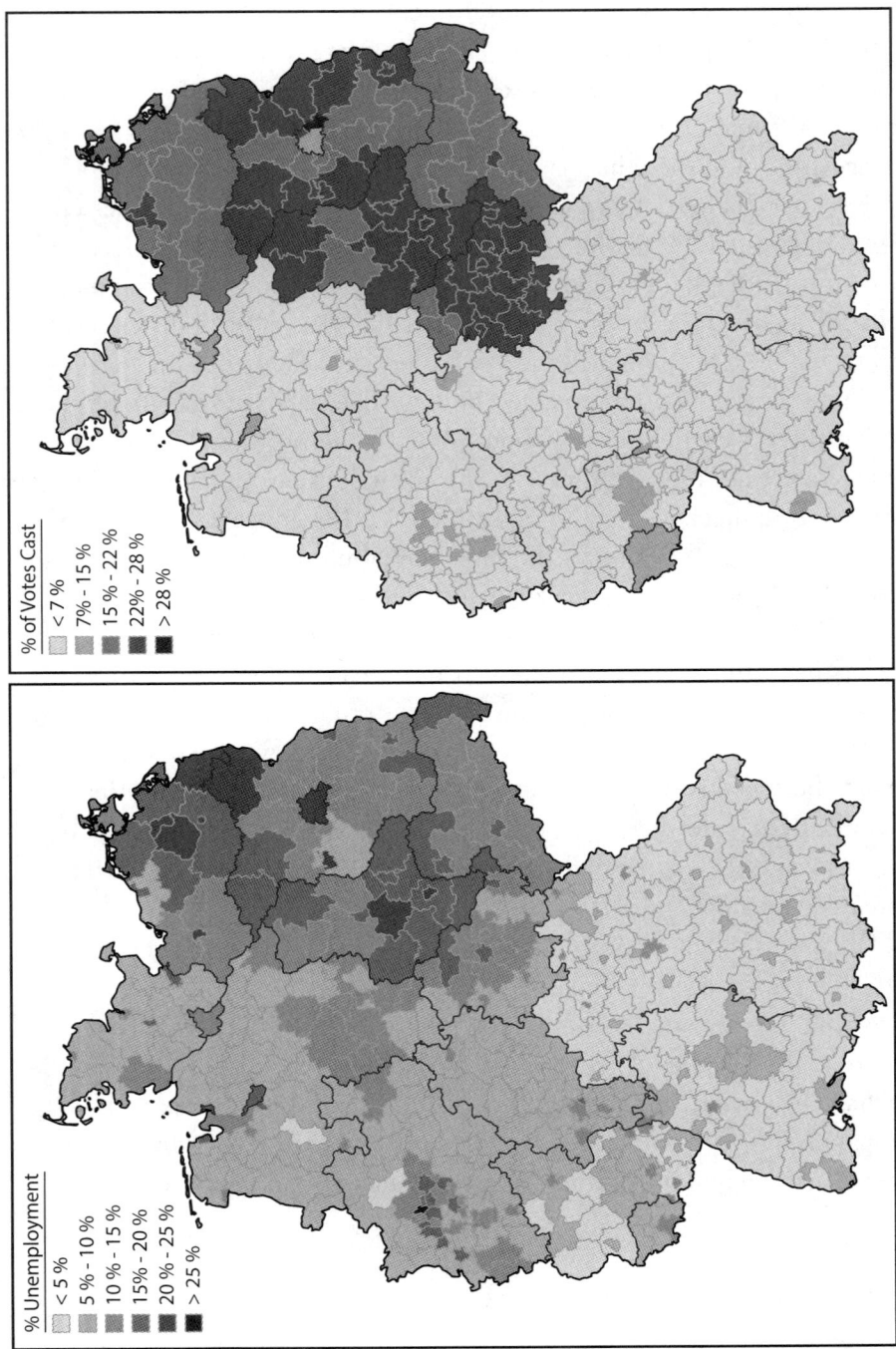

Fig. 11 and Fig. 12. Unemployment in Germany, 2011 (*left panel*); Percent voting for the Left Party, 2013 (*right panel*). Maps by Jim DeGrand.

Whether it is particularly weak in northern housing markets is unclear, though given that this area is where demand is most intense, that would seem to be a reasonable inference.[8]

The contrasts with the politics of the American Rust Belt, discussed in the first chapter, should be evident. It is not just the fact of the institutionalized mechanisms of redistribution, which might have worked more to the advantage of the depressed Rust Belt states if the United States did not have such a radical federalism—a federalism that makes the regional solidarity payments of the German case stand out. It is also the fact of centralized wage determination mechanisms.[9] Again, American labor law, like its fiscal system, is highly fragmented: another condition for the explicitly territorialized nature of the American politics and for the initial strategy of business interests in the Rust Belt states to press for revisions, including the introduction of right-to-work legislation. Of course, one can say in retort that the German politics of reunification has been equally territorialized: a case of a regional cross-class coalition imposing a solution to its own advantage and aggravating geographically uneven development to boot. But that is not the way it has been imagined, at least by the labor movement. And as we will now see, the way conflicts and tensions *have* been imagined plays a central part in how the Western European politics stands in nice counterpoint to the American one. How the state is structured has provided a significant context for contrasting discourses.

8. This particular configuration of effects connecting housing markets and interregional migration recalls current issues in Great Britain. London and the South East are the most rapidly growing areas of the country, while elsewhere local economies, particularly in the North, can be quite depressed. Differentials in housing prices can be huge—as of September 2015 a house in London cost two-and-a-half times the price of a house elsewhere in the country (Bloomfield 2015)—and restrictive land use planning laws are typically identified as a major reason for housing scarcity in London and the South East. This is an obstacle to moving in the direction of the jobs, since liquidating one's assets in the North will not provide the money to buy much housing in the Southeast. Aside from those who do not own homes, particularly the young and unmarried, this is a serious deterrent to movement.

9. Though these mechanisms have weakened considerably more recently (Dustmann et al. 2014).

5. Garden Grabbers!

> Labour MPs in southern England have started lobbying government ministers to stop creating new jobs in their constituencies, warning of a crisis in prosperity. The lobbying has centered on the Thames Valley corridor where demand is pushing up house prices and leading to hundreds of vacancies in key public sector jobs, such as teaching, nursing, policing and bus driving. MPs report an increasing number of complaints from constituents about a crisis of prosperity, including transport congestion, massive public sector recruitment problems and excessive housebuilding. (Wintour 2000)

This story, which appeared in the British newspaper the *Guardian* in December 2000, would be bizarre by American standards, where local growth coalitions in pursuit of inward investments would refuse to let a silly thing like a housing shortage get in their way. The area it referred to, the Thames Valley corridor, lies just to the west of London and is part of Great Britain's major boom area in southeastern England. A boom in employment in towns like Reading, Bracknell, Newbury, and Slough had not been accompanied by proportional additions to the housing stock. In trying to explain this, public attention was focused on the difficulties of getting greenfield sites approved by the local planning authorities who, in turn, were responding to the outrage expressed by those already resident there. Much of the land is in the hallowed green belt, where it is difficult to obtain planning permission anyway. Meanwhile, in the Thames Valley there were complaints from local government about the difficulties of hiring teachers, firemen, police, nurses, and other public servants. Housing prices were rapidly increasing, but restrictions on national pay standards for the civil service meant there was no way of offering higher salaries to compensate.

Within the next ten years though, a solution of sorts to the regional housing question began to take shape. This took the form of a sharp increase in the purchase by developers of existing housing on relatively large lots, its demolition, and then its replacement with a larger number of units, sometimes a multi-story block of apartments. In fact, between 1997 and 2008 the proportion of new housing units built on existing residential land, like back gardens, increased from one in ten to one in four. By 2010 this was generating something of a moral panic, with developers stigmatized as "garden grabbers": something bound to resonate in a country that takes its gardens seriously. There were issues of aesthetically inappropriate development: inserting a modern-looking block of flats in a street of late nineteenth century housing. This was sometimes on streets that were not constructed to take the extra traffic or indeed parking. Something of a domino effect then ensued as other home owners on the street sold out to developers; though it was never clear whether this was to avoid the subsequent congestion or to take an attractive offer when it was made.

The issue quickly turned into a party political one. The uproar, it should be noted, came largely from the better-off home owners since they were the ones most likely to be living on streets with the sorts of large lots prized by the developers. The Conservative Party quickly smelled pay dirt, identifying the problem as stemming from a change in planning policy that had been introduced by the Labour government in 2000. In an attempt to mitigate the housing shortage, which was most acute in areas like the Thames Valley, the government had tried to encourage the use of brownfield sites, but brownfield sites had been defined as including the gardens of existing housing. As it turned out, these sites were the ones preferred by the developers, since they rarely required the expense of environmental remediation; hence the glee with which the Conservative Shadow Communities secretary could proclaim: "Thanks to regulations issued by John Prescott,[10] leafy gardens (!) across the country are being dug up, and replaced with blocks of flats and high-density buildings that spell disaster for the local environment and local infrastructure."[11]

On the other hand, as Figure 13 suggests, if the question was one of mitigating a housing shortage, then garden grabbing was occurring in the right places, with a noticeable concentration in, indeed, the Thames Valley area to the west of London, but also in favored retirement areas to the

10. The Labour Party Minister immediately responsible.

11. "Government Promises Action to Stop 'Garden-grabbing,'" *BBC News*, Jan. 19, 2010, accessed May 5, 2016, http://news.bbc.co.uk/2/hi/uk_news/politics/8468511.stm.

southwest. And whether they liked it or not local planners were defenseless because they had to obey national planning law as well as directives from London urging the use of brownfield land as a way of increasing housing supply. Therefore, although the problem was fairly localized, the question of what to do about it was, like many development issues in Western Europe, a national one, so other national organizations got involved, including the Royal Horticultural Society. A spokesperson averred that "Gardens, like parks, are the green lungs of cities, improving air quality, controlling air temperature and flood risk, and providing a haven for wildlife."[12] The Labour government felt itself forced to act, and brownfield land was redefined to exclude gardens. Thus, garden grabbing came to a screeching halt.

This sort of redevelopment of existing lots is occurring elsewhere in Western Europe and in some parts of the United States and is encouraged as a contribution to the creation of compact cities. It has also generated an equal unhappiness among existing residents, though not with the degree of publicity it has received in the British case.[13] What is interesting, however, is the way the controversy so generated underlines contrasts with the American one; in particular, it becomes a national issue. In the British instance, it was given space in serious major newspapers like the *Guardian* and the *Daily Telegraph*, and the BBC website offered copious commentary. But there is also a sense in which it *had* to be a national issue, since national legislation was at stake. First, there was the planning legislation itself for which local planning authorities are merely agents; they are legally obliged to obey what is laid down at the center. In the United States, and quite aside from the fact that as far as planning is concerned, there *is* no center, this sort of intervention at the federal level is rare. Even something like *Kelo v. City of New London*, which, coming from the US Supreme Court applied to the whole country, was quickly countermanded by amendments to the existing legislation in many of the individual states.

12. "Councils to Get Help to Stop 'Garden Grabbing,'" *BBC News*, June 9, 2010, accessed Feb. 21, 2016, http://news.bbc.co.uk/2/hi/uk_politics/8728633.stm.
13. For the French instance see Vacquerel (2011, 51–52) and Petitet (2013), and on the Netherlands, De Haan (2005).

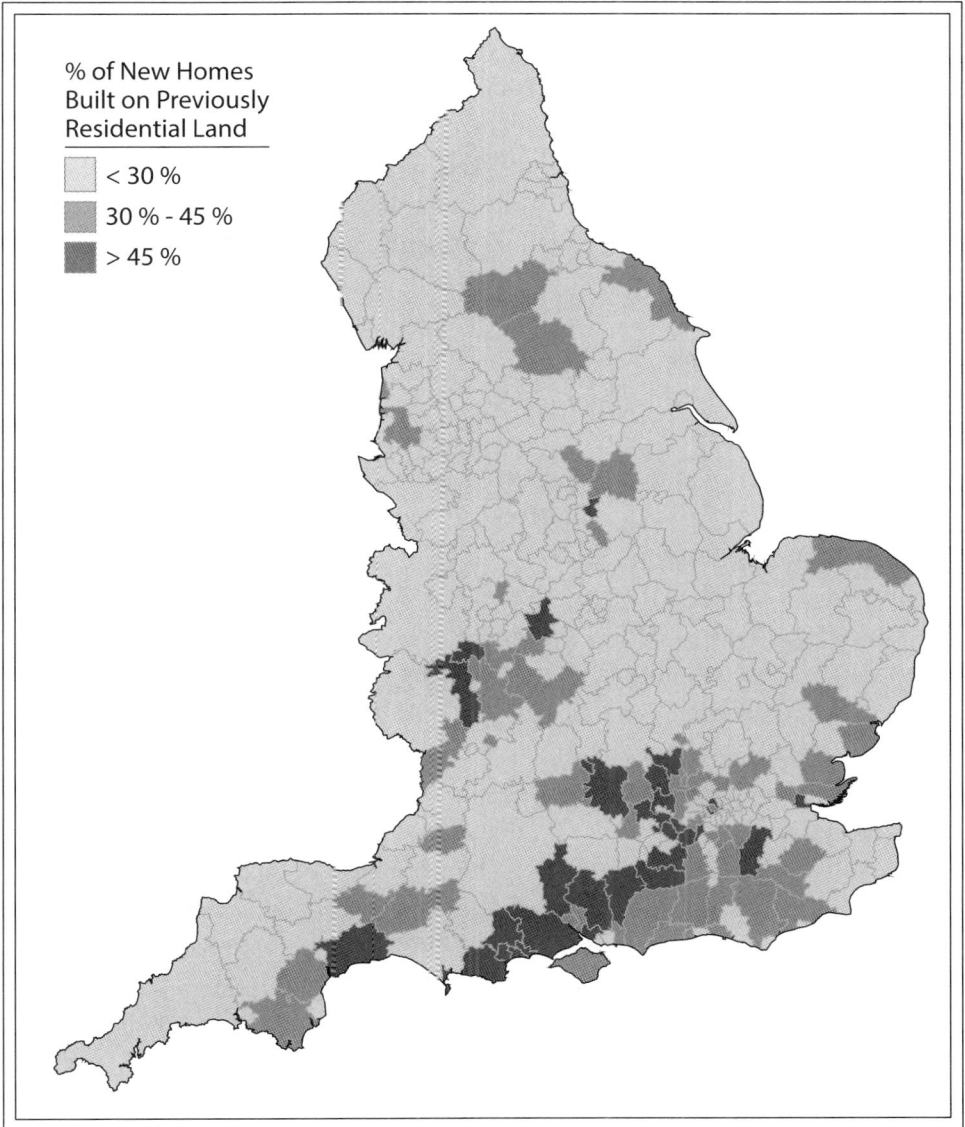

Fig. 13. Garden grabbing, 2005–2008. Based on "Councils to Get Help to Stop 'Garden Grabbing,'" BBC News, June 9, 2010. Map by Jim DeGrand.

Second, though, is the fact that other sorts of national legislation were contributing to the severity of the housing crisis for which garden grabbing was seen, by some at least, as a solution. Rapidly increasing housing prices collided with national pay scales for civil servants. So although the severity of the housing crisis was quite localized, any solution had to be found at the national level. And there was in fact a national debate, even while it did not get much above the banalities of "leafy gardens" and "green lungs."

6. The Urban Question

Obviously there *is* an urban question in Western Europe, but it differs from the US urban dilemma in some important ways. Anything attached to the jurisdictional fragmentation of metropolitan areas in the United States—fiscal disparities, inner versus outer suburbs, massive social inequalities in a territorial guise—tends to be at the very least quite weak. Likewise, in Western Europe it is harder to detect the sort of competition for positions in what I called the spatial division of consumption. In part, such competition is precluded by the centralization of school finance and national pay scales for teachers. Privileged educations lie, for the most part, in private or church schools and not in exclusive suburbs. That does not preempt the jostling of parents to get their children into a state school of repute; something that *does* show up in how urban housing markets work, and consequently in home values, but it is harder for the development industry to exploit—aside, that is, from densification—since it is a question of areas that are already built up, and compact city policies make the creation of new, self-sufficient suburban developments with their own high schools very difficult: the balance between peripheral and infill development is different.

There is exclusion, and sometimes this has assumed forms very similar to the American case; the vexed relation between the inner and outer boroughs in the old Greater London Council (Young and Kramer 1978a, 1978b) was an example. Regardless of a jurisdictional mesh that is typically much coarser than in the American case, social differentiation is clear. Aix is not Marseilles, just as Solihull is not Birmingham, Heidelberg is not Mannheim, nor even is Neuilly Paris (Pinçon and Pinçon-Charlot 2007).

Differential home values continue to sort people out by household income while at the same time providing a tendency for whatever exclusionary strategies can be marshaled: Charmes's reference (2013) to what he calls "clubbisation"—localities as exclusionary clubs of the self-selecting—in the *zones pavillonaires* around French cities recalls Wingo's (1973) discussion of the American case. But there are limits imposed from the center that provide far less scope for managing social composition than what is available to local governments in the United States. In Great Britain it would be very difficult to find a local authority that had no public housing. The same applies to any French commune above a threshold of, say, ten thousand residents. Likewise, and again unlike the United States, the concentration of public housing in the central city is much less evident. Rather it is often found toward the periphery of the built-up area alongside privately owned units but resulting in its own sort of marginalization.[14]

Conspicuously absent is the scorched-earth effect attendant on the typically American pattern of a low-density form pushing into the surrounding countryside seemingly without end, and leaving behind a wasteland of devalued homes, redlining, brownfields, and fiscal shortfalls, to be colonized only slowly by the footprint of the postindustrial city. Accordingly, redlining has not been a political issue in Western Europe. The obverse of this, though—relatively high housing costs, and sometimes extraordinarily so—has been an issue, and one now aggravated by the increased policy emphasis on the compact city; this, alongside the speculative diversion of money into existing housing, seems to have created a bonanza for property companies. Housing costs are an issue to a degree that is not the case in the United States, except on the West Coast and in the major metropolises of the Northeast, and housing scarcity has had important compounding effects on the topography of conflict.

How this has been expressed has varied. In London the demolition of public housing stock has become a massive political issue. Pushed by a diversity of challenges—lack of money to build new public housing, a

14. The "grands ensembles" or *cités* toward the periphery of major French cities or the huge public housing estates south of Glasgow, like Drumchapel or Easterhouse, are notorious as warehouses for the weak and deprived.

desire to increase local revenue streams—individual boroughs have been persuaded that the solution lies in redevelopment: tear down the public housing, sell the land to private developers for redevelopment at higher densities, but with an understanding that the needs of the poor will be taken care of through provision of units at affordable rents. The developers, however, have learned to deceive, seeking a midstream renegotiation of the numbers of affordable units by claiming their own poverty.

Likewise, in London and other Western European cities experiencing rapid growth and housing scarcity—Paris, Barcelona, Berlin, Amsterdam, Brussels—gentrification is an issue, sometimes generating violent protests, that it is not in the United States, except again in the West Coast cities and the big metropolitan areas of the Northeast. Infill development, on the other hand, like the British garden grabbing or the French *densification pavillonaire* or the insertion of new housing on small brownfield spaces is a very Western European phenomenon with only faint echoes in the United States,[15] and one capable of generating massive heat in the neighborhood.

The housing issue in major cities is in part a result of the way in which since the 1970s national governments have tended to favor them as "national champions" through their regulatory and infrastructural policies (Crouch and Le Galès 2012), as was discussed in chapter 5. This, however, as Crouch and Le Galès have made clear, has had regional repercussions that make the urban question a national one in another way altogether; merging, as it were, with a regional question. The British case is well-known and was discussed earlier. The disparities in infrastructural spending have been huge, generating dismay in the major cities elsewhere—particularly in the north, where fortunes have tended to lag—as well as a great deal of publicity.[16] One result has been their organization as

15. Though beginning to appear as a public issue in Los Angeles and the Bay Area in the form of densification and what are called "backyard homes." On the latter see, for example, Mukhija, Cuff, and Serrano (2014).

16. According to one report from 2014, central government per capita spending on infrastructure in London amounts to 5,426 pounds in comparison to the next ranked region, the North West which includes Manchester, of 1,248 pounds per head of the population. See, for example, "London Gets 24 Times as Much Spent on

the "core cities" to bring pressure on the government with a view to altering the imbalances. As Crouch and Le Galès (2012) discuss, Finland and Norway are other instances where a government focus on major cities as "national champions" fit for international purpose has been controversial in the regions. The rise of Nokia as a national champion in another sense led to government investments in Helsinki in education and infrastructure that worked to the disadvantage of historically poorer areas in the north and east of the country, generating opposition there.[17]

Aside from the superordinate role of central states in the Western European politics of the city, including the way in which questions of housing costs become national ones, even when they tend to be concentrated in the larger cities, partisan divisions can also play a role that is largely foreign to the American case. In Great Britain, garden grabbing rapidly became a national issue and was fought out there on the terrain of division between a Labour government and a Conservative opposition. The stakes are lower for local governments, but they are still contested along party lines, and voting in local elections closely follows national party identifications.[18] Local governments have priorities that mirror national party preferences. French communes with a Socialist majority are much more likely to promote social housing than those without.[19] Issues in particular cities or communes, whether it is that of expanding social housing or resisting demolition to make way for a development of private homes and rentals, attract partisan division and this can focus the attention of the center. Mrs. Thatcher's governments famously used nationally constituted urban

---

Infrastructure per Resident than North-east England," *The Guardian*, Aug. 7, 2014, accessed Oct. 11, 2015, http://www.theguardian.com/news/datablog/2014/aug/07/london-gets-24-times-as-much-infrastructure-north-east-england.

17. Opposition from the regions to French policies aimed at building up Paris's competitive capacities on a global stage has been less evident. But see Wendeln (2014, 4).

18. Accordingly, local elections are viewed by the national parties as barometers of respective electoral prospects in national elections.

19. Compare Preteceille: "The political traditions of the left at the municipal level, being oriented toward public housing and public facilities, are . . . opposed to 'growth coalitions' of a capitalist kind, except in a few cases, perhaps" (1990, 41).

development corporations that could act independently of local government to force her vision of local development onto municipal councils where a Labour majority was resisting through, in particular, resort to "local socialism" and Enterprise Boards (Le Galès 1990).

It may be that as the interest in economic development has become more prominent in local government agendas, so traditional partisan divisions have tended to retreat, but making way for new ones; that at least was the view of Bernard Jouve:

> This transition has some important consequences. In effect, this (local development) agenda is henceforth a common one across all metropolitan areas, whatever might be the partisan orientation of the city council, and this leads to a depoliticization of the debate and an erosion of the political cleavage between left and right. On the part of the elected officials claiming to represent parties of the left one result has been a weakening of the organic ties with their traditional electoral base among those groups situated toward the bottom of the social structure. In countries like France, this recentering of local political life partly explains the importance assumed by extreme parties, notably the National Front, which have succeeded in attracting an orphaned electorate through a discourse that is xenophobic, anti-European and opposed to globalization.[20] (2005, 188; author's translation)[21]

20. "Cette transition a des conséquences importantes. En effet, cet agenda est désormais commun à l'ensemble des métropoles, quelle que soit l'orientation partisane des exécutifs en place, ce qui conduit à une dépolitisation du débat et à une érosion du clivage politique droit/gauche. De la part des élus se revendiquant des partis situés historiquement à gauche sur l'échiquier politique, on a ainsi observé une remise en question des liens organiques qui existaient avec leur clientèle électorale traditionnelle c'est-à-dire les groupes sociaux situés à la base de la structure sociale. Dans des pays comme la France, ce recentrage de la vie politique locale explique en partie l'importance qu'ont pris les partis extrémistes, essentiellement le Front National, qui ont réussi à attirer, en faisant valoir un discours xénophobe, anti-européen et anti-globalisation, une électorat orphelin."

21. Haila and Le Galès (2005) have shown how this relationship between strong partisan divisions, on the one hand, and the challenges of territorial competition on the other, is playing out in the Helsinki area. See also Gough and Eisenschnitz: "[I]nternationalization elicits a localistic ideology. This can build on the day-to-day interdependences

And of course the National Front has its equivalents elsewhere in Western Europe, with parties like the British National Party, the Freedom Party in the Netherlands, the United Kingdom Independence Party, or even Italy's Northern League and the Flemish Independence Movement all providing very different slants on the material salvation of the masses.

This sort of explicit politicization of local government would be inconceivable in most cities in the United States. It is not just the difference between a system in which bottom-up forces dominate over the top-down. Partisan forces count for much less. The reforms of the Progressives at the turn of the century tended to severely limit the expression of party political identities in local politics. The nonpartisan ballot was adopted, particularly in the independent suburbs, and mayors who might conceivably have represented a party replaced by professional city managers who were appointed rather than elected. Even in the central cities, the partisan character of politics was diluted as a result of the widespread replacement of election of city councilors by ward by elections at large. Party labels persisted, but now citywide visibility and money tended to assume a larger role, and in order to compete, this tended to pull the Democratic Party away from more radical positions toward the center: not so much a de jure irrelevance of party, therefore, but a de facto one and one, moreover, which tended to favor growth coalition interests as Elkin (1987) has shown in his discussion of the Dallas case.[22]

---

between individuals and firms within localities" (1998, 762). Another symptom of the weakening of partisan contestation at the local level has been the emergence of what has been called "the post-political condition": a condition in which local issues and land use planning, which have been to the fore in the literature, are engaged in a seemingly democratic process, including public participation, but one that is stage managed in various ways so as to achieve a deceptive consensus. This proceeds in part through recourse to a hegemonic discourse of technical expertise and definitions of who is a "stakeholder" in an issue. See Allmendinger and Haughton (2012), MacLeod (2013), and Swyngedouw (2009). This is a primarily European literature but it has received some attention in the United States (see Mitchell, Attoh, and Staeheli 2015).

22. In Dallas these institutional arrangements lasted for most of the twentieth century and until well into the 1970s. Their principal advocate was the Citizens' Charter Association, dominated by local businesses: "The Citizens' Charter Association was the

Superficially, these six vignettes might suggest that Western Europe has at least some of the same sorts of development conflicts as the United States: conflicts around gentrification, around plant closures, and the same NIM-BYism (Barlow 1995; Renau and Lozano 2015). Closer inspection, however, reveals not only a somewhat different topography of conflict; the structuring forces are also quite different. It is a very different world, as American corporations discover when they try to establish branch plants or networks across the Atlantic, and as Wal-Mart discovered to its regret when it tried to enter the German market (Christopherson 2007, 469). This is the case even while, since the 1980s, Western Europe has tended to shift somewhat in a more American direction.

Instead of a diffused, decentralized politics where conflicts get worked out locally, there is a much more centralized one in which central government officials play crucial, make-or-break roles,[23] as indeed Arcelor Mit-

---

principal means by which leading businessmen sought to ensure that elected officials would share their views on the importance of city growth and how it was to be fostered. The association only supported candidates who were committed to the continuation of the council-manager system. . . . What the association wanted was amateurs who would be happy to leave the day-to-day running of the city to the city manager and his staff. Full-time politicians would seek and require independent bases of support in the electorate, whether through party organization or through personal followings, and would thus likely be independent of businessmen's counsel" (Elkin 1987, 30). A major pillar of the system was election of councilors at large. This gave the advantage to people of money who were visible and could command support throughout the city—business people for the most part. Just how significant this could be has been made clear by Cummings and Snider in another study of the Dallas case: strategic and geographically focused housing code legislation was used to transfer land from small landlords to developers, and there was little public opposition to the plan "due to the fact that council members were elected primarily on an at-large basis, many being themselves representatives of business and real estate interests" (1988, 166).

23. Compare Mayer in a discussion of local citizen movements in the former West Germany: "Given the relatively centralized West German federal system, and the integrated party structure, but especially given the highly statist and corporate system of interest regulation, most German citizens' initiatives, while locally based, frequently become

tal discovered when it decided to close the blast furnaces at Florange. Instead of a pragmatic politics in which, while not absent, notions of what would be a just outcome are off the shelf—almost matters of convenience to justify the outcome of a bargaining relationship—there is a much more ideological one: a politics governed more by ideals of the "good geography" as an essential part of the "good society" than of a government in the service of diverse private interests competing one with another. And instead of the primacy of growth coalitions and developer networks putting together plans for how to direct value through their own social relations, in Western Europe it is far more likely to be the central planners and government departments that take the initiative, and not with an eye to rents. If, on the other hand, state agencies do not take the lead, it is essential that developers have them on their side, and that is not at all to be taken for granted. Even at the local level, planners keep their distance from the developers. Planning s a more deliberative than a bargaining process: informed by a belief that one can arrive at some sense of the public interest and then enforce it.[24]

Continuities

The centralized nature of Western European states has been a key condition for differences in the sorts of conflicts emerging there and even allowing for the fact of federal institutions in the cases of Belgium, Germany, and Spain. One consequence is that the incentives for the territorial competition so much a feature of the American instance are limited by the geographically homogenizing effects of state institutions, particularly those governing the employment relation, including national determination of pensions, but also specific territorially equalizing policies, as

---

nationally based. Whenever opposition to a local issue emerges—be it a large scale industrial or nuclear plant, a highway, toxic wastes, plant closure or even urban renewal—the protest immediately confronts the whole state and the whole party apparatus" (1987, 352).

24. Something noted by Elkin (1974) in a study of London many years ago and which still applies.

discussed in the case of Germany's fiscal equalization policy. The idea of regions or localities competing in terms of business climate has made limited sense. The same applies to the sort of competition for positions in the spatial division of consumption in metropolitan areas so common in the United States, as noted above.

Most crucially, centralization has paved the way for the state planning of locations to play a predominant role. Growth coalitions, to the extent that they exist, and in virtue of the highly qualified degree to which there is a market in locations, as in the United States, have a much diminished role. The central branches of the state lay down land use planning guidelines, issue directives as to what the thinking of their local level counterparts should be, scrutinize local plans, and bring them into conformity with some central vision. They make decisions on heritage sites, conservation areas, airports, high-speed rail lines, new container ports, and, in some instances where electricity is a publicly owned enterprise, the location of power stations, too, and they impose severe limits on the construction of new suburban shopping centers.

Accordingly, debate about location policy is much more national. There is debate, relatively insulated from the cut-and-thrust of local-level pressures, about what would constitute an ideal geography: not just the good society, therefore, but the good geography as an essential part of it. In contrast, one is reminded of Theodore Lowi's (1969) claims about the American state in his book *Beyond Liberalism*: how its utter fragmentation and colonization by special interests precluded any sustained reflection on what the national interest might be. Rather, in his view, it emerged by default as the outcome of a quasi-market process of bargaining and horse trading.

What has resulted from this process of debate, informed in part by government-constituted commissions of inquiry as well as through parliamentary deliberation, the opinion pages of a national press, and media discussions, has been a different set of balances or priorities. There has been a greater emphasis on preservation over development, heritage over progress, including the preservation of the countryside and historic townscapes. Views are to be protected against the intrusiveness of high-rises or of any change to the built environment for that matter. Freeway routes and high-speed railroad routes get scrutinized and fought over to a degree that would surprise an American, though there can also be a degree of cynicism here as, in a sort of "*patrimoine* creep," the heritage status of an area or the historical significance of a landscape gets redefined. This means a different balance between the rights of the individual land or property owner as opposed to the public at large. There is an important sense in which development rights have been nationalized. If the planners say that land should not be changed from agricultural to urban uses or that a building should not be demolished, then so be it, even while there might be opposition, as there was in the case of the creation of the Calanques national park in the south of France.[25] There is no takings clause as there is in the United States; no right to develop, and therefore no compensation if you should find, for example, that your land happens to be in a national park and subject to all the limits to land use change that go along with that.[26]

Likewise talk of competition between places does not resonate like it does in the United States. Competition between one government and another is something to be regulated so that the public does not have to foot the bill: something that played a role in the EU decision to rein in the subsidies being offered by small airports to low-cost airlines; and also in the decision on Germany's attempt to influence the Magna Consortium to refrain from plant closures. If there are regional inequalities, then there should be some redistribution as in the case of Germany's fiscal equalization program. Solidarity is a watchword of development-speak in Western Europe: solidarity with those less well-off, those marooned in areas of declining employment or threatened by plant closures.[27]

25. "Rebellion in Provence at Paris Plan for National Park," *Guardian*, July 26, 2009, accessed Jan. 1, 2016, http://www.theguardian.com/world/2009/jul/26/paris-calanques -national-park-rebellion.

26. National parks in Western Europe are different. They are not owned by the state. Rather people continue to live and work there but under a stricter planning regime designed to protect the environment from what is judged to be intrusive development.

27. Compare Hudson (2015, 25) in a discussion of recent trends: "Growing economic polarization affects social conditions, while in turn the evolution of the economic

Given the predominance of the specifically national media in the lives of respective countries, something that is scarcely possible in a country as big and diverse as the United States, it is difficult not to be aware of these debates—debates about plant closures, about the construction of high-speed rail routes, about the location of suburban shopping centers (whether to allow them and under what constraints), even about a third runway at Heathrow or Munich, or an entirely new airport at Nantes.[28]

In addition, because these debates occur at the national level, and therefore at the level of party political competition, the conversations and claims can come to reflect wider party political positions. Given the relative strength of left-leaning political parties in Western Europe, and however much their radicalness has been blunted in recent years, this inevitably gives contestation around location in the broadest sense a class edge that is lacking in the United States, yielding compromises that express that very different political balance. There is a rhetoric of "national interest," "solidarity," "social partnerships" and a different balance between individual rights and social obligation that is missing on the other side of the Atlantic. This informs practice in very clear ways, as in chapter 4's discussion of "the fair city."

Yet even while these are policies that can be interpreted as favoring those less well-off and without property or, in the case of legislation about plant closures, the unemployed, what is interesting and what can only be understood in terms of a deeper set of national values is the broad party

---

development process is influenced by these socially-produced spatial differences. As a result, national states (and now the EU) see it as necessary to seek to limit socio-spatial polarization and keep inequality within 'acceptable' limits." Whether this commitment is honored more in the breach is an issue. What is not an issue is that a statement like this could *not* have been written about policy toward uneven development in the United States. "Solidarity" is a foreign word.

28. Germany, with its federal structure, has been somewhat different, but, at least as far as airport expansion is concerned, that may be changing ("A New Third Runway at Munich Airport?" *Young Friends of the Earth Europe*, May 16, 2012, https://www.foe europe.org/node/896). And the issue of suburban shopping centers and the terms on which they can compete with city center retailing has always been a national question.

consensus that usually tends to surround them. The same can be said about the compact city policy, even if it has its class biases: a coalition of town center retail interests, left party interests in equalizing accessibility by making mass transit more feasible, and the privileged classes in the small surrounding villages who want to keep the masses at bay.

On the other hand, the major role assumed by central branches of the state can leave national governments isolated and exposed. They are the automatic focus of appeals when things go wrong. Plant closures are seen as matters for central government, which is expected to act. Expectations for its mediating role are high, and it becomes an easy target for blame. In the United States, given the priority accorded to a market in locations, this exposure is greatly reduced. The more central branches, whether federal or state government, have to concern themselves with the rules governing competition and the "leveling of the playing field," but this diffuses the tensions downward away from the state toward the localities and regions. Hence the idea that central states are somehow culpable is much weaker.

During the golden years of the 1950s and 1960s, this exposure was of no great moment, but it became highly problematic after the economic crisis of the 1970s. This helps to explain the devolution, limited as it was, of central functions in a number of Western European states during the 1980s, as discussed in chapter 5. This narrowing of the central state's role, however, would unleash new tensions particularly in combination with the neoliberal turn that became the favored strategy for exiting the crisis. These tensions would then be reinforced by developments in the European Union, notably the move to a single market and the expansion after 1990 into Eastern Europe.

Americanizing the Western European Politics?

In a book about the changing nature of the politics of local and regional development in France, Philippe Subra (2007) bemoaned the changes that had been taking place. What he thought of as a more consensual politics under the aegis of the central state and operating in terms of a strong sense of national coherence—the pattern prevailing during the 1950s and

1960s—was being displaced by one of increased territorial conflict and relative *in*coherence.[29]

While Subra's characterization of the earlier period might have been a rhetorical device to foreground the particularities of the present, Body-Gendrot (1987) in a much earlier publication supported it: the fundamental notion, that is, of a central government planning for the public good that was widely accepted and fairly immune to grassroots challenge. In this regard, the French experience was very similar to that of other West European countries. As in France, the generally buoyant economic times allowed central governments to divert employment to disadvantaged areas without serious threat to those regions from which it was being diverted, and the idea of sunset industries in what would be sunset regions was

29. "À la représentation qui prévalait du temps de Trente glorieuses—celle d'un territoire national et d'une communauté nationale unique et unifié, dont toutes les parties bénéficiaient, bien qu'à des degrés divers, du processus général de modernisation et d'enrichissement—s'est substituée, au moins partiellement, celle d'une collection de territoires locaux et de populations locales, aux sorts tragiquement différents, certains gagnants, d'autres perdants dans le grand jeu de l'intégration européenne et de la mondialisation. Á un schéma relativement simple qui voyait coexister une identité territoriale dominante, la Nation, et des appartenances de classes très tranchées, a succédé un tableau bien plus confus où la première est en concurrence avec de multiples identités territoriales, certains supranationales (la planète, l'Europe), d'autres infra-nationales (la région, la commune, le quartier)—tandis que les identités de classes et les clivages générationnels semblent jouer un rôle moins important" (Subra 2007, 8). [In contrast to the idea which dominated during France's thirty year period of rapid growth after the Second World War—that of a united national community in which all areas benefited, if to different degrees, from the general process of modernization and growth—has been substituted, at least partially, that of an aggregation of places and their populations, each with a very different destiny, some winners and some losers, in the great game of European integration and globalization. A very simple framework of coexistence between one dominant territorial identity, that of the nation, and clear class affiliations, has given way to a much more complex picture: one in which the nation is competing with other territorial identities, including supranational ones like the earth and Europe and infra-national ones like the region, the commune and the neighborhood; and in which class identities and inter-generational cleavages seem to play a less important role] (author's translation).

barely on the horizon. They also shared the strong sense of national unity around postwar reconstruction.

The devolutionary measures discussed in chapter 5 were part of the response to the changing economic climate subsequent to the early 1970s. As I suggested, this was one of the ways in which central governments tried to reduce the pressures they were experiencing— pressures that were detracting from their legitimacy. There were other measures designed to relaunch national economies into a new age of prosperity. Not least was the rise of neoliberalism and a retreat from state intervention and toward the view that the further development of the common market of the European Union would facilitate competitive advantage on a global scale. All these moves had unintended consequences, including territorial contradictions and responses to them. The overall impression was that a politics of development that was more American in character was beginning to emerge. This tendency should not be exaggerated. Much of the distinctiveness outlined in the previous section remains. But the Western European politics is no longer quite what it was.

In the first place, then, the retreat of the state has been apparent in the dismantling of much of the regional planning apparatus which, for a long period after the Second World War, tried to even out employment rates between the regions in the countries of Western Europe. To some degree this is a result of EU restrictions on the subsidies offered to firms thinking of opening branches in depressed areas; but it would have happened anyway as governments have sought to reduce their expenditures and allow businesses in the "winning" regions to thrive where they are rather than having to expand elsewhere. Regional aid still exists, but not under the old guise. Now it targets "winning" regions rather than the deprived.[30] The deregulation of the British stock market in 1986 is an outstanding case of this, since it ignited a boom in the London stock market, attracting international banks and reviving the city's fortunes as a, if not *the*, major financial center in the world. As congestion has hit with a vengeance, so more public money has been invested in the capital for relief measures,

30. The Belgian story is fairly typical. See Vanthillo and Verhetsel (2012).

as in the Crossrail project, which promises to stoke the fires still further. Calls to decentralize airport capacity to cities outside of the favored South East fall on deaf ears, even while the more general rhetoric is about "rebalancing" the economy, including its territorial aspects.

As states have tried to run down their responsibilities and looked to the market as salvation, nationalized industries have also been sold off, but in order to make them attractive to private investors they typically had to be drastically slimmed down first. These moves often hit hard regions that had historically been vulnerable to unemployment. As Hudson (1986) has shown for the British case, the nationalized industries of coal, iron and steel, and shipbuilding tended to be heavily concentrated in areas that, even during capital's golden age, had experienced relatively higher rates of unemployment.[31] It was for that reason that they had also been over-represented among areas eligible for subsidies to new employment-creating investments. But as states tried to reduce their costs, the qualifying areas contracted.

The tendency has been toward an intensification of geographically uneven development (see Dunford 1994, 1997): boom areas like London and the South East in contrast to the old industrial North; the growth of France's Ile-de-France in contrast to the declining fortunes of the old coal and iron and steel regions of northeastern France; the growth of Brussels and Antwerp and the decline of the Charleroi-Namur-Liege axis in Belgium; the rise of southern Germany and the decline of the Ruhr; and the shifts in the center of gravity of the Scottish space economy from the west of Scotland to Aberdeen and, in particular, Edinburgh with its vast weight of banking and the growth of government employment subsequent to devolution. As the state has withdrawn the supports that propped up those regional economies heavily concentrated on declining sectors, privatized industries, and abolished investment subsidies, there has been little to take

---

31. Coal mining areas in Western Europe in general have been hard hit and now suffer from unusually high levels of unemployment. Closures had been occurring long before those subsequent to the privatization of British pits in the second half of the 1980s in response to the heightened competition of cheaper coal from Australia and South Africa and of oil and natural gas in electricity generating stations. In France, the competition of nuclear power was also important.

their place. Rather the growth sectors, like financial services, the airplane manufacturing industry, computers and software, biotech, specialty chemicals, even higher education, have tended to concentrate elsewhere.

This has had political consequences. Geographically uneven development has been on the agenda to a degree that was unusual in Western Europe prior to the 1970s and has generated tensions that would not be foreign to the American politics In part, though, and in contrast to the American case, these tensions have been expressed in a new regionalization of support for political parties that are ostensibly national in their appeal. The most notable case of this is the Left Party in Germany discussed earlier. In the 1980s there was a suggestion that the British Labour Party was becoming a party of those regions that had lost out on the Thatcher boom, whereas the Conservatives tended to do unusually well in southern areas of the country (Savage 1987).[32] In France, on the other hand, it is the far right National Front that has been the beneficiary of regionally concentrated unemployment.[33] It has found a new base for itself among the unemployed in the Northeast in addition to its old heartland along the Mediterranean littoral (Figure 14). The correspondence with the unemployment map (Figure 15) is striking.[34] This support is partly on the basis of its calls for restrictions on immigration, but the idea of withdrawal from the EU on the grounds of the way it is conditioning a relocation of French industry to Eastern Europe has to be equally seductive. Meanwhile the far right has also found fertile soil in the rust belts of the big cities. But at least in these instances the appeal has not been explicitly territorial and has been pitched more in terms of a national debate as to what, for example, would improve the lives of working people.

32. The argument was one about working-class home ownership. In the weak labor markets of the old industrial North home values had declined. Only with the promised expansionary policies of the Labour Party did it seem that there might be salvation. In the South, however, working-class home owners had seen the value of their property improve under Thatcher, her austerity policies notwithstanding.

33. On this intensified uneven development in France, see Davezies (2012).

34. I am not claiming that it is the unemployed who are voting for the FN; merely that depressed economic conditions in general make people susceptible to its message.

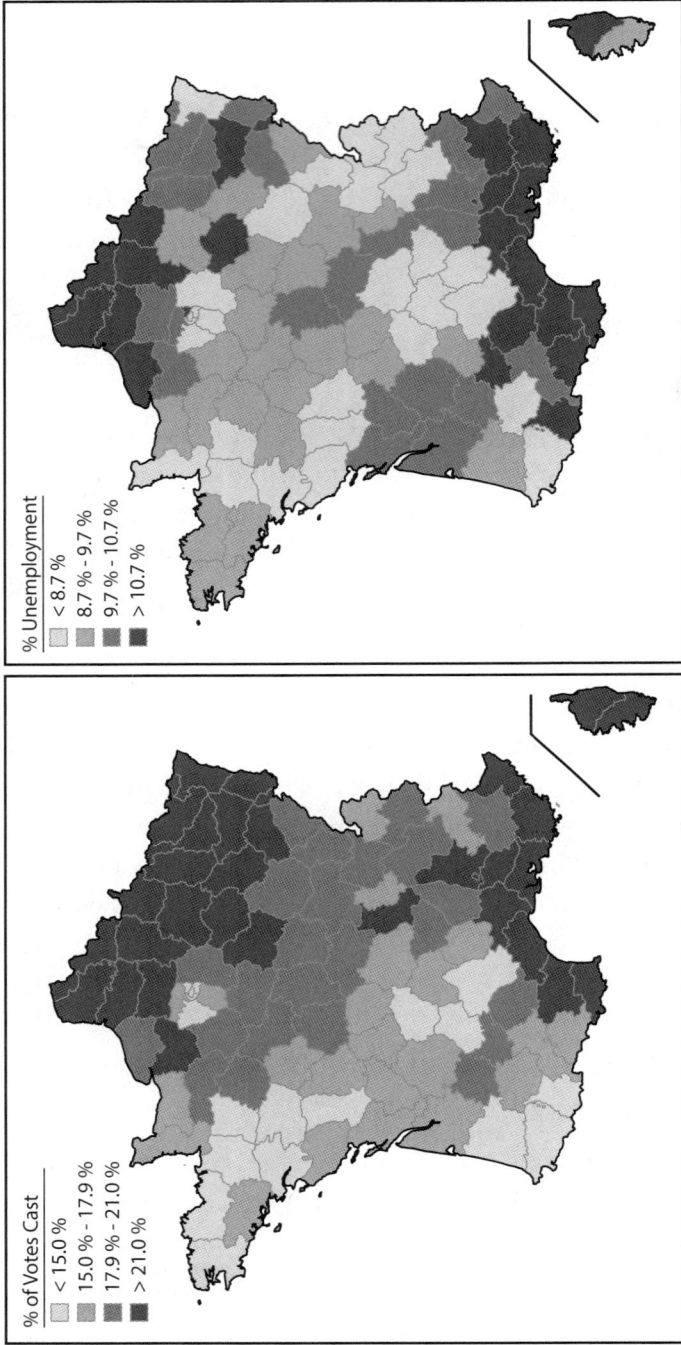

Fig. 14 and Fig. 15. The vote for the Front National, presidential election, France, 2012 (*left panel*); Unemployment rates by department, France, 2011 (*right panel*). Maps by Jim DeGrand.

Rather different have been those cases where it is the centralized welfare states of Western Europe that have come under pressure. Under conditions of geographically uneven development, the welfare state has become an increasingly important vehicle for redistribution from the more prosperous regions to the less so. This is an important condition for the separatist demands of the Northern League in Italy and the New Flemish Alliance in Belgium, as well as for the tensions in Germany that led Charles Jeffery to conclude that "increasingly, competition, rather than cooperation, has become the organizing principle of territorial politics" (1999, 153).

In Great Britain a major issue has been the future of the so-called Barnett formula, according to which local authorities in Scotland and Wales get considerably higher per capita grants than local authorities in England (this was introduced in 1976 in order to dampen down separatist sentiment).[35] Along similar lines, cities are now making calculations of the difference between the share of national taxes that their residents provide and the share of national domestic spending that they receive. This was an issue raised by all candidates for the 2012 mayoral election in London, a historic first in British local politics. But in short, these calculations signify a politics of territorial exploitation quite similar to that which is commonplace in the United States and which was so vividly apparent in the politics of the American Rust Belt, reviewed in chapter 1.

Along with these ideas of territorial exploitation has gone a new emphasis on territorial competition. Symptomatic in Great Britain has been the establishment of the Core Cities Group discussed in chapter 5, which aims at attracting more government money for purposes of embellishing local economies: a response to the huge amounts of money that have been lavished on London. Issues as varied as interest rate policy and the expansion of Heathrow are now passed through the prism of London dominance.[36]

35. These are not insignificant differences. Scotland receives 25 percent more per capita in public expenditure per year than the English regions, and Wales, 15 percent.

36. There has long been concern in Scotland at the way interest rate policy tends to disadvantage growth there. Inflationary pressures in an overheated London and the South East have been met by increases in interest rates, while in Scotland, where overheating

In addition to these territorial tensions within countries, the development of the European Union has led to new ones between them. This development can be interpreted as one response to a failure to restore profitability to the levels characteristic of the 1950s and 1960s—internalizing, for example, a new low-wage periphery in Eastern Europe for outsourcing purposes[37]—but it has injected its own dynamic into the politics of geographically uneven development. In particular, and crucially, it is this which has tended to make the Western European politics of local and regional development more similar to that which prevails in the United States. For as in the case of the states of the United States, there are now no restrictions to the movement of goods, capital and, to an increasing degree, labor, between the EU member states. This means that firms now locate with respect to the EU as a whole rather than with respect to the space economies of individual members. Likewise, location patterns get rationalized on the basis of the geography of the EU taken in toto, as discussed in chapter 5.

The big concern of labor movements and most of the national governments of the more prosperous EU members, has been what has come to be defined as "social dumping"; achieving some gain in employment or investment by taking advantage of an "uneven playing field," though the evenness desired by the more prosperous members would be at a level closer to their own labor, taxation, and welfare standards. These concerns have markedly intensified with the enlargement of the EU to include most of the Eastern European and Baltic states.

Social dumping assumes several forms. In the case of "fiscal dumping" the big issue has been relative rates of corporate taxation. This first

---

would be a pipe dream, the concern is keeping them down so as to facilitate investment. The recommendation to expand Heathrow has also been met with dismay by Scottish taxpayers, who do not want to help fund a project that is of very limited utility to them. Glasgow and Edinburgh airports enjoy limited international routes beyond Europe, and these are complemented only in part by London since airlines operating out of Amsterdam and Quatar have extended connecting links to Scotland so as to channel traffic through *their* hubs.

37. See Hudson (2003; 2015) for a discussion of this.

gained attention through Ireland's relatively low corporate tax rates and subsequent success in attracting American investment. But now the new members want to follow the same path. The Czech Republic, Estonia, Latvia, Lithuania, Hungary, Poland, and Romania have all cut the maximum corporate tax to 20 percent or below. This compares with Belgium, France, and Germany, where the rates are currently in the low thirties. Accordingly, the latter countries have revived the idea of a minimum corporate tax rate for the whole of the EU, and significantly closer to their current rates. There has also been a highly controversial proposal that countries which refuse to co-operate could be deprived of the EU's regional aid to poorer regions, and these are increasingly located in the Eastern European members.

Another concern has been "wage dumping," which came into sharp focus with a 2005 proposal by the EU Commission that would allow service providers like construction companies, catering, and security firms, to compete anywhere in the twenty-five-member EU. A major issue has been the "country of origin principle." This would allow a business to operate in another country under the laws of its own and so undercut local workers by ignoring the local minimum wage and health and safety standards. Labor unions in Germany, France, and some member states with highly developed social welfare structures, including Belgium, France, Germany, and Sweden, have vigorously opposed this proposal. The conflict is ongoing.

Still, a single market does not make the institutional context of the European Union anything close to that of the United States. The introduction of a common currency, the euro, was intended to do that. Not all EU member countries have joined the Eurozone; Great Britain and Sweden are major exceptions even while, unlike the Eastern European countries that are also outside it, they could have qualified in terms of the fiscal thresholds imposed by the European Union. But of those who did join there have been serious problems, underlined by the crisis in Portugal, Ireland, and Greece after the great recession of 2007. The issue has, quite correctly in my view, been presented as one of the proper conditions for a currency zone. The United States has them, but there is considerable doubt about the Eurozone. Just as none of the American states has control over monetary policy, the same applies to those countries belonging to the Eurozone. In its interest-rate-setting powers, the European central bank functions like the Federal Reserve. This works if the economies of member units move in tandem or if there are strong compensatory tendencies to variations in inflationary pressures, but that does not apply to the Eurozone. For some countries, and prior to the great recession, interest rates were too low to restrain inflationary tendencies (notably in Ireland and Spain), and elsewhere they were too high (notably in Germany; instead of spending, Germans were saving, which gave impetus to German firms to export to booming countries like Greece and Spain). In turn the latter borrowed in order to consume, creating imbalances in national accounts that could not continue. In the United States a similar pattern can apply: interest rates may be too high for some state economies and too low for others. The difference is that there are compensatory mechanisms. Despite its deficiencies as a welfare state, regional distress is countered to some degree by the federal taxation system, reducing taxes in the affected areas, and by the loans that the federal government makes to state unemployment compensation programs. And people move away from areas of unemployment to ones where local economies are experiencing something closer to boom conditions. Within the European Union, and *pace* the fuss in countries like Great Britain about migrants from Eastern Europe, these tendencies are quite weak. And, of course, there is no EU welfare state that could counter the disequilibrating tendencies of uneven development.

Wolfgang Streeck (2015) has pointed to another issue—one of different national capitalisms. The southern Eurozone countries are different. Historically, growth has depended on the expansion of domestic demand. This has occurred through budget deficits and wage concessions to relatively strong labor unions. The result has been inflation, but prior to currency union, the problems of external balance that this generated could be, and were, taken care of by periodic devaluations. The northern European model was different: more export-led and in consequence more cost-competitive, much less inflation-prone, therefore, and so able to eschew devaluation. In each instance there is a concomitant moral economy; different growth policies are justified by distinct moral orders: which helps explain why Germans can talk of "lazy Greeks" and the Greeks in turn complain of people who live to work rather than the other way around. The euro, however, in combination with extremely tight monetary policies, has put the Northern countries, notably Germany, the Netherlands, Austria, and Finland in the saddle, putting pressure on governments in Italy, Greece, and Spain to "mend their ways" and adopt a policy model, like more flexible labor markets, which in light of deeply held expectations would be difficult to introduce, at least in the short to moderate term. Again, this is not an issue in the United States: the individual states do not have a history of different economic policies, and the federal government has always played a central role in conditioning views as to what is the appropriate moral economy—which again suggests that the Americanization of local and regional development policy in Western Europe still has a very long way to go.

Concluding Comments

As we saw in chapter 6, and congruent with the institutional forms of local and regional development policy there, in the United States the forms and empirical associations of conflict around it are highly distinctive. Again the comparison with the Western European countries helps throw this distinctiveness into relief. Instead of the localized forms assumed by conflict in the United States, in Western Europe conflicts around development tend to get pushed upward to higher levels of the state since this is where power tends to reside, and in clear contrast to the American case. Meanwhile to the extent that in the United States they *do* get projected upward in the political system, it is likely to be in a bipartisan, territorialized way, as in the struggles around the Rust Belt in the 1980s. In the Western European case, forms of consciousness are much less territorial and, concomitantly, the role of stratification and class clearer, as in Germany's Left Party and France's National Front. This is not to be exaggerated. Electoral struggle modifies positions. The garden grabbing issue in Great Britain was very clearly one for home owners. But the concentration of resentment in the South East, where the Labour Party needed to prevail in close election contests to remain in power, trumped what should have been a response in favor of increasing the housing supply and lowering prices for those struggling under conditions of severe scarcity. Electoral issues aside, the attempt to achieve some national consensus around development issues has always been strong: not just protecting "leafy gardens," therefore, but also the values of the welfare state. Where territory does take over, and explicitly in struggles around development, it expresses itself in a different way than in the United States. The separatist tendencies in Flanders and northern Italy have not been the way out in the United States since the Civil War, which suggests that there is something about the form of the state in the Western European countries that cannot handle issues of severe uneven development of a geographic sort.

This in turn affords some clues as to how we might begin the process of shedding explanatory light on the American case. It is not just the form of the state, though. There is also the political strength of the working class, as in the different priority accorded the ideals of the welfare state. However, any single variable or even multivariable explanation is not going to suffice, as we will see in the final chapter.

8

A Very American Practice

Introduction

All of the advanced capitalist countries have some policy provision for local and regional development. One hundred years ago it would have been very different. But by the immediate postwar period, institutional frameworks to that purpose—ways of publicly addressing what in more abstract terms might be referred to as urban and regional questions—were being elaborated and given coherence. Yet what emerged in the United States as a public responsibility was clearly very different from the way local and regional development was conceived on the other side of the Atlantic.

Viewed close up, there were certainly differences between France, Great Britain, Germany, Italy, the Scandinavian countries, and so on. But the differences paled almost into insignificance when set beside the very, very different American case. In the United States, local and regional development has been a matter for the cities and to a lesser degree the states, both working in close conjunction with and prodded by those firms whose goal, sometimes superordinate and sometimes subordinate, is rent in the various forms yielded by development and control of real estate. Local development has been, not to put too fine a point on it, a free-for-all determined by the competition of one territorially defined entity, one cluster of state-supported rent-seeking interests, with another.

In Western Europe, despite recent and very modest shifts in the direction of the American model, there has been a much stronger central coordination on the part of the state, even planning, when dealing with those locations judged to have implications for jobs, housing, and well-being more generally; something calibrated, at least in national debate, in terms of the "good geography." How, therefore, is this contrast, a contrast that remains very apparent, to be explained? Is this one more instance of American exceptionalism? Is there something distinctive about the American social formation that sheds light on the contrast? And if so, why is it indeed so distinctive?

Obviously, and these contrasts notwithstanding, there are some crucial similarities. It is the capital accumulation process which imparts its distinctive logics to development in both cases, creating possibilities, as in the case of the new spatial divisions of labor of firms discussed in chapter 2, notably in the form of employment generators that could be moved around, as well as imposing constraints. At a very high level of generality, the same goes for the state, class relations, and beliefs. It is always a capitalist state, structured by capitalist logics and by that ongoing struggle between capital and labor that is the other side of the accumulation coin. Part of that struggle is inevitably around understandings, but understandings that are grounded in the material realities (and, therefore, the practical experiences) of capital and wage labor respectively.

And yet, the American state, while remaining a capitalist state, is very different from the more unitary[1] and parliamentary states of Western Europe. It differs not just in its structure, but also in the division of labor arrived at with civil society. How the class relation is experienced, how the classes are represented politically is also at variance, not least the absence of the sort of labor-based party that is taken for granted in Western Europe but also that of a Western European–style conservative party. And this, in turn, comes with a different set of beliefs about the nature of respective social formations: the balance between individual and society, capital and the state, and so on.

None of these specificities stands alone. Class relations and the beliefs that they have entailed, state forms, and divisions of labor are all internally related aspects of a capitalist development process; state forms can only

---

1. "More" unitary, since some of the states, notably Belgium, Germany, Spain, and Switzerland have a federal form, but one that in its structure falls far short of the federation that is the United States.

be understood in terms of class relations and vice versa. There is a set of views embedded in distinct class relationships about the relation of citizen to state, about competition, distinct to the American case that makes its state form meaningful; a necessary consistency, even if there are slippages, contradictions that have to be constantly attended to in order to maintain it. It is not, therefore, with regard to class relations or state forms taken separately as independent forces that we can make any sense of the distinctiveness of the American politics; rather, we must regard it as a social formation *in toto*. I am going to argue, though, that it is differences in class relations, differences embedded in distinct processes of capitalist development, that have been the decisive condition; and that with state forms so conditioned, they help us understand just why development policy and the subsequent politics of development in the United States have been so different; in other words, a very peculiar practice.

The State

In thinking about the state, we need to foreground its capitalist nature and the way in which, in consequence, it is an object of class struggle. It is separate from the economy, which means that it relies on the accumulation process for its revenues, a fact that is, as we have seen, exploited by growth interests in the United States as they push their agenda with state and local governments. All capitalist states share certain functions, including the definition and protection of private property rights and contracts, management of the money supply, and facilitating commodity exchange in other ways (e.g., reducing transaction costs and countering the monopoly power of land owners so as to create those massive pieces of land-consuming public infrastructure so crucial to the operation of a capitalist economy). But while sharing these functions, exactly *how* states are capitalist states, how they advantage the capitalist class and facilitate the accumulation process, is a variable. In this instance, the American state is quite different from those of Western Europe, even granting some differentiation among the latter.

What is at stake here are two major sets of relationships, one having to do with those between the state and the rest of society; and the other with its own institutions. In the first place, therefore, there is the matter of the division of labor between state and civil society. This is partly a question of who gets to do what, like the balance between public and private provision. It is also a matter of how and in what ways those areas of competence are shared, how capitalists and their sidekicks are consulted, recruited into government positions or not, as the case may be, and the legitimacy accorded their claims and arguments. In part, this is about the relation between government and governance.

Second, there is the institutional form of the state. Following Jessop (1990) and his distinction between the respective institutions governing the "inputs," "throughputs," and "outputs" that define the state, I have found it helpful to consider this under three headings:

- The institutionalized practices through which demands are made on the state: political parties, elections, commissions of inquiry taking public evidence, consultation with the public as in rezoning hearings, and lobbying of government officials, elected or otherwise.

- How the state is organized in terms of its own internal division of labor and the coordination of that division of labor. This includes the relations between the three principal branches of the state— the executive, the legislative and the judicial—and the relations between the executive and legislative branches are very different in the United States. There is also the division within the executive to consider, the division into departments and their moral ordering— that is, which ones are defined as more critical to the work of the government: Defense versus housing, perhaps? Production versus the welfare state?

- Modes of intervention include the extent to which the state is reactive rather than *proactive*. I have already suggested that in the matter of local and regional development the American state and its various branches, particularly the more central ones, have tended to be quite passive compared with their Western European cousins. According to Jessop (2002), the degree to which and the ways in which states intervene has recently shifted: he has talked about a displacement of the Keynesian welfare state by a Schumpeterian workfare state in which, while the state withdraws from some functions, its mode of intervention also shifts toward the more regulatory pole and away from that of financial inducement. Again, this is germane to this discussion.

In practice, of course, it is not always easy to separate questions of the division of labor between state and capital from the state as an institutional ensemble. Struggles around state institutions are often also struggles around defining the boundaries of the state, as in the debate that can surround the creation of new government departments—whether or not the state should indeed be intervening in the sphere of activity carved out for it. The same applies to what sorts of representational practices get legitimated; for example, debates in the United States about campaign finance. So to repeat: state forms differ, as does the division of labor between state and civil society. The discussion now turns to an examination of those differences.

The State and Society

In talking about the separation of state from civil society, the most obvious, even notorious distinction in the American instance is the relative weakness of the welfare state: the capacity of the state to supplement private incomes, to provide a social safety net, and to provide for the health and shelter of even the most impecunious. Public housing has had a major presence in the countries of northern and northwestern Europe, excepting Germany, while in the United States the state has been much more assiduous in promoting provision through the private market and relying on trickle down for the housing of the masses. And in Western Europe, universal health insurance with varying articulations within a (strongly regulated) private insurance industry has long prevailed: an interesting contrast with the only recently enacted Affordable Health Care Act, where proposals for establishing the state as a source of insurance, disciplining the private insurance industry, fell by the wayside. Housing vouchers, as in Section 8, are another case of acceding to private interests, and the attempt to diffuse the idea of vouchers into the school system, exchangeable either in the public or private sector, is ongoing. In short, it is not just a matter of the degree to which the welfare of the masses is provided for; it is also the manner of that provision.

Another expression of a distinct division of labor between state and civil society has been the degree to which the state owns or has a majority stake in respective economies. In Western Europe, publicly owned industry has tended to play a much more important part in economic life. As discussed in chapter 4, historically this provided important leverage in urban and regional policy, and to some degree it still does, as in the development of France's TGV network and decisions on the location of routes and stations. Privatization since the 1970s, though, has reduced the extent of public ownership, and in some cases very significantly indeed (notably that of Great Britain with the sale of the nationalized coal, iron and steel, and shipbuilding industries). This does not mean that in the United States the state has not provided public financial support to industry. The most obvious beneficiaries of this are the various defense industries and through them, their suppliers;[2] and given the significance of US arms exports around the world, not to mention the spillovers into the production for civil consumption of airplanes and computers, it would be incorrect to see this spending as merely a matter of national defense.

Also distinctive of state-society separation in the United States has been the peculiar way in which the state functions as a regulatory state. Regulatory functions have grown enormously since the late nineteenth century in all the advanced capitalist societies and clearly predate the impetus given to them by the growth of the welfare state: public health, housing standards, urban planning, waste disposal, the handling of industrial chemicals, health and safety in the workplace, and transportation are just a few of many examples. What is different about the United States, though, is the way in which this has tended to occur not just through government departments, as elsewhere, but also through specialized agencies and commissions, and with legislative committees as quite crucial intermediaries, at least at state and federal levels.

---

2. As Ann Markusen (1991a) has pointed out in her work on what she has called the "Gunbelt," this has had quite clear implications for regional development.

Lowi's (1969) critique of this is well known. He drew attention to the way in which organized groups representing particular business interests, perhaps representing specific sectors of the economy, benefited from the actions of federal and state agencies and commissions, even stimulated their creation to start with, and how their interests were represented in legislative committees: what he called an extension of representation into the executive branch. Well before Lowi, though, what was referred to as the "iron triangle" had attracted attention: a relation between those to be regulated, the agency or other government bureaucracy supposed to regulate them, and a legislative committee through which, in various ways, the regulated determine, in effect, how they will be regulated. A classic instance is that embracing irrigation interests in the West, what used to be the House and Senate Committees on Interior and Insular Affairs, and the Bureau of Reclamation.[3] In some cases private interests actually "help" in drafting legislation. This, it will be recalled from chapter 3, was how NAREB got the stiffening of zoning regulations that it sought into the FHA rules governing federal mortgage insurance.

These connections are then reinforced by what has come to be known as "the revolving door": former elected officials or their assistants go to work for business interests and their lobbying groups providing advice and connections to help them achieve their goals with government bureaucracies, committees, and agencies. It works in the reverse direction as well. Business people get appointed to positions in the government or seconded, and then acquire capacities that can be turned to profitable purpose when they leave it.

The whole bizarre situation obviously rests on a particular structuring of the state: the proliferation of nonelective agencies, the committee system, and the weakness of political parties so that individual legislators are not tied to a strong party line and can be, in effect, bought.[4] It also,

3. Now respective House and Senate Committees on Natural Resources.

4. There is evidence that the revolving door at least is now catching on in Western Europe and is certainly raising concerns and attempts to rein it in. So long as party discipline remains strict and the use of committees is limited, though, so too will be this particular practice.

and obviously, depends on a legitimacy accorded to business that is alien on the other side of the Atlantic. The public justification is that those to be regulated are the ones who know most about their particular line of business; they have the expertise. But this is clearly giving the matter a benefit of the doubt that could be challenged and often is by a muckraking press, but not to a point that makes much difference.

The more positive view of these arrangements, of course, particularly when the way they are heavily loaded toward business interests can get bracketed out of the conversation, is that they are evidence of that nice, neutral-sounding idea "governance": a democratization of the state that encourages concertation of government with groups representative of civil society, or at least those with a stake in a particular issue. This is an idea that has been of particular interest in the literature on local development through what is known as urban regime theory, even while it is recognized that most urban regimes are much more accommodating of business interests than of more popular and progressive ones (Stone 1987). Royce Hanson (1974), in what is now a fairly old but still relevant paper, pointed out just how, in detail, this can and often does work out.[5]

State Institutions and the Territorial Structure of the State

In talking about the state as an institutional ensemble, and as outlined earlier, Jessop has suggested that we think of it in terms of an articulation between three different types of institution: those governing, respectively, what he has called "inputs," "throughputs," and "outputs." Before focusing more narrowly on the way the state is structured territorially and the

---

5. "From the point of view of land development, the functional or special-purpose agencies and intergovernmental bureaucracies may be as important as the general-purpose local jurisdictions. Major public works are often the responsibility of independent, special purpose authorities . . . For the most part, these special agencies have direct contact with client groups, not with the public at large. It is not strange, then, that those interested in development take special care to cultivate the bureaucrats in the agencies, who naturally tend to care for 'their' public, which in turn protects the agency from criticism or curtailment of operations" (Hanson 1974, 17). See also Piven and Friedland (1984).

difference that might make for the politics of urban and regional development, it is helpful to think of these in relatively aspatial terms (see Table
5). Some of the differences essential to the argument here can be captured
through a set of oppositions and an emphasis on the different balances
between the two poles. Historically, political parties in the United States
have been relatively weak: party discipline is weaker as are the national
party organizations with respect to state and local ones. In legislative
determinations, bipartisan coalitions, shifting in their composition from
one issue to another, are relatively common. This means that the degree
to which elections are contested around a shared platform is much more
variable: the fact of the primary election elicits somewhat heterogeneous,
more locally responsive positions that are alien to the Western European
case. On the other hand, the American state has proven itself much more
open to interest groups and to lobbying, something conveyed by the attention that American political science has given to them for a very long time
and to the associated idea of pluralism. The other thing to notice is the
historic role of governance in the American case. Governance is often
treated as something that arrived with the post-Fordist state (Jessop 2002),
but as I pointed out in chapter 5, it has a long history in the United States.
The notion of the iron triangle originated there and was clearly operating long before it was discovered by academics. Meanwhile, the idea of
"government," of governing at some remove from those being governed,
has enjoyed a much greater legitimacy in Western Europe than in the
United States: something that was clearly puzzling to the American political scientist Stephen Elkin (1974) when he conducted research on land
use planning decisions in London.

In terms of the way the state is organized internally, what is most striking about the American case is the radical fragmentation of formal power:
the famous "checks and balances." This contrasts with the much greater
concentration in the European case—something captured by the way in
which executive and legislative branches overlap so that the ruling party in
the executive branch is also the ruling party in the legislature and depart-
mental ministers vote on the legislation that they themselves have proposed.
Meanwhile, in the United States legislation has to make its way through an
appropriate committee. This creates centrifugal forces which have only a

Table 5

Comparative State Structures

	United States	Western Europe
Inputs	• Political parties: weaker • Interest group representation: stronger • Greater emphasis on governance	• Political parties: stronger • Interest group representation: weaker • Greater emphasis on government
Throughputs	Fragmentation of formal power	Concentration of formal power
Outputs	• Weaker levels of state coordination: creating a "level playing field." • Favoring provision through the market.	• Stronger levels of state coordination: creating the "good society." • Favoring provision through the state.

limited counterpart in Western Europe where, in effect, the cabinet serves as a grand committee. On top of all that, of course, there is the fact that the United States is a very, very radical federation: not the confederation that it replaced but still according quite massive powers to the individual states. Not all the Western European states are unitary, but their federations— Belgium, Germany, Spain, and Switzerland—are in comparison weak tea.

Finally there are the different modes of intervention. What one notices in the American instance is the way in which legislative provision so often favors the private sector. Health care was long a matter for provision through employers, and recent reforms have given a privileged position to the private insurance industry quite at odds with the Western European case. Providing services in-house is seen as just another case of "big government" rather than something judged, through careful deliberation within the government itself, at a distance from interest groups, to be better provided through the state than through the market. Rather, what the American state should be doing, or so the common argument goes, is "creating a level playing field": making sure that the state, through its legislation, does not favor one firm/worker/region/sector over another. In other words, the market is the best possible aggregator of popular demand—a view that in Western Europe has been far from the accepted view, even with the recent neoliberal turn.

Table 6

The Territorialization of the American State

	United States	*Western Europe*
Inputs	More territorialized	More deterritorialized
Organization	• More decentralized (powers and responsibilities) • Flexibility in local government	• More centralized (powers and responsibilities • A central template for local government
Outputs	• In their explicitly territorial aspects, unplanned: a result of the quasi-market relations of decentralized powers. • Implicitly territorial: policies for people that are geographically heterogeneous	• In their explicitly territorial aspects, planned: the good geography • Implicitly indifferent to territory: policies for people that are geographically invariant.

When projected onto a territorial plane (Table 6), what these contrasts amount to are very different contexts for a politics of urban and regional development. In the American case, state structure provides a formidable set of tools for local and regional growth interests to pursue their agendas (Christopherson 2010).[6] In the Western European case, it is the center that tends to get advantaged both in setting an agenda and in implementing it. A major fact to consider here is that, territorially, formal power in the American state is also quite extraordinarily fragmented. On the one hand, American federalism is unusually strong; and on the other, the states have to a very considerable degree, delegated to their respective local governments powers that are quite crucial from the standpoint of local economic development.

All states have what might be called a scale division of labor. Different areas of authority are allocated to different, geographically defined branches: central and local, and in some cases regional as well. There

6. For a worked out statement of this position, see Cox (2004). Brenner (2008) has underlined the significance of some aspects of this for the American case.

is also an allocation of responsibilities in terms of what has to be done and how the execution of those responsibilities is to be financed. These relations have asymmetries. States monitor local governments. Intergovernmental grants are made from more central to more local branches, but always with conditions. However, the degree to which the different, geographically defined branches of the state can act independently of one another varies tremendously. This is typically conceived along a unitary/federal dimension; in federal states, different areas of sovereignty are assigned to the federal government and to the governments of the component units respectively, whereas in the unitary form the central state is sovereign and the powers and responsibilities of local branches are delegated to them. But there are different degrees of federalism. The number of powers reserved for the federal branch is relatively high in the Australian and Swiss cases and much lower in the US instance. To underline: American federalism is of an extreme nature.

American states have unusual powers and responsibilities. But the fragmentation of the state receives further impetus by the fact of delegation to local governments. Local governments dispose of their own ensemble of statutory capacities, and many of these can be turned to the purpose of "expanding local economies." Among the more significant of these one would have to include: a land use regulation process that is subject to very little in the way of state oversight; control of water and sewer line extensions; powers to annex unincorporated land; the ability to make tax concessions to investors; the ability to raise money on the private bond market to finance public works projects like airports, convention centers, sports stadiums; and—certainly important for those typically suburban growth interests trying to carve out positions in local geographic divisions of consumption—the provision of schooling.[7] One should emphasize that these functions are delegated by the states and not constitutionally prescribed. But as a result of the way in which different local forces acquire a vested

---

7. Which helps to explain why, in cases of referenda on local school bond levies in the suburbs, realty interests will often be prominent in their support of those pressing for passage.

interest in at least some of them taking them away can in practice be politically very difficult indeed.[8]

Even after this delegation though, the states retain very considerable powers of the highest significance for the accumulation process. Their fiscal, labor law, and welfare responsibilities are a case in point. To reiterate, the American welfare state is more accurately defined as the American welfare states. This is because the individual states retain major competencies with respect to, inter alia, taxation, unemployment compensation, workers' compensation, minimum wages, so-called "right-to-work" laws,[9] education, and aid to single parent households. All these can be, and are, used in the struggle to attract inward investment and to retain existing industrial bases, though the specifics can vary a great deal depending on whether one is hitching state economic futures to low-wage work or to more knowledge-intensive forms of labor process. And while this is to foreground the struggle for positions in the geographic division of labor, state powers can also be turned to attracting in wealthy consumers, like retirees; Nevada's zero inheritance taxes are an extreme and graphic case of this, though highly effective given its long border with California, a state with relatively heavy taxes of all sorts.

This is not to marginalize other aspects of state structure, which enhance the powers available to local growth coalitions. There is, in particular, a remarkable territorialization of representation that also plays into the hands of local growth coalitions. Local representatives in state and federal legislatures have a quite extraordinary power to get things done and to turn central powers to local advantage.

One of the reasons for this is the committee system. Under the US Constitution, it is the legislative branch that has the sole power to introduce legislation. This does not mean that the executive level cannot have its own legislative agenda; rather, any bills it proposes have to be introduced by a member of the legislature. Legislators also retain the right to amend any such bills. But before any bill is considered by the

---

8. But it can happen. Only municipalities gain from the annexation power. Unincorporated areas are the losers and this can unleash struggles around placing limits on it.

9. Laws forbidding the closed shop.

full assembly—the House of Representatives and the Senate—it must first be assigned to respective committees for study, hearings, revisions, and approval. If the bill does not move out of committee then it dies. Committees will include members of both majority and minority parties, and they play a part in enabling legislators to achieve constituency-specific ends, a part whose significance cannot be overemphasized.

This is because senators and congresspersons typically get to sit on those committees most relevant to their constituencies. In this way, not only is there a strengthening of local influence on committee deliberations—a conflict of interest which again those who worship at the altar of the American constitution would prefer to ignore—but also a strengthening of the power of particular business interests. As mentioned above, the House Committee on Interior and Insular Affairs (now the Committee on Natural Resources) occupies a gatekeeper position with respect to the authorization of federally funded irrigation projects (see Berkman and Viscusi 1971; Reisner 1986). Committee membership is typically dominated by those Western states that have the most interest in them. Farming areas are overrepresented on the various agriculture committees, and those representing constituencies that contain major military installations on armed services. The House Committee on Merchant Marine and Fisheries is drawn almost exclusively from districts bordered by the ocean or the Great Lakes. On the House Financial Services Committee, the current representation of major banking centers is overwhelming. Of New York State's twenty-seven representatives, the five who sit on that committee all represent districts in the New York City metro area. Of North Carolina's thirteen representatives, the two on the Financial Services Committee represent districts taking in or bordering Charlotte, another major banking center, if not of the same order as New York City.

This puts committee members in a strategic position not just to block legislation that will be to the disadvantage of constituent interests, or at least those which have some clout; but also to add to bills special provisions that meet some local need. The Wright Amendment, discussed in chapter 1 in the context of the travails of DFWI and the struggle with Southwest Airlines, is a nice illustration. Congressman Wright represented a district that took in Fort Worth, and was a member of the House Committee on Public Works and Transportation, which got to consider air transport legislation; hence his amendment to the ironically titled International Air Transportation Competition Act of 1979.

In fact this type of concession may be the price of obtaining a committee member's support for a bill that, in terms of overall thrust, is not one that he or she feels comfortable with. This may not be obvious. Provisions are often articulated in a universalistic language that can be misleading. The local thresholds in terms of economic conditions that make states or congressional districts eligible for certain types of aid will be artfully designed to take care of the constituencies of committee members, which helps to explain the tendency to spread federal largesse around, to the detriment of achieving the program goal. Or definitions will be specified sufficiently broadly as to cater to some local need.

Because of their power in the legislative process, the committees also attract around them a variety of other interests that stand to gain from the decisions made. Foremost are the various agencies of the federal government itself. Something like the Army Corps of Engineers or the Bureau of Reclamation will have a lot at stake simply because their funding and their ability to keep people employed will depend on whether or not a bill leaves committee for consideration on the floors of the House and Senate. As a result they form close relations with committee members, anxious to provide the data, appropriately selected and massaged, that will advance the claims of pieces of legislation of particular interest to members; or to facilitate a justification of those bills the committee opposes and which also threaten to diminish the role of the agency in question.

In short, committees are a major focus of interest for legislators because of the power they afford to deliver benefits to their immediate constituents, or at least those constituents who are able to command their attention. Many of these benefits may well harmonize with party programs, strictly or loosely expressed, but the point is: It is not necessary that they do so. And when it comes to consideration of bills on the floor of the House or Senate, the same balance of power between individual legislator and party asserts itself. Party discipline over the voting of those who claim the party label tends to be relatively weak. Members' positions on particular issues tend to be influenced more by the balance of advantage for the home district, or for some interests there, than by any calculation of party gain (Kau and Rubin 1982). For the individual legislator, the state or congressional district they represent is a significant horizon for roll call votes, and one with which the claims of party must compete. By the standards of parliamentary democracies, this sensitivity to constituency pressures is nothing short of extraordinary. The position taken on roll call votes is influenced as much if not more by social and economic conditions "back home" than by party affiliation, as numerous studies of roll call voting have demonstrated. This means that voting on many issues pertaining to urban and regional development is seriously bipartisan, as Bensel (1984) has indicated in his study of American sectionalism. At the same time, the weakness of party in determining positions on legislative issues opens up the way for logrolling: the exchange of favors between one group of legislators and another, sometimes belonging to the same party but sometimes not. So the weakness of party creates a space for the consummation of all manner of deals having constituency implications.

Yet if constituency interests are paramount in the calculus of representatives and senators, whether in committee or on the House and Senate floors, respectively, this begs the question of why local rather than national party agendas are able to dominate? An immediate answer lies in the way in which candidates are selected. Unlike the case of parliamentary democracies, national parties in the United States exercise much less power over the selection of candidates. Rather the selection process is highly localized in terms of both where it is staged and the influences to which it is subject. And among these influences, those with money loom large owing to the way in which election campaigns, including the primaries through which candidates are selected, are funded.

The effect of the direct primary, introduced as a Progressive reform around 1900 as part of their general horror of monopoly and its supposed implications for party corruption, was to amplify these localizing effects (Epstein 1986). In the direct primary, choice of candidates is carried out in a state-regulated election. The list of candidates cannot be limited by the dictates of any party organization. Rather, anyone who wants to claim the party label can stand. This approach results in a more candidate-centered politics and a less party-centered one. It consequently creates a space for support bases for party candidates that, taken as a whole, are much more geographically varied than would otherwise be the case. In the primary election each candidate tries to carve out a distinct position for him/herself in an attempt to appeal to a particular social base that is not shared with the other candidates. The positions represented by the different candidates—for the same party, that is—in the subsequent *general* election, are therefore likely to be far more varied than could ever be encompassed by a common political platform. So the allegiance to such a platform and what is viewed as good for the nation is likely to be quite weak. By the same token, locally specific coalitions of forces get assembled, and it is to those coalitions that the elected representative will tend to feel more responsible than in a situation where the party exercised more control over candidate selection: the coalition, after all, comprises the people who elected them to office and funded their primary campaign, and the party label was of relatively minor significance. The local representative therefore has an incentive to deliver, to answer to specifically local interests. She herself has an intense interest in the economic fortunes of "her" locality.[10]

And so too does local government. Local governments participate in growth coalitions, get seduced by the projects of particular property developers, collaborate with counterparts in the wider urban region, and support the introduction of those institutional mechanisms that will facilitate the provision of the sort of physical and social infrastructures demanded by inward investors, because they see gains for themselves. This in turn is because of the very substantial degree to which they depend for their revenues on local taxes: property taxes, sales taxes, and income taxes. This dependence varies somewhat from state to state. In terms of education, some states, like New Hampshire, have quite radical measures for ensuring

---

10. According to David Mayhew in his book *Congress: The Electoral Connection* (cited by Ellwood and Patashnik 1993) Congressional life consists largely of a "relentless search" for ways of claiming credit for making good things happen back home and so increasing the likelihood of re-election. Federally funded infrastructure, awarding an Enterprise Zone, cheap loans for inward investors are all things for which the individual congressperson can claim credit—credit, moreover, that they will not shy away from but rather will advertise through media events.

equality of per-pupil expenditures between school districts of quite highly differentiated fiscal capacity, but they are the exception. The general picture is one of uneven abilities to generate revenues—an unevenness that is alleviated by the state only to a very limited extent.[11]

Local governments look to the states for favorable legislation on development issues, and the states have their own reasons for providing support. Quite aside from the way in which unemployment levels factor into state election contests, particularly for governor, the fact is that states too enjoy (if that is the appropriate term) high levels of fiscal home rule. They depend on state taxes and fees for the bulk of their expenditures, and this dependence is intensified by the absence of any provision at all for territorial redistribution on the part of the federal government. Significantly, and among the established federations, only the United States does *not* have a policy of fiscal transfers designed to at least narrow differences in fiscal capacities across its component units. This concern for tax base, at both state and local levels, is then intensified by the characteristic mode of raising money for capital expenditures, which (and again in sharp contrast to other advanced industrial societies) is through the private bond market. The result is a vulnerability to the rating process and, in consequence, a strong interest in embellishing that state or local tax base out of which bonds must ultimately be repaid. And of course, those local governments most in need of bond monies are the ones whose paper is typically downgraded by the rating agencies, and so they have to pay a higher rate of interest (see Table 7 for examples from some Midwestern cities).

The radically decentralized form of the American state has deep historical roots. Obviously, it was constitutionally entailed, but it has also been substantially deepened over the years. The Progressive movement at the end of the nineteenth century was the culmination of a strong tradition of populism. It entrenched fragmentation and compromised in various ways, often inadvertently, the possibility of a strong, centralizing labor movement. The significance of the primary election for the territorialization of

11. This accounts for the widely felt concern, inter alia, for fiscal disparities between the local governments comprising metropolitan areas.

Table 7

Local Economic Conditions and Bond Ratings for Midwestern Cities

	Population Growth, 1990–2000	Unemployment Rate, 2000	Retail Sales Per Capita, 1997	S&P Bond Rating, 2005*
Chicago	+ 4.0	5.6	4944	AA–
Cincinnati	– 9.1	5.1	8871	AA+
Cleveland	– 5.4	8.7	4751	A
Columbus	+ 11.8	2.8	12852	AAA
Dayton	– 8.9	6.5	6072	***
Detroit	– 7.5	6.6	3269	BBB
Indianapolis	+ 6.9	3.0	13751	AAA
Louisville	– 5.0	3.7	8061	AA+
Milwaukee	– 5.0	6.7	5785	AA
Minneapolis	+ 3.9	3.2	6588	AAA
Pittsburgh	– 9.6	4.1	7922	BBB–
St. Louis	– 12.2	6.6	6856	A–

* Fourth quarter; order of rating categories: AAA, AA, A, BBB, BB, B; the addition of a plus or minus sign indicates relative standing within those major rating categories.
*** Not available.

formal political power in the United States has already been noted. The view of state and city government as corrupt was also a significant element in the Progressive view (Weir 2005). Not least, it was a condition for the liberalization of laws allowing the incorporation of new cities. These rules included small population thresholds and a tightening up of those governing annexation. In turn, these provisions facilitated the growth of independent suburbs around the larger cities and so allowed people, or so it was believed, to become independent of the big city machine—another way in which competition would trump monopoly but without an awareness of what the consequences would ultimately be. For it created the extraordinary jurisdictional fragmentation that is a hallmark of the contemporary American metropolitan area, laying a basis for a competition not in the provision of "good government" as the Progressives intended, but for privileged positions in geographic divisions of consumption. At the same time, the addition of city manager government and the nonpartisan ballot helped seal off vast urban areas from the class politics that accompanied party rule, so subverting serious challenge to the dominance of territorial imaginaries. As Newton (1978) has pointed out though, jurisdictional fragmentation itself served the same purpose because fragmentation precluded the formation of any political arena in which class issues, or more accurately those of social stratum, might be rehearsed. Rather, the antagonist was located somewhere else in the metropolitan area and beyond the redress afforded by municipal ordinance.[12]

Not only, therefore, do congresspersons and senators see themselves as responsible to local interests owing to the nature of the candidate selection process, but the committee system and weak party discipline in floor votes means that they can also be responsive. From the standpoint of the electorate, this in turn signifies that between party and candidate as cues for voting choices, the balance tends much more in the direction of the candidate than it does in parliamentary systems like those of Great Britain, France, or Germany.

The same sort of constellation of relations between legislator, party and constituency repeats itself at the state level. As at the federal level, candidates for election to state houses need a local support base; the party label just will not suffice. They must run the same gauntlet of the primary and have to distinguish themselves from other candidates by appealing to a particular, place-specific cluster of interests. And once elected, legislators attempt to consolidate their local support base by soliciting proposals for state legislation from local interest groups (Shefter 1978).

12. "The creation of a large number of political arenas has a tendency to reduce political conflict and competition. Social groups can confront each other when they are in the same arena, but this possibility is reduced when they are separated into different arenas. Political differences are easier to express when groups occupy the same political system and share the same political institutions, but this is more difficult when the groups are divided by political boundaries and do not contest the same elections, do not fight for control of the same political offices, do not contest public policies for the same political units, or do not argue about the same municipal budgets" (Newton 1978, 84).

If the weakness of the parties facilitates local deal making, so too is this the case at the state level. Logrolling between the representatives of different areas of the state is the norm rather than the exception. To some degree this has been formalized in a reciprocity rule: state assemblies will not reject legislation relating to a particular city submitted by the state delegation from that city so long as there is support from the delegation in question.[13] Historically in Illinois, Chicago could exercise power by striking bargains with downstate Republicans and Democrats, leaving the Republican-dominated suburbs out of the deal (Weir 1996). This allowed Chicago to acquire support for local development projects and a broader base for financing many city costs, including social spending. A common pattern was that the city agreed to support the governor's budget in exchange for major economic development initiatives. This was how a regional transportation authority joining Chicago and its independent suburbs came into being, even though suburban representatives opposed it fearing that they would become responsible for the costs of the insolvent Chicago Transit Authority.[14]

The openness of the American state—the deal making to which it lends itself—also creates space for new forms of state structure at the local level: new ways of administering, of spreading fiscal risks, of affording access to larger tax bases, all of which are looked to as still more ways of creating a competitive advantage in the ongoing struggle for inward investment and more generally for the money that will irrigate the investments of property companies. So-called urban delegations to state legislative assemblies are crucial vehicles in the construction of new forms of urban government by clearing away obstacles and sponsoring the enabling legislation, if it should be needed. Metropolitan areas in the United States exhibit a huge variety of governmental forms, and that is

13. As Burns et al. (2009) have shown, the unity of those representatives from a particular urban area is important in securing the consent of the legislative assembly as a whole.

14. This power of the City of Chicago working through its state representatives is no longer what it once was. See Margaret Weir (1996).

only in part to do with the fact that they are in separate states, since many of them are not. Columbus, by virtue of state enabling legislation that neutralized the opposition of suburban school districts (Cox and Jonas 1993), has been able to continue to expand by annexation in ways that have not been possible for Cincinnati and Cleveland, since they were already surrounded by other municipalities: something that has paid off in terms of its ability to raise money for capital projects (see Table 7).[15] The Los Angeles area is unique among metro areas in California in its so-called Lakewood system, an arrangement through which small municipalities are able to take advantage of the economies of scale accruing to Los Angeles County by contracting out for various services. Without it, it is unlikely that the area would have experienced the suburban development in the form that it has (Connor 2013). In upstate New York, the Niagara Frontier Transportation Authority brings together airports and mass transit in the Buffalo area and through its subsidiaries, like the Buffalo Niagara International Airport, raises money for its expansion through the sale of its own bonds. One effect of this is to reduce the bonded debt of Buffalo itself and so give it more room in which to raise money for other projects.

In Western Europe the highly centralized form of the state, corresponding to the way the state concentrates power, means that in contrast to the American case, the scope for local and regional development forces advancing their agendas is much, much more limited. Local governments lack the sorts of formal powers available to local governments in the United States. There will certainly be a local planning apparatus, but unlike the American case, it is typically subject to strong central oversight powers. As discussed in chapter 4, local plans are scrutinized for consistency with those of neighboring local governments. Local planning offices are subject in their recommendations to local councils to advisories and various bits of "guidance," or simply orders coming down from the center.

15. High retail sales per capita (Table 7) are a result of the way in which Columbus has managed, in virtue of its aggressive annexation, to corral all the major regional shopping centers within its boundaries. This in turn generates relatively large streams of sales tax revenue.

Raising money for local public works depends on negotiations with the central state and not, as in the American instance, selling bonds to private investors as the occasion arises. Annexation again means working through central government offices rather than operating within some loose set of rules that typically favor municipalities. And one of the reasons for the relative absence of the territorial competition that is taken for granted in the United States is the fact that the sorts of concessions that local governments can make there, either on their own or through the cooperation of state governments, simply are not possible or are not attractive.[16]

In the same way, the vehicles for mobilizing central branches of the state, harnessing its offices to local purposes, are by and large missing. Political parties are much more centralized, territorial representation more nominal, and party discipline of a strength that makes the assembling of bipartisan coalitions around regional issues much harder.[17] And there is nothing like the American committee system. There are some qualifications. In France, the practice of le *cumul des mandats*, as discussed in chapter 2, has been a crucial means of funneling state largesse to local purposes.[18] But by and large the wriggle room for those wishing to pursue local or regional programs of development is very limited.

One result is the way in which, in the wake of the intensification of geographically uneven development under neoliberal dispensations, separatist movements have either been reinvigorated or, where they did not already exist, emerged as with the Northern League in Italy and the various Flemish nationalist parties in Belgium. Their antagonism is toward respective welfare states, which, in a context of increasing uneven development, have,

16. In the British case, if a local government offers a reduction in business taxes, it has to compensate the central government. This is because the business component of the local property tax is subject to a national rate that is common across the country as a whole and is collected by the national government. This preempts offering financial incentives to new investors. But keeping existing investment can be problematic as EU law, as we saw in the last chapter, forbids the offering of state incentives to keep plants open where the company concerned has plants in other EU member countries.

17. Though not impossible. For a British case see Bassett and Hoare (1984).

18. For some striking cases see Subra (2007, chapter 3).

or so the arguments of the interested parties go, put them in the position of net donors. I also noted the emergence of new, non-separatist parties that have regional support bases, as in the case of the German Left party and the Front National in France. But the point is, none of this would be likely to happen in the United States. Rather, the way in which political parties function in virtue of the structure of the American state, makes them broad churches, seemingly infinitely expansive in terms of the factions and interests, including regional ones, that they can accommodate. The weakness of interregional redistribution mechanisms also makes a difference: it is these, after all, that are at issue in Belgium and Italy.

What the Western European states *have* been able to do, though with increasing difficulty since the 1980s, is impose some vision of the "good geography": programs designed to redistribute employment so as to even out unemployment rates, and to alleviate local economic distress. And this is a point that merits more intensive discussion and illustration, since it underlines so clearly how and why the American politics is so distinct. For there have been and continue to be more top-down sorts of initiative aimed at alleviating geographically uneven development. But in practice they have been subject to centrifugal forces of such an intensity as to compromise, even undermine, their original intent. Through the committee system legislators get to structure the criteria according to which areas will qualify for government assistance and, given the fragmentation of powers in the American state, that means doing it so as to benefit their own districts or states, and any central vision be damned.

A case of this originated in the initiatives of the Economic Development Administration (EDA), a federal agency accountable to the secretary for commerce (Barnekov, Boyle, and Rich 1989). From 1965 on, the EDA was required to promote the development of areas of persistent unemployment. This was to be accomplished through grants and loans for physical infrastructure, job training programs, and long-term, low-interest loans to firms willing to establish plants in the eligible areas. But the ultimate goal of alleviating pockets of severe economic distress was compromised by the way in which Congress manipulated the various criteria as to what constituted eligibility for these funds. The desire of individual congresspersons, of course, was that their own constituencies would be included (Barnekov, Boyle, and Rich 1989, 111). The result was that about 80 percent of the US population found themselves in the areas eligible.[19]

Ellwood and Patashnik (1993) comment in similar vein on the outcome of the Model Cities program of the mid-1960s. Originally intended to funnel billions in demonstration grants to the nation's ten most severely distressed cities to see if comprehensive aid could alleviate urban poverty, by the time the bill became law the number of eligible cities had increased by a factor of fifteen! In Great Britain's town expansion schemes of the 1950s and 1960s, not all the towns identified as eligible took the offer up. In the US context that simply would not have happened. In fact, it would have been hard to resist the claims of any and all towns to be on the list of those qualified for centrally subsidized expansion.

The same tendencies can be observed in respective enterprise zone legislation. Whereas in the British instance local authorities were asked to bid for a very limited number of enterprise zone designations, in the American case the legislation of the individual states has been extraordinarily permissive. In Britain there have only ever been eighteen, and in France never more than thirty-eight; but there are currently thirty-nine in California, ninety-one in Illinois, fifty-two in New York State and in the state of Ohio, with just under a sixth of the population of Great Britain, there are well in excess of an already remarkable three hundred.[20]

These tendencies are not confined to the policies of federal and state governments. City councils are subject to similar sorts of pressures. If

19. Barnekov, Boyle, and Rich (1989) quote from Grasso: "There is little evidence that the agency's programs have succeeded in promoting the economic development of chronically depressed areas. Rather, the agency seems to have concentrated on achieving the goal of a wide geographic dispersal of aid, with a disproportionate share of the funds channeled to States with disproportionate representation in Congress" (79). Arnold (1981) provides an excellent discussion of how local influences tend to prevail and trump federal visions of how local development should proceed.

20. Ireland, though, is an exception to these arguments about the implications of a decentralized state. Even with a highly centralized one, it is very vulnerable to centrifugal tendencies working through local representatives. See Breathnach (2010).

money is set aside to revive an ailing retailing strip it is in practice hard to resist claims that the same money should also be allocated to other retailing strips elsewhere in the city, though clearly what stands for "ailing" gets redefined and watered down in the process. The same goes for gentrification projects. The result is that the money delivers less because it is less spatially concentrated in its effects, less capable of generating the sorts of externality effects that might lift redevelopment above that threshold at which it becomes self-sustaining.

If property capitals and the representatives of the growth coalitions to which they often belong were asked to design a set of state institutions conducive to the way they practice their trade, it is hard to imagine how they could have improved on what they already have. Even so, it is also the case that without that particular ensemble of institutions, those particular ways of accessing the state and restraining its power, the susceptibility of local and state governments to developer and property company blandishments, all the while exploiting the revenue extraction capacities of the federal government, the various coalitions of forces that they form, including growth coalitions, would not have existed in the first place. More centralized state structures of the sort characteristic of the Western European politics would certainly have been the condition for something quite different.

Yet states clearly do not exist in a vacuum. Their boundaries with civil society, their internal structures, territorial organization, modes of representation and the like are fought over. They are social stakes; more specifically they are class stakes even while the effects of class are typically highly mediated. A crucial question to ask, therefore, is how these different state structures might reflect different ensembles of class relations; but class relations as they are experienced rather than simply read off from the production relations of a capitalist society, since in that regard we are talking about very, very similar formations. And furthermore, how, in the context of those state structures, do class relations make a difference to the politics of local and regional development? It is to these questions that we turn next.

The Question of Class

> Nowhere in the advanced capitalist world is the working class as disorga-
> nized and depoliticized as in the US, where, unlike Europe or Australia,
> dozens of millions of workers are excluded from basic social and labor
> laws. (Hylton 2007, 2)

> The American Revolution sharply weakened the *noblesse oblige*, hier-
> archically rooted, organic community values which had been linked to
> Tory sentiments, and enormously strengthened the individualistic, egal-
> itarian, and anti-statist ones which had been present in the settler and
> religious background of the colonies. These values were evident in the
> twentieth century fact that, as H G. Wells pointed out close to ninety
> years ago, the United States not only has lacked a viable socialist party,
> but also has never developed a British or European-type Conservative
> or Tory party. Rather America has been dominated by pure bourgeois,
> middle-class individualistic values. (Lipset 1996, 31–32)

In virtually all the advanced capitalist countries a major political cleav-
age along the classic right-left terms is very clear: on the right, a party
representing capital and the more privileged of the working class that is
pushing an agenda of reducing taxation, limiting welfare spending, com-
modifying state functions or resisting further decommodification, and
restricting labor rights; and on the left, a party or parties pushing for
enhanced labor rights, transferring market functions like public transport
and housing to the state, and increased welfare spending to be funded
by taxation bearing more heavily on the wealthy. In short, it is a matter
of a struggle around the distribution of material privilege and, to a lesser
degree, the production relations underlying those unequal outcomes. But
just how that material privilege has been defended, how the challenge
has been met, has varied according to the dynamics of the class struggle.
In this regard it is not an exaggeration to say that the United States has
indeed been quite exceptional, particularly when compared with Western
European counterparts.

It is not just that the United States has lacked a Socialist Party or,
heaven forbid, a Communist Party attracting the sort of substantial

support that it did in France and Italy in the postwar years.[21] It is also, as Lipset (1996) pointed out, that it has never had its European counterpart to these: a conservative party of the sort exemplified by the Gaullist tradition in France, the Christian Democrats in Germany and Italy, the Conservatives in Great Britain, or the Swedish Moderates. The conservatism of the Republican Party is different, and that provides an essential clue to how and why class relations vary and in ways that shed light on differences in the politics of urban and regional development. In particular it takes us back to contrasting histories of capitalist development. This is because while we know that conservatism is by definition "conserving," exactly what is to be conserved has varied.

In the United States, what conservatism has meant most centrally has been the preservation of market relations, the dominance of commodity exchange, and the rule of capital, and it has been like that for a very long time. Even back in the 1920s when Calvin Coolidge made his famous proclamation about America's business being business, it is unlikely that any Western European counterpart would have felt comfortable saying that about his or her own country. It is as simple as that, which helps to explain the shrillness of opposition to anything that smacks of "socialism," as in the campaigns against public housing, or some limit on individual rights and the much-touted "freedom." Accordingly, it is an anti-statist conservatism, enduringly suspicious of seemingly any and all state intervention and forever casting around for new ways of dismantling state functions and assigning them to corporations. The state, it is claimed, is a monopoly provider and that is a bad thing. Markets are to be celebrated because they are competitive and provide what people want at the lowest possible price. And even if these views reach their apogee in the Republican Party, they have had an enduring impact on the national discourse and its center of gravity.

In the countries of Western Europe, things have been more complicated. Whereas in the United States capitalist development proceeded

---

21. But not in West Germany, where the Communist Party was banned in 1956, and despite—possibly because of—the fact that it had reached levels of popularity approaching those of the Weimar republic years.

virtually on a tabula rasa, on the other side of the Atlantic this was far from being the case. Rather, capitalism emerged within the context of various sorts of pre-existing social formation: feudalism, certainly, and even while it bent before the rule of the absolutist state; but then in some parts, like much of Germany west of the Elbe, France outside the Ile-de-France and the northeastern quadrant, and parts of Italy and Spain, an enduring peasant form of agriculture and *its* distinctive social relations. This in turn has meant coexistence and interaction between two different forms of social opposition.

First, and like the United States, there is the division between capital and labor: a division that finds clear political expression on both sides of the Atlantic. Just like the Republicans, the Christian Democrats and the British Conservatives will defend the rights of private property and of employers against the claims of the parties supposedly representing the working class and the labor movement. Major stakes have been labor rights and the welfare state, but it is a conflict that, as should be clear from earlier chapters, is expressed in the living place as well as at the point of production.

There is, though, a second tension in Western Europe that, while of declining weight, still has significant discursive effects, and through discourse on how people interpret events and so come to act. This is the division, constantly at work in Western European societies at all manner of levels—utterly penetrating them—a crucial aspect of national frames of understanding between the modern and the traditional; between commodification and what are seen as incorruptible use values; between individualism and more collective values redolent of older forms of community; between equality and hierarchy; and between capital's moral relativism and an insistence on inviolable absolutes. It is what many Americans, particularly on the right, feel uncomfortable about, and what they bring together under the heading of "elitism," even while they can rail at the same time about the sins of "socialism" rampant across the Atlantic. And it is often their riposte to what they perceive as "anti-Americanism."

This helps to explain two aspects of class relations in the Western European countries. First, the labor movement has received sustenance from precapitalist discourses critical of the commodification of social relations, of the destruction of older forms of community (hierarchical as they might have been), of the atomization of market relations, and of capital's amorality. At the same time, those discourses have weakened capital's arguments about the superiority of markets in the organization of social life. As Edward Heath, then British prime minister, famously claimed in 1973 when referring to the actions of a particular British multinational, capitalism could have an "unpleasant and unacceptable face": a public statement inconceivable for an American president.

The second point is that, while indeed the state in Western Europe is capitalist, capital has felt compelled to seek refuge in distinctive forms of tradition in order to respond to the challenges of the labor movement, legitimate its rule, and create an illusory sense of national community. This is very clear in Great Britain and the role of the royal family, but all the Western European countries have their symbols recalling a glorious past—a past that is indissociable from social forms of an equally precapitalist character, like France's *la sémeuse* (long a feature of its postage stamps) or the pomp of the republican guard. Obviously, all forms of "illusory community" draw on unifying symbols from the past. But again the United States is different: the founding fathers are a crucial point of reference in justifying what are seen as the virtues of a "free" market, even capitalist, sort; none of the sort of embarrassment that an Edward Heath might have, therefore.

These contrasts help shed light on some of the differences raised earlier in the book. In the countries of Western Europe, there is a valorization of what has been lost, what has been reinvented as the past, even while people do not necessarily recognize it as reinvented, or what is in danger of being lost. One result is the elevated significance of the rural in the prehistory of Western European development policy, as discussed in chapter 2: something that was very clear in the arguments of Jean-François Gravier when arguing for a decentralization of activities from Paris to the rest of the country; or even more radically in German arguments for emptying out the cities—plans that were not exclusive to the Nazis. Its enduring significance would be an anti-urbanism apparent in postwar new town policies and in calls for their revival.

Reverence for the past, or for what is believed to be the past, also gets expressed in a preservationism foreign to the United States, where the land tends to be viewed more unambiguously as a commodity,[22] and where old buildings are simply to be cleared away to make way for developments that will generate a higher rent; unless, that is, gentrification beckons. The common European pattern is to preserve working landscapes but to restrict development there. These restricted areas cover large parts of the countryside. In Germany, nature parks cover a quarter of the country's land surface. In England and Wales, and in addition to green belts and national parks, Areas of Outstanding Natural Beauty—a misnomer if ever there was one, since these are intensely humanized landscapes—amount to 18 percent of the land surface. In France, protected areas include one fifth of the country. Buildings get a similar treatment. Old country houses become converted into expensive retirement homes, not so much because the retired are in love with the past, though clearly some are, but because there is a preservation order on the building, which of course vastly increases development costs. In cities there can be restrictions on old buildings, perhaps Regency-style buildings in old spa towns, or the Wilhelmine buildings in Germany that the blitz spared, but seemingly anything representative of a particular period, including the brutalist public architecture of the postwar years. And then there are the urban views. The city of Paris has long been divided over the skyscraper and has imposed severe restrictions on their construction; and in vivid contrast to anything one might imagine in the United States, there are continual complaints about the changing London skyline.

Perhaps of more general significance where the importance of the state for urban and regional development is concerned is the way the more untrammeled capitalist morality of the United States, unhindered by anxieties about limits to commodification and pushing aside any values other than those of the market, has affected its operations. There is

22. Or as, and consonant with the frontier mythology, preserved by the federal government as wilderness.

a sense in which the American state is more commodified, more open to capitalist interests and in harmony with what they want to accomplish— it is almost a corporation in its own right, as state or local governments worry about the business climate over which they preside. Lobbying on individual items of legislation can be furious, and legislators held to account (no more money *unless* . . .). Election campaigns are driven by money and, in consequence, by those *with* money, which means corporations and the fundraising groups to which they contribute. Referenda are a common feature of the urban development scene, but the money thrown into the battle is stunningly unequal so that the developers typically prevail even though every vote they gain will be far more expensive than what the resistance "pays" for each of its votes. And those who are willing to play the game—those who are willing to prostitute themselves, who can be corrupted in ways other than the grubby packet under the table—are the ones who put their names forward for elective offices: the lawyers all too common in legislative assemblies who can expect future business from the firms whose interests they agree to push; the insurance agents who are so frequently city councilors in the suburbs (and why not, given that that developers will need insurance once they get their rezonings?).

American government can often seem to be in thrall, even in hock, to corporate pressures, as Lowi (1969) made so strikingly clear, and his arguments still resonate. One of the ways they make their influence felt is through "governance" and the bargaining that can go on between business and public officials in committees or special commissions. Here the contrast with Western European countries continues: in Western Europe, the state has proven more impervious to the efforts of capital, including property capital, to harness government to its purposes; in part due to an ambivalence regarding the corporatization of the state, even while it is proceeding at its own, slower, pace; in part a resistance to the seductions of governance.

These different positions are partly an expression of much stronger labor movements in Western Europe. In contrast, and to repeat Hylton's claim at the beginning of this section, "Nowhere in the advanced capitalist world is the working class as disorganized and depoliticized as in the US, where, unlike Europe or Australia, dozens of millions of workers are excluded from basic social and labor laws" (2007, 2). Oddly, therefore, it might seem that it is where capitalism has been able to generate its own culture—a culture that expresses its inherent nature, and without the limits imposed by the residues of an aristocratic or peasant society, each with its own distinct anticapitalist ethos—that the capitalist class has been most successful in subsuming labor, and in internalizing it as an aspect of itself economically, culturally, and politically. In turn this helps to shed light on the relative weakness of the welfare state in the United States as well as the way in which the American working class is more susceptible to the siren songs of territorialization and trickle-down. Nowhere in the capitalist world has there been greater success in separating the individual from the social integument, both materially and in the imaginary. Without a strong welfare state, and once assimilated and cast loose from the immigrant community, the individual has to rely on him or herself; and in a society where there is no competing vision born of deep precapitalist roots and conveyed through the media, political parties, and literature, he or she seems to believe that is exactly how it should be. So long as the state keeps its nose out of it, the market provides opportunities for all. If you are ambitious, careful with your money, and work hard then you too can realize the American Dream. To put it in an ironic light, it would seem that everyone can be a lawyer, doctor, engineer, or successful businessperson; and if you are not, then it is your fault: in other words, a fantasy land in which the division of labor seems to have been abolished.[23] The upward mobility of

---

23. Going back to Horatio Alger stories, there has long been a belief that it is a country that is unusually open to upward mobility (as mythical a claim as the Horatio Alger stories themselves: see Lipset and Bendix 1991)—that it is a country in which the rise from humble origins is not only accepted but is encouraged. This combines with an extraordinary emphasis on individual effort and enterprise. In turn, this has helped to create a working class that sees organization as a mere means to individual ends; something to be discarded as individual goals of material improvement and social status are achieved.

the individual trumps class. This is a world in which class struggle is irrelevant because there is no reason for it.[24]

But the reason that in the US capital has been so successful in incorporating labor and defanging the labor movement is more complex. The Republican Party has never had to fight elections with a European-style social democratic party backed up by a strong, sometimes militant, labor movement. In Western Europe it has been otherwise. Instead of the aggressive posture of a self-confident right-wing party of the Republican sort, the political right has had to proceed more carefully, preserving for the most part, when it wins elections, the reforms made by its left party predecessors: accepting the sort of Western European welfare state for which the Republican Party has such contempt—a contempt it can afford since the challenge to it from a self-confident political left, threatening a serious curtailment of capital's prerogatives, has been so relatively weak.

Giddens has suggested that degrees of mobility closure are important in class formation, by which one has to assume he means the formation of classes that are aware of themselves; he focuses on the presence of barriers to interclass mobility in relation to what he calls market capacities, like the possession of educational qualifications or the means of production (1973, 107). I think that the idea of closure is pertinent but with two qualifications: it is the perception of equality of opportunity—always heightened in the United States—which has been important; and closure needs to be understood more broadly to include political[25] and cultural dimensions. The political dimension would include exclusion from the franchise. In the United States the relative earliness of the white male suffrage across all the states of what was then the union, 1856, and prior to the full blossoming of industrial capital, removed what would prove to be an important

---

24. The kneejerk reaction of the right in the United States, whether in the public statements of politicians, in the media, or in letters to the editor, to any hint of redistributive reform is to claim that people are trying to introduce class conflict into the debate. Aside from the fact that class struggle is there already regardless, this is a very US-specific rhetoric; you will struggle to find its counterpart in any Western European country.

25. Something the importance of which Parkin recognized in his discussion of class and closure (1979, chapter 4).

target for labor movements in Western Europe. In the latter, a mix of property, literacy, and tax-paying requirements provided a grievance around which organization could continue to be energized (Przeworski 2009): an important condition for the sense of "us" and "them" that still affects party politics in a way alien to the United States.

Once more, there is a consistency with historical context. The sense of social superiority, of a landed class born to rule that was common in Western Europe, and that was therefore reluctant to share it with the rising bourgeoisie, let alone the great unwashed, did not apply. This made the extension of the franchise to all white males, regardless of income or education, and by the relatively early date of 1856, that much easier. In Western Europe it would be much later and only after protracted working-class struggle. Those same working classes would then be emboldened by an historical legacy of skepticism towards the rule of the commodity and of the individual shorn of connection to wider collectivities. This, in turn, would generate an equal skepticism toward individual uplift through upward mobility and an embrace of mass uplift through the welfare state.

The territorial structures of the state discussed in the earlier part of this chapter have then tended to reinforce these distinctive class relations, both materially and discursively. In the United States, the decentralization of powers and responsibilities to the states and then to local governments has tended to enhance the possibilities of territorial discourse that, by invoking cross-class alliances against similar ones elsewhere, simultaneously undermines class identities. It becomes possible, rather, to invite workers to compete with workers elsewhere for inward investment and to make concessions to business with that in mind; or to protest against an exploitation which, rather than along class lines, is territorial in character—an exploitation of cities by suburbs, of downstates by upstates, of rust belts by the new growth areas.

The structure of the state would be of no great moment—no more than an opportunity structure—if there were not, in fact, strong incentives to take what it offers. In American cities, property capitals have long held pole position in urban politics, not just by virtue of the powers that local governments dispose of with regard to development but also because of the incentives stemming from their own embeddedness in particular metropolitan areas or towns;[26] historically they have been supported by others with an interest in land rent, like the utilities, locally owned newspapers, and the banks. This has then been transferred upward via local delegations at state and federal levels to influence policy in locally enhancing ways. But this has meant countering the opposition of more popular forces through discourses of territorial competition and exploitation; something for which the territorial structure of the American state is an ideal tool, as was elaborated on in chapter 6. This insistence on channeling value through particular places can then be reinforced by the rent-seeking goals of others, like the coal mining companies discussed in the context of the Clean Air Act in chapter 1, or the Sagebrush rebels who have made common cause with small town retailers and developers across the West.

In Western Europe it has worked the other way around: highly centralized territorial structures have worked to facilitate class mobilization and to suppress more territorialized forms of development politics. Although legislators nominally represent geographic areas, their first allegiance is to a highly centralized party—and centralized because it is at the center that the major decisions are made, including those affecting local development. But even if legislators wanted to press some constituency-specific issue that was of no interest to anyone else, the weakness of the committee system would preclude them advancing their agenda. On the other hand, at local levels of the state, the powers that property capitals can mobilize in the United States are simply not there.

One can reasonably ask whether the outcome in the Western European countries would have been different if other conditions for the

26. Compare Mason Gaffney's vigorous, if somewhat reductive, claim: "[T]he LG (local government) . . . is a group of landowners in league to preside over the collective capital that they use jointly. The LG is a halfway house between the individual landowners and the state. Landowner control is modified by democracy, which gives the whole system some of its characteristic tensions and compromises. But landowners, as the permanent party of every LG, take a strong and steady interest in local government out of all proportion to their numbers. It is reasonably accurate for many purposes to think of the LG as a collective landowner, maximizing land income" (1973, 117).

emergence of local growth coalitions had been more favorable. Banks have long been absorbed into national chains and lost any dependence that they might once have had on lending in particular places. It is true that small retailers clustering around local chambers have been active in trying to preserve a local monopoly, though the advent of chain retailing makes them decreasingly significant, and in any case their positions were defensive rather than expansionary: the last whimper of a dying class of locally owned, family-run businesses. Provincial newspapers rarely attain the significance that they have in the United States. There is no national press in the United States[27] and newspapers like the *St. Louis Post-Dispatch* or the *Chicago Tribune* are gatekeepers not just for local and regional news but also national and international news in a way rarely duplicated in Western Europe. Even so, there *are* local real estate interests and developers who surely stand to gain from local growth and who always formed the core of American growth coalitions. They have, though, been curiously quiescent. The sort of clearly defined and aggressive local capitalist classes, forming around a local development agenda, have therefore been by and large absent.

I am going to suggest that this contrast owes in large part to the powers over development available to local government in the United States, which makes it a power center for property companies and developers. It also helps that local government has its own interests in seeing the local economy and therefore its tax base grow. The same sort of capacity is rare in Western Europe. However, the ability to use these powers depends on the local balance of political forces, and in the United States these have tended to favor the local growth interest. Despite David Harvey's (1989a) arguments about a shifting balance in local government between what he called managerialism and entrepreneurialism, which he extended to the Western European countries, they remain quite different. Local government was always more managerial there, always more dedicated to social provision of a redistributional sort. This remains the case even with

---

27. Some might argue that *USA Today* is national, but I do not think that it is taken seriously as such: more a freebie for distribution by hotels and, at one time, airlines.

some recent shift in a more entrepreneurial and neoliberal direction. An important reason for that is the vastly superior political weight of the working class. In the United States, the weakness of the labor movement, the attraction toward the pole of upward mobility, and the private advantage coming from increased home values or a desirable local school district makes workers, particularly the more "successful" of them, available for mobilization into territorial, cross-class coalitions to a degree that does not apply to the same extent in France, Germany, Great Britain, or Western Europe as a whole.[28]

If the territorial structure of the American state has served to underpin a particular class settlement that works to the advantage of capital, particularly its property sector, and which helps select in a politics of local and regional development of a distinctive sort, it also expresses and reinforces crucial aspects of the national discourse that have the same effect. It helps here if we keep in mind some of the discursive contrasts with the West European case: market versus planning; market versus the state; competition versus monopoly; bargaining as opposed to deliberation; and interest groups versus classes. Accordingly, if the state is to function more adequately then it should mimic as far as possible the rules of the market. The decentralization of the American state is seen for that reason as an unmitigated "good." The role that competition plays in local and regional development policy, guiding firms to locations where they can maximize their profitability and so increase the wealth of the country, is

28. In discussing what he called the "Have Rebellion" of the more affluent classes at the end of the 1970s and the early years of the 1980s, Davis refers to how, "exemplified in the innumerable property owners' and suburban residents' movements . . . [it] was a defensive participation of skilled workers and the lower salariat in support of their threatened prerogatives of social mobility and consumption (home-ownership, superior suburban education, nepotistic apprentice systems, and so on.) Faced with genuinely collapsing standards of living in many sectors of the traditional white working class, these groups increasingly visualized themselves—even if their own concrete situation was one of appreciating property values and rising wages—as locked in a desperate zero-sum rivalry with equality-seeking minorities and women" (1984, 35).

testimony to the wisdom of these arrangements if not to that of the found-ing fathers.[29]

In Western Europe, on the other hand, the sort of competition for inward investment taken for granted in the United States is viewed much more skeptically and as a threat to what is called "solidarity": an extension of welfare-state thinking into the criteria that it is believed should under-pin local and regional development policy, which in turn acts as a brake on arguments in favor of a greater decentralization of state competences. That same rhetoric of concern for working-class people also crops up in anxieties in the European Union about social dumping, and however dis-honored they might be in the breach. Neither competition, the bargaining that comes with it, nor a diminished role for the state have the popular appeal that they do in the United States. On the other hand, in the United States, it is not the business of the state to try to determine the broad outlines of the country's geography; that would be one more example of it "choosing winners and losers," which is a negative in the discourse of American public life, and one more instance of where state pretensions have to be curbed.

The people's right to choose has to be protected, and the radical decentralization of the American state serves that purpose. This means that the jurisdictional fragmentation of the metropolitan area is a "good thing." No matter that it plays into the hands of the development industry by creating new possibilities for Harvey's (1974) "class monopoly rents," people looking for housing can, in the classic way given academic sanc-tion so many years ago in the work of the economist Charles Tiebout (1956), pick and choose. Some local governments supply particular mixes of public goods and others, different ones. If you are retired and on a fixed income and your children have left home, it makes sense to live in a school district that spends little on the education of its children; and for those with children and concerned about their education, the reverse

---

29. Who are, of course, central to this story of the superiority of the American way of doing things.

applies. This is far from academic fantasy. The theory of public choice is empirically grounded in the views expressed whenever the prerogatives of the more materially privileged to choose to live in their own enclaves are threatened. The Lakewood Plan facilitated the creation in the Los Angeles area of numerous jurisdictions of that sort, and not to mention the City of Vernon discussed in chapter 1, which was justified in exactly that way (Connor 2013).

More generally, and Tiebout and public choice aside, there is the view that inequalities in school spending are less to do with variations in property tax revenues—lower spending per pupil where people tend to be poorer—than with the choices people make: improving one's material circumstances is a choice. The variations are, incidentally, of magnitudes that would certainly go against the grain in Western Europe: an affront to the ideals of the welfare state and, ironically, to assumptions of equality of opportunity.

Yet while there is an impressive consistency between class relations and the particular imaginaries that they have entailed, on the one hand, and state structures, including their territorial aspects, on the other, it is important not to lose sight of other forces of a quite exogenous nature. One can certainly argue that without strong labor movements of the sort that have characterized Western Europe the centralization of state functions would have been less impressive, and the converse applies to the United States. But even prior to the emergence of industrial capital, we are talking about states that, in comparison to the United States at the same time, were unusually centralized.[30] This centralization owed at least in part to old military anxieties and preparations for war with European neighbors that would continue well into the twentieth century; anxieties and preparations that would be absent in the United States until well into that same century. In consequence, while strong central states were attractive to labor movements because of their desire to prevent capital playing one locally or regionally constituted group of workers off against another,

---

30. For some of the background to the British and French cases, see Meiksins Wood (2016).

a pre-existing state structure was already in place. In the United States, on the other hand, the attempt of the labor movement to forge a national welfare state foundered on decentralized structures similarly inherited from the past and with a strong momentum of their own.[31]

Summing Up

The idea of development policy in the United States and in Western Europe was long in the making. It would not emerge fully formed until after the Second World War, but notions of distinct urban and regional questions had been taking shape well before then. The particular practices that would be the necessary conditions for the policies that would eventually take shape made seemingly independent appearances. They would include: urban and regional planning; the beginnings on the part of local governments to promote inward investment; some tentative interventions by more central branches of the state, particularly during the 1930s, when the regional question was assuming aggravated forms; new forms of real estate products, like the industrial park and the shopping center; and the birth of property capital as provider of the real estate needs of industry, commerce, and finance, and with its own distinct interest in rent. A new mobility on the part of industrial firms in particular, a liberation from old sites on the coalfields and estuaries, and the navigable rivers that might give access to coal, would then create enhanced possibilities of moving investment around; and to some degree this would be paralleled by the increasing mobility of the residents of the metropolitan areas, creating scope for citywide housing markets and the growth of a speculative housing industry.

But only after the Second World War would policy emerge as a recognizable and articulated ensemble of these elements and opportunities targeting urban and regional questions. How the different conditions would combine to form the basis of urban and regional development policy

---

31. On how and why, in the course of the New Deal, the attempt to create a single, national welfare state fell afoul of the mobilization of decentralized state structures by those opposed to it, see Gordon (1991) and Farhang and Katznelson (2005).

would be quite different in the United States than in the countries of Western Europe: comparatively, therefore, a very peculiar practice. In the United States, policies would be primarily a matter for local government and, to a lesser degree, the states. A dominant motif would be competition for inward investment across a range of activities; in essence anything that promised to increase the flow of revenues to property companies though local government retained its own interest in rent in the form of the property tax. Meanwhile, more central forms of planning locations to counter the emergent market form were vigorously rejected. The federal government, and the states to a lesser degree, were regarded as resources rather than stimulators or orchestrators.

This would be in sharp contrast to the countries of Western Europe, where central governments would play a heightened role. The balance between central planning and the market would be very different, inspired in part by welfare state ideals of redistribution so as to mitigate uneven development; but also by a more critical anxiety about urbanization. Urbanization policy would be almost the antithesis of the market-dependent form it assumed in the United States. Attempts to stem the growth of large cities through the imposition of limits to their geographic expansion have been accompanied by attempts to accommodate it through the creation of new towns, and then to control expansion elsewhere through centrally managed planning policies. If there is a blanket term for these different policies it would be the "good geography": a geography of development that responds to priorities determined at central levels; priorities that in turn have been seen as the proper object of deliberation, in which certain moral absolutes about the welfare state, the compact city, and what is fair have held sway. This is a world in which opportunities have certainly been available to the property companies but not in the unfettered way that has been the case in the United States. Meanwhile, they have been able to console themselves quite nicely with the high rents that have been an offshoot of quite strict planning regulations.

As discussed in chapter 5, these are policy regimes that under the very different conditions subsequent to the early 1970s have undergone mutations. There is a view that the Western European version is assuming more of the contours of the American model, and there is certainly some evidence for that, not least the way in which the EU has been a condition for greater competition of a territorial sort. There have been other institutional changes, including a much-hyped enhancement of local responsibilities. But if anything the American model under neoliberalism has become more about a market in locations than it ever was. What continues to impress, therefore, is the extraordinary strength and durability of the trans-Atlantic contrast.

Policy has been contested but, again, in different ways and against very distinct discursive backgrounds and with very distinctive forms of resolution. Two sorts of contrast, albeit related ones, seem clear. The first is, not surprisingly, the way in which in the US struggles around urban and regional development tend to get territorialized: conflicts between one locality, one growth coalition or even a single property capital, along with some popular support, including those who are persuaded by rhetorics of employment or property tax advantages, and one elsewhere with a different network of allies, but all focused on what the outcome will be for a particular place. This is a scale-independent matter. It is immaterial whether one is talking about the plight of inner suburbs, of local economies in the Rust Belt, or of Dallas and Southwest Airlines versus Fort Worth and American Airlines. This sort of territorialized response is far less likely in the West European instance, even while its distinctiveness in that matter has tended to become more blurred as geographically uneven development has intensified. Conflicts around gentrification and urban rents are more likely to mushroom into demands for renewed attention to public housing—something likely to be resisted by forces of the right. Requests for shopping center development on the edge of the urban area are often countermanded by the need to preserve downtown shopping and its accessibility advantages for the poor and others who are less mobile.

The second contrast to note is the way in which the landscape of conflict in the United States is much more dispersed: more matters for local or possibly state government than for the federal government.[32] In Western

---

32. Aside from cases like the Sagebrush Rebellion, where the federal government *had* to be at the center of the issue, it is often a last resort for those who have not been able to gain salvation at local or state levels. The community builders (Weiss 1987) only

Europe, conflicts around land use and development are more likely to become national issues, as in the case of Florange or the garden grabbers, which is entirely appropriate given that that is where power tends to lie. The British miners' strike in 1984–85 had a strong class dimension but was also national: a matter for central government and underlining the historic significance of public ownership in Western Europe, not just as an expression of a class politics but also of its importance in the support of particular regional economies.

In trying to come to terms with the distinctiveness of the American case, I have emphasized three interrelated elements: the division of labor between state and civil society; the structure of the state itself; and what I have called class relations. The latter comprise the dominant determinant element. The division of labor between state and civil society, or more accurately, between state and capital, has been quite distinctive in the United States. The welfare state has been much more limited in its scope. One expression of this in development policy has been the comparative weakness of forms of redistribution designed to mitigate geographically uneven development. The sorts of federal programs found in Canada and Germany, where the better-off provinces fund transfers to the less well-off, are absent. Within the states, and with the notable exception of New Hampshire, inequalities in the funding of public education can be vertiginous, with corresponding implications for the appropriation of class monopoly rents by the developers. These inequalities have no parallel in Western Europe, where central state redistribution tends to mitigate variation in the resources available between local education authorities. Furthermore, particularly during the 1950s and 1960s, the division of labor between state and capital in Western Europe—the division between private and state ownership of banks, industry, and transport companies—has permitted the sorts of regionally or locally targeted

---

got interested in what the federal government could do for them with respect to protection from spot zoning and the curbstoners when they failed to make an impression on local government. Likewise, the federal Clean Air Act, reviewed in chapter 1, came about because environmental protection agencies in the states producing the high sulfur smokestack exhausts had dragged their feet.

interventions that would have been difficult in the United States, even if the will had been present.

As for the structure of the state itself, what jumps out is the quite remarkable fragmentation, including territorial fragmentation of formal power. American local governments dispose of a formidable armory of competences to be used, if so desired, in pursuing local development. The states in their turn have been major agents in the formulation of policies typically falling under the welfare state heading, presiding over major elements of labor law and social spending that can be, and have been, turned to the purpose of local and regional development as aspects of "business climate." Meanwhile, state power in the Western European countries, including the federal states, has tended to be much more concentrated at the center, making possible the top-down development policies that have tended to prevail there even since the changed circumstances after the beginning of the long downturn in the early 1970s. And the idea of local business climates, aside from what is transpiring at the level of the EU, is simply a nonstarter.

In a very famous quotation about capitalist ideology,[33] Marx, in *Capital Volume 1*, referred to commodity exchange as "a very Eden of the innate rights of man" and among which he listed "Freedom, Equality, Property and Bentham." But while he drew heavily on his experience of living in Great Britain and the industrial revolution there, his claim seems much more applicable to frames of self-understanding in the United States than in any of the Western European countries, including Great Britain. This in turn is due to a different history of capitalist development; one

33. "The sphere of circulation or commodity exchange, within whose boundaries the sale and purchase of labor-power goes on, is in fact a very Eden of the innate rights of man. It is the exclusive realm of Freedom, Equality, Property and Bentham. Freedom, because both buyer and seller of a commodity, let us say, of labor-power, are determined only by their own free will. They contract as free persons, who are equal before the law. Their contract is the final result in which their joint will finds a common legal expression. Equality, because each enters into relation with the other, as with a simple owner of commodities, and they exchange equivalent for equivalent. Property, because each disposes only of what is his own. And Bentham, because each looks only to his own advantage" (Marx 1867, 280).

that has entailed equally different class relations, by which I mean not just the material relation of capital and labor in work- and in living-place but also a more general interpretive framework through which that relation is understood.

In this regard it is widely acknowledged that the United States lacks the sort of political left characteristic of the Western European countries. Less appreciated is the fact that it also lacks the sort of conservative party typically found there: one that is dedicated not just to the reproduction of capitalist social relations, commonly seen as those of "the market" or "free enterprise," but which also reflects values of a precapitalist era: an ethos less suspicious of the state, more critical of the rule of commodity exchange and cognizant of its limits, less egalitarian, but also expressing solidarities that stand at some remove from the unqualified individual rights specified in the US constitution. Accordingly, the moral center of gravity of Western European societies is different.

It is one, moreover, which has—and paradoxically—allowed labor movements to flourish as they have not in the United States. Ruling classes in Western Europe yielded slowly to the political demands of the working class, engendering a lasting feeling of exclusion. Social democratic parties then found fertile ground in the more general suspicions of commodity exchange bequeathed by aristocratic societies, and in some cases by the slow liquidation of the peasantry. In the United States, on the other hand, the more egalitarian "rights of man" were taken more seriously, clearing the way for a subsumption of labor to capital that has been quite unique among advanced industrial societies.

The common idea that it is a country where class thinking counts for less, where the individual has the opportunity to "make it" on his or her own, where the ability to compete on a level "playing field" is what counts, has then been reinforced by distinctive features of the American state. It is one where, as a result of the fragmentation of state power, both territorially and within the center itself, the central state is indeed weak. The way in which its structure provides a condition for a certain form of pluralism also suggests a state that works to counter the centralization of power and supposed threats to the individual. On the other hand, as well as expressing an understanding of class relations more appropriate to a market society, state structure has also reinforced them. In particular, the structure of the American state has made possible a territorialization of social relations, the organization of cross-class coalitions, and at all manner of geographic scales—within cities, between them, between regions—that has served to counter class as a key to understanding the social world.

There are commonalities; otherwise the international circulation of ideas by the consultocracy, transmitting models of best practice between cities in the developed world (McCann and Ward 2011), would make no sense. Capital's mutations, not least its new spatial divisions of labor, have provided a common horizon for the planners and the local economic development people. Particular real estate innovations move across the ocean, though more in the European direction than in the other—an odd parallel to the movement in the academy of ideas about the politics of local development! But the way they are incorporated into developmental practice remains very different. The interests that have grown up around particular models, the way they draw strength from the institutional status quo, the manner in which the claims they make resonate, and the way in which cumulative causation has tended to reinforce divergence, makes any Americanization of development politics in Western Europe very unlikely, and underlines the continual distinctiveness of the American case.

References

Abrams, Mark, Richard Rose, and Rita Hiden. 1960. *Must Labour Lose?* Harmondsworth, Middlesex: Penguin.

Agnew, John A. 1995. "The Rhetoric of Regionalism: The Northern League in Italian Politics." *Transactions of the Institute of British Geographers*, n.s., 20: 156–72.

Allen, John, Doreen Massey, and Allan Cochrane. 1998. *Rethinking the Region.* London and New York: Routledge.

Allmendinger, Philip, and Graham Haughton. 2012. "Post-Political Spatial Planning in England: A Crisis of Consensus?" *Transactions of the Institute of British Geographers*, n.s., 37: 89–103.

Alt, John. 1976. "Beyond Class: The Decline of Industrial Labor and Leisure." *Telos* 28: 55–80.

Ambrose, Peter, and Bob Colenutt. 1975. *The Property Machine.* Harmondsworth, Middlesex: Penguin Books.

Ancien, Delphine. 2005. "Local and Regional Development Policy in France: Of Changing Conditions and Forms, and Enduring State Centrality." *Space and Polity* 9 (3): 217–36.

Anderson, James. 1990. "The 'New Right,' Enterprise Zones and Urban Development Corporations." *International Journal of Urban and Regional Research* 14 (3): 468–89.

Anton, Thomas J., and Rebecca Reynolds. n.d. "Old Federalism and New Policies for State Economic Development." Discussion paper, A. Alfred Taubman Center for Public Policy and American Institutions, Brown Univ.

Arnold, R. Douglas. 1981. "The Local Roots of Domestic Policy." In *The New Congress*, edited by T. E. Mann and N. J. Ornstein, chap. 8. Washington, DC: The American Enterprise Institute.

Association of Bay Area Governments. 2016. "Housing Supply." Accessed Feb. 21. http://www.abag.ca.gov/planning/theoryia/houssvmg.htm.

Axford, Nicholas, and Steven Pinch. 1994. "Growth Coalitions and Local Economic Development Strategy in Southern England." *Political Geography Quarterly* 13: 344–60.

Aydalot, Philippe. 1986. "Trajectoires technologiques et milieux innovateurs." In *Milieux Innovateurs en Europe*, edited by P. Aydalot, 347–61. Paris: GREMI.

Baeten, Guy, Erik Swyngedouw, and Louis Albrechts. 1999. "Politics, Institutions and Regional Restructuring Processes: From Managed Growth to Planned Fragmentation in the Reconversion of Belgium's Last Coal Mining Region." *Regional Studies* 33 (3): 247–58.

Baing, Andreas. 2010. "Containing Urban Sprawl? Comparing Brownfield Reuse Policies in England and Germany." *International Planning Studies* 15 (1): 25–35.

Baker, Peter. 1995. "Land and Property in Local Economic Development." *Local Government Studies* 21 (3): 360–75.

Barlow, James. 1995. "The Politics of Urban Growth: Boosterism and Nimbyism in European Boom Regions." *International Journal of Urban and Regional Research* 19: 129–44.

Barnekov, Timothy, Robin Boyle, and Daniel Rich. 1989. *Privatism and Urban Policy In Britain and the United States*. Oxford: Oxford Univ. Press.

Barr, John. 1969. "Durham's Murdered Villages." *New Society* (April): 523–25.

Bassett, Keith, and Anthony Hoare. 1984. "Bristol and the Saga of Royal Portbury: A Case Study in Local Politics and Municipal Enterprise." *Political Geography Quarterly* 3: 223–50.

Baudelle, Guy. 2008. "Construire ensemble les territoires: les transformations récentes du modèle français d'aménagement." In *Construire ensemble les territoires*, edited by Paul Arnould, Guy Baudelle and Roland Pourtier. Historiens et Géographes, Comité national français de géographie, Congrès de l'Union géographique internationale, Tunis.

Baumol, William, and William G. Bowen. 1966. *Performing Arts: The Economic Dilemma*. New York: Twentieth Century Fund.

Beauregard, Robert. 2005. "The Textures of Property Markets: Downtown Housing and Office Conversions in New York City." *Urban Studies* 42 (13): 2431–45.

Bell, Trevor. 1986. "The Role of Regional Policy in South Africa." *Journal of Southern African Studies* 12 (2): 276–92.

Bensel, Richard F. 1984. *Sectionalism and American Political Development 1880–1980*. Madison: Univ. of Wisconsin Press.

Bentley, Gill, David Bailey, and John Shutt. 2010. "From RDAs to LEPs: A New Localism? Case Examples of West Midlands and Yorkshire." *Local Economy* 25 (7): 535–57.

Berge, Wendell. 1946. *Economic Freedom for the West*. Lincoln, NE: Univ. of Nebraska Press.

Berkman, Richard L., and W. Kip Viscusi. 1971. *Damming the West*. New York: Grossman Publishers.

Beynon, Huw, Ray Hudson, and David Sadler. 1986. "Nationalised Industries and the Destruction of Communities: Some Evidence from Northeastern England." *Capital and Class*, no. 29: 27–57.

Blair, John P, Rudy H. Fichtenbaum, and James A. Swaney. 1984. "The Market for Jobs: Locational Decisions and the Competition for Economic Development." *Urban Affairs Quarterly* 20 (1): 64–77.

Bloomfield, Ruth. 2015. "Mind the Gap: How the London Property Market Compares to the Rest of Britain." *Homes and Property*, Apr. 15. Accessed Sept. 26. http://www.homesandproperty.co.uk/property-news/news/mind-gap -how-london-property-market-compares-rest-britain.

Body-Gendrot, Sophie. 1987. "Grass Roots Mobilization in the Thirteenth Arrondissement of Paris: A Cross-National View." In *The Politics of Urban Development*, edited by Clarence N. Stone and Heywood T. Sanders, chap. 6. Lawrence, KS: Univ. of Kansas Press.

Bouneau, Christophe. 1990. "Chemins de fer et développement régional en France de 1852 à 1937." *Histoire, Économie et Société* 9 (1): 95–112.

Boyle, Mark. 2000. "Euro-Regionalism and Struggles over Scales of Governance: The Politics of Ireland's Regionalization Approach to Structural Fund Allocations 2000–2006." *Political Geography* 19: 737–69.

Boyle, Mark. 2003. "Scale as an 'Active Progenitor' in the Metamorphosis of the Waste Management Hierarchy in Member States: The Case of the Republic of Ireland." *European Planning Studies* 11 (4): 481–502.

Breathnach, Proinnsias. 2010. "From Spatial Keynesianism to Post-Fordist Neoliberalism: Emerging Contradictions in the Spatiality of the Irish State." *Antipode* 42 (5): 1180–99.

Brenner, Neil. 1998. "Global Cities, Glocal States: Global City Formation and State Territorial Restructuring in Contemporary Europe." *Review of International Political Economy* 5 (1): 1–37.

Brenner, Neil. 2004. *New State Spaces*. Oxford: Oxford Univ. Press.

————. 2008. "Is There a Politics of 'Urban Development'?" In *The City in American Political Development*, edited by R. Dilworth, chap. 6. London and New York: Routledge.

Brenner, Robert, and Mark Glick. 1991. "The Regulation Approach: Theory and History," *New Left Review*, no. 188: 45–119.

Brenner, Robert. 1998. "The Economics of Global Turbulence." *New Left Review*, no. 229: 1–265.

————. 2004. "New Boom or New Bubble?" *New Left Review*, n.s., 25: 57–100.

Burns, Nancy, Laura Evans, Gerald Gamm, and Corrinne McConnaughy. 2009. "Urban Politics in the State Arena," *Studies in American Political Development* 23: 1–22.

Buyst, Erik. 2009. "Reversal of Fortune in a Small, Open Economy: Regional GDP in Belgium, 1896–2000," Discussion paper no. 8, Research Center for Regional Economics, VIVES Univ. College, Courtrai, Belgium.

Buzzelli, Michael, and Richard Harris. 2006. "Cities as the Industrial Districts of Housebuilding," *International Journal of Urban and Regional Research* 30 (4): 894–917.

Byrne, David. 1980. "The Standard of Council Housing in Inter-War North Shields—A Case Study in Reproduction." In *Housing, Social Policy and the State*, edited by John Melling, chap. 6. London: Croom Helm.

Caldera Sánchez, A., and Å. Johansson. 2011. "The Price Responsiveness of Housing Supply in OECD Countries." Working paper no. 837, OECD Economics Department, OECD Publishing. Accessed Sept. 27, 2015. http://dx.doi.org/10.1787/5kgk9qhrnn33-en.

Cannadine, David. 1977. "Victorian Cities: How Different?" *Social History* 2 (4): 457–80.

Cannari, Luigi, Francesco Nucci, and Paolo Sestito. 2000. "Geographic Labor Mobility and the Cost of Housing: Evidence from Italy," *Applied Economics* 32 (14): 1899–906.

Caprotti, Federico. 2007. "Destructive Creation: Fascist Urban Planning, Architecture and New Towns," *Journal of Historical Geography* 33 (3): 651–79.

Caudill, Harry. 1963. *Night Comes to the Cumberlands: A Biography of a Depressed Area*. Boston: Little, Brown.

Charmes, Eric. 2010a. "L'explosion périurbaine." http://www.adef.org/COLLOQUE_ADEF/2010/colloque2010/Etudesfoncieres_148_dossierperiurbain.pdf.

———. 2010b. "Le Malthusianisme foncier." http://hal.archives-ouvertes.fr/docs /00/32/75/96/PDF/malthusianisme_foncier_charmes.pdf.

———. 2013. "Les communes périurbaines face à la métropole: sécession ou intégration fonctionnelle?" *Métropolitiques*, July 1. http://www.metropoli tiques.eu/Les-communes-periurbaines-face-a.html.

Charney, Igor. 2001. "Three Dimensions of Capital Switching within the Real Estate Sector." *International Journal of Urban and Regional Research* 25 (4): 740–58.

Chester, Paul C., and Christian Hilber. 2008. "Office Space Supply Restrictions in Britain: The Political Economy of Market Revenge." *Economic Journal* 118 (June): 185–221.

Chinitz, Benjamin. 1961. "Contrasts in Agglomeration: New York and Pittsburgh." *American Economic Review* 51 (2): 279–89.

Christopherson, Susan. 2007. "Barriers to 'US Style' Lean Retailing: The Case of Wal-Mart's Failure in Germany." *Journal of Economic Geography* 7: 451–69.

———. 2009. "Manufacturing: Up from the Ashes." *Democracy* 14 (Fall). http:// democracyjournal.org/magazine/14/manufacturing-up-from-the-ashes/.

———. 2010. "Afterword: Contextualized Comparison in Local and Regional Economic Development: Are United States Perspectives and Approaches Distinctive?" *Regional Studies* 44 (2): 229–33.

Clark, Gordon L. 1981. "The Employment Relation and the Spatial Division of Labor: A Hypothesis." *Annals of the Association of American Geographers* 71 (3): 412–24.

Clark, Greg, Alexandra Notay, and Gareth Evans. 2010. *Leveraging Public Land to Attract Urban Investment: A ULI Urban Network Investment Report*. London: Urban Land Institute Europe.

Clarke, Simon. 1988. "Overaccumulation, Class Struggle and the Regulation Approach." *Capital and Class*, no. 36: 59–92.

Clavel, Pierre. 1986. *The Progressive City*. New Brunswick, NJ: Rutgers Univ. Press.

Clawson, Marion. 1971. *Suburban Land Conversion in the United States* Baltimore: Johns Hopkins Univ. Press for Resources for the Future.

Cobb, James. 1982. *The Selling of the South*. Baton Rouge, LA: Louisiana State Univ. Press.

Cochrane, Allan. 1999. "Redefining Growth Politics for the Twenty-First Century." In *The Urban Growth Machine*, edited by Andrew E. G. Jonas and David Wilson, chap. 7. Albany: State Univ. of New York Press.

Coing, Henri. 1966. *Rénovation urbaine et changement social*. Paris: Les Éditions Ouvrières.

Connor, Michael A. 2013. "'Public Benefits from Public Choice': Producing Decentralization in Metropolitan Los Angeles, 1954–1973." *Journal of Urban History* 39 (1): 79–100.

Cooke, Philip. 1983. "Regional Restructuring: Class Politics and Popular Protest in South Wales." *Environment and Planning D: Society and Space* 1: 265–80.

Cotterau, Alain. 1970. "Les débuts de la planification urbaine dans l'agglomération parisienne." *Sociologie du travail*, special issue: 362–92.

Cottour, Claude. 2008. *Une brève histoire de l'aménagement de Paris et sa région*. Accessed May 1, 2016. http://www.driea.ile-de-france.developpement-durable .gouv.fr/IMG/pdf/Chapitre4_de_Breve_histoire_de_amenagement_de_Paris _DREIF_Auteur_Claude_Cottour_cle05a227.pdf.

Cowell, Richard, and Jonathan Murdoch. 1999. "Land Use and the Limits to Regional) Governance: Some Lessons from Planning for Housing and Minerals in England." *International Journal of Urban and Regional Research* 23 (4): 654–69.

Cox, Kevin R. 1973. *Conflict, Power and Politics in the City*. New York: McGraw-Hill.

———. 1981. "Capitalism and Conflict around the Communal Living Place." In *Urbanization and Urban Planning in Capitalist Society*, edited by Michael Dear and Allen J. Scott, chap. 16. London and New York: Methuen.

———. 1984. "Social Change, Turf Politics, and the Concept of Turf Politics." In *Public Service Provision and Urban Development*, edited by Andrew Kirby, Paul Knox and Steven Pinch, chap. 12. Beckenham, Kent: Croom Helm.

———. 1985. "Housing Tenure and Neighborhood Activism." *Urban Affairs Quarterly* 18 (1): 107–29.

———. 1998. "Spaces of Dependence, Spaces of Engagement and the Politics of Scale, or: Looking for Local Politics." *Political Geography* 17 (1): 1–24.

———. 2004. "The Politics of Local and Regional Development, the Difference the State Makes and the US/British Contrast." In *Governing Local and Regional Economies*, edited by Andrew Wood and David Valler, chap. 10. Aldershot: Ashgate.

———. 2009. "'Rescaling the State' in Question." *Cambridge Journal of Regions, Economy and Society* 2 (1): 107–21.

———. 2010. "The Problem of Metropolitan Governance and the Politics of Scale." *Regional Studies* 44 (2): 215–27.

Cox, Kevin R., and Andrew E. G. Jonas. 1993. "Urban Development, Collective Consumption and the Politics of Metropolitan Fragmentation," *Political Geography* 12 (1): 8–37.

Cox, Kevin R., and Andrew J. Mair. 1988. "Locality and Community in the Politics of Local Economic Development." *Annals, Association of American Geographers* 78 (2): 307–25.

Cox, Kevin R., and Alan R. Townsend. 2005. "The English Politics of Local Economic Development and the American Model." *Regional Studies* 39 (4): 541–53.

Cox, Kevin R., and Andrew M. Wood. 1997. "Competition and Cooperation in Mediating the Global: The Case of Local Economic Development." *Competition and Change* 2 (1): 65–94.

Cronon, William. 1992. *Nature's Metropolis: Chicago and the Great West.* New York: W. W. Norton.

Crouch, Colin, and Patrick Le Galès. 2012. "Cities as National Champions." *Journal of European Public Policy* 19 (3): 405–19.

Cummings, Scott, and Edmond Snider. 1988. "Municipal Code Enforcement and Urban Development: Private Decisions and Public Policy in an American City." In *Business Elites and Urban Development*, edited by Scott Cummings, chap. 7. Albany, NY: State Univ. of New York Press.

Cybriwsky, Roman A. 1978. "Social Aspects of Neighborhood Change." *Annals of the Association of American Geographers* 68 (1): 17–33.

Davezies, Laurent. 2008. *La République et ses territoires. La circulation invisible des richesses.* Paris: Seuil.

———. 2012. *La crise qui vient: la nouvelle fracture territoriale.* Paris: Seuil.

Davezies, Laurent, and Thierry Pech. 2014. "La nouvelle question territoriale." *La Fondation Terra Nova.* Accessed Dec. 28, 2015. http://tnova.fr/etudes /la-nouvelle-question-territoriale.

Davis, Mike. 1980. "Why the U.S. Working Class is Different." *New Left Review* 123: 3–44.

———. 1984. "The Political Economy of Late Imperial America." *New Left Review* 143: 6–38.

———. 1992. *City of Quartz.* New York: Vintage Books.

———. 1997. "Sunshine and the Open Shop: Ford and Darwin in 1920s Los Angeles." *Antipode* 29 (4): 356–82.

Dawley, Stuart, Neill Marshall, Andy Pike, Jane Pollard, and John Tomaney. 2014. "Continuity and Evolution in an Old Industrial Region: The Labour

Market Dynamics of the Rise and Fall of Northern Rock." *Regional Studies* 48 (1): 154–72.

De Decker, Pascal. 2008. "Facets of Housing and Housing Policies in Belgium." *Journal of Housing and the Built Environment* 23 (3): 155–71.

De Haan, Henk. 2005. "Social and Material Appropriation of Neighborhood Space: Collective Space and Resistance in a Dutch Urban Community." Paper presented at the international conference "Doing, Thinking, Feeling Home: The Mental Geography of Residential Environments," Delft Univ. of Technology, Delft.

Deas, Iain, and Kevin G. Ward. 2000. "From the 'New Localism' to the 'New Regionalism': The Implications of Regional Development Agencies for City-Regional Relations." *Political Geography* 19 (3): 273–92.

Dessus, Michel G. 1953. "Les origines de l'aménagement du territoire." *Économies rurale* 16 (1): 3–8.

Dietz, Bernhard. 2008. "Countryside-versus-City in European Thought: German and British Anti-Urbanism between the Wars." *The European Legacy: Toward New Paradigms* 13 (7): 801–14.

Domhoff, William G. 2005. *Power at the Local Level: Growth Coalition Theory.* Accessed May 2, 2016. http://www2.ucsc.edu/whorulesamerica/local /growth_coalition_theory. html.

Downie, Leonard. 1974. *Mortgage on America.* New York: Praeger.

Duhl, Leonard J., and Nancy Steetle. 1968. "Newark: Community or Chaos?" In *A Symposium on the Urban Crisis,* edited by Leonard J. Duhl, 408–45. Berkeley: Center for Planning and Development Research, Univ. of California.

Dunford, Michael. 1994. "Winners and Losers: The New Map of Economic Inequality in the European Union." *European Urban and Regional Studies* 1 (2): 95–114.

———. 1997. "Divergence, Instability and Exclusion: Regional Dynamics in Great Britain." In *Geographies of Economies,* edited by R. Lee and J. Wills, chap. 20. London: Edward Arnold.

Dustmann, Christian, Berndt Fitzenberger, Uta Schönberg, and Alexandra Spitz-Oener. 2014. "From Sick Man of Europe to Economic Superstar: Germany's Resurgent Economy." *Journal of Economic Perspectives* 28 (1): 167–88.

Dyer, Stephanie. 1998. "'Holding the Line against Philadelphia': Business, Suburban Change, and the Main Line's Suburban Square, 1926—1950." *Business and Economic History* 27 (2): 279–91

Dykstra, Clarence. 1937. *Our Cities: Their Role in the National Economy*. Washington, DC: Research Committee on Urbanism, US National Resources Committee.

Ebeid, Michael, and Jonathan Rodden. 2006. "Economic Geography and Economic Voting: Evidence from the US States." *British Journal of Political Science* 36 (3): 527–47.

Eickmann, Andrew J. 2009. "Dutch Spatial Planning: The Coordination of Compact Development and Affordable Housing." Master's thesis, Department of Urban Studies, Portland State Univ.

Elkin, Stephen L. 1974. *Politics and Land Use Planning: The London Experience*. Cambridge: Cambridge Univ. Press.

———. 1987. "State and Market in City Politics: Or the 'Real' Dallas." In *The Politics of Urban Development*, edited by Clarence N. Stone and Heywood T. Sanders, chap. 2. Lawrence, KS: Univ. of Kansas Press.

Ellwood, John W., and Eric M. Patashnik. 1993. "In Praise of Pork." *The Public Interest*, no. 110: 19–33.

Epstein, Leon. 1986. *Political Parties in the American Mold*. Madison: Univ. of Wisconsin Press.

Esser, Josef, and Joachim Hirsch. 1989. "The Crisis of Fordism and the Dimensions of a 'Postfordist' Regional and Urban Structure." *International Journal of Urban and Regional Research* 13 (3): 417–37.

Evans-Cowley, Jennifer. 2006. "Development Exactions: Process and Planning Issues." Working paper, Lincoln Institute of Land Policy.

Fainstein, Susan S. 2001. *The City Builders: Property Development in New York and London, 1980–2000*. Lawrence, KS: Univ. of Kansas Press.

Farhang, Sean, and Ira Katznelson. 2005. "The Southern Imposition." *Studies in American Political Development* 19 (1): 1–30.

Feiock, Richard C. 2002. "A Quasi-Market Framework for Development Competition." *Journal of Urban Affairs* 24 (2): 123–42.

Fishman, Robert. 1999. "The American Metropolis at Century's End: Past and Future Influences." *Housing Facts and Findings* (Winter).

Florida, Richard. 2002. *The Rise of the Creative Class*. Basic Books: New York.

———. 2015. "The U.S. Spends Far More on Homeowner Subsidies Than It Does on Affordable Housing." *Atlantic CityLab*, Apr. 17. http://www.citylab.com/housing/2015/04/the-us-spends-far-more-on-homeowner-subsidies-than-it-does-on-affordable-housing/390666/.

Fogelson, Robert. 2001. *Downtown: Its Rise and Fall, 1880–1950*. Yale Univ. Press: New Haven, Conn.

Frankestein, Robert. 1980. "Intervention étatique et réarmement en France 1935–1939." *Revue économique* 31 (4): 743–81.

Fried, Marc. 1966. "Grieving for a Lost Home: Psychological Costs of Relocation." In *Urban Renewal: The Record and the Controversy*, edited by James Q. Wilson, chap. 6. Cambridge, MA: MIT Press.

Friedricks, William B. 1987. "Henry E Huntington and Metropolitan Entrepreneurship in Southern California, 1898–1917." *Business and Economic History* 16: 199–203.

Frymer, Paul. 2004. "Race, Labor and the Twentieth-Century American State." *Politics and Society* 32 (4): 475–509.

Furlough, Ellen, and Rosemary Wakeman. 2004. "La Grande Motte: Regional Development, Tourism and the State." In *Being Elsewhere: Tourism, Consumer Culture and Identity in Modern Europe and North America*, edited by S. Baranowski and E. Furlough, chap. 14. Ann Arbor, MI: Univ. of Michigan Press.

Gaffney, Mason. 1973. "Tax Reform to Release Land." In *Modernizing Urban Land Policy*, edited by M. Clawson, 115–52. Baltimore: Johns Hopkins Univ. Press.

Galimberti, Deborah. 2013. "Des variétés de régulation de la ville compétitive." *EspacesTemps.net*. Accessed Sept. 7, 2015. http://www.espacestemps.net/en/articles/des-varietes-de-regulation-de-la-ville-competitive/.

———. 2015. *Gouverner le développement économique des territoires: entre politique et société. Une comparaison des régions de Lyon et Milan (1970–2011)*. Thèse, Université de Lyon, Lyon, France.

Gendron, Robert, and William G. Domhoff. 2009. *The Leftmost City*. Boulder, CO: Westview Press.

Giblin, Béatrice. 2005. "La région: enjeux de pouvoirs." *Quaderni* 59: 97–108.

Giddens, Anthony. 1973. *The Class Structure of the Advanced Societies*. New York: Harper and Row.

Ginsberg, Yona. 1975. *Jews in a Changing Neighborhood: The Study of Mattapan*. Glencoe, IL: Free Press.

Goodman, Robert. 1979. *The Last Entrepreneurs*. New York: Simon and Schuster.

Gordon, Colin. 1991. "New Deal, Old Deck: Business and the Origins of Social Security, 1920–1935." *Politics and Society* 19 (2): 165–208.

Gough, Jamie. 1996. "The Contradictions of Neo-Keynesian Local Economic Strategy." *Review of International Political Economy* 3 (3): 434–58.

———. 2012. "Capital Accumulation in Space, Capital-Labor Relations and Political Strategy." In *Territory, the State and Urban Politics*, edited by A. E. G. Jonas and A. M. Wood, chap. 6. Farnham: Ashgate.

Gough, Jamie, and Aram Eisenschnitz. 1998. "Debates and Reviews: Theorizing the State in Local Economic Development." *Regional Studies* 32 (8): 759–68.

Graff, Harvey. 2008. *The Dallas Myth*. Minneapolis: Univ. of Minnesota Press.

Gray, Mia, and James DeFilippis. 2015. "Learning from Las Vegas: Unions and Post-Industrial Urbanization." *Urban Studies* 52 (9): 1683–1701.

Grit, S., and Piet J. Korteweg. 1976. "Perspectives on Office Relocation in the Netherlands." *Tijdschrift voor economische en sociale geografie* 67 (1): 2–14.

Guy, Clifford. 1998. "Controlling New Retail Spaces: The Impress of Planning Policies in Western Europe." *Urban Studies* 35 (5–6): 953–79.

Habermas, Jürgen. 1975. *Legitimation Crisis*. Boston: Beacon Press.

Haila, Anne, and Patrick Le Galès. 2005. "The Coming of Metropolitan Governance in Helsinki?" *Cahiers du pole Ville/Métropolis/Cosmopolis*, no. 5.

Halbert, Ludovic. 2010. *L'avantage métropolitain*. Paris: Presses universitaires de France.

———. 2013a. "Les deux options métropolitaines des politiques de développement territorial." *Annales de Géographie*, no. 689: 108–21.

———. 2013b. "Les acteurs des marchés financiers font-ils la ville?" *Espaces-Temps.net*. Accessed Sept. 9, 2015. http://www.espacestemps.net/en/articles/les-acteurs-des-marches-financiers.font-ils-la-ville/.

Hall, Peter. 1974. "The Containment of Urban England." *Geographical Journal* 140 (3): 386–408.

Hall, Peter, and Marion Clawson. 1973. *Planning and Urban Growth*. Washington, DC: Johns Hopkins Univ. Press for Resources for the Future.

Hall, Peter, Ray Thomas, Howard Gracey, and Roy Drewett. 1973. *The Containment of Urban England*. London: Allen and Unwin.

Hancké, Bob. 2003. "Many Roads to Flexibility: How Large Firms Built Autarchic Regional Production Systems in France." *International Journal of Urban and Regional Research* 27 (3): 510–26.

Hanson, Royce. 1974. "Land Development and Metropolitan Reform." In *Reform as Reorganization*, edited by L. Wingo, chap. 1. Washington, DC: Resources for the Future.

Harding, Alan. 1991. "The Rise of Urban Growth Coalitions UK-Style?" *Environment and Planning C* 9 (3): 295–318.

Harris, Richard. 1991. "Self-Building in the Urban Housing Market." *Economic Geography* 67 (1): 1–21.

Harris, Richard, and Robert Lewis. 2001. "The Geography of North American Cities and Suburbs, 1900–1950: A New Synthesis." *Journal of Urban History* 27 (3): 262–92.

Harvey, David. 1973. *Social Justice and the City*. Baltimore, MD: Johns Hopkins Univ. Press.

———. 1974. "Class-Monopoly Rent, Finance Capital and the Urban Revolution." *Regional Studies* 8 (3–4): 239–55.

———. 1979. "On Planning the Ideology of Planning." In *Planning Theory in the 1980s*, edited by Robert W. Burchell and George Sternlieb, 213–33. Center for Urban Policy Research, Rutgers Univ., New Brunswick, NJ.

———. 1982. *Limits to Capital*. Chicago: Univ. of Chicago Press.

———. 1985a. "The Geopolitics of Capitalism." In *Social Relations and Spatial Structures*, edited by D. Gregory and J. Urry, chap. 7. London: Macmillan.

———. 1985b. *The Urbanization of Capital*. Oxford: Blackwell.

———. 1989a. "From Managerialism to Entrepreneurialism: The Transformation of Urban Governance in Late Capitalism." *Geografiska Annaler* 71B, 3–17.

———. 1989b. *The Urban Experience*. Baltimore: Johns Hopkins Univ. Press.

———. 1996. *Justice, Nature and the Geography of Difference*. Oxford: Basil Blackwell.

———. 2005. *A Brief History of Neoliberalism*. Oxford: Oxford Univ. Press.

———. 2012. *Rebel Cities*. London: Verso.

Hayden, Dolores. 2001. "Revisiting the Sitcom Suburbs." *Land Lines* 13 (2). http://www.lincolninst.edu/pubs/253_Revisiting-the-Sitcom-Suburbs.

Hefeker, Carsten, and Nobert Wunner. 2003. "Promises Made, Promises Broken: A Political Economic Perspective on German Unification." *German Politics* 12 (1): 109–34.

Hewitt, Lucy E. 2011. "Towards a Greater Urban Geography: Regional Planning and Associational Networks in London during the Early Twentieth Century." *Planning Perspectives* 26 (4): 551–68.

Hill, Richard C. 1983. "Crisis in the Motor City: The Politics of Economic Development in Detroit." In *Restructuring the City*, edited by Susan S. Fainstein et al., chap. 3. New York: Longman.

Howley, John. 1990. "Justice for Janitors: The Challenge of Organizing in Contract Services." *Labor Research Review* 1 (15): 61–71.

Hoyler, Michael, Tim Freytag, and Christoph Mager. 2006. "Advantageous Fragmentation? Reimagining Metropolitan Governance and Spatial Planning in Rhine-Main." *Built Environment* 32 (2): 124–36.

Huber, Joe. 2012. "The Life and Death of Great St Louis Malls." *NextSTL*, Dec. 5. Accessed Jul. 7, 2015. http://nextstl.com/2012/12/life-and-death-of-great-st-louis-malls/.

Hudson, Ray. 1982. "Accumulation, Spatial Policies, and the Production of Regional Labor Reserves; A Study of Washington New Town." *Environment and Planning A* 14 (5): 665–80.

———. 1986. "Nationalized Industry Policies and Regional Policies: The Role of the State in Capitalist Societies in the Deindustrialization and Reindustrialization of Regions." *Environment and Planning D: Society and Space* 4 (1): 7–28.

———. 2003. "European Integration and New Forms of Regional Development." *European Urban and Regional Studies* 10 (1): 49–67.

———. 2015. "Uneven Development, Socio-spatial Polarization and Political Responses." In *New Geographies of Central and Eastern Europe. Socio-spatial Polarisation and Peripheralization in a Rapidly Changing Region*, edited by Thilo Lang, Sebastian Henn, Kornelia Ehrlich, and Wladimir Sgibnev, chap. 2. London: Palgrave.

Hull, Dana. 2015. "Reno Bets Tesla Gigafactory Will Erase Image as Downmarket Vegas." *Bloomburg*, June 22. Accessed Sept. 14. http://www.bloomberg.com/news/articles/2015-06-22/reno-bets-tesla-gigafactory-will-erase-image-as-downmarket-vegas.

Hylton, Forrest. 2007. "U.S. Labor and Working-Class History 101: Questions and Some Answers." Unpublished manuscript.

Jackson, Kenneth. 1987. *Crabgrass Frontier*. Oxford: Oxford Univ. Press.

Jeffery, Charlie. 1999. "Party Politics and Territorial Representation in the Federal Republic of Germany." *West European Politics* 22 (2): 130–66.

Jessop, Bob. 1990. *State Theory*. Cambridge: Polity Press.

———. 2002. *The Future of the Capitalist State*. Cambridge: Polity Press.

Jezierski, Louise. 1996. "Pittsburgh: Partnerships in a Regional City." In *Regional Politics: America in a Post-City Age*, edited by Hank V. Savitch and Robert K. Vogel, 159–81. Thousand Oaks, CA: Sage Publications.

Jouve, Bernard. 2005. "La contribution des réformes institutionnelles des métropoles à la transformation de l'état keynésien: un bilan des expériences ouest-européenne." *Géographie, économie, société* 7 (2): 177–92.

Kaal, Harm. 2009. "Running the Big City: The Dutch Prewar Mayoralty Under Construction." *European Review of History* 16 (4): 437–52.

Kafkoula, Kiki. 2013. "On Garden-City Lines: Looking Into Social Housing Estates of Interwar Europe." *Planning Perspectives* 28 (2): 171–98.

Katznelson, Ira, and Bruce Pietrykowski. 1991. "Rebuilding the American State: Evidence from the 1940s." *Studies in American Political Development* 5 (2): 301–39.

Kau, James B., and Paul H. Rubin. 1982. *Congressmen, Constituents, and Contributors*. Boston: Martinus Nijhoff Publishing.

Keating, Michael. 1991. "Local Economic Development Politics in France." *Journal of Urban Affairs* 13 (4): 443–49.

Kellett, John R. 1969. *The Impact of Railways on Victorian Cities*. Toronto: Univ. of Toronto Press.

Key, Valdimer O. 1949. *Southern Politics in State and Nation*. New York: Alfred A. Knopf.

Koistinen, David. 2013. *Confronting Decline: The Political Economy of Deindustrialization in Twentieth-Century New England*. Gainesville, FL: Univ. Press of Florida.

Krätke, Stefan. 2007. "Metropolization of the European Economic Territory as a Consequence of Increasing Specialization of Urban Agglomerations in the Knowledge Economy." *European Planning Studies* 15 (1): 1–27.

Kushner, James A. 2014. "Comparative Urban Governance: Why the United States is Incapable of Reform." *Fordham Urban Law Journal* 41: 20–28.

Lazare, Daniel. 1998. "America the Undemocratic." *New Left Review*, no. 232: 3–40.

Le Galès, Patrick. 1990. "Crise urbaine et développement économique local en Grande-Bretagne: l'apport de la nouvelle gauche urbaine." *Revue française de science politique* 40 (5): 714–35.

———. 1991. "Les facteurs sociaux locaux d'une politique de développement économique local: l'exemple de Coventry." *Sociologie du Travail* 334: 503–27.

Le Galès, Patrick, and Alan Harding. 1998. "Cities and States in Europe." *West European Politics* 21 (3): 120–44.

Lee, Timothy B. 2011. "Zoning Laws Are Strangling Silicon Valley," *Forbes*, Sept. 19. http://www.forbes.com/sites/timothylee/2011/09/19/zoning-laws-are-strangling-silicon-valley/#2f7f1d31568b.

Leven, Charles, James Little, Hugh Nourse, and R. Reed. 1976. *Neighborhood Change: The Dynamics of Urban Decay.* New York: Praeger.

Liberto, Jennifer. 2012. "Fiscal Battle over Mortgage Deduction." *CNN Money,* Nov. 27. Accessed Sept. 24, 2015. http://money.cnn.com/2012/11/27/real _estate/housing-mortgage-interest-tax/.

Lipset, Seymour M. 1996. *American Exceptionalism: A Double-Edged Sword.* New York: W. W. Norton.

Lipset, Seymour M., and Reinhard Bendix. 1991. *Social Mobility in Industrial Society.* Brunswick, NJ: Transaction Publishers.

Lo, Ruth. 2013. "The Architecture and Planning of Fascist New Towns in Sardinia." *Society of Architectural Historians Newsletter* (Mar. 14). Accessed June 16, 2015. http://www.sah.org/about-sah/sah-news/2013/03/14/the-architecture -and-planning-of-fascist-new-towns-in-sardinia.

Lowi, Theodore. J. 1969. *The End of Liberalism.* New York: W. W. Norton.

Lucifora, C., and F. Origo. 1999. "Wage Differentials and Unemployment in Italy: A Regional Perspective." Accessed Oct. 17, 2015. http://ftp.zew.de/pub /zew-docs/sws/origo.pdf.

Mackay, R. Ross. 2001. "Regional Taxing and Spending: The Search for Balance." *Regional Studies* 35 (6): 563–75.

Mackinder, Halford J. 1919. *Democratic Ideals and Reality.* London: Constable.

MacLeod, Gordon. 1999. "Place, Politics and 'Scale Dependence': Exploring the Structuration of Euro-Regionalism." *European Urban and Regional Studies* 6 (3): 231–53.

———. 2013. "New Urbanism/Smart Growth in the Scottish Highlands: Mobile Policies and Post-Politics in Local Development Planning." *Urban Studies* 50 (11): 2196–221.

Magri, Susanna. 1986. "Le mouvement des locataires à Paris et dans sa banlieue, 1919–1925." *Le Mouvement social,* no. 137: 55–76.

Magri, Susanna, and Christian Topalov. 1987. "De la cité-jardin à la ville rationalisée: Un tournant du projet réformateur, 1905–1925: Etude comparative France, Grande-Bretagne, Italie, Etats-Unis." *Revue française de sociologie* 28 (3): 417–51.

Mair, Andrew. 1988. *Private Planning for Economic Development: Local Business Coalitions in Columbus, Ohio 1858–1986.* PhD diss., Ohio State Univ.

Marchand, Bernard, and Joelle S. Cavin. 2007. "Anti-Urban Ideologies and Planning in France and Switzerland: Jean-François Gravier and Armin Meili." *Planning Perspectives* 22 (1): 29–53.

Markusen, Ann R. 1991a. *The Rise of the Gunbelt: The Military Remapping of America.* New York: Oxford Univ. Press.

———. 1991b. "The Military-Industrial Divide." *Environment and Planning D: Society and Space* 9 (4): 391–416.

Markusen, Ann R., and Jerry Fastrup. 1978. "The Regional War for Federal Aid." *The Public Interest* 53: 87–99.

Markusen, Ann R., and Gregory Schrock. 2003. "Cities as Hierarchists or Specialists? Evidence from Occupational Profiles." Working paper no. 258, Project on Regional and Industrial Economics, Humphrey Institute of Public Affairs, Univ. of Minnesota.

Marshall, J. Neill. 2007. "Public Sector Relocation Policies in the UK and Ireland." *European Planning Studies* 15 (5): 645–66.

Marshall, Tim. 2011. "Planning at the National Level in Europe in Relation to Major Infrastructure." *European Planning Studies* 19 (5): 887–905.

Marx, Karl. 1867; republished 1976. *Capital Volume 1.* Harmondsworth, Middlesex: Penguin.

Massey, Doreen. 1984. *Spatial Divisions of Labor.* London: Macmillan.

———. 2005. *For Space.* London: Sage Publications.

Massey, Doreen, and David Wield. 1991. *High-Tech Fantasies: Science Parks in Society, Science, and Space.* London: Routledge.

Matless, David. 1993. "Appropriate Geography: Patrick Abercrombie and the Energy of the World." *Journal of Design History* 6(3): 167–78.

Mayer, Margit. 1987. "Restructuring and Popular Opposition in West German Cities." In *The Capitalist City,* edited by M. P. Smith and J. R. Feagin, chap. 6. Oxford: Basil Blackwell.

McCann, Eugene, and Kevin G. Ward. eds. 2011. *Mobile Urbanism: Cities and Policymaking in the Global Age.* Minneapolis: Univ. of Minnesota Press.

McCrone, Gavin. 1969. *Regional Policy in Britain.* London: Allen and Unwin.

McDougall, Glen. 1979. "The State, Capital and Land." *International Journal of Urban and Regional Research* 3 (3): 361–80.

Meiksins Wood, Ellen. 1988. "Capitalism and Human Emancipation," *New Left Review* 167: 1–20.

———. 2016. "Britain versus France: How Many Sonderwegs?" *Historical Materialism* 24 (1): 11–29.

Meyer, Peter. 1991. "Meaning and Action in Local Economic Development Strategies: A Comparison of Policies in Britain and the United States." *Environment and Planning C: Government and Policy* 9 (4): 383–98.

Meyers, Andrew. 1998. "Invisible Cities: Lewis Mumford, Thomas Adams, and the Invention of the Regional City, 1923–1929." *Business and Economic History* 27 (2): 292–306.

Mezerik, Avrahm G. 1946. *The Revolt of the South and West*. New York: Duell, Sloan and Pearce.

Mishan, Edward J. 1969. *The Costs of Economic Growth*. Harmondsworth, Middlesex: Penguin Books.

Miszczyk, Agata. 2013. "Specialized Growth: Planning and Politics in Rochester MN and the Growth Machine Theory," *Cities in the 21st Century* 3 (1), article 4. http://digitalcommons macalester.edu/cities/vol3/iss1/4.

Mitchell, Donald, Kafui Attoh, and Lynn Staeheli. 2015. "Whose City? What Politics? Contentious and Non-Contentious Spaces on Colorado's Front Range." *Urban Studies* 52 (14): 2633–48.

Mitchell, Stacy. 2006. *Big-Box Swindle*. Boston: Beacon Press.

Mohl, Raymond A. 2002. *The Interstates and the Cities: Highways, Housing and the Freeway Revolt*. Research Report: Poverty and Race Research Action Council. Accessed Jul. 8, 2015. http://www.prrac.org/pdf/mohl.pdf.

Mollenkopf, John H. 1983. *The Contested City*. Princeton: Princeton Univ. Press.

Molotch, Harvey. 1973. *Managed Integration: Dilemmas of Doing Good in the City*. Berkeley and Los Angeles: Univ. of California Press.

———. 1976. "The City as a Growth Machine: Toward a Political Economy of Place." *American Journal of Sociology* 82 (2): 226–38.

Morgan, Kevin. 2001. "The New Territorial Politics: Rivalry and Justice in Post-Devolution Britain." *Regional Studies* 35 (4): 343–48.

Moskowitz, Marina. 1998. "Zoning the Industrial City: Planners, Commissioners, and Boosters in the 1920s." *Business and Economic History* 27 (2): 307–17.

Mukhija, Vinit, Dana Cuff, and Kimberly Serrano. 2014. *Backyard Homes and Local Concerns*. Los Angeles, CA: cityLAB, UCLA Department of Architecture and Urban Design.

Mullin, John R. 1982a. "Ideology, Planning Theory and the German City in the Inter-War Years Part 1." *Town Planning Review* 53 (2): 115–30.

———. 1982b. "Ideology, Planning Theory and the German City in the Inter-War Years Part 2." *Town Planning Review* 53 (3): 257–72.

Musgrove, Frank. 1963. *The Migratory Elite*. London: Heinemann.

National League of Cities. 2015. "First Tier Suburbs Council." Accessed Oct. 13. http://www.nlc.org/build-skills-and-networks/networks/committees-and-councils/first-tier-suburbs-council.

Newkirk, Margaret. 1995. "Where the Road Money Went." *Columbus Monthly* (March): 35–40.

Newman, Peter, and Andy Thornley. 1995. "Euralille: Boosterism at the Centre of Europe." *European Urban and Regional Studies* 2 (3): 237–46.

Newton, Kenneth. 1978. "Conflict Avoidance and Conflict Suppression: The Case of Urban Politics in the United States." In *Urbanization and Conflict in Market Societies*, edited by Kevin R. Cox, chap. 3. Chicago: Maaroufa.

Nicolaides, Becky M. 1999. "'Where the Working Man Is Welcomed': Working-Class Suburbs in Los Angeles, 1900–1940." *Pacific Historical Review* 68 (4): 517–59.

Nozeman, Eduard F. 1990. "Dutch New Towns: Triumph or Disaster?" *Tijdschrift voor Economische en Sociaale Geografie* 81 (2): 149–55.

Paparella, Domenico, and Vilma Rinolfi. 2003. "Social Partners Oppose Government's Devolution Proposals." Eurofound (European Foundation for the Improvement of Living and Working Conditions) website. Jan. 8. Accessed July 16, 2015. http://www.eurofound.europa.eu/eiro/2002/12/feature/it02121 07f.htm.

Parkin, Frank. 1972. *Class, Inequality and Political Order*. London: Paladin.

———. 1979. *Marxism and Class Theory: A Bourgeois Critique*. London: Tavistock Publications.

Parson, Don. 2005. *Making a Better World: Public Housing, the Red Scare, and the Direction of Modern Los Angeles*. Minneapolis: University of Minnesota Press.

Pasquier, Romain. 2003. "La régionalisation française revisitée: fédéralisme, mouvement régional et élites modernisatrices (1950–1964)." *Revue française de science politique* 53 (1): 101–25.

Peck, Jamie. 1995. "Moving and Shaking: Business Elites, State Localism and Urban Privatism." *Progress in Human Geography* 19 (1): 16–46.

Peck, Jamie, and Adam Tickell. 1994. "Searching for a New Institutional Fix: The After-Fordist Crisis and the Global-Local Disorder." In *Post-Fordism: A Reader*, edited by Ash Amin, chap. 9. Oxford: Blackwell.

Petitet, Sylvain. 2013. "Densifier l'habitat pavillonnaire: des démarches individuelles aux projets collectifs." *Métropolitiques* (March 20). Accessed Aug. 23, 2015. http://www.metropolitiques.eu/Densifier-l-habitat-pavillonnaire.html.

Phelps, Nicholas. 2009. "From Branch Plant Economies to Knowledge Economies? Manufacturing Industry, Government Policy and Economic Development in Britain's Old Industrial Regions." *Environment and Planning C: Government and Policy* 27 (4): 574–92.

Pickvance, Chris G. 1977. "Physical Planning and Market Forces in Urban Development." *National Westminster Bank Quarterly Review* (August), 41–50.

———. 1981. "Policies as Chameleons: An Interpretation of Regional Policy and Office Policy in Britain." In *Urbanization and Urban Planning in Capitalist Society*, edited by Michael J. Dear and Allen J. Scott, chap. 10. London: Methuen.

———. 1985. "Spatial Policy and Territorial Politics: The Role of Spatial Coalitions in the Articulation of 'Spatial Interests' and in the Demand for Spatial Policy." In *Political Action and Social Identity*, edited by Gareth Rees et al., chap. 6. Basingstoke: Macmillan.

———. 1990. "Council Economic Intervention and Political Conflict in a Declining Resort: The Isle of Thanet." In *Place, Policy and Politics: Do Localities Matter?* edited by Chris G. Pickvance and John Urry, chap. 8. London: Unwin Hyman.

Pinçon, Michel, and Monique Pinçon-Charlot, M. 2007. *Les ghettos du gotha: au cœur de la grande bourgeoisie* Paris: Seuil.

Pinson, Gilles. 2009. *Gouverner la ville par projet: Urbanisme et gouvernance des villes européennes.* Paris: SciencesPo. Les Presses.

Piven, Frances Fox. 1970. "Comprehensive Social Planning." *Journal of the American Institute of Planners* 36 (4): 226–28.

Piven, Frances Fox, and Richard A. Cloward. 1971. *Regulating the Poor.* New York: Pantheon Books.

Piven, Frances Fox, and Roger Friedland. 1984. "Public Choice and Private Power: A Theory of Fiscal Crisis." In *Public Service Provision and Urban Development*, edited by Andrew Kirby, Paul Knox and Steven Pinch, chap. 15. Beckenham, Kent: Croom Helm.

Preteceille, Edmond. 1976. "Urban Planning: The Contradictions of Capitalist Urbanization." *Antipode* 8 (1): 69–76.

———. 1990. "Political Paradoxes of Urban Restructuring: Globalization of the Economy and Localization of Politics." In *Beyond the City Limits: Urban Policy and Economic Restructuring in Comparative Perspective*, edited by John R. Logan and Todd Swanstrom, chap. 2. Philadelphia: Temple Univ. Press.

Przeworski, Adam. 2009. "Conquered or Granted? A History of Suffrage Extensions." *British Journal of Political Science* 39 (2): 291–321.

Puentes, Robert. 2006. "The State of Organizing in Midwestern First Suburbs." *Opolis* 2 (1): 53–64.

Quadagno, Jill S. 1984. "Welfare Capitalism and the Social Security Act of 1935." *American Sociological Review* 49 (5): 632–47.

Reisner, Mark. 1986. *Cadillac Desert*. New York: Viking Penguin.

Renard, Vincent. 2015. "La question foncière, une clé pour agir sur les politiques du logement." Accessed July 20. http://vincentrenard.eu/index.php/articles/11-la-question-fonciere-une-cle-pour-agir-sur-les-politiques-du-logement.

Renau, Luis del Romero, and Antonio Lozano. 2015. "From NIMBYsm to the 15M: A Decade of Urban Conflicts in Barcelona and Valencia." *Territory, Politics, Governance* 4 (3): 375–95.

Rifkin, Jerry, and Randy Barber. 1978. *The North Will Rise Again: Pensions, Politics and Power in the 1980s*. Boston: Beacon Press.

Rosevear, Stephen. 1998. "Balancing Business and the Regions: British Distribution of Industry Policy and the Board of Trade." *Business History* 40 (1): 77–99.

Rosser, Colin, and Harris, Christopher. 1965. *The Family and Social Change: A Study of Family and Kinship in a South Wales Town*. London: Routledge and Kegan Paul.

Rousseau, Max. 2010. "Gouverner la gentrification." *Métropoles* 7. Accessed Sept. 8, 2015. http://metropoles.revues.org/4257.

Salisbury, Robert H. 1964. "Urban Politics: The New Convergence of Power." *Journal of Politics* 26 (4): 775–97.

Savage, Lydia. 2006. "Justice for Janitors: Scales of Organizing and Representing Workers." *Antipode* 38 (3): 645–66.

Savage, Mike. 1987. "Understanding Political Alignments in Contemporary Britain: Do Localities Matter?" *Political Geography Quarterly* 6 (1): 53–76.

Saxenian, AnnaLee. 1984. "The Urban Contradictions of Silicon Valley: Regional Growth and the Restructuring of the Semiconductor Industry." In *Sunbelt/Snowbelt: Urban Development and Regional Restructuring*, edited by Larry Sawers and William K. Tabb, chap. 7. New York: Oxford Univ. Press.

———. 1985. "Let Them Eat Chips." *Environment and Planning D: Society and Space* 3 (1): 121–27.

Schmidt, Stephen, and Ralph Buehler. 2007. "The Planning Process in the US and Germany: A Comparative Analysis." *International Planning Studies* 12 (1): 55–75.

Schmidt, Vivienne. 1988. "Industrial Management under the Socialists in France: Decentralized Dirigisme at the National and Local Levels." *Comparative Politics* 21 (1): 53–72.

———. 1990. *Democratizing France: The Politics and Administrative History of Decentralization*. Cambridge: Cambridge Univ. Press.

Schnargl, Wilfried. 2012. *Bayern kann es auch allein*. Berlin: Quadriga.

Schubert, Dirk. 2004. "Theodor Fritsch and the German (*völkische*) Version of the Garden City: The Garden City Invented Two Years before Ebenezer Howard." *Planning Perspectives* 19 (1): 3–35.

Scott, Allen J. 1988. *New Industrial Spaces: Flexible Production Organization and Regional Development in North America and Western Europe*. London: Pion.

———. 2008a. "Production and Work in the American Metropolis: A Macroscopic Approach." *Annals of Regional Science* 42 (4): 787–805.

———. 2008b. "Resurgent Metropolis: Economy, Society and Urbanization in an Interconnected World." *International Journal of Urban and Regional Research* 32 (3): 548–64.

Scott, Peter. 2001. "Industrial Estates and British Industrial Development, 1897–1939." *Business History* 43 (2): 73–98.

Self, Robert O. 2003. *American Babylon: Race and the Struggle for Postwar Oakland*. Princeton: Princeton Univ. Press.

Shapiro, Edward S. 1972. "Decentralist Intellectuals and the New Deal." *Journal of American History* 58 (4): 938–57.

Shefter, Martin. 1978. "Local Politics, State Legislatures, and the Urban Fiscal Crisis: New York City and Boston." In *Territorial Politics in Industrial Nations*, S. Tarrow, P. J. Katzenstein, and L. Graziano, chap. 6. New York: Praeger.

Shermer, Elizabeth T. 2013. *Sunbelt Capitalism: Phoenix and the Transformation of American Politics*. Philadelphia: Univ. of Pennsylvania Press.

Smith, Michael P., Gregory A. Guagnano, and Cath Posehn. 1989. "The Political Economy of Growth in Chicago: Whose City?" In *Unequal Partnerships*, edited by Gregory D. Squires, chap. 14. London and New Brunswick: Rutgers Univ. Press.

Smith, Neil. 1979. "Toward a Theory of Gentrification: A Back to the City Movement of Capital not People." *Journal of the American Planning Association* 45 (4): 538–48.

———. 1987. "Gentrification and the Rent Gap," *Annals of the Association of American Geographers*, 77 (3) 462–65.

Stone, Clarence N. 1987. "Summing Up: Urban Regimes, Development Policy, and Political Arrangements." In *The Politics of Urban Development*, edited by Clarence N. Stone and Heywood T. Sanders, chap. 14. Lawrence, KS: Univ. Press of Kansas.

Storper, Michael, and Richard A. Walker. 1989. *The Capitalist Imperative.* Oxford: Basil Blackwell.

Stovall, Tyler. 1989. "French Communism and Suburban Development: The Rise of the Paris Red Belt." *Journal of Contemporary History* 24 (3): 437–60.

Stovel, Katherine, and Mike Savage. 2005. "Mergers and Mobility: Organizational Growth and the Origins of Career Migration at Lloyds Bank." *American Journal of Sociology* 111 (4): 1080–121.

Streeck, Wolfgang. 2015. "Why the Euro Divides Europe." *New Left Review,* n.s., 95: 5–26.

Subra, Philippe. 2007. *Géopolitique de l'aménagement du territoire.* Paris: Colin.

Swyngedouw, Erik. 2009. "The Antimonies of the Post-Political City: In Search of a Democratic Politics of Environmental Production." *International Journal of Urban and Regional Research* 33 (3): 601–20.

Tarrow, Sidney. 1978. "Regional policy, Ideology, and Peripheral Defense: The Case of Fos-sur-Mer." In *Territorial Politics in Industrial Nations,* edited by Sidney Tarrow, Peter J. Katzenstein and Luigi Graziano, chap. 4. New York: Praeger.

Teaford, John C. 1979. *City and Suburb: The Political Fragmentation of Metropolitan America, 1850–1970.* Baltimore: Johns Hopkins Univ. Press.

Team Britannia Hungary. 2014. "The Fires of Perfect Liberty: Labouring Men and Women of England, 1851-1951: Part Five." October. Accessed June 29, 2015. https://chandlerozconsultants.wordpress.com/2014/10/29/the-fires-of -perfect-liberty-labouring-men-and-women-of-england-1851-1951-part-five.

Thiesse, Anne-Marie. 1992. "L'invention du régionalisme à la Belle Époque." *Le Mouvement social,* no. 160: 11–32

Tickell, Adam, and Peter Dicken. 1993. "The Role of Inward Investment Promotion in Economic Development Strategies." *Local Economy* 8: 197–208.

Tiebout, Charles. 1956. "A Pure Theory of Local Public Expenditures." *Journal of Political Economy* 64 (4): 16–24.

Trigilia, Carlo. 1992. *Sviluppo senza autonomia: effetti perversi delle politiche nel Mezzogiorno.* Bologna: Il Mulino.

Tuppen, John N. 1983. "The Development of French New Towns: An Assessment of Progress." *Urban Studies* 20 (1): 11–30.

Ulam, Alex. 2014. "How a Widely Beloved Tax Deduction Really Just Benefits the Well-Off and Exacerbates Inequality." *American Prospect,* Aug. 20. Accessed

Sept. 20, 2015. http://prospect.org/article/how-widely-beloved-tax-deduction-really-just-benefits-well-and-exacerbates-inequality.

Vacquerel, Bénédicte. 2011. *Dalle et dédale en Seine-Saint-Denis.* Université Paris-Est Créteil: Institut d'urbanisme de Paris.

Vandermotten, Christian. 1998. "Dynamiques spatiales de l'industrialisation et devenir de la Belgique." *Le Mouvement social,* no. 185: 75–100.

Vanthillo, Ties, and Ann Verhetsel. 2012. "Paradigm Change in Regional Policy: Towards Smart Specialization? Lessons from Flanders (Belgium)." *Belgeo* 1–2: 2–16.

Veltz, Pierre. 1996. *Mondialisation, Villes et Territoires.* Paris: Presses Universitaires de France.

Vercellone, Carlo. 2006. "The Anomaly and the Exemplariness of the Italian Welfare State." In *Radical Thought in Italy,* edited by M. Hardt and P. Virno, chap. 6. Minneapolis: Univ. of Minnesota Press.

Vicari, Serena, and Harvey Molotch. 1990. "Building Milan: Alternative Machines of Growth." *International Journal of Urban and Regional Research* 14 (4): 602–24.

Vogel, David. 1978. "Why Businessmen Distrust Their State: The Political Consciousness of American Corporate Executives." *British Journal of Political Science* 8 (1): 45–78.

Walker, David. 2002. *In Praise of Centralism.* London: Catalyst Forum.

Walker, Richard A. 1978. "Two Sources of Uneven Development Under Advanced Capitalism—Spatial Differentiation and Capital Mobility." *Review of Radical Political Economy* 10 (3): 28–38.

Walker, Richard A., and David Large. 1975. "The Economics of Energy Extravagance." *Ecology Law Quarterly* 4: 963–85.

Ward, Stephen V. 1986. "Implementation versus Planmaking: The Example of List Q and the Depressed Areas, 1922–1939." *Planning Perspectives* 1 (1): 3–26.

———. 1990. "Local Industrial Promotion and Development Policies 1899–1940." *Local Economy* 5 (2): 100–118.

Watson, William. 1964. "Social Mobility and Social Class in Industrial Communities." In *Closed Systems and Open Minds,* edited by Max Gluckman, 129–57. London: Oliver and Boyd.

Webb, Walter Prescott. 1937. *Divided We Stand.* New York: Farrar and Rinehart.

Weir, Margaret. 1996. "Central Cities' Loss of Power in State Politics." *Cityscape* 2 (2): 23–40.

———. 2005. "States, Race, and the Decline of New Deal Liberalism." *Studies in American Political Development* 19 (2): 157–72.

Weiss, Marc A. 1980. "The Origins and Legacy of Urban Renewal." In *Urban and Regional Planning in an Age of Austerity*, edited by Pierre Clavel, John Forester, and William W. Goldsmith, chap. 4. New York: Pergamon Press.

———. 1987. *The Rise of the Community Builders*. New York: Columbia Univ. Press.

Wendeln, Matthew. 2014. "Territorial Equality in France: A Historical Perspective," *Metropolitics* (June 4). Accessed Oct. 11, 2015. http://www.metropoli tiques.eu/Territorial-Equality-in-France-A.html.

Werthman, Carl, Jerry Mandel, and Ted Dienstfrey. 1965. *Planning the Purchase Decision: Why People Buy in Planned Communities*. Univ. of California at Berkeley: Center for Planning and Development Research, Institute of Urban and Regional Development (Preprint 10).

While, Aidan, Andrew E. G. Jonas, and David Gibbs. 2004. "Unblocking the City? Growth Pressures, Collective Provision, and the Search for New Spaces of Governance in Greater Cambridge, England." *Environment and Planning A* 36 (2): 279–304.

Williams, Raymond. 1973. *The Country and the City*. Oxford: Oxford Univ. Press.

Williams-Ellis, Clough. 1928. *England and the Octopus*. London: Geoffrey Bles.

Wilson, William J. 1987. *The Truly Disadvantaged: The Inner City, the Underclass and Public Policy*. Chicago: Univ. of Chicago Press.

———. 1996. *When Work Disappears: The World of the New Urban Poor*. New York: Knopf.

Wingo, Lowdon. 1973. "The Quality of Life: A Micro-Economic Definition." *Urban Studies* 10 (1): 3–18.

Wintour, Patrick. 2000. "South MPs Warn of 'Prosperity Crisis' as More Jobs Force Up Home Prices." *Guardian*, Dec. 26. Accessed Sept. 25, 2015. http://www.theguardian.com/politics/2000/dec/27/uk.britishidentity.

Wolf, Eleanor P., and Charles Lebeaux, C. 1969. *Change and Renewal in an Urban Community*. New York: Praeger.

Wood, Andrew M. 1993a. "Local Economic Development Networks and Prospecting for Industry." *Environment and Planning A* 25 (11): 1649–62.

———. 1993b. "Organizing for Local Economic Development: Local Economic Development Networks and Capitalist Investment in the US City." PhD diss., Department of Geography, Ohio State Univ.

———. 2004. "The Scalar Transformation of the U.S. Commercial Property-Development Industry: A Cautionary Note on the Limits of Globalization." *Economic Geography* 80 (2): 119–40.

Woods, Ralph L. 1939. *America Reborn: A Plan for Decentralization of Industry.* New York: Longman's, Green and Co.

Wright, Gavin. 1986. *Old South, New South.* New York: Basic Books.

Yglesias, Matthew. 2012. "George Lucas, Facebook, and the Crisis of NIMBYism," *Slate,* May 23. http://www.slate.com/articles/business/moneybox/2012/05/facebook_george_lucas_and_nimbyism_the_idiotic_rules_preventing_silicon_valley_from_building_the_houses_and_offices_we_need_to_power_american_innovation_.html.

Young, Kenneth, and John Kramer, J. 1978a. "Local Exclusionary Policies in Britain: The Case of Suburban Defense in a Metropolitan System." In *Urbanization and Conflict in Market Societies,* edited by Kevin R. Cox, chap. 10. Chicago: Maaroufa Press.

———. 1978b. *Strategy and Conflict in Metropolitan Housing.* London: Heinemann.

Young, Michael, and Peter Willmott. 1957. *Family and Kinship in East London.* London: Routledge and Kegan Paul.

Zepf, Marcus, and Andres, Lauren. 2011. *Enjeux de la planification territoriale en Europe.* Lausanne: Presses polytechniques et universitaires romandes.

Index

Italic page number denotes illustration.

Kevin R. Cox is Distinguished Emeritus Professor of Geography at The Ohio State University. He has been a Guggenheim Fellow and is the author of numerous books, including, most recently, *Making Human Geography*.